Transnational Perspectives on
Latin America

Transnational Perspectives on Latin America

The Entwined Histories of a Multi-state Region

LUIS RONIGER

OXFORD
UNIVERSITY PRESS

Oxford University Press is a department of the University of Oxford. It furthers
the University's objective of excellence in research, scholarship, and education
by publishing worldwide. Oxford is a registered trade mark of Oxford University
Press in the UK and certain other countries.

Published in the United States of America by Oxford University Press
198 Madison Avenue, New York, NY 10016, United States of America.

Library of Congress Cataloging-in-Publication Data
Names: Roniger, Luis, 1949– author.
Title: Transnational perspectives on Latin America : the entwined histories
of a multi-state region / Luis Roniger.
Description: New York, NY : Oxford University Press, [2022] |
Includes bibliographical references and index.
Identifiers: LCCN 2021027751 (print) | LCCN 2021027752 (ebook) |
ISBN 9780197605318 (hardback) | ISBN 9780197605332 (epub) |
ISBN 9780197605325 | ISBN 9780197605349
Subjects: LCSH: Latin America—Politics and government—21st century. |
Latin America—Foreign relations. | Transnationalism.
Classification: LCC F1410 .R634 2022 (print) | LCC F1410 (ebook) |
DDC 980.04—dc23
LC record available at https://lccn.loc.gov/2021027751
LC ebook record available at https://lccn.loc.gov/2021027752

DOI: 10.1093/oso/9780197605318.001.0001

1 3 5 7 9 8 6 4 2

Printed by Integrated Books International, United States of America

Contents

Acknowledgments

I would like to thank many individuals and institutions that helped me bring this book together. I am indebted to the colleagues of the research group and international conference on Contesting Liberal Democracy held at the Institute of Advanced Studies of Jerusalem; the participants in the seminars at the Department of Politics and International Affairs at Wake Forest University; participants in the conferences of the Consortium on Political Exile; the Latin American Studies Association; the International Political Science Association; the Middle Atlantic Council of Latin American Studies; the workshop on trans-nationalism at American University; and the research group on migration and exile at CLACSO. The fruitful discussions in these venues have been important in the formulation of several chapters. I am grateful to Leonardo Senkman and Daniel F. Wajner for their approval of including here part of our joint work as chapters 5 and 8. Special thanks are due to Henry Parkhurst for his outstanding research and editorial assistance starting in January 2020, and to Omri Elmaleh for his advice on Muslim Latin Americans.

Some of the essays in this book incorporate and expand on work published in articles and chapters elsewhere. The core of chapter 2 derives from an article published in the journal *Protosociology, an International Journal of Interdisciplinary Research* (Frankfurt), directed by Gerhard Preyer, 26 (2009): 71–100. Part of chapter 5 on the Chaco War relies on an article published in the *Journal of Politics in Latin America* (Sage, CC-BY-NC license), 11 (2019): 1–20, and the section on the War of the Pacific relies on analysis first developed in the book *América Latina tras bambalinas* (Latin American Research Commons, 2019). Parts of chapter 7 derive from an analysis first developed in the *Journal of Latin American Studies* (Cambridge University Press), 43 (2011): 693–724. Chapter 8 was published originally as an article in *Latin American Research Review* (LASA), 54 (2019): 458–475. Chapter 9 incorporates Venezuelan materials first published in the ACTA Paper "Antisemitism: Real or Imagined? Chávez, Iran, Israel and the Jews" (Vidal Sassoon International Center for the Study of Antisemitism, Jerusalem) in July 2009. I am grateful to these journals and publishers for their permission to use these materials. The texts are set here in new form as part of a systematic project highlighting aspects of Latin American development in a framework broader than that of individual nation-states, developing analyses on the entwined histories of this multistate region.

Abbreviations

ALADI	Latin American Integration Association
ALBA	Bolivarian Alliance for the People of Our America
ALBA-TCP	Bolivarian Alliance for the Peoples of Our America-People's Trade Treaty
ALCA	Free Trade Area of the Americas
APRA	American Popular Revolutionary Alliance
CAIS	Central American Integration System
CALC	Summit of Latin America and the Caribbean
CAN	Andean Community of Nations
CAOI	Andean Coordination of Indigenous Organizations
CARICOM	Caribbean Community
CELAC	Community of Latin American and Caribbean States
COICA	Coordinating Body for Indigenous Organizations of the Amazonian Basin
CONAIE	Confederation of Indigenous Nationalities of Ecuador
CONIVE	Consejo Nacional Indio de Venezuela
CSN	South American Community of Nations
FMLN	Farabundo Martí National Liberation Front (El Salvador)
FSLN	Sandinista Front Army of Liberation (Nicaragua)
FTAA	Free Trade Area of the Americas
IAC	Ibero-American Community
IACHR	Inter-American Commission on Human Rights
IGO	intergovernmental organization
IIRSA	Initiative for South American Regional Integration
OAS	Organization of American States
ONECA	Network of Central American Black Organizations
PEMEX	Petróleos Mexicanos (Mexico's Oil Company)
RAPIM	Meeting of Indigenous Authorities of MERCOSUR
SAIIC	South American and Mesoamerican Indian Rights Center
SOA	School of the Americas
TBA	Triborder Area (South America)
TIFA	Framework Agreement for Trade and Investment
UNASUR	Union of South American Nations

Introduction

The chapters in this book explore the historical development of Latin American societies in terms of the twin processes of nation-state building and transnational connections. Latin America is a multistate and polyglot region with a diversity of races, ethnicities, and cultures, at the same time that the region shares historical legacies, institutional frameworks, and political and socioeconomic challenges. At various historical junctures, important social, intellectual, and political forces led political and cultural strategies of mutual recognition in the region.

Crystallizing as the "farthest West" in global expansion, the shared characteristics and inner diversity of Latin America made it a setting for comparative-historical analysis, starting with Iberian transatlantic colonialism and its forced intercivilizational encounters. This perspective has enabled enlightening analyses of geopolitical processes encompassing multiple countries and affecting the political, social, and cultural experience of these societies in the Western Hemisphere. I claim that, in addition to approaching this multistate region with a comparative lens, one should also address it from a transnational perspective. Only then can analysis fully account for the articulation of local and national dynamics with international and global dynamics. Before describing in detail how this perspective informs the chapters of the book, let me briefly explain how my own interest in these issues developed over the span of four decades of academic research and publication.

As a comparative political scientist, I started working with comparative-historical sociologist Shmuel Noah Eisenstadt and began my own work on clientelism, producing systematic studies of these relations and networks. Those studies highlighted how the regulation of power and the construction of trust and legitimation had different articulations in societies across the globe, giving rise to diverse modes of control of access to human and material resources, some of which were mediated while others were more open to universal principles. At that stage, while paying full attention to the comparative analysis of patron-client relations and clientelism, I did not address transnational processes.[1]

In parallel to that research, I participated in several interdisciplinary efforts with historians, sociologists, political scientists, and cultural analysts to analyze Latin American development as part of multiple modernities. As the region crystallized out of various expansionist and imperialist projects in addition to intercivilizational encounters, it was "born" global and remained part of wider

Transnational Perspectives on Latin America. Luis Roniger, Oxford University Press. © Oxford University Press 2022.
DOI: 10.1093/oso/9780197605318.003.0001

frameworks of global exchange and interaction, yet exhibited its own peculiar trends. Due to their historical configuration, the societies of Latin America both are and are not part of the West. They incorporated European religions, cultural ideas, and practices, yet at the same time had distinctive cultural and demographic makeups, developing specific institutional trends and cultural notions. At that stage in my studies, I was particularly interested in tracing the interplay between the public structuring and regulation of identities and the creative processes of collective identification, appropriation, and evasion of identities. A major dimension of those studies involved evaluating how these societies influenced each other and evinced different demonstration effects as they followed the road to multiple forms of modernity and globalization.[2]

Those studies moved me increasingly to focus on the shifting frontiers of citizenship and the consolidation of human rights and alternative discourses and practices in Latin America.[3] Nonetheless, my focused interest in transnational processes can be traced back to the mid-1990s, when, together with political scientist Mario Sznajder, I studied how the Cold War dictatorships of South America coordinated their policy targeting leftist activists transnationally. We quickly began to assess the crucial implications of such repressive coordination as these countries transitioned back to democracy. At that stage in their development, they could not ignore the legacies of human rights violations and had to adopt policies of transitional justice that relied on cross-country assessments; they endured human rights crises that, due to the transnational character of repression, reverberated and spilled over from one state to another.[4]

The émigré networks of those individuals forced to flee their countries of residence and the advocacy networks they established in the diaspora emerged as crucial factors in confronting the dictatorships and their authoritarian legacies. We thus conducted a series of studies of political exile as a mechanism of institutionalized exclusion, then published *The Politics of Exile in Latin America*. In that book we systematically assessed the historical significance and transformed functionality of networks of political exile in the region and beyond its borders.[5] The work continued subsequently in cooperative work and research also with historians Pablo Yankelevich, Silvina Jensen, Leonardo Senkman, and James N. Green; cultural analyst Saúl Sosnowski; and philosophers Arturo Aguirre and Antolín Sánchez Cuervo. Analyzing the transnational impact of émigré networks and the transformation of political exile, we all contributed to what is now a major focus of research in the Americas.[6] In *Exile, Diaspora and Return*, the most recent book written in that line of analysis, we explored how post-exilic relocations, transnational migrant displacements, and diaspora communities affected Argentina, Chile, Paraguay, and Uruguay. Specifically, we provided a comprehensive analysis of diasporic experiences and the impact of returnees on the public life, culture, institutions, and development of post-authoritarian politics in the Southern Cone of the Americas.[7]

I gained further understanding of the transnational dynamics of Latin America's multistate system of nations as I explored the dialectical tug of war that unfolded in Central America between the process of distinct state consolidation and processes of transnational engagement and disengagement in the region. In *Transnational Politics in Central America*, I examined the connected history, close relationships, and mutual impact of the countries in the Americas' isthmus. These nations have shared not only a close geographical relationship and history, but also a geopolitical interdependence. This relationship has formulated profound effects on the construction of political identities and the type of challenges faced, both within the countries and in their exile communities, including several short-lived attempts at reunification and, more recently, their articulation in regional interstate organizations.[8]

All these interests and lines of analysis have found their way into this book. In it, I have tried to show the Janus-like character of distinct state formation and transnational linkages in Latin America. Due to their shared background combined with multiple and diverse identities, the region has long provided a framework for comparative analyses. While this remains true, adding a transnational analysis provides deeper understanding of the region's political, cultural, and social dynamics. Transnational dimensions remained strong throughout the process of crystallization of nation-states. With its porous borders and a series of diasporas, migrations, and relocations while facing similar challenges of postcolonial development, Latin America experienced a profound spillover of people and ideas. The region has long witnessed cross-border movements and struggles, prompting international agreements on issues of common concern, including human rights, working out mechanisms regionally even before those principles reached a global scale. Cold War tensions and post–Cold War mechanisms of transitional justice heightened shared experiences, further muddling strong notions of completely separate collective identities and disconnected policies and cultural trends. Social scientists, political theorists, and historians often analyzed these countries either as individual nation-states or as the pawns and victims of global insertion and international intervention. While these aspects are very relevant, in this book I also focus on the transnational linkages operated by exile networks that cross borders and reformulate political projects, the transnational spillover of coercion and narratives of liberation, the character of democratization processes, the crystallization of new transnational movements, and various processes of legitimation and delegitimation of minorities with transnational connections. My first step is to define what is in a name, and what analytical perspectives can best account for the development of this multistate region.

1

Latin America as a Multistate Region

The idea of regions is a highly contested analytical concept and can be subject to criticism from both the optic of distinct nation-states and global perspectives. Due to the constructed conceptual character of regions, attempts at attributing a fixed or essential nature to them are pitfalls. Moreover, the contested and shifting nature of boundaries and borders, particularly under the impact of globalization, beleaguer area studies. Indeed, a series of processes of global interdependence has further called into question the very idea of regions possessing identifiable boundaries and relatively stable sociodemographic configurations. Among them, the heterogeneous process of globalization and multiculturalism stands out; its conceptualization has constantly shifted under the impact of the ebbs and flows of transnational migration, the transference of ideas, the proliferation of diasporas, and the crystallization of increasingly complex identities, commitments, and international alliances.[1] Peter A. Hall and Sidney Tarrow called attention to this trend decades ago, stressing the capacity of area studies to provide context-rich knowledge as well as develop propositions of general applicability.[2]

It is not surprising, then, that the labels usually used to describe the region at the center of this book vary and include Latin America, Hispanic America, Lusoamerica, Iberoamerica, and Francophile America, among others. All of these terms are loaded with diverse historical and political significance, as they were coined by diverse geopolitical projects intended to shape the horizons and political boundaries of the Western Hemisphere. These various conceptual constructs are claims put forward by intellectual and political elites who promoted geopolitical projects envisioning a bridging of the various social, historical, economic, and political contexts of different subregions in the Americas. Debates developed about the very terms used to address a region of fluid boundaries whose connotations have shifted repeatedly in the course of the last two centuries. Yet as stressed by contextual constructionism, though arising in specific contexts, some of those claims have been projected and endorsed recurrently in the region, thus conferring real transnational impact and validation on the contrasting images of Latin American solidarity and fratricide.

Transnational Perspectives on Latin America. Luis Roniger, Oxford University Press. © Oxford University Press 2022.
DOI: 10.1093/oso/9780197605318.003.0002

What Is in a Name? The Conceptual Constructs for a Multistate Region

"Latin America" is the umbrella term I use hereafter. The concept usually encompasses Brazil, Haiti, and the eighteen Spanish-speaking states of the Americas and has come to be used by intellectuals and others in those nations. Writ large, intellectuals, diplomats, activists, and other elites coined the term in the mid-nineteenth century, when the region first witnessed North American expansionism, a generation after the Monroe Doctrine.

With independence, the self-referential term for the region remained Americas and soon Hispanic America and Lusoamerica, to distinguish it from the United States or Anglo-America. In their *Voyage aux régions équinoxiales du nouveau continent* (1816–26), Alexander von Humboldt and Aimé J. A. Bonpland used the term "Latin race" to refer to peoples living in those parts of the Western Hemisphere. Two generations later, a sense of transnational solidarity was generated across the region after the US victory over Mexico in the Mexican-American War (1846–48), followed by the 1856 takeover of power in Nicaragua by William Walker and his North American adventurers. As analyzed in chapter 3, Walker's intention to expand his control across Central America galvanized a coalition of forces in Nicaragua, Costa Rica, and neighboring states to wage a "national war" that in fact was fought by transnational forces. The chance of losing territory again, which was contrary to the principles of Bolivarianism (equal standing of American states and resistance to territorial gains by war, predicated by Simón Bolívar), galvanized the peoples of the Western Hemisphere. In a detailed analysis of "the invention of Latin America," historian Michel Gobat indicated how such developments motivated Spanish Americans to imagine their region as a geopolitical community. Fears of US expansionism mobilized Central Americans and brought South Americans to draft plans for an anti-US alliance, geared to activate South American aid for the war against Walker, while envisioning the creation of a confederation of states resisting US expansion in any part of the continent.[3] In parallel, diplomats and exiles living in Paris coined the term Latin America to represent discursively, and in some cases diplomatically, their home countries vis-à-vis the intellectual and political circles of Europe. At that time, the French state envisioned itself controlling parts of the region, particularly Mexico.

Lusoamerica and Hispanic America are terms with a more restricted denotation than Latin America. Lusoamerica stresses the cultural connection of Brazil, the core seat of the global Portuguese Empire for a short period in the early nineteenth century, to the home country, once the two empires followed their separate paths without engaging in war. The term Hispanic America, while older, grew strongest by the end of the nineteenth and early twentieth centuries.

Following the Spanish-American War of 1898, the modernists resumed a spirit of Hispanic or Iberian rapprochement on which to base their rejection of US expansionism. As for Iberoamerica, that term received support from German Latin Americanists, leaving French *latinité* aside.

In addition to the twenty states usually included, the term Latin America also embraces other territories: Puerto Rico; the French-speaking territories of Canada (mainly Quebec and parts of New Brunswick); parts of the United States (primarily in the South, as in the case of Louisiana); and France's overseas Caribbean departments of Martinique, Guadeloupe, and French Guiana. Likewise, almost half of the continental United States is territory that was conquered—and its population annexed—in the Mexican-American War, which erupted in the wake of US annexation in 1845 of Texas, a state whose secession in the 1830s Mexico refused to recognize. The Latin presence persisted throughout these territories in people's names and sites; in food, customs, and practices; and in historical records and personal memories. Later on, the waves of transnational migration from Latin America—primarily from Mexico, the Caribbean, and Central America—into the United States recreated the meaning of being Latin@ and the boundaries of the "Latin American" region in novel ways.[4]

I retain the term Latin America as a label for the countries of South, Central, and North America shaped by the global expansion of continental Europe into the Western Hemisphere. That turn in history affected the political and economic structures and the collective imagination of the Old World while reshaping the institutions and collective visions of millions living and settling in the Americas. The conquest, settlement, and extraction of riches in the New World would shape the forms of state formation, the development of capitalism, and the construction of civilization by a new type of modernity.

The very existence of a region defined as Latin America or as Iberoamerica is nonetheless problematic. Latin Americans consider themselves Americans, and many oppose the arrogant cooptation of the continent's name by the United States, only one of the thirty-four countries that share the Western Hemisphere.[5] Moreover, one can easily deconstruct the notion by merely indicating the huge differences that separate the component states from one another, in terms of both their demographic composition and their distinct ecological, institutional, and historical development. Students of Latin America stress time and again the inner variability of the region: the huge distance that separates the Afro-Caribbean and Afro-Brazilian areas from the Indo-American mountain ranges and valleys covering the Andes from South to North, and the Euro-American complex of much of the Southern Cone and *mestizo* America as constructed in Mexico, parts of Central America, Venezuela, and so forth. Similarly, from an institutional perspective, the area has lived through a multiplicity of political and institutional experiences, on a spectrum that varies enormously as one goes, for instance, from Cuba, Venezuela, and Bolivia through Brazil, Chile, Argentina, and Mexico, to Colombia and Central America.

Accordingly, it might be wiser to use "Latin Americas" in the plural, provided the term did not sound so awkward. Nonetheless, I claim that with all the aggregative distortion of referring to Latin America in the singular, the term and the images it evokes are highly important. They are significant because they enable the retention of a trans-state and transnational perspective on the region, its institutions, and its political culture. Indeed, the continued use of "Latin America" is justified by the many geopolitical, sociological, and cultural trends that have shaped a contiguity of influences, leading sometimes to confrontations, but overall shaping *a transnational arena of connected histories, interactions, and visions*. Addressing such entangled histories and dynamics requires considering the process of nation building itself, while moving away from methodological nationalism. Only then can one fully understand the dynamics of a region of multiple "sister nations" sharing historical and cultural connections and developing divergent paths while *unable to fully disengage from one another*, thus experiencing persisting processes that cross over international borders.

In Latin America, nation-state horizons increasingly superseded the transnational domain imagined by intellectuals, writers, and activists, but never forced its disappearance. Since Bolívar the Liberator envisioned, yet failed to achieve, his "Bolivarian" vision of a South American political union in the early nineteenth century, the idea of a regional consciousness and identity has never disappeared; rather, it has remained persistently relevant. Independence leaders moved across American territories. José de San Martín became the "Protector of Peru," in addition to liberating Chile after crossing from Cuyo, an area recently incorporated into the realm of Buenos Aires. A native of New Granada, Antonio José de Sucre was head of state of Bolivia. Honduran liberal Francisco Morazán ruled over the entire Central American Republic. Guatemalan Antonio José de Irisarri fulfilled public functions in Chile; as a Chilean diplomat, he served in Buenos Aires, Central America, and Peru, and as a Guatemalan and Salvadoran diplomat, in Ecuador and Colombia, before moving to Curaçao and the United States.

Moreover, based on common roots, culture, and institutions, Latin American societies not only struggled over the porous borders of independent states but also moved to establish international norms of regional interaction and coexistence. The transnational point of departure also led to repeated attempts to create multistate confederations, such as Great Colombia, the Central American Republic, and the Peruvian-Bolivian Confederation, and to the later emergence of international regional organizations, for example, the Andean Community, the Central American Common Market, and Mercosur, and broader regional organizations such as the Bolivarian Alliance for the Peoples of Our America

(ALBA), the Union of South American Nations (UNASUR), and the Community of Latin American and Caribbean States (CELAC).

The transnational domain has remained present in a series of recurrent phenomena. Among them are the repeated emergence of intellectuals and leaders claiming to be speaking not only for their nations but also for their sister nations, as well as the emergence of intellectual and social movements committed to continental horizons, be they reformist or revolutionary. Take for instance Latin American modernists such as José Martí, Rubén Darío, or José Santos Chocano. During his long exile, Cuban poet, essayist, and activist Martí relocated to New York, yet his voice became known transnationally through his columns in periodicals published in Buenos Aires, Caracas, and Mexico. Nicaraguan poet Darío published his book of stories and poems *Azul* in Valparaíso, and he was able to read and find inspiration in French authors consulted while working in a private library in San Salvador. Peruvian poet and diplomat José Santos Chocano published not just in his native Perú but also in Guatemala, Nicaragua, Mexico, and Chile. Moreover, intellectuals were also political figures, whose writings mobilized others to action and whose activism inspired their cultural work. Argentine president Bartolomé Mitre wrote history, and his successor, Domingo F. Sarmiento, was an accomplished essayist. Colombian presidents Rafael Núñez and Miguel Antonio Caro started their careers as men of letters. Even Guatemalan dictator Estrada Cabrera was a poet and patron of poets.[6]

The crystallization of regional practices and legal doctrines imbued with the spirit of Bolivarianism is similar. Ideally, these doctrines were geared to regulating international relationships and reducing tensions between states in the region, as evidenced in the precocious elaboration of principles of nonintervention, rejection of territorial gains by war, treaties that dealt with the widespread presence of political exiles, mechanisms of mediation, and diplomatic negotiation. Last, but not least, has been the recurrent drive to create a myriad of regional and subregional organizations, even if they are overlapping and segmented. Such transnational trends and forces at work justify developing a region-wide analytical perspective, in spite of cross-country variation and the socioeconomic and cultural diversity that prevails within the territorial boundaries of countries.

Another common characteristic in the region, again cloaked in debate, has been the drive of these countries to develop and modernize, an idea that— even if interpreted in contrasting ways, for instance by liberals, Marxists, or neoconservatives—has trickled down from elites and permeated, from very early on, even the lower echelons of society. Again, the issue of Latin American modernities has led to recurrent controversy and discussion. There is much debate about the modernity of Latin America: when, where, and how Latin America is or has been modern. The controversy and subsequent debate has been going on for two centuries, transforming the region into one of the most exciting loci of thought and reflection on collective identities in the world.

Hereafter I attempt to tackle some of the transnational and comparative dimensions of the region, the global connections, and the ways in which collective identities have been constructed and reconstructed. My analysis devotes special attention to the major challenges of *a region "born" global* out of colonialism and intercivilizational encounters, followed by its insertion into global economic circuits in postcolonial times. Seen as the "farthest West," the region maintains an ambiguous and often conflict-ridden relationship with Western modernity and hegemony. Yet, as discussed later in detail, the relatively open-ended character of modernity and its vision of potential material and cultural progress have been major assets for the endorsement of future-oriented perspectives in Latin America. I suggest that in Latin America the confrontation with Western modernity has been a confrontation with roots, discourses, and institutions that turned out to be their own because of colonial and postcolonial domination. Accordingly, from very early on the dynamics of Western development have linked those American territories to global and transnational arenas, turning modernity into an ever-fleeting reality and leading to recurring attempts to reconstitute and attain its unfulfilled promises in the region. Recently, some of these attempts have led to reappraisals of Native American cultural heritages, as in Ecuador and Bolivia, albeit coined also in terms of those unfulfilled promises.

Comparative and Transnational Perspectives on Latin America

Latin America has long been an ideal laboratory for comparative analysis, as it is a multistate and polyglot region with a diversity of races, ethnicities, and cultures, as well as shared historical legacies, institutions, and developmental challenges. Such a perspective has allowed breaking out an excessive focus on individual nation-states, enlightening processes that encompass multiple countries and uniting many political, social, and cultural experiences throughout the Western Hemisphere. It is my claim that notwithstanding the importance of comparative research, we should add a transnational perspective when analyzing Latin America. When combined with a comparative optic, such a perspective enables a richer, multilayered analysis that enlightens the existence of circum-Latin American processes of circulation, transmission, and articulation among subnational, state, regional, and wider arenas and networks.

The transnational perspective stems from finding interlocking approaches between the move to global history and the discussions that such a move has generated among supporters of historical distinctiveness.[7] These discussions have opened the way for bringing comparative analysis and transfer/transnational studies closer and have triggered the analysis of what Sanjay Subrahmanyam has defined as connected histories,[8] or what Michael Werner and Bénédicte Zimmermann have called *histoire croisée*.[9] Indeed, my approach benefits from paradigmatic shifts in history and the social sciences, as developed by Akira Iriye and others, which are of great importance for regional studies.[10]

These developments inform a renewed interest in the emergence of regional frameworks; the redrafting of trans-state exchanges; and the burgeoning presence of transnational movements and networks, both those that support contemporary processes of globalization and many others that oppose it. As Michelle Pace has indicated, regions involve practices of boundary production that construct regions discursively and cannot fully discard contestation and disagreement.[11] From an international relations (IR) perspective, Thomas Risse-Kappen similarly called attention to the multilayered character of transnational interactions across national boundaries "when at least one actor is a non-state agent or does not operate on behalf of a national government or an intergovernmental organization." Increasingly, transnationalism has evinced itself worldwide in thousands of international nongovernmental organizations (IGOs), transnational movements, and transgovernmental issue networks with a growing impact on normative frameworks and ideas such as human rights, the environment, and institutional probity.[12] Accordingly, IR scholars have suggested moving beyond a dichotomist reading of Global North-South relations to engage in an intellectual dialogue across the virtual or imagined North-South divide. According to Arie Kacowicz and Daniel F. Wajner, such dialogue will necessarily challenge the usual hegemonic assumption that only world order scenarios enacted by Northern scholars, politicians, and practitioners have a global reach, whereas the Southern inputs and agency are minimal or nonexistent.[13]

The transnational turn also builds on anticolonialist and postcolonial scholarship, contributing to the analysis of "units that spill over and seep through national borders, units both greater and smaller than the nation-state."[14] Social constructivism has been instrumental in drawing attention to transnational practices, as analyzed by Craig Calhoun and others, along with feminist works elaborated following the seminal notion of the "politics of location," coined long ago by Adrienne Rich.[15]

Within this framework, we discern the vibrant transnational turn to analyses neither fully determined by the whims and primacy of developed countries' geopolitical priorities and visions nor driven fully by globalization. Thus, for instance, by following comparative inquiries into intercrossings between societies, these perspectives provide awareness of how processes and reflexivity about them are—to follow Pierre Bourdieu—socially constructed. That is, we see how they reflect networks, mutual impacts, resistances, inertias, new combinations, and transformations "that can both result from and develop themselves in the process of crossing" social and physical borders. As such, this turn in history and the social sciences conceives the transnational level as interacting with the others, yet creating its own logics and feedbacks: "from being limited to a macroscopic reduction, the study of the transnational level reveals a network of dynamic interrelations whose components are in part defined the links they maintain among themselves and the articulations structuring their positions."[16] In this new stage, there is awareness of the constructed character and multilayered structure of regions. When applied to Latin America, this perspective opens ground for recognizing the existence of shared, distinct, and mutually impinging forms of institutional building and crystallization of civilizational patterns. These can be traced back to the models projected into the transatlantic world with the expansion of Iberian colonialism into the Americas starting in the late fifteenth and early sixteenth centuries. These projections have been reconfigured through three centuries of colonial rule and recreated after political independence, with mutual impact across countries in spite of the process of construction of separate states and nationalities.

In this framework, we can consider several key transnational aspects. Among them are the connections between sister nations, particularly when nonstate actors are involved; the protracted and only partial disengagement from one another's affairs, carried out by political exiles and other wandering individuals; the rise of intellectuals and politicians prioritizing international law and institutions as a way to preserve sovereignty from foreign intervention; and the spillover effects of geographical and historical closeness. All these factors prompt us to realize that by confining our attention only to separate nation-states, we may lose rather than gain perspective on Latin America.

Beyond the question of the appropriate focus of analysis for empirical work, there is much sense in embracing a regional perspective for this set of societies in the Americas, looking also for forces and processes that have connected them beyond their variance, even as we try to understand localized developments and trends. One may easily identify at least three such dimensions of analysis in which the regional perspective may be instrumental in addition to case studies focused on specific countries and subnational arenas. The first is the bridging of scholarly compartmentalization. The second can be seen in the recognition of transnational dimensions that have existed in the region since colonial times but remained largely ignored in the heyday of consolidation of nation-states. Third is the connectedness of historical processes affecting a region, such as political trends, cultural visions, and economic ideas spreading from beyond the boundaries of single states and societies.

A pan–Latin American perspective also provides an ideal framework for comparative analysis. It is instrumental in bridging trendy gaps separating the societies of Latin America in terms of their separate languages, for instance separating Brazil from Spanish- or French-speaking parts of the Americas. Historian Barbara Weinstein has called attention to the ongoing tensions in the field of Latin American history between Spanish America and Portuguese America, asking to what extent they together constitute a coherent subject of study.[17] In spite of Brazil being the biggest, most populous, and until recently, wealthiest and most industrialized country, Weinstein has indicated that at least among historians, Brazilianists often bemoan the reluctance of most Hispanic Americanists to fully integrate Brazil in their analyses. The rather idiosyncratic character of Brazil's postcolonial experience, revealed in its comparative territorial lack of fragmentation, the intensification of plantation economies and slavery (Brazil was the last nation in the Americas to end slavery, in 1888), and the structure of imperial Brazil that contrasted with republican Spanish-speaking countries, prompted the use of separate lenses to approach both areas. Yet as Weinstein shows, by limiting discussion—for example, in colonial/postcolonial studies, to specific subaltern groups, mostly the indigenous populations in most Spanish Americas—rather than addressing many existing and often-blurred categories and conventional boundaries, much is lost.

The dilemmas implied in the construction of national identities and their implications for the marginalization of subaltern groups have been shared across the continental divide between Brazil and Spanish America, beyond specificities due to the demographic composition of the countries. Weinstein discusses, for instance, parallels in the negotiation of inclusion and exclusion that followed the same logic in early postcolonial times. Thus, in Brazil, free persons of color asserted their rights as citizens and resisted the racialization of political status while acquiescing to the limits on citizenship in the form of slavery, much as *mestizo* and *ladino* populations in the Andes, Mexico, and Central America resisted policies that would reduce them to the same status as indigenous populations. By approaching such varied configurations within a shared analytical framework, new understandings of state and nation building are achieved.

A regional perspective also enables defining the national realm in ways that do not endorse essentialism, but rather reconstruct the evolving meanings of being national as often embedded within transnational implications. A classic example is Central America. From a geopolitical perspective, the isthmus is a region composed of small republics standing in relative proximity to one another, making it prone to be affected by political processes in neighboring societies and polities. The core states of Central America trace their origins back to the disintegration of a single state, established in the early nineteenth century, based on a previous colonial jurisdiction. Accordingly, research can trace the parallel processes of construction of separate nation-states and the intricate transnational connections among them, which affected the modes of adoption of institutional and cultural trends identified with modernity. This is crucial for understanding past developments and envisioning the future of that region. Emerging from imperial disintegration, the states eventually strove to create their own nations, attempting to "render them real" by using official accounts and rituals; the elaboration of hegemonic material and symbolic practices; and the structuring of images of peoplehood, connected to spatial and temporal boundaries. Such strategies of nation building involved the partitioning of territories that once belonged to the same political entity, the formation of confined membership, and the delineation of borders, organized according to principles of national sovereignty. Born out of shared colonial administrative jurisdictions and a short-lived attempt at unification following independence, these states have striven to construct their national identities and idiosyncrasies, as well as to develop their institutional distinctiveness. All the while, they have been unable to completely disengage themselves from the "sister republics" and are constantly learning from one another.[18]

The creation of separate nations also involved systems of cultural representation that legitimized or delegitimized different access to the resources controlled by the nation-states.[19] Once separate, the republics faced the dual task of consolidating their territorial control and domination while constructing a sense of collective identity through their policies, practices, and ceremonies. They had to define and create national membership and boundaries, which implied recognizing certain categories of citizenship as paramount, while replacing, ignoring, or denying—without fully eradicating—earlier forms of identification, including the pan-isthmian identity, and subsuming more localized and ethnic identities.

For decades after their separation, the states had porous and poorly defined territories and were not able to seclude themselves from regional interventions, driven by either the prospect of taking power on their own turf or the wish to expand their hold on wider territorial spaces. Overshadowing the construction of sovereign realms and separate identities were their common origins, which left a legacy of cross-national networks of kinship, economic, social, and political ties and an image of an alternative project of regional nation building. Individuals could rely on such an image when relocating to sister countries or challenging current institutional arrangements and political divisions. From the perspective of the symbolic enactment of separate national identities, primordiality—in the form of ethnicity or race—was secondary to the political and civic strategies adopted while constructing nationhood. From early on, elites were fully aware that local identifications existed, but they also recognized that there were no strong lines necessarily separating republics from one another or portraying the others as unalterably different in an incommensurable manner. Moreover, the way in which these states declared independence implied that they envisioned their collective identity not as naturally given, but rather as a civic accomplishment.

These trends draw attention to the importance of keeping a regional perspective as the basis for the analysis of specific countries. In the case of the Southern Cone, it took civil wars over several generations to consolidate the porous and poorly defined territories and unify the different regions into countries. In fact, the formation of Uruguay was intended to conclude the endless struggle between the Portuguese and Brazilian empires and the Spanish-speaking territories. Likewise, in the Andean area, Bolivia, Peru, and Chile became involved in cross-national confrontations that would change their physical and cultural boundaries, with exiles participating in the process of construction of distinctive nation-states. In the northwestern corner of South America as well, Venezuela, Colombia, and Ecuador remained entangled for many decades after the dismemberment of Great Colombia. In the case of the republics of Central America, the process of nation building was also complicated by their shared origins, the complex process of promulgation of independence, and the protracted mutual involvement of each state in the affairs of its neighbors. Thus, for instance, the intervention by North American filibusters in the mid-nineteenth century led to a war fought by what today we would define as a "transnational" alliance of nationals of all isthmian countries. Still, paradoxically—or perhaps not, since it fit the logic of state claims—this war became known in local historiographies as "the National War." Repeatedly, the national angle has been embedded with a transnational dimension. That is, the transnational realm has often supported and superseded the meaning of being part of a nation in the isthmus. A similar dynamic was present in South America.[20]

The concept of transnationalism, as considered in this work, addresses the interconnectivity between individuals, groups, and nations that is often triggered by social processes, political movements, and cultural ideas and networks extending beyond national boundaries and state borders that have in turn conditioned such dynamics.[21] Such interconnectivity may develop—although not necessarily—along organizational lines. Often it becomes equally visible in cultural bonds, historical memories, cross-border networks, and unstructured migration flows. Diaspora networks have been a major instance of such dynamics.[22] Likewise, travels and waves of expatriation and forced migration are also crucial, as they have generated experiences and lifestyles that encompass multiple national spaces and territories, as if they were intertwined or "halfway" ("betwixt and between" was anthropologist Victor Turner's concept, originally used to describe rites of passage). Such varied forms of human mobility have created transnational networks that span several countries and participate in various types of activity, ranging from solidarity and advocacy to illegal and violent social networks, which also operate on a transnational scale. Equally important is the formation of new forms of consciousness and decentered attachment and the correlated appearance of hybrid and multiple identities, as well as cultural spaces that encompass syncretism, bricolage, and cultural translation. Take for example the grassroots movements of both right- and left-wing orientations that maintain transnational contacts and support local networks. In parallel, planetary concerns—with ecology, air pollution, energy, health, and sustainable development—have become increasingly relevant, as evidenced by the growing number of international NGOs. The participation of individuals and nonstate actors in these organizations is a reflection of a growing concern for the human condition in broader terms than ethnic attachments or membership in a nation-state.

The transnational perspective is also important in contemplating how intellectuals, diplomats, jurists, and practitioners have elaborated and promoted norms of international law and international institutions as related to international peace and security, with implications not only for their region, in this case Latin America, but also for the world order as a whole. Arie Kacowicz and Daniel F. Wajner indicate how over two centuries of political sovereignty, Latin American countries developed a strong rejection of external intervention and a distinctive juridical tradition of principles of national sovereignty, nonintervention, and peaceful settlement of disputes among themselves. In addition, the region has pioneered international normatives. Thus, "norms of arms control, collective security, and confidence-building measures have been implemented in Latin America well before Europe. Likewise, the Treaty of Tlatelolco in 1967 established the first nuclear-free zone in the world, setting a precedent for other regions."[23] Equally evident is the precocious role of Latin American countries in developing international humanitarian and human rights law. The region's support for such progress has been shown in the treaties enshrining policies of asylum and in the American Declaration of the Rights and Duties of Man, approved by the Ninth International Conference of American States (Bogotá, 1948), which preceded the United Nations declaration by six months. Moreover, as they made up a third of the initial members of the UN, Latin American delegates were also key actors pushing for a universal recognition of social and economic rights in addition to political and civil rights. Latin American countries have also been pioneers in the global recognition of native rights, as reflected in their majoritarian presence among the signatories of Convention C169 on indigenous and tribal peoples of the International Labor Organization (ILO). In addition, in recent years several of these countries have even incorporated international covenants and human rights law into their own legislation, granting them constitutional precedence over their laws.[24]

The role these states and societies have played in contemporary processes of globalization and trans-state migration, human trafficking, and criminal networks is also relevant. A case in point is the transnational illicit networks that, following migration to the United States in the period of the civil wars in the isthmus and after being socialized into crime there, have been deported or returned to the societies of origin to project their new know-how and transnational contacts into the establishment of illicit networks. These networks cross nation-state boundaries and require a transnational approach on the part of those willing to control their social and political impact.[25] The capacity of these states to cooperate beyond the economic realm, where they have carried out a lifting of custom regulations, depends on long-term memories, suspicions, and commitments. These factors cannot be reduced to economic processes, even if the latter are a highly important component. Social orientations, political culture in a broad sense—which includes narrative constructions, discourse, and practices—and institutional design are also central to such an inquiry on transnationalism.

Another important dimension suggesting the relevance of an approach to Latin America broader than that of nation-states is the connectedness of historical processes affecting the region and its political trends, cultural visions, and economic ideas beyond the boundaries of individual states and societies. Thus, major developments in the history of these countries have occurred due to shifting policies led by hegemonic powers. Latin America went from connecting to an international division of labor under British economic hegemony to joining the US sphere of influence throughout most of the twentieth century, through the Cold War period, subsequent democratization, and the onset of neoliberal policies in the 1990s. Only recently, with the decline of US hegemony and the engagement of Latin America in a multipolar and rather anarchical world order, has this scenario changed radically.

In parallel, anti-Americanism remained salient in Latin America, particularly after the 1890s, when the United States rose to hegemonic status in the Western Hemisphere. This was a reflection of geopolitical conflict—starting as early as the 1840s in Mexico—and the recurrent disappointment with US actions that were not commensurate with the values that many would come to admire in the neighbor in the North. This is what Max Paul Friedman detailed when pointing out an extreme case of that reflection, what he termed the "Nicaraguan paradox":

> Why was the most Americanized country in Central America, whose inhabitants went to far as to prefer baseball to soccer, also home to two of Latin American's most successful revolutionary movements of the twentieth century—bringing down the wrath of the United States upon Sandino in the 1930s and the Sandinistas in the 1980s?[26]

As Friedman elaborates, it was the aggressive US policies and the gap between them and the ideals that the United States claimed to defend—not psychological hatred or irrational paranoia—that stood behind the wary reactions of intellectuals and political activists throughout the region, which provided the transnational banner of solidarity with Latin American sister nations.

One particularly grim part of this interconnectedness in the Americas has been the role played by the United States during the Cold War, as it trained Latin American military officers in The School of the Americas and bolstered repression of leftist activists and presumed sympathizers under the guise of doctrines of national security. The transnational methods of counterinsurgency projected a legacy of human rights violations onto the reconstructed democracies of the region for decades thereafter. In this new stage, any human rights crisis in one country reverberated in the others transnationally.[27]

Another transnational angle of that period of confrontation, repression, deportation, and escape abroad is the phenomenon of massive political exile and the formation of transnational diasporas. The study of political exile shows that individuals forced to relocate in the region have made important contributions to the construction and reconstruction of national narratives since independence. For instance, Edward Blumenthal has shown how the very ideas of Argentine or Chilean nationality were shaped when nineteenth-century exiles and émigrés had to address two different publics by appealing to public opinion through images of a shared history and common past.[28] When states had consolidated there, as elsewhere in the Americas, exiles claimed they were the true representatives of the national spirit and thus redefined repeatedly what it meant to be a national of the country of origin, sometimes even challenging the conception of the national within established borders.[29]

Similarly, recent studies have traced how the transnational gaze between Brazil and neighboring Spanish-speaking countries has impacted ideas not just at the level of knowledge, but also and most effectively at the levels of moral judgment and action, affecting key political and social "national" events. Historian Ori Preuss has shown how the institution of the monarchy loomed large in the self-image of Brazil's intellectual and political elite, as Brazilian stability generated a sense of superiority compared to most Spanish-American republics. Looking at the turmoil and civil wars that had torn apart those republics since independence in the early nineteenth century, Brazilians felt complacent for decades. Those attitudes changed while cooperating with Argentina in the Triple Alliance War against Paraguay (1864–70), challenging the idea of Brazilian superiority and raising concerns about imperial rule and the institution of slavery, which was pervasive in Brazil. Preuss discussed how these concerns led to defiance of the monarchy by Brazilian republicans and liberals in the 1870s and to the eventual fall of the monarchy in 1889. Brazil thus experienced a series of fundamental changes in which Spanish American countries such as Argentina and Chile functioned as a "significant other," being reframed repeatedly by both monarchist and republican leaders into a positive model and playing an important role in redefining regional projects and alliances.[30]

A further focus of recent interest is the study of frontiers as shifting areas of encounter and interaction between societies, economies, and political networks, which underscore the tug of war between modernist projects of state control and the creativity and practices of local peoples moving across borders.[31] There are various fascinating examples of such dynamics and optics leading to new readings of Latin American history. Among them is how to understand the debacle in the Pacific War (1879–83) as developing out of the dynamics of frontier societies rather than as a war resulting from a British conspiracy against Peru and Bolivia with Chile as the proxy partner. In the war, Chile defeated Bolivia and Peru, occupying territory of both countries. Peru and Bolivia lost much territory, including 480 kilometers of coastline, thus closing Bolivia's access to the sea. That war left deep marks on all three countries. Each of the belligerent countries then developed its own narrative to explain and justify the outcome of the war and the basis of what each considered its legitimate rights over the disputed territories. Beyond the conflicting narratives and mutual grievances, professional historians have reconstructed the roots of the conflict in the explosive socioeconomic dynamics of the Bolivian frontier territory of Antofagasta (the so called Provincia Litoral), which was inhabited mostly by Chilean *rotos*, and whose nitrate resources had been leased to the Compañía de Salitres y Ferrocarriles de Antofagasta, backed by mixed Chilean-British capital (more on this in chapter 5).

Of similar historical transcendence is how the porous frontier society between the Dominican Republic and Haiti, exhibiting a mixed Haitian-Dominican background and culture, became targeted by the Trujillo administration in 1937, which manifested in the massacre of thousands of its members in a drive to consolidate borders and fix national identities.[32] Other, more recent cases include the border regions of the Patagonia or Araucanía, the original lands of the Mapuche, where long-lasting connections and crossings survived the imposition of territorial sovereignty by Chile and Argentina;[33] and the Miskitu of Central America. Their kingdom was lost by 1893, when Nicaragua militarily occupied its territory and forced its incorporation into the national territory. Yet in the 1980s the Nicaraguan revolutionary state targeted the Miskitu because it resented their transnational location along the Caribbean coast, which led it to suspect their commitment to the Sandinista government in Managua.[34]

Additionally, standing out in recent years is the growing importance of diaspora studies that place the binomial of being simultaneously national and transnational at the center of inquiries into citizenship and its relationship to the construction and reconstruction of collective identities. In the past, the main concern of academics studying migration was to follow patterns of sociocultural integration within national fabrics and the emergence of hyphenated identities of migrants as both citizens and members of ethnocultural communities. In recent years, new perspectives have emerged that stress the role of expatriate communities in both the home countries and the countries of relocation as well as in the formation of new transnational identities, be they political, religious, or ethnic.[35] A paradigmatic case is that of the Caribbean island societies, whose dynamics of dispersal have raised awareness of the intricacies of diaspora life. Tracing the new optic on new national spaces in the Spanish Caribbean, historian Blanca G. Silvestrini indicated that a major challenge of the new historical studies is the question of borders, blurred by transnational mobility, remittances, and multiple cultural and physical transfers:

> How do we understand nations that are on the move, with large portions of their population living outside the traditional national boundaries; nations whose social classes subsist a world apart; national spaces complicated by Creole languages and linguistic accents and whose people belong to cohorts that experience the national spaces in radically different terms?[36]

Only relatively recently have the transnational dimensions seriously been taken into consideration. Historically, attention focused on how nation-states defined the nature of citizenship and how the global insertion dictated a pattern of belated, uneven development. The impact of the Cold War and the subsequent wave of democratization, with their subsequent spillover across the continent; the massive character of migration and exile; the rising role of diasporas; and the problematic projection of illegal transborder networks have changed that perspective. All these processes have promoted an increasing awareness of the importance of transnational factors in shaping the historical and contemporary development of Latin American countries and mindfulness of the impact of those living lives in motion, beyond the boundaries of national home territories.

The transnational optic has thus reshaped how we approach the societies in the region, studying how they have interacted with and envisioned each other, at once in complementary and competitive ways. From that perspective, we can follow how the national domain has been constructed in tandem with intellectuals' and political actors' reshaping of knowledge, images, and moral judgment, affecting others transnationally across state borders. Such an approach calls into question the older ways of approaching Latin American history by focusing just on separate states or by stressing a postcolonial situation. Adding to those lines of analysis, important as they are, the transnational perspective calls attention to a no less important dimension: the persistent yet changing connections and interactions between states, nations, and societies in the region. This work suggests that much can be gained by following such a perspective as we look for clues about the Latin American historical experience, starting with these societies' entangled global insertion.

2

Latin American Modernities

Global, Transnational, Uneven, Open-Ended

As a concept used by academics, modernity has been associated with a series of sociological, political, economic, and cultural trends that altered the forms of space/time constitution of many societies worldwide. In the Western world, many conceived of the concept as intimately connected to the development of new forms of rationality, novel institutional frameworks, capital accumulation, and mercantile capitalism, starting in the age of discovery and later encompassing processes of growing urbanization, bureaucratization, rapid transportation, and communication. Less emphasized, though no less essential, were the imperialist designs of the core nations of the West, geared both toward global domination and taking control of human and material resources. As such, modernity shaped a stratified and hierarchical international system, buttressed by a cultural program predicating civilizational superiority over other Latin American societies, placed in a "trans-European penumbra."[1]

Modernity involved both a cultural program and multiple institutional processes that affected societies across the world. It involved a forward-looking attitude, shifts in the conception of human agency, the assumption of a stable self, a reflexive consciousness geared to innovation, and the creation of new institutions—trends that would be projected worldwide. Modernity also exhibited dark sides. Evidence of this is in the ultramarine, imperialist expansion and colonialist domination of subjugated Native American populations, along with the enslavement of African populations, accomplished through violence and with genocidal consequences. Since early colonial times, the legacies of colonialism and internal exclusion continued to shape many aspects of these societies, as reflected in their institutions, social order, and self-reflection, including in the religious and cultural domains. Yet one should stress at the outset that Latin America has also been a pioneer region in which those exclusionary and discriminatory trends have been contrasted with ideas of republican citizenship, rights, and social justice.

Accordingly, Latin America has maintained an ambiguous and sometimes conflict-ridden relationship with the poles of Western development and expansion since colonial times. In spite of such tension-ridden and even contradictory implications, the relatively open-ended character of modernity and its élan

Transnational Perspectives on Latin America. Luis Roniger, Oxford University Press. © Oxford University Press 2022.
DOI: 10.1093/oso/9780197605318.003.0003

of material and cultural progress, the promise of expanding access and relative freedom from traditional and confined ties, have been a major source of appeal for its upwardly mobile elites and popular sectors. Even if the term "modern" was seldom claimed by parties or social movements in the region, the plethora of correlates of modernity has long attracted the imagination and shaped the agendas of Latin American countries, albeit in varied ways, sometimes wrangling with deep concern about their problems and at other times defending their civilizational standing on the global scene. The correlates of such confrontation with modernity have ranged from openness to new ideas and technical knowledge to republican politics and the crystallization of new collective identities opened to public opinion and celebration of freedoms.

Atlantic Modernity and Colonialism

In the context of transatlantic development, the uses and analysis of Latin America in terms of modernity have led to controversy and debate. As these societies crystallized as a result of Western European colonial expansion and, once independent, remained for long in a postcolonial bind, the discourse of modernity—or its translation into notions such as the promotion of civilization or progress—often has been suspected of being an instrument of what Aníbal Quijano called the "coloniality of power."[2] Thus, for example, as a political credo, liberalism was suspected of serving the expansionist drives of capitalist, imperialist, and globalizing interests, starting in the 1920s and acting more forcefully in later decades.

Many observers that the discourse of modernity served to disguise exploitation and control by external powers and forces over the societies and economies of the region. Traditionally, these societies have had a marginal position in global geopolitics; they were at the periphery and semiperiphery of the world system, to use the terminology of world-system theory. Their geopolitical position in the international system was also replicated within each society, through a series of hierarchical controls aimed at dominating the subaltern classes, exploiting them and relegating them to the realm of the "traditional," despising and marginalizing them.[3]

The debate on modernity in Latin America is also tied to the question of whether we can use a generic term to pool together the distinct societies and states of the region, whose internal structures and developmental trends are as varied as their external differences. Such use is sometimes contested by those who claim that the divergent configuration, composition, and institutional development of these societies do not merit their analysis as part of a supposedly "empty" label created out of Western Europe and North America. Thus, as

I tackle the focus of this discussion, I need to address both the ways their modernity or lack thereof can be conceptualized, particularly in connection with globalization, and the lenses through which the societies of Latin America have been
categorized and interpreted. It is to this double task that I turn in this chapter.

The discussion of the relationship between Latin America and the globalizing
trends of modernity has a long tradition in sociology and history, as well as in the
humanities.[4] The very rise of the West cannot be explained except in terms of the
multiple colonialist and imperialistic interactions with the Americas and Africa.
For over three centuries, the American territories under consideration turned to
be in the orbit of Iberian and other West European powers and then under the
rising hegemony of the United States, which *claimed the name "America" exclusively for itself.*

The existence of an Atlantic modernity, to use Jeremy Smith's term,[5] has been
stressed time and again both by scholars of world history and by researchers
of both colonialism and intercivilizational encounters. Even though analysts
differ in their premises and lines of inquiry, claiming that the supporters of
perspectives other than their own ignore the basic lines of structuring of
interactions between the Americas and the centers of world development,
diverging scholars nonetheless converge in recognizing the centrality of such
interactions in enabling or even triggering modernity. In other words, even if
working from distinct perspectives, there is widespread support for the view
that modernity as an expanding structural phenomenon—with all its new
forms of space/time constitution—started with the so-called discovery and settlement of the Americas.[6]

In contrast, the uneven development and sociopolitical configuration of the
region led some observers to question the seemingly globalized and modern
Western physiognomy the societies of Latin America exhibited, which their
leaders often professed to endorse. This awareness brought a number of scholars
and activists to challenge the truisms about Latin America being part of a universal mode of modernity and ask the question in a bold way: "[W]hen [and
where] was Latin American modern?"[7] Historian Alan Knight even asserted that
the concept of modernity is not of much help as a heuristic device for understanding Latin America, unless we define it in terms of a discernible set of ideas
associated with the Enlightenment, rationalism, secularism, humanism, and ma-
terialism, and measure how these survived in Latin America, "like galaxies in the
void of space."[8] Other scholars, such as political scientist Laurence Whitehead,
have claimed otherwise. Namely, they have suggested that Latin Americans' self-
constructions are projected as belonging to the West and accordingly have been
wide open to modern ideas and innovations. This has distinguished this region
from others in the Global South, in that the notions and expectations associated with what we understand as modernity have rather early "become part of

the 'tacit knowledge' used by local actors and their external interlocutors alike in their routine praxis."[9]

In order to assess what modernity has denoted in Latin America, I next review the constructs and images attributed to the region, subsequently addressing the frames and perspectives on modernity in the region and their relationship to global processes taking place on the world scene.

Latin America and Its Multiple Modernities

Beginning in the nineteenth and into the twentieth centuries, the image of Latin America was often assembled by contrasting the historical reality in the region with a stylized ideal of Western societies, so that Latin America emerged as exhibiting a long history of pathologies and dwarfed institutions. Sometimes this even occurred in the form of a caricature, as in the image of "banana republics" attributed to Central America. Latin American intellectuals also fell into the trap of sometimes depicting European and North American societies in an idealized way, even if the latter were "as littered with grandiose but ultimately incomplete modernization projects [as] Latin America."[10] As James Dunkerley showed in *Americana*, from very early on there were mutual flawed constructions of these societies' images, both across the Atlantic and along the North-South axis in the Americas.[11]

The discourses of modernity and the debates around them addressing Latin America in many ways resemble earlier discussions on the program of modernity as envisaged by the Enlightenment in Europe, yet they go beyond them by stressing that the category of Western modernity does not fully encompass their historical path. For instance, Latin America shared with the United States a sense of being a land of utopia, a promised land, the target of dreams, a land of open opportunities, which was built up around the ideals and expectations of the Enlightenment and even pioneered its implications for expanding liberty, equality, and universal fraternity.[12]

Due to their historical configuration, *the societies of Latin America are and are not part of the West*. They have endorsed modern notions of republicanism, citizenship, representative democracy, civic associations, elections, public debate and public spheres, justice, and equality before the law, wrangling with them as part of their own colonial traumatic origins. Yet at the same time, these societies have had distinctive cultural-demographic setups, developing specific institutional trends and notions and adapting political ideas as they took over positions of power, often betraying those ideas to be able to rule in societies that also opened their public arenas to wider social strata, at least de facto. From a worldwide perspective, they have pioneered notions of modern republicanism, social justice, and human rights, even if many observers in the Global North have ignored these trends, depicting Latin America as a caricature of itself or overlooking these trends' eclectic, multiple, and varied manifestations.

Human societies differ widely, due not only to their structural setup but also to the different civilizing and soteriological visions that infuse life in society with meaning. While comparing societies, we should recognize—as Ernest Gellner reminds us—that various societies have developed different answers and solutions to the same questions about human existence and life in society.[13] Shmuel Noah Eisenstadt, Jóhann Páll Árnason, and other scholars have defined such a view as a perspective of multiple modernities, entailing the idea that while modernity could be viewed as a distinct civilization, related to distinct institutional trends in politics and the economy, it has unfolded in multiple patterns worldwide. As a distinct civilization, *modernity evinces certain premises*, among which stand out a continuous reconstruction of roles and identities, a growing autonomy from ascribed frameworks, an increased reflexivity, and the decline of markers of certainty. Yet that program of modernity has met with varied forms of contestation, appropriation, and transformation, thus creating not one but *multiple patterns of modernity*. In other words, as it turned global, modernity became plural. Even those movements that usually claim to fight modernity and predicate a fundamentalist return to pristine culture—for example, contemporary Islamic radicalism—are in fact redefining the meanings of their path into the global scene, which is none other than modern.[14]

In this framework, it is important to stress that—beyond all the colonial and postcolonial violence, as well as the mercantilist and capitalist integration into world circuits as producers of primary wealth ranging from minerals to cattle products, crops, and consumers of manufactured products—the societies of Latin America have developed global, multiple, and yet often truncated modernities. These tendencies started to develop very early throughout the region, albeit at different rhythms. From their very inception, elites connected those societies to external centers and global circuits, as part of the economic and political, religious, cultural, and ideological centers of an emerging Atlantic modernity.

Atlantic modernity attempted to replace and obliterate—with variable success—the memory of successive imperial waves of autochthonous modernization. Those previous waves are epitomized in the astronomical discoveries of the Maya, the advanced uses of landscape and urban design by the Aztecs, and the forward-looking modes of redistribution of agricultural surpluses and symbolic organization of space and society orchestrated by the Incan political center. In this sense, we should consider Western-originated globalization another cycle in an ongoing process triggered by earlier imperial expansions and reinforced by the shifting and expanding unfolding of the capitalist system, a process neither peculiar nor limited to recent and contemporary historical conditions.[15]

A kind of global awareness crystallized and provided parameters of institutional building and reflection in these societies, led by upper classes and elites who thought they were pioneering new ideas and practices, while struggling with and subjugating subaltern populations as they envisioned being part of the upward mobile strata of Atlantic modernity.[16]

Yet while imagining themselves as taking part in Atlantic modernity, these elites soon realized that their demographics and identities, their social problématique and the construction of political order, were not identical to those of Europe. Being at the crossroads of Western European expansion into the New World, individuals in the Americas realized very early on that their experience differed from that of their Old World contemporaries. Many of the descendants of non-Western civilizations, such as the peoples of the Inca Empire, the historical Maya kingdoms, and the forcibly displaced members of African societies enslaved in the Americas, attempted to keep their cultural distinctiveness alive. Those arriving from Europe and their Creole descendants could not avoid reflecting on the distinctiveness of their new social environment, even as they attempted to share the culture, values, and lifestyles that Iberians followed in the peninsula.

By being in a different world, interacting with others not found in the societies of origin or in precolonial times, along with being exposed to diverse tastes, illnesses, sounds, and sights that triggered awareness of such differences, neither settlers nor subject populations could avoid considering that their markers of certainty did not fit exactly those of the "mother countries." Whether supporting social and moral principles that they considered universally valid or particular to them, the experience of the New World gave rise to reflexivity, rebellion, and struggle, typical of modern contexts and frames of mind.

This reflexivity had global referents, yet underwent a twist as these societies entered fully the period of construction of self-constituted—mostly republican—polities in the nineteenth century and went through new transformations in the late nineteenth and twentieth centuries. Even very early in colonial times, there were several sources of reflexivity. First, the colonists were part of multiple frameworks of identity, of expansive powers that were in fact just a composite of monarchies, to use John H. Elliott's depiction of Spain, and of intersecting and diverse ways of life.[17] This prompted *intersectionality* and precluded the formation of uniform criteria of membership. Rather, crosscutting criteria prevailed: being Catholic; being subjects of a composite monarchy ruling over different kingdoms; being members of local settlements and yet separated by their standing in social hierarchies; being Whites and non-Whites; and being free, semi-free, and non-free individuals, among many other criteria.[18]

Elites interpreted those criteria in a nonorthodox manner, creating an elasticity that the distance from the centers of power in the Iberian Peninsula shaped into a persistent gap between the letter of the law and its implementation for centuries to come. For example, while in theory non-Christians could not migrate to the Americas, in practice many (among them crypto-Jews and crypto-Muslims) crossed the Atlantic and became members of local communities, especially during Castile's annexation of Portugal between 1580 and 1640.[19] Similarly, as Tamar Herzog has shown, while there was a distinction between Whites and non-Whites, the criteria were not strictly racial, but rather embedded biological considerations within cultural and socioeconomic cultural traits, "thus allowing dark-skinned people to become 'White' and 'darkening' [some of] those with a fair complexion."[20]

This trend of crosscutting criteria of membership and multiple intersectionality, as well as the gap between social practices and formal institutional rules, which were always subject to negotiation, persisted in various forms well into contemporary times. The result has been the recreation of dynamics of confrontation and debate between "purists"—be they conservatives, liberals, or revolutionaries attempting to reach power—and the more pragmatic orientations that, once they reached power, social and political forces adopted, even betraying the ideals they had held before.

Adding complexity was miscegenation, religious syncretism, and emerging hybrid identities. In Spanish and Portuguese America, peoples and traditions from Europe, the Americas, and Africa met on unequal ground, yet they impinged upon one another from the start. Hierarchical domination and colonial controls were imposed on subaltern sectors by a minority of conquerors, settlers, and patrons. However, societies became complex very early on, due to factors such as the gender ratio of colonizers to the colonized and the sequel generations of mixed offspring, the dynamics of mutual accommodation and negotiation, the distance from the metropolitan centers of power, and the frontier-like character of settlements dispersed in territories larger than anything known in the Old World. Thus, despite the destruction of earlier social systems, annihilation of entire populations, and shattering of aboriginal cultures, the conquest and colonization of the Americas opened room for syncretism and alternative modes of identity formation.

Challenges were common from very early on, originating in the descendants of the settlers; the heirs of native nobility; the Indian commoners; the slaves, runaway slaves, and freemen; and the growing sectors of mixed backgrounds. Miscegenation (*mestizaje*) implied much disappointment for those eager to climb the upper echelons of the social hierarchy, yet integrationist images did not disappear but rather merely amalgamated in new forms as part of the Bolivarian and republican ethos that became dominant in the nineteenth century.[21] Since then, and into the twenty-first century, miscegenation has become a pervasive trait that has generated ambiguity, in tandem with religious syncretism and hybrid structures, all constituting major trends in the social composition, the stereotypes and discrimination of subaltern sectors, and their collective reflexive images. In the heyday of racism, miscegenation prompted doubts about the ability of these societies to embrace "civilization," while mixed demographics proved to be key in producing more assertive visions of self-representation such as those of the *raza cósmica* in twentieth-century postrevolutionary Mexico or the *homem cordial* in republican Brazil. Such visions condensed sets of values deemed by elites to be crucial for maintaining social unity and order under real-life conditions of disaggregation, submerging conflicts and containing violence.

Another axis of reflexivity involved the continuous questioning of and need for legitimizing societies' collective identity, which was in part triggered by cultural transformations and the internal controversies led by various parts of colonial and postcolonial society, and due also to inter-European struggles such as those centered on the so-called Black Legend of the conquest of America. In the eighteenth century, Americans found themselves increasingly entangled in controversies about the nature of their societies. Some, like the Jesuits exiled to Europe, looked for the indigenous roots of the distinctive American identities and tried to establish the image of Aztecs and Incas as civilized nations far more advanced than the Romans in Gaul and England.[22] In this endeavor, those authors continued a line perhaps initiated by Bartolomé de las Casas and Peter Martyr's letters (which influenced Montaigne's and Europe's mythical image of the "noble savage" in the sixteenth century). As analyzed in detail by Antonello Gerbi and Leopoldo Zea, the displaced Jesuits were opposing Europeans who, seduced by visions of their Enlightenment, portrayed the New World as a feeble version of Europe.[23] Whether defending or deploring the condition of the Americas and their people, or struggling to uphold the seemingly "pristine values" of their countries, those Jesuits—like many in the Western Hemisphere—thought themselves part of a global scenario, and as such reflected on their place among world societies.

The perception of those growing up in the Americas underwent many changes in the following centuries, while at the same time the view of being part of a globalizing trend of modernity persisted. The sense of tilting toward modernity, however, came with an awareness of difference, lending itself to what we now define as part of a road of multiple modernities. At the core of this approach is the view that these societies combined a global insertion, being fully integrated into world circuits, and sharing with other societies in the West basic premises of political and economic order, while simultaneously evolving their own path. In the case of Mexico, anthropologist Claudio Lomnitz defined this path as that of an "Indian modernity."[24]

Collective identities are predicated on a varied mixture of universal and particularistic themes, symbols, and representations.[25] In 1810, the American delegates complained of injustice when the Cortes of Cádiz did not fully take into account the size of the American population—unlike that of Spaniards residing in the peninsula—in determining the number of representatives. The argument used was that, as the indigenous population was said to lack an education, they could not be considered full members of a civilized society. As the American territories disengaged from the Spanish monarchy and the political classes promulgated independence, they adopted republican models of political organization and resorted to the mythology of claiming to be descendants of Incas, Aztecs, and others, as the basis for their claimed legitimacy, mainly—yet not only—in the areas densely populated by indigenous peoples. Contrasting their republican polities based on democratic principles with the monarchical and despotic turn of Europe after 1815, they portrayed pre-Columbian civilizations as models of political wisdom, tolerance, and even individualism.[26]

Since then, Latin American societies have tended to downplay the primordial elements in their collective representation, giving primacy to civil-political criteria of full membership. Political actors and intellectuals split over how to integrate the indigenous populations and whether to respect their communal organization or suppress it forcefully in the name of universal inclusion, with the covert agenda of taking over their lands. In Mexico or Paraguay, national identities were constructed around the idea of fusion of races (or languages in the latter case), intimately connected to images of Latin Americanism and universalism.[27] By the late nineteenth and early twentieth centuries, social Darwinism had bent earlier paternalistic indigenism into a more racialized vision of unequal races. Nonetheless, social and revolutionary struggles launched expansive cycles of recognition. Starting with the Mexican Revolution in the 1910s, societies would again assert the symbolic salience of their autochthonous roots, reaching by the late twentieth century a cycle of official recognition in the "aspirational constitutionalism" of countries such as Colombia, Bolivia, and Ecuador, which amended and redrafted their constitutions in the spirit of plurinationalism. In these and other cases, the basic charters followed a future-oriented perspective, without necessarily being a reflection of their present situations. According to Mauricio García Villegas, who coined the term, aspirational constitutionalism thrives in situations of inconformity with the present and a strong aspiration for a change and a better situation in the future. In that future-oriented option, the drafters hoped that the promulgated clauses would become reality, even if that depended on the commitment of political forces and social movements, the mobilization of public opinion, and a judicial activism aimed at making them effective.[28]

Latin American symbolic self-representations also drew on other images. Sometimes those representations reflected the imposing nature of landscapes, which were immortalized among others in the *Canto general* (1950) of Chilean poet Pablo Neruda, and the universal aspirations of important sectors in these societies, which prompted a continuous search for universal models of development and institutionalization. The universal, global orientation implied a tension between political ideas and the social and political dynamics—either demographic-cultural or socioeconomic-geopolitical—that, at various historical moments, were interpreted as placing these societies at a structural disadvantage vis-à-vis other societies of the expanding global system.

As soon as these societies attained political independence, their elites saw themselves at the forefront of modern world politics, as independent, mostly republican states. As Eduardo Posada-Carbó and Iván Jaksić pointed out in a comprehensive historiographical essay, the early nineteenth-century Hispanic liberal wave constituted a third revolution, after that which had occurred in the thirteen North American colonies and the French Revolution. Following Armando Martínez Garnica, Posada-Carbó and Jaksić indicated that the liberal agenda

> covered a wide programmatic spectrum: freedom of the press, division of powers, popular sovereignty and representative government, abolition of privileges and legal exemptions (fueros), elimination of Indian tribute, manumission of slaves, and constitutional designs that in New Granada, Venezuela, and Chile actually preceded the liberal [Spanish] Constitution of Cádiz in 1812.[29]

However, as there was little division of labor between intellectuals and politicians in the nineteenth century, while that ideology served those elites aspiring to reach power, "once in power Liberals found themselves confronted with their own convictions,"[30] adapting those ideas into a mere instrument of power and sometimes even betraying them. Unsurprisingly, a basic tension crystallized between their optimistic future-oriented outlook, on the one hand, and the ensuing deep sense that modernity did not fully develop but rather was truncated, on the other, along with a growing reason for concern due to the current state of their societies. Simón Bolívar the "Liberator" expressed such concerns as his conscious effort to create a liberal nation composed of "good citizens" seemed to fail.[31] Due to the particular modes of insertion into the global system and configuration of rather open public spheres in the process of detachment from Spanish rule and subsequent civil wars, many of the high expectations led to a sense of disappointment and lack of fulfillment, witnessing impaired accomplishments and a peripheral standing surrounded by the global scene. Yet it is worth stressing that such a sense inhered in the character of the ideals they had pioneered and pined to materialize. Moreover, liberalism had long-term consequences, as reflected in the emancipation of slaves in most countries—with the exception of Cuba, Puerto Rico, and Brazil—at the latest around the mid-nineteenth century, before US abolition, which took a major war to occur.

In the nineteenth century, as they emerged from the initial wave of revolutionary wars, Latin American states pioneered Enlightenment ideas of republicanism, democratic practice, and social rights, and tried to implement them as an alternative to European old regime institutions and practices. Posada-Carbó and Jaksić called attention to the initial pull of that philosophy in 1808–25, with lasting impact in the nineteenth century. James Dunkerley and James E. Sanders, among others, have analyzed liberalism there as the model adopted for shaping the future in Central America and for Mexico, Colombia, and Uruguay in the 1840s to 1870s, respectively. Elites and sectors participating in the public sphere imagined Latin America in future-oriented terms and through the prisms of civilization and modernity, envisioning a universal and global project. Grounding that initial organization was the principle of popular sovereignty, based on which they claimed legitimacy for the new states in the name of republican representation. Even in provincial areas, such as Yucatán in Mexico, there was already a buoyant celebration of progress in the mid-1840s, as traced by James Dunkerley:

> We have literary, scientific, commercial and political journals. There are today in Mérida philanthropic societies, reading groups and scientific academies. Pioneering businesses have triumphed; we have a stagecoach network, cafés, hotels and recreational associations. Primary education has acquired new energy; the government is improving and makes efforts to develop agriculture; roads have been built and repaired. In short, we are on the road to progress.[32]

Similarly, James E. Sanders pointed out how biased and prejudiced the often accepted master narrative that Latin America remade itself in the image of Europe has been, when in fact Latin America, at least in part of the nineteenth century, developed what he calls a "countervision of modernity," seeing itself as embodying "the future":

> A Mexican provincial newspaper argued that instilling "democracy" and "having triumphed among us the latest progresses of human learning" had "made us equal to the old civilizations" of Europe. . . . [Francisco Bilbao] proclaimed that Europe, lacking true liberty . . . would have to wait for [Latin] America "to regenerate the spirit of Old Europe."[33]

At one point the elites proclaimed that vision as a means for the construction and reconstruction of their nations within the framework of innovation while addressing Iberian and European ideas, and they saw themselves as starting an open-ended path of renewal of ideas and institutional innovation.[34] Liberalism had to contend with conservative ideas and with the persistent power and appeal of Catholicism among wide sectors of the population, leading to most violent confrontations and civil wars, for example in Colombia. Liberalism came under attack and underwent various up-and-down cycles, with different countries diverging in its rhythms and impact, though generally declining toward the 1920s. However, some of the ideals it introduced can be identified as reemerging as a discursive tool for those resisting and censuring the repressive regimes of the 1970s to 1980s, and even influencing the rhetoric of populist and revolutionary movements predicating alternative paths of modernity.

With the passing of time, and as societies engaged in internal struggles and civil wars and lagged behind in institutional and economic development, it became common to view the problems of truncated modernity in terms of an internal fight around progress or, as epitomized in the renowned work of Domingo Faustino Sarmiento, of civilization against barbarity. When Sarmiento wrote *Civilización y barbarie* (1845), he was fully aware of the French periodical literature of his period; knew the work of historians such as Guizot, Michelet, and Thierry; and in his prologue observed that South America as yet lacked a work comparable to Alexis de Tocqueville's *Democracy in America*, which was published only shortly before Sarmiento's piece.[35] According to him, the political conditions of independence created an environment in which only the despotism of harsh *caudillos* could prevent society from lapsing into civil war, anarchy, and banditry. Yet such despotic order was inimical to progress and indeed expressed a struggle between rural *caudillismo* and urban culture, with Buenos Aires as the epitome of future order and civilization. Both Sarmiento and his critics (e.g., Juan Bautista Alberdi) agreed that their country should emulate European paths to civilization, drawn by the binary opposition between liberal progress—as exemplified by France, Great Britain, and the United States—and Catholic Spain, the source of conservatism and stagnation in the Americas.[36]

Throughout Latin America, seclusion from global forces and currents was in most cases not considered an option, and seclusion from neighboring sister nations and states or provinces was a structural impossibility. Elites purposely looked to maintain a dialogue with the ideas and practices of Western modernity, not mimicking them, but rather adapting them eclectically and innovating according to their own experience.[37] The reflexive concern with the inner fabric and dynamic of their societies led them to develop ideas and practices in their own way. Threatened by the presence of the masses, once in power, liberalism soon turned elitist ("moderate"), whereas conservatism admitted the caducity of some of the old regime's ideological foundations. The rather conservative vein of liberalism (lacking much of the pragmatic orientation that it exhibited in the United States) and the liberal vein of conservatism agreed on the need to lead change. They differed mainly in the pace and agency of the change and the progress they envisioned: Would history dictate organically the rhythm of change, as claimed by Latin American conservatives, or should social forces promote it actively, imprinting a progressive shift in history, as claimed by liberals?

Later on, as civil wars waned and institutional stability could be foreseen, the drive toward modernity continued in societies that had turned elitist and oligarchic. Positivism was adopted—more Comtean and authoritarian in Mexico, Chile, Brazil, and Venezuela, and more Spencerian and Darwinian in Argentina, Uruguay, and Colombia—for its promise of order toward the consecution of industrial and scientific progress. Likewise, as positivism was adopted in the region, its corollaries underwent transformations. Whereas in Europe positivism became connected with racist trends, in Latin America it predicated progress through miscegenation and assimilation of subaltern sectors into a "Creole race," a process to be pursued by whatever means, even by force or by replacement— that is, by welcoming massive flows of immigrants.[38]

At times the lack of signs of progress induced pessimism and a sense of failure. Elites followed, interacted, and hoped to have an impact on global models and ideas, turning them into institutional guides and converting Latin America into what Laurence Whitehead has called a "mausoleum of modernities." This notion conveys the idea that each wave of modernity reached a truncated end or just reinforced previous imbalances in society and was soon followed by another wave of innovation and new ideas struggling to accomplish the uneven fulfillment of the promises of modernity.

Historian Tulio Halperin Donghi also stressed that intellectual and political elites incorporated selectively ideas and modern institutions as they coped with specific challenges in their societies.[39] In connection with Brazil, Roberto Schwarz once questioned whether these modern epitomes were merely "ideas out of place."[40] We may assume that due to their global immersion, leading elites and social strata used globally fashionable idioms and symbolic markers to interpret reality and compete for political power and cultural hegemony, often translating these notions into oppressive forms of domination of the subaltern groups, yet meeting a continuing struggle of civil sectors demanding greater equality and social justice. As these struggles took place in societies that differed from those in which the ideas originally crystallized, the cultural lenses themselves shifted and metamorphosed into more eclectic—or perhaps I should say "multiple"— frameworks of analysis.

It is important to realize that even if most Latin American projects of modernity had external referents, they were not necessarily derivative, as stressed by Nicola Miller in her analysis of key intellectual figures of the early twentieth century in the region:

> In any case, the creation of the Latin American 'other' was as complex and variegated as its creation of self: these intellectuals sought inspiration not only

from Britain, France, and the United States, but also from Russia, Spain, Italy, Germany, Japan, China, Australia, and New Zealand. Experiences within Latin America were also crucial: Buenos Aires became a touchstone of modernity for the rest of Latin America; after the Mexican Revolution of 1910–1920, Mexico City became another major point of reference. All advocates of modernity in Latin America have made reference to external examples—as often as not, in order to illustrate what *not* to do.[41]

Also crucial was the transnational communication and exchange of ideas between nationals of different societies that shared the same language, had a common past, and faced similar challenges in the present, which prompted learning from each other. Illustrative of this is how, in the nineteenth century, South American historians participated in a republic of letters, as Argentine historian Bartolomé Mitre maintained an active exchange with Chilean Benjamín Vicuña Mackenna after they spent time together in prison, and with Diego Barros Arana; the latter was in contact with Colombian José María Restrepo, and Restrepo with Venezuelan Rafael María Baralt. Bolivian Gabriel René-Moreno studied with Chilean Miguel Luis Amunátegui, Peruvian Felipe Paz Soldán maintained an exchange with Mitre and Vicuña Mackenna, and Ecuatorian Federico González Suárez was in contact with Colombian José Manuel Groot.[42] In addition, Spanish and Latin American liberals maintained an active political and cultural dialogue, particularly in the 1857–86 period,[43] laying the ground for a pan-Hispanic revival in parts of the twentieth century.

The transnational gaze of sister nations also explains why multiple societies entered cycles of authoritarianism or democratization, as they contemplated the experience and policy decisions and calibration of those nations. For example, such a bias was evident in the last wave of democratization, as societies in the region maintained a mutual gaze, learning from each other's experiences transnationally as they faced similar challenges. When the Southern Cone societies shifted away from repressive authoritarianism and embraced civilian democracy, they all confronted similar grim legacies of human rights violations. Each society looked for precedents and tried to assess the adequacy of the institutional path followed by the other countries, finding inspiration and recognizing dangers while observing and interpreting the experience of the others, as I discuss in greater detail in chapter 7.[44]

The idiom of Western modernity did not go unchallenged, in part due to the inner ambivalence between liberty and equality, and between representation and participation, yet also as alternative traditions coexisted with the mainstream patterns of organization in the Americas. Among them, indigenous traditions that persisted over time, even if it took time to fully recognize their concepts of "good living" and sustainable development—for example, Andean *sumak kawsay, suma qamaña,* and *allin kawsay*—appeared in official charters and in multicultural and intercultural directions, including education and alternative medicine, as research by David Lehmann, Deby Babis, and John Stolle-McAllister has shown[45] African beliefs, customs, rhythms, and flavors were contributed by the uprooted descendants of forced laborers and slaves. In addition, a range of ideological views was brought by immigrants as they arrived massively in the second half of the nineteenth and first quarter of the twentieth centuries. More recently, various postmodern forms of social disaggregation, misinformation, and disinformation have added complexity as well.

The confrontation between elite imagination and those alternative perspectives has been a long-lasting experience in Hispanic America and Lusoamerica. We can trace it back to as early as colonial times as it spread through a wide variety of realms, most importantly, however, as a religious quest for salvation.[46] It acquired new forms in the last two centuries, as elites faced contradictions between their models of political legitimacy (ordered according to republican and liberal principles) and the mechanisms necessary for governance (which included concentration of powers in the executive and the use of clientelism). This confrontation can be followed as well in the reactions to the implementation of positivist and capitalist ideas and developmental models, as seen in peasant revolts; in a full-fledged social and political revolution in Mexico in the 1910s and 1920s; and subsequently in the 1952 Bolivian Revolution, the 1979 Sandinista Revolution, and the Zapatista uprising in Chiapas. Many of these trends were rephrased in the idioms and markers of new ideologies, borrowing from and changing Marxism-Leninism, Trotskyism, and Maoism in the spirit of indigenous and Afro-American grievances.

A crucial aspect of the indigenous models has been the quest for the protection of collective ownership of lands rooted in the collective memory of the Andean Tahuantinsuyu and the Mesoamerican regions, which provided a strong source of resistance to the capitalist encroachment and privatization of lands. Driven by this logic of pre-Columbian origins, even modernists such as Peruvians Pedro Zulen and José Carlos Mariátegui in the early twentieth century, concerned with progress and development and attuned to global idioms, were able to transcend the European bias of their ideologies. Both rephrased their ideas in terms of the revolutionary potential they identified in the *indigenista* movements of Peru. Later on, radical movements such as the Shining Path in Peru embraced those ideas, although in a very authoritarian and violent manner. Similar trends of confrontation, connected with the decline of support for liberal democracy and neoliberal policies, have been developing more recently in different ways in Bolivia, Ecuador, Mexico, and Central America.[47]

The backlash against macroeconomic adjustment policies, which elites embraced in the 1990s to face the crisis created by economic stagnation, inflation, and debt-ridden budgets, and which openly discarded the étatist legacies of earlier decades, soon erupted, not only in the countries already mentioned. The backlash was directed against both the economic policies and, in many countries, the liberal principles of representative democracy that seemed to have failed to lead the countries into more than a truncated pattern of modernity and development. The policies of macroeconomic stabilization and liberalization dismantled corporatist frameworks of representation, curtailed subsidies, changed the regulation of labor markets, and affected rural communal lands. Unsurprisingly, indigenous and popular movements rose to fight those policies and even depose rulers, after denouncing their policies and mobilizing transcommunal support for alternative models of development opposed to neoliberal privatization and changes in labor conditions. In some countries, such as Venezuela, the reaction was potent. Carlos Andrés Pérez, a respected president in the 1970s, the years of the oil bonanza, was again elected as head of state in the late 1980s. As he started his presidential term (1989–94), Pérez implemented major economic reforms supported by the International Monetary Fund, despite having insisted as a candidate that he would not bend to the IMF prescriptions. The neoliberal policies he adopted dramatically increased the cost of gas and public transportation, and the impact came in February 1989 in the form of nine days of protests, rioting, vandalism, and shootings, known as the Caracazo.[48] The security forces and the military repressed the protests forcefully, with hundreds of casualties. Soon Colonel Hugo Chávez organized a secret cell within the military, known as MBR-200, and launched a short-lived, failed coup in February 1992. After he landed in prison, his actions made him a martyr-like, revolutionary leader for many, particularly lower class citizens, After his release, Chávez continued building support until 1998, when he won the presidency with 56 percent of the vote. With his reaching power in Venezuela, the backlash against neoliberal policies spread transnationally through the region, this time linked to the renewed appeal of leftist and socialist ideas, while the state remained as étatist, polarizing, and mobilizing as the classical populist precedents of past generations.[49]

This analysis indicates that these societies patterned their political institutions and public spheres according to models that they considered the epitome of global progress and advanced modernity. Second, it suggests that the multiple models of modernity became hybrid in Latin America, due to the tensions in their inner logic and between such logic and their subordination to local history and prevailing social and political patterns. Third, in this process modernity often appeared truncated; accordingly, the carriers of models of modernity struggled to impose their vision of global insertion upon wider sectors, competing with each other and with the carriers of indigenous models in the symbolic arenas. Fourth, the policies adopted by the upper classes and those in power generated strong countervailing forces that contested the visions and policies imposed and looked for alternative ways of development. It is in terms of such interplay between history, politics, and culture that we should try to understand the unfolding of Latin American modernities, as global and transnational and yet uneven and often truncated.

Latin America on the Global Scene

Latin America was "born" global. Since the early days of the emergence of Atlantic modernity, the languages, religions, institutions, and symbolic markers of Western Europe were imposed by colonial rule on the Americas, often in brutal ways, and enthusiastically adopted by the local elites. As Peter Winn accurately pointed out, despite resistance by natives and slaves, "no other region of the Third World was colonized for so long or penetrated so deeply by Europe."[50]

Even though at first Western institutions, ideas, and practices were part of an imposed order, they transformed the region in permanent ways through the adoption of Christianity, capitalism, bureaucratic structures, and later on, political institutions at the forefront of Western-led modernity. Paradoxically, yet in full congruence with this pattern of development, often seemingly traditional areas in contemporary Latin America that were once the spearheads of modernity were left behind as modernization shifted gears, moving to other sectors and areas. In Latin America, *often tradition is merely a form of left-behind modernity* as it turned peripheral and shifted to new poles and waves of development.

For centuries, the West and its tenets of modernity have been reference points for projects, designs, and ambitions on the part of those living in these societies, yet triggering reactions and imprinting great ambiguity in society. Still, while turning hegemonic in certain periods and countries, the institutions, ideas, and practices of Atlantic modernity faced resentment due to their unfulfilled promise and biased appropriation, and accordingly could not prevent defiance and the eruption of confrontation and struggle.

On another level, however, there is a major difference between Latin America and other cultural areas of the world such as China or the Islamic world. In the case of Latin America, with the exception of perhaps some of the Andean areas and other pockets of Native and Afro-American identity, the confrontation with Western ideas and institutions became not just a confrontation with an alien culture, as in Islam, China, or perhaps India during British imperial rule. It has been rather *an ongoing confrontation with their own conflict-ridden origins and development.* This confrontation has been intertwined with long reflections on collective identities and has led to an amalgamation of forms. Modern institutions and idioms have also become part of the language and structures of aboriginal societies, the descendants of the slaves, and the children and grandchildren of immigrants. They have become the makeup of the absolute majority of sectors and countries in Latin America. Let me repeat this: what is striking is that the confrontation is not a confrontation with visions and institutions external to these societies, but rather a conflict-ridden confrontation that became an intrinsic part of the constitution and configuration of these societies, which have amalgamated even autochthonous trends within future-oriented perspectives of progress, justice, development, and equality.

The meaning of being modern and of modernity has changed with the passing of time. Latin America has changed radically, in a process that has redefined repeatedly the meaning of being modern on the continent. Yet as it changed, Latin America did so by replicating neither the European experience nor that of the United States, but rather in multiple and distinctive ways that amalgamated social groups, redefined cultural hybridity, and projected religious syncretism, with institutional consequences that shaped collective identities, political order, and public spheres. The region also praised itself for having developed a distinct sensibility to global human issues shared transnationally on the continent, thus leading to the creation of multiple regional organizations devoted to articulating shared positions on the global scene.

Latin American intellectuals have claimed to have distinctive cultural traditions integrating reason, spirituality, and passion. That image was romanticized mainly in opposition to the rising economic star of the United States and its expansive geopolitical position, interpreted as derived from the materialistic perspective endorsed by its elites and institutions. In her book *Reinventing Modernity in Latin America*, Nicola Miller indicated perceptively that well into the twentieth century, Latin America exhibited a long tradition of critique of pure, instrumental reason, as evident in various domains:

> [I]n literature (the "marvelous real") and criticism (the "critical closeness" of Carlos Monsiváis); in philosophy, particularly in the idea that critique can be a basis for liberation and solidarity; in Liberation Theology, which sought to accommodate social science and theology; in educational theory, for example, Paulo Freire's pedagogy of consciousness-raising; and in Che Guevara's concept of the new man. In all these areas, reason was conceived as more encompassing and less absolute than instrumental reason.[51]

Interestingly, that perspective was shared both by Spanish American modernist thinkers—for example, José Enrique Rodó in his renowned work *Ariel*, which impacted generations of Latin American intellectuals—and by widespread voices in Francophone Quebec geared to resist the pull of Anglophone Canada and the United States.[52]

In addition, the multiplicity of cultural traditions that amalgamated in Latin America made religious syncretism be paramount, leading to a lack of autochthonous or Catholic religious fundamentalism, despite constant religious change and the resurgence of social movements among the indigenous sectors and more recently, also among the Black populations. In countries with monotheistic religions, as typical of the region, one could expect to have some sort of fundamentalism, as found in the United States, but the phenomenon is rather negligible in Latin America. In contrast, the region has exhibited other religious trends. Among them is liberation theology, a vision that promised to fulfill the unfulfilled dream of human equality. Another trend is the crystallization of Afro-Brazilian and Afro-Caribbean religions that amalgamated Catholic saints and African *orixás* (spirits). In addition, there has been a sustained rise of Protestant and especially Pentecostalist groups, which in Central and South America became less grounded in messianic messages and more oriented toward healing, possession trances, and the reconstitution of personal behavior and family life.[53] It is mostly among Orthodox Jews and some Muslim networks that some sort of revivalist fundamentalism has taken hold in recent years.[54]

When compared to Europe, for instance, until recently there has been a weakening of the primordial criteria of collective identity and an emphasis on civil and political membership, as evident in the relatively rare occurrence of racial wars amid multiple political confrontations and civil war. In spite of profound ethnic tensions, racial wars have been rather exceptional: Túpac Amaru in the Andean area in the 1780s, in Haiti in the 1790s, and in Yucatán in the nineteenth century. Such occasions have been rare, and their socioeconomic causes have been crucial. Many civil wars have taken place, but they have developed a different character, typically following a socioeconomic, class-driven direction rather than being structured as cultural wars, as was the case in the United States, and not in the direction of racial or ethnic wars, as in sub-Saharan Africa or the Balkans. Sometimes civil wars have degenerated into ethnic conflicts, as in Guatemala in the 1980s, but these occasions have been rather exceptional until recently. Certainly, more recently there have been signs of leaders such as the late Hugo Chávez in Venezuela using or allowing close circles to use a polarizing political rhetoric, spreading xenophobic messages as a mobilizing tool among the popular and previously marginalized sectors. However, even these trends— with all their danger, which I discuss in detail in chapter 8—have been contained so far.[55]

In parallel, a new type of transnational, diasporic, and postcultural Latin Americanism also emerged, linked to the Latinx diaspora(s) in the United States and the emergence of a critical consciousness going back to the 1960s and fully articulated starting in the 1990s.[56] Since the dawn of the new millennium, the democratic systems have shown resilience, albeit shifting from one end of the political spectrum to the other through a series of mass protests, violence, scandals, and a series of popular impeachments deposing elected presidents accused of corruption or abuse of power.[57]

There has been a continuous search in Latin America to deliver the visions and unfulfilled promises of modernity. This has led to the emergence of competitive models, of alternative and multiple modernities, with one model of modernity carrying the day and replacing previous ones, all of them voiced in attempts to accomplish and fulfill the unfulfilled promise of modernity, while in many cases resisting ferociously the implications of contemporary globalization. Indeed, the history of the region exhibits a continuous confrontation with the unfulfilled promises of modernity, a trend I see as being derived from the truncated character of modernity there. Toward the mid-twentieth century, views crystallized that built a critique of geopolitical dependency and capitalism's unequal terms of international exchange. Many intellectuals and academics embraced dependency theory, while global decolonization and the revolutionary Left, inspired by the Cuban Revolution, Che Guevara, and other models of insurgency, gained momentum. The reform option led by the Alliance for Progress in the 1960s had declined, as it did not solve the deep internal socioeconomic imbalances of Latin American societies, denounced by both dependency theory and liberation theology. Soon the revolutionary option failed as well, crashing in South America in the 1970s and 1980s under the repressive wave coordinated transnationally by Operation Condor, and also producing massive crimes against humanity in Central America in the 1980s and into the mid-1990s.[58]

When the region started returning to democracy, many of the countries embraced the Washington Consensus with high expectations, hoping to join the First World, only to be disappointed by the results of neoliberal policies of privatization and state and economic restructuring. One repeatedly witnesses social movements and new leaderships confronting ideas originating in the Western centers, assuming their implications while addressing their shortcomings, demanding equality, recognition, and a fuller political participation. Illustrative is the Shining Path in Peru, which incorporated Maoist ideas and related them to earlier precolonial, Inca ideas, predicating Maoist revolution and enforced social equality by launching, beginning in the 1980s, guerrilla war that attempted to accomplish the complete severance of connections between the Peruvian countryside and the circuits of capitalist commercialization and liberal state control. Their own brutal authoritarianism, together with the bold reaction of the government and armed forces, brought down the Senderistas, but their message appealed to sectors of the Peruvian rural countryside.

Thus, as deep inequalities and systemic crises increased, the region witnessed the renewed appeal of alternative visions of political order and solidarity, which presented once again as standing up to US policies and denouncing imperialist designs.[59] As it launched its rebellion in January 1994, the Ejército Zapatista de Liberación Nacional (EZLN) claimed to oppose the North American Free Trade Agreement (NAFTA) in the name of those very principles professed by other modern revolutionaries and unfulfilled in the case of the rural populations of Chiapas. With their antiglobalization ideas, the Zapatistas did not just use modern techniques of communication. Rather, they incorporated the idiom of human rights to call into question the generations-long disregard of subaltern sectors in the state of Chiapas and other Mexican states. In the late 1990s, the rise of Hugo Chávez in Venezuela, who soon added allies with new electoral victories of left-wing candidates, spearheaded the "Pink Tide." The shift, however, was not universal and thus, in the 2000s and 2010s, the region remained more divided than ever, between what Jorge Castañeda, a former foreign minister of Mexico and professor of politics, defined in 2010 as Americas-1 and Americas-2 countries—that is, countries and sectors supporting Venezuelan Chavismo and those openly opposed to the "Bolivarian" wave and the Pink Tide.[60]

The distinctive yet multiple patterns of modernity in Latin America have recurrently reinforced the consciousness of the unfulfilled promises of Western-led modernity; its core ideas; and its institutional derivatives of progress, development, equality, and justice. In the region, this became connected to the consciousness of being at the margins of global development, being part of an unfulfilled dream of modernity, living a truncated form of modernity, whose imbalances have deepened in recent waves of globalization. As indicated, in Latin America there has been a continuous search for fulfilling such visions of modernity. This has led to the constant search for more successful models of development, competing with one another, and yet all those emerging models can be seen as attempts to fulfill that promise of modernity, while in many cases resisting ferociously the implications of contemporary globalization.

Historically, as in any other society, a gap developed between the ideas of modernity and their unfolding in practice, which resulted in their incomplete implementation. In theory, from the nineteenth century onward, these countries have defined themselves as representative democracies. In practice, they have often become plebiscitary and "majoritarian" democracies, exhibiting a strong presidentialism and a lack of institutional checks and balances. This, in turn, has led to the recurrent emergence of military and civilian leaders ruling through the exclusion, persecution, and exile of the opposition, while claiming to represent the common will of the people.[61] According to the proclaimed ethos, these polities have been ruled constitutionally and within the bounds of the law. Yet in practice, the informal structures and illicit frameworks and networks have been interlinked and have affected the implementation of the law, disseminating institutional distrust and reinforcing patterns of mediated clientelism, favoritism, and bending of the rule of law.

In the past few decades, the area has witnessed new and increasing divergence and diversification of its multiple modernities. There are countries that have tried to diversify their economies and have succeeded in launching inclusionary policies that respect pluralism and create modules of participatory regulation of civil society, while linking such policies to their integration in contemporary processes of globalization. There are some countries, most notably Chile, Peru, Mexico, and most Central American and some Caribbean nations, that while showing variable structural economic differentiation, have opted to become integrated in the model of globalization and transnational commercial exchange led by the United States. Other countries, led by Venezuela, have chosen self-proclaimed revolutionary, modern models that curtail free markets, threaten pluralism, reinvigorate radical nationalism, and radicalize the interlinking of national and global strategies in the direction of South-South alliances contesting US hegemony in the region. Recently, Chavismo has entered a phase of erosion and contestation from within, and the free-market model supported by IMF loans (e.g., Argentina under Mauricio Macri in 2015–19) has led to a dead end. Recent years have also witnessed a renewed impetus for a politics of identity, evinced in such varied trends as widening constitutional recognition of multiculturalism, a growing presence of indigenous and Black leadership, and heightened mobilization of subaltern groups.

Beyond the contrasting and multiple models, whose lines of development are still uncertain, all contemporary Latin American countries are trying to face the forces of globalization in a multipolar global arena, in which China, Russia, and other countries have a growing presence in the Americas alongside the United States and the European Union. They are doing so while redefining and reinstitutionalizing what they perceive as their own traditions, rooted in the universalistic and participatory legacies of the Great Revolutions and the discourse of modernity, equality, and social justice. They continue to evolve on the global scene within a framework of regional optics, being a multistate region immersed in transnational trends and in regional dialogue and conflict.

3

The Interface of Nation-State Building and Transnationalism

How did separate nation-states crystallize, turning Latin America into a multistate region subject to persistent transnational trends? The story of Latin America as a multistate region is one of contested territorial boundaries and a tension-ridden consolidation of separate collective identities out of a tapestry of transnational interaction. In Spanish America, political independence was the result of imperial implosion, a process initiated with the Napoleonic invasion of the Iberian Peninsula, which affected traditional principles of royal legitimacy. Brazil avoided this impact, as the Portuguese ruling house of Braganza fled and crossed the Atlantic, turning its American territory into the center of its global empire, and then transitioning to independence peacefully under a Braganza scion years later. In contrast, Spanish American territories awoke to a de facto autonomy that, as a result of accelerated events in the peninsula and wars in the New World, evolved into independent statehood. Being independent, however, individuals lacked the sense of belonging to a nation-state. Rather, they had a strong sense of belonging to their *patria chica* (little homeland) as well as of being Americans. The sense of belonging to a nation could take much longer to develop, with much depending on contingent developments and the crisscrossing pull and push of multiple forces and centers of power.

Constructing State Identities and Narrating the Nation

The disintegration of imperial Spanish America produced undefined borders, where deep transnational forces pulled emerging states into persistent struggles, wars, and territorial losses. The Southern Andean and the Río de la Plata expanses are outstanding examples of the historical process of crystallization of new territorial nation-states amid transregional connections. In many cases, independence opened a long-fought process of newly established states imposing their rule and citizens opting to disengage or learning to "live together," as Marie-Danielle Demélas masterfully described for Bolivia, Ecuador, and Peru.[1] Thus, the nineteenth century witnessed the labor pains of Bolivia and Ecuador, as they attempted to disengage respectively from Lima and Buenos Aires in the case of

Transnational Perspectives on Latin America. Luis Roniger, Oxford University Press. © Oxford University Press 2022.
DOI: 10.1093/oso/9780197605318.003.0004

Bolivia, and from Santa Fe and Lima in the case of Ecuador. In the latter case, Quito and Guayaquil also pulled in different directions for many decades. The protracted consolidation of Bolivia and Ecuador contrasted with the greater initial legitimacy of Peru or Mexico, which as former imperial capitals could assert a greater claim to nation-state standing after independence.

Like Mexico, Peru reluctantly transitioned to independence. In fact, independence was forced upon the colonial elites of Peru and Bolivia by the armies of José de San Martín and his allies, coming from Cuyo and Chile in the South, and those of Simón Bolívar and his lieutenants, arriving from New Granada in the North. During the wars of independence (1810–25), Lima lost its imperial grandeur, immense wealth, and primacy as a viceregal seat. Even if it had a stronger claim over its territory based on the principle of *uti possedetis*,[2] Peru's territorial boundaries remained disputed for decades. Its ill-defined borders with Brazil did not result in clashes due to the vast unexplored Amazon lands. However, delimiting the territorial boundaries with Ecuador, Bolivia, Colombia, and Chile resulted in war and numerous confrontations, with *caudillo*-led armies and exile networks crossing back and forth over those ill-defined borders, forcing people to define distinct nation-state identities out of rather fluid, nonexclusive networks.

Since the sixteenth and seventeenth centuries, the booming economic cycle around Potosí's silver mines had brought Southern Peru closer to Bolivia than to Northern Peru. In turn, Bolivia had to disengage also from Buenos Aires, as the Spanish Bourbon monarchy tore away Alto Perú (Upper Peru) from Lima's orbit in 1776, close to the end of colonial times, and transferred it to the realm of the newly created Viceroyalty of the Río de la Plata.

Following independence, a Peruvian-Bolivian confederation led by Bolivian president Andrés de Santa Cruz in 1836–39 reflected the shared culture, landscapes, and commercial and family connections linking Bolivia and Southern Peru. Northern Peruvian elites and neighboring states opposed and defeated that confederation, yet the idea of a South Andean confederated unity retained its allure for decades and led to the establishment of a defensive alliance. That vision was also key to the policies of President Ramón Castilla, a native of Arica in Southern Peru (now Chile), who held power for nearly twenty years starting in 1845. Later on, in 1873–74, Bolivia and Peru signed a secret alliance treaty of mutual support against Chile, as a developmental rush for guano and saltpeter started, similar to the California "gold rush" a few decades earlier.[3]

In this context, local interests with a transnational reach played a decisive role in territorial shifts of sovereignty. A major actor in Bolivia's littoral province along the Pacific Ocean was the Compañía de Salitres y Ferrocarriles de Antofagasta (CSFA), the company of nitrates and railroads of Antofagasta (Bolivia). The joint

Chilean-British company operated under tax exemption in accordance with a Chilean-Bolivian treaty of 1874. It was led by Chilean Agustín Edwards, who also owned *El Mercurio*, an important media outlet. With the opening of economic opportunities in the region, a huge number of poor and adventurous Chilean workers settled in the area, transforming Antofagasta and Caracoles into populous cities. Soon enough, the so-called Littoral Province—a true Bolivian Far West—found itself under the weak but no less despotic control of a few Bolivian armed forces stationed there. These forces were supposed to impose order over a massive conglomerate of Chilean *rotos* (lower class, poor individuals), who were prone to engage in violence, banditry, and street altercations.

Following two earthquakes, in 1973 and 1874, Bolivian president Hilarión Daza Groselle decided to impose a tax of ten cents for each quintal of nitrate extracted by the CSFA in the province, despite the legal obligation of exempting it from taxation. That decision had long-lasting implications. When the English manager, with the full support of the Chileans, refused to pay the tax, as he considered it unfair and illegal, the Bolivian authorities tried to arrest him, causing him to flee to Chile. Faced with the reluctance of the CSFA to pay the tax, Daza decided to confiscate the company's properties and auction them off, a scenario in which Peruvian capital could prevail.

During the War of the Pacific, Chile took control of extensive territories and maritime domains, including Bolivia's Littoral Province, turning Bolivia into a landlocked nation-state, with no access to the Pacific Ocean, and occupied Lima and the Peruvian provinces of Tacna, Arica, and Tarapacá. In October 1883, Chile and Peru signed the Treaty of Ancón, which established the terms for concluding armed hostilities. Under the terms of that treaty, in addition to paying compensation, Peru ceded the province of Tarapacá to Chile and granted it possession of Tacna and Arica for ten years, at the end of which it committed to hold a plebiscite or popular consultation to decide the final sovereignty of both provinces. In 1929, under the Treaty of Lima, both countries reestablished diplomatic relations and solomonically divided the disputed territory. Tacna returned to Peru, and Chile retained Arica and Tarapacá.

The effects of the war continued to reverberate into the twenty-first century. In both defeated nations, the war opened a cycle of long crisis that heightened the nationalistic rhetoric and popular mobilization. In Chile, victory over the indigenous soldiers of the South Andean nations heightened a sense of national pride. In turn, that self-confidence led Chilean elites to launch an internal war against the native Mapuche people to take control of their territories, decimating them and pushing them further back into the Patagonian south. In the case of Bolivia, its traumatic defeat in the War of the Pacific left a collective scar that in 1932–36 led the government to start another adventurous military confrontation, this time with Paraguay over control of the northern Chaco, and face a new defeat.

Every March 23, Bolivia commemorates the Day of the Sea in memory of the loss of approximately 120,000 square kilometers of its Littoral Department. The country also maintains a navy that symbolically operates commemorations in the waters of Lake Titicaca. In the Plaza Abaroa of La Paz and in other towns, events take place with the participation of civil and military authorities, to keep alive the memory of the usurped national territory and the fallen heroes.[4] In Chile, May is the Month of the Sea, and in the Tarapacá region, all schools hold parades on May 21 in commemoration of the war and its heroes, with the explicit objective of promoting youth patriotism. In Peru, on the other hand, on October 8, the country remembers the loss of the ship *Huáscar* and the death of Admiral Miguel Grau, their war hero.[5]

The lack of insularity and natural borders separating an emerging state from its neighbors also characterizes Uruguay, leaving its nation-state formation open to the impact of transnational forces and historical contingency. In late colonial times and in the transition to political independence, there was no certainty about the promulgation of a separate state there. Would Uruguay become independent or remain attached to the provinces of the River Plate? Alternatively, would it turn into a state in the Brazilian federation or be annexed by one of its member states?

Uruguay shared much of its cultural, environmental, class, and political structure with the territories that became part of Argentina as well as with the Southern Brazilian territory of Rio Grande do Sul. It crystallized as a separate country like other Latin American states following the Napoleonic invasion of Iberia, the ensuing crisis of authority in the Americas, and the subsequent disintegration of the Spanish Empire. Still, unlike Mexico, which had historical Aztec and Spanish imperial roots from which to develop a long-lasting center of power and a *mestizo* identity, Uruguay's development as a separate nation-state was, in the words of historian Tulio Halperin Donghi, an awkward creation that few expected would last.[6]

Several macrohistorical factors made it unlikely for such a distinct nation-state to emerge. The first hurdle was the late colonial development of the region amid fragmented jurisdictions and conflicting claims to authority, which led to civil and transnational wars in the first half of the nineteenth century. Unlike other regions of Spanish America that by the sixteenth century were subject to the control of urban centers such as Santo Domingo, Mexico, or Lima, the eastern bank of the Uruguay River was left to the control of the indigenous populations until the late seventeenth and eighteenth centuries. The native residents relied mostly on hunting, fishing, and some agriculture and included groups as diverse as the fierce Charrúas and the more peaceful Guaraníes. Only in 1680 did the Portuguese establish their first major settlement in Colonia do Sacramento, and in 1726 the Spanish authorities of Buenos Aires founded Montevideo in an attempt to protect the South Atlantic basis of their empire against the Portuguese and the Anglo-Portuguese alliance.

Sparsely populated, the territories on the eastern bank of the Uruguay River were split among several jurisdictions, each pulling in diverse transnational directions. These included clusters that would soon complicate state consolidation in the wake of the imperial crisis; first was the southern parts of the eastern bank of the Uruguay River, under the influence of Buenos Aires. The second complication was the Spanish military control over the northern districts of the eastern bank, as well as over large areas of contemporary northeastern Argentina and southern Paraguay, including large tracts transferred in the nineteenth century to Brazil. Third, a Spanish Navy governorship with authority over the walled fortress port city of Montevideo and its rural hinterland proved challenging to consolidation efforts.

The territories of the future state were known as the Banda Oriental, the eastern bank of the Uruguay River. Those fertile lands of moderate hills and a plateau covered by tall prairie grass did not differ much from the environment of neighboring Río de la Plata and Brazil's region of Rio Grande do Sul. As in the neighboring Argentine and Brazilian territories, the land supported large numbers of cattle and horses, whose populations were thriving from those left by the early Spanish settlers. The cattle served as a basis for the export of salted beef to industrialized Britain, where it would sustain the poor working classes, and to Cuba and even Brazil, where it was the basis of the slaves' diet. Leather and wool were also exported, primarily to Britain. The fertility of the land also served to support the transterritorial mobility of the armies wrangling for control of Uruguay in the early nineteenth century. Likewise, in terms of its ethnic or socioeconomic composition, Uruguay closely resembled the structure of those neighboring territories. Moreover, in cultural terms, nothing distinguished the so-called Orientals from the inhabitants of some of the future Argentine provinces. The notion of a "national" territory emerged only in a protracted manner.[7]

Other factors proved to have a centrifugal impact. Located on strategic sea trade routes, the port cities of Montevideo and Buenos Aires prompted the early interest in the region of France as well as of the maritime hegemonic power, England. Rivalry and disputed authority soon colored relations between Montevideo and Buenos Aires. Buenos Aires became the imperial capital of the Viceroyalty of the Río de la Plata, carved out of the early Viceroyalty of Peru, in 1776. Following a short-lived British occupation in 1807, Montevideo increasingly developed rival claims over recognition and trade interests. Montevideo had supported resisting the British invasions and advertised that resistance as supporting its claims of autonomy, requesting Spanish colonial authorities to end its "humiliating dependence" on Buenos Aires, as stated in a letter from the *cabildo* (city council) of Montevideo to the Spanish king following the British defeat. That letter asked the king to make Montevideo the headquarters of an intendancy, to give it a *consulado* (commercial council) of its own, and to extend the limits of its authority to include the entire Banda Oriental.

The territory was in a constant transterritorial dispute. It served as the target of mounting intervention by the Portuguese and Spanish Crowns, and later on by the Brazilian empire and the United Provinces of the Río de la Plata, which replaced them, respectively. The Portuguese wanted to extend Brazilian control to its "natural" frontier in the River Plate, while the Spanish, and later on the Buenos Aires authorities, considered the region one more province in their disintegrating jurisdiction, a territory occupied or relinquished according to tactical considerations. These conflicting demands and the constant predation on local resources triggered the early emergence of local landed interests willing to master their own affairs and eventually attain self-determination.

A momentous step in the birth of Uruguayan collective identity occurred as the result of a sense of defeat and forced migration of thousands of Orientales across transnational landscapes. The major figure galvanizing the population into collective action was a native-born second commander of the rural gendarmerie founded by the authorities in Montevideo in the 1790s to keep order in the countryside. José Gervasio Artigas served under Spanish royalist authorities and later shifted his allegiance to the authorities in Buenos Aires. He soon became disappointed when Buenos Aires, under mounting pressure, negotiated a truce that returned the Banda Oriental to royalist control. In November 1811, resenting the decision, Artigas led over four thousand Oriental militia and an equal number of fleeing civilians on a month-long trek beyond the armistice lines, across the Uruguay River, to an eight-month encampment in the future Argentine province of Entre Ríos. Fearing Spanish reprisals and Portuguese depredations, the civilians had joined the withdrawing militias en masse in what at that time people called a defeat (*redota*, a rustic transposition of the Spanish word *derrota*). Many saw it as one of the earliest visible signs of the birth of the Uruguayan nation, born out of loss and expatriation.[8]

One can trace those early signs of a sense of Uruguayan nationhood back to the declarations and statements of Artigas. The emerging leader endorsed ideas of resumption of popular sovereignty when facing an acephalous royalty. These ideas date back to a sixteenth-century Spanish school of thought, expressed in the pages of the *Gazeta de Buenos Ayres* by the radical autonomist Manuel Moreno, who also translated parts of Rousseau's *Contrat Social*. In 1812, Artigas popularized these ideas in Uruguay and the neighboring provinces, stressing the "primitive [that is, original] rights" of sovereignty of the Orientales, who constituted themselves as a people by electing him as their *jefe*. Peoples left to fend for themselves, accordingly, had the right to organize themselves.

As Protector of the Free Peoples in a transnational landscape that extended from Uruguay to the littoral provinces of Argentina and beyond, however, his ideas evolved during the next several years. He first explicitly supported self-determination and federalist ideas, leading to a still undefined confederacy of peoples. That confederacy was to involve not only the Banda Oriental but also parts of contemporary Argentina, primarily the provinces of Entre Ríos and Corrientes, and eventually was to include Santa Fe and even Córdoba (1813). He then moved to a more autocratic and paternalist attempt to keep control of the unruly population of his own native territory (by 1815). Ultimately, he lost and left Uruguay for a thirty years in exile and isolation in Paraguay.[9]

Already in the 1810s and 1820s there were incipient signs of the emergence of such a sense of collective identity. The first such signs were visible in the 1810s in the use of official papers, still carrying the insignia of Spanish imperial rule, with the added inscription "4th and 5th years of The Liberty." A similar token of the construction of a new collective identity in the Artigas camp was the use of playing cards with the written mottoes, "Long live the Fatherland" (*viva la Patria*) or "With persistence and fatigue, Artigas liberated his Fatherland" (*con la constancia y fatigas, libertó su Patria Artigas*). These were part of a conscious attempt to strengthen the inner conviction of the rebellious camp. Equally illustrative was the January 1816 decision of the "Governing Cabildo" called by Artigas, which admonished suspicious activities and forced support, demanding "that every Patriot citizen should use a ribbon [with the colors] of the Oriental Province."

By the mid-1830s, shortly after independence, popular expressions of nation building emerged, most significantly led by poets. These expressions took the form of the publication of anthologies of poetry, a process similar to those of other Spanish American territories emerging into independent life. *El Parnaso Oriental* was an anthology compiled by Luciano Lira in 1835. Following the neoclassical style of similar anthologies in Argentina (1824) and Brazil (1829), it attempted to create the nation by the word. It started with a song that eventually was recognized as the national anthem: "Orientales, la Patria o la tumba! Libertad o con Gloria morir!" (Orientals, the fatherland or the tomb! Freedom or a glorious death!). The subject of its discourse was the citizen, envisaged as a universal and public category, from which, notably, most feminine voices and all Black and indigenous voices were absent. The community was discursively constituted by the act of liberation, signaled by the autonomous subject singing about the glory of the free people born in the territory of the Eastern Band of the Uruguay River. Thorny dissent and polemics were silenced, and an image of the unity and harmony of those belonging to the nation and struggling for its freedom was projected as reality. A nation in the making seemed already under way.[10] This trend can be traced throughout Latin America, with its multiple societies soon developing a genre of domestic romances and novels instrumental to nation-building, exemplified—as Doris Sommer pointed out—in Argentina's *Amalia*, Cuba's *Sab*, Colombia's *María*, Chile's *Martín Rivas*, Brazil's *Iracema*, Peru's *Aves sin nido*, and the Dominican Republic's *Enriquillo*. From very early on, an intimate connection developed between fiction and history, wherein the use of narrative in foundational novels became a useful replacement for the lack of a complete and rigorous archival documentation.[11]

The Banda Oriental remained highly divided for many decades. In the wake of Spanish imperial disintegration, the patrician and learned circles of Montevideo, the landed and mercantile classes, and the officers in the armed forces and the rural militia, as well as the lower classes, reacted to and coalesced with one another. They all faced the contrasting transnational pressures put forward by the Spanish royalists (and then independent Buenos Aires) and Portugal (and then independent Brazil). Uruguay's independence was facilitated by the role of Great Britain as the dominant sea power, which was willing to mitigate the rivalry between Argentina and Brazil by creating a buffer state in the Southern Cone of the Americas. By 1828, Britain had struck a successful mediation between the rival countries, in which both sides, exhausted by transnational war, renounced their claims to annexation of the Banda Oriental. Motivated by its interest in maintaining some stability for the sake of British trade, British diplomats played a crucial role in creating this buffer state. In 1828 an independent state was established, officially known as the Republic to the East of the Uruguay River (República Oriental del Uruguay), a state soon recognized by its neighbors, with the rival countries occupying a transnational space of rather fluid boundaries.

This creation did not put an end to the borderline arena, which would be a scene of successive territorial conflicts. It took a long time to define the "national" realm as distinct from its embedment in the transnational landscape. At least until the end of the Great War in 1851, these distinctions were largely irrelevant in the Southern Cone. The parties waging civil wars in Uruguay continued to mobilize the support of transterritorial coalitions, reaching out to the radical autonomists of Rio Grande do Sul in southern Brazil, to the imperial house in Rio de Janeiro, and to the *caudillos* in Buenos Aires and other Argentine provinces.

Nonetheless, state independence implied an important shift, as it created long-standing institutions that increasingly focused the rival energies of the Orientales on the shared public arena and, in this process, managed to constitute the nation-state as distinct from other nation-states in the region. Thus, the promulgation of a constitution in 1830 was conceived as an anchor of stability, in the spirit of the Enlightenment. That constitution—which remained the institutional charter until 1919—made the legislature the dominant authority of the Oriental Republic and granted the body the power to elect the president. The intention was to create oligarchic rule led by a political class anchored in the patrician and learned circles of Montevideo. The political parties, led by *caudillos* (military warlords) and their rural followers, imposed authority by force. A gap was thus created between the legal structure and the "real" structure of power, which prompted recurring rebellions, assaults on power, and civil wars. The Catholic Church and the army, which were the institutional pillars of conservatism elsewhere in Spanish America, were weak in Uruguay. The foci of real power turned out to be the competing political factions or parties. The main opposition was between the Blancos, headed by General Juan Antonio Lavalleja and soon by General Manuel Oribe, and the Colorados, initially headed by General Fructuoso Rivera. These parties, which in a simplistic way can be characterized as built around the conflicting interests of Montevideo versus the countryside districts, soon became the focal points of popular commitment and were instrumental in institution building and nation building—after they almost exhausted themselves and the country during the civil wars.

By the mid-nineteenth century, the parties were tired of waging war and had to recognize that they were almost indistinguishable in terms of their ideologies, blending classical republicanism and modern liberalism. Yet an attempt to abolish them for the sake of national reconciliation in the 1850s proved ephemeral. As pointed out in the classic study by historian Juan E. Pivel Devoto, the political parties persisted, albeit under new physiognomy, as the most powerful defining institutions of public life in Uruguay, a trend unrivaled until recently in South America, with the exception of Colombia.[12] Uruguay's transnational involvement became evident once again in the War of the Triple Alliance (1864–70), when the country joined the powerful countries of Brazil and Argentina, eager to defeat the rising star of Paraguay and its autarchic economy, in what many saw and continue to see as the crushing of an autonomous, nondependent model of development.

The focal points for defining the nation turned out to be the republican virtues of citizenship and the principle of political order and rights guaranteed by the state. By the late nineteenth and early twentieth centuries, these images were constructed in rather universal terms. The National (Blanco) Party leader, Wilson Ferreira Aldunate, expressed this view when emphasizing the role of the state and its principles in the definition of the nation, as he addressed the Chamber of Deputies of Ecuador in 1983. Speaking from exile during military rule in his home country, he claimed that Uruguay was "a most authentic country" not because of its genetic composition or geography, but because it was a community imbued with spiritual values, namely, "equality before the law, the representative character of the organs of government, the periodic election of the rulers, the subordination of any authority and power center to the civilian government, the strict obedience to the guarantees of freedom, of political freedom and individual freedom."[13] Ferreira Aldunate added that when those spiritual values are undermined, "the very existence of the country is put under risk."

Even though there are still open debates and controversies about the role that individuals and institutions played in the nineteenth century in the constitution of the Oriental nation, this view became widely accepted by the early twentieth century, "routinized" as Uruguay structured its modern state under President José Batlle y Ordóñez (1903–1907, 1911–15). It is important to emphasize, however, that the initial criteria of citizenship were rather restrictive, limiting representation according to several conditions: personal status (slaves and dependent workers were not granted electoral rights), gender (females were excluded), age (minors under the age of twenty-one did not enjoy the franchise), and education (analphabets were precluded from the electoral process after 1840). Moreover, even though they were formally abolished, slavery and indebted work continued into the second half of the nineteenth century.[14] It was only with massive immigration that the physiognomy of the country changed. In the period 1835–42 alone, an estimated 30,000 to 48,000 immigrants arrived to join a country that had only 74,000 inhabitants in 1830. The influx of immigrants contributed to population growth: the number of inhabitants grew to 132,000 by 1852 and to 438,000 by 1879. Immigrants constituted 48 percent of the population in 1860 and 68 percent in 1868.

Large landed estates, or *latifundios*, still predominated in the countryside, and husbandry recovered after its decline during the civil wars. Yet society became more differentiated, especially in the urban centers. By 1853, in Montevideo there were 2,200 merchants and manufacturers, 80 percent of whom were "foreigners," that is, born abroad. Workers' unions and philanthropic and philosophical organizations proliferated, especially after 1870. The city modernized: gas service was installed in 1853, the first bank opened its doors in 1857, sewage works were initiated in 1860, a telegraph was established in 1866, railroads to the interior were started in 1869, running water was available in 1871, an arts section was created in the National Museum in 1872, and a society for the promotion of science and the arts was founded in 1876. A new generation came of age in the 1860s and 1870s and combined new models of bourgeois privacy and public activism, replicating European upper-class claims and standards. Modernizing landowners established a rural association in 1871, charged with the task of improving livestock-raising techniques, and it soon gained considerable influence over policymakers. A huge gap separated the upper classes from the lower classes, who lived in rented quarters and multiroom, crowded buildings (*casas de inquilinos* and *conventillos*). A similar gap separated natives from immigrants and rural from urban sectors.[15]

The 1870s and 1880s witnessed a plethora of decisions aimed at the creation of some sort of "civil religion" to support an increasingly secularized state and society. Civic institutions were created to replace the role played by religious ones, and civic liturgies and rituals were launched.

Fundamental in this transformation was educational reform carried out by José Pedro Varela, which structured primary and normal schooling in the 1870s and 1880s, driven by US liberal pedagogy and Spencerian positivism. Under Batlle y Ordóñez, after another civil war that ended in 1904, the political and pedagogical ideas spreading transnationally between Santiago de Chile, Buenos Aires, Montevideo, and Porto Alegre informed the continuing process of educational reform and became part of the secular credo of the leading political and cultural elites.[16] Sacredness was transferred from the religious to the secular public realm, with legislation minimizing religious formation in state schools; the creation of a civil state register; the establishment of civil matrimony as obligatory and prior to religious marriage; the law of secondary and higher education, which established state control over educational institutions; and the decision to close monasteries.

Until the turn of the twentieth century, the history of Uruguay resembled that of other South American countries, having been clustered around a long series of both civil and transnational wars. Yet unlike neighboring Argentina, by the early twentieth century Uruguay had succeeded in reaching a wide agreement among political forces and a shared vision of the nation centered upon the recognition of citizenship and universal entitlements, thus giving birth to a stable democracy. The political class promoted a melting-pot vision through an expanding educational system that raised the standards of literacy. It aimed at instilling a sense of nationality and common destiny, constructed in terms that traced the notion of Oriental nationality back in history to Artigas and the founding fathers of the independent state.

This nation-state project upheld civilian rule and instilled the values of citizenship, republicanism, and consensus among major segments of the population. For decades thereafter, Uruguayans endorsed the state narrative of civility, public peace, and development, buttressed by universal education, welfare benefits, and the promotion of public culture. Grounded upon this shared vision, the state encouraged the adoption of narratives that praised the nation as the Switzerland of the Americas, a content nation often referred to as the "happy Uruguay." These images and the collective consensus that supported them suffered a blow during the Cold War in the third quarter of the twentieth century, while having far-reaching consequences for the process of redemocratization, as analyzed for the entire region in chapter 6.

Nation-States and Transnational Visions

For the new states, independence meant a separation from the Crown of Castile and Aragon rather than decolonization, as initially the rising elites were mostly descendants of the Iberian settlers. Moreover, the process of growing self-determination leading to independence did not reflect a burgeoning sense of national identity. Certainly local patriotism existed, as evident in the way in which many Jesuits wrote elegiac narrations of the home territories they had left behind, after they were expelled from the American territories in the late 1760s. Those feelings were equally salient in the patriotic pride of the local militias fighting British invasions in the River Plate in 1806–1807. They were just as emphatically professed by the members of the *cabildos*, who in the 1810s assumed self-government in the name of the imprisoned monarch and later on resented the attempt by Spain's forces to undo the achieved autonomy, be they conservative forces (1814), liberal (1820), or once again conservative (1823). Despite the sense of local patriotism, political independence was not the result of a sense of nationhood. Rather, it involved a series of decisions and dilemmas that the higher echelons of those societies in the Americas (White, well born, Catholic, and mostly wealthy) faced once the old principles of legitimate rule on which they had relied for their secure social positions entered a period of crisis.

In most cases, initially the boundaries of the new states followed closely previous colonial administrative jurisdictions, although sometimes these contained conflicting territorial claims. The new states adopted new principles of legitimacy relying on popular sovereignty, which collided with the mechanisms needed to sustain them. Most states became republican, recognizing a division of powers and the principle of representation, while in practice they relied on authoritarian rule, the negotiation between contending forces and *caudillos*, and their clientelistic networks of support. The challenge of imposing and maintaining order was compounded by the lack of administrative and financial capacity of the new states. Most emerging polities abolished old colonial taxes, and the elites resented the imposition of new ones, with the exception of customs fees, which were then imposed on society in an unequal manner. This created what Miguel Angel Centeno once defined as the "institutional dwarfism" of the new states. This notion implied that they had to resort to either printing money and triggering inflation; taking out loans internationally, thus creating foreign debt; or selling access to commodities, thus opening the door to imperialist interventions.[17]

In addition, and most crucially for our analysis, the celerity of the process of political independence meant that the new states were charged with eventually creating nationhood. Creating a sense of nationality would be a long-term task, involving attempting to "render it real" by launching official narratives and rituals, elaborating hegemonic views and symbolic practices, and structuring images of peoplehood connected to spatial and temporal boundaries. In some cases, the strategies of nation building would involve the partitioning of territories that once belonged to the same administrative realm; the formation of confined membership; and the delineation of borders, organized according to principles of national sovereignty.[18] The creation of nations also involved systems of cultural representation that attempted to shape discriminating boundaries of inclusion and exclusion, legitimizing or delegitimizing the access of different sectors of the population to residence and the resources available to each nation-state.[19]

The societies of Central America found it especially hard to articulate distinct nation-state identities disengaged from transnational regional processes. As they reached independence hesitantly by joining the Mexican Empire of Iturbide and then joined a shared Central American Republic (1823–38), they developed distinct principles of statehood and nationhood belatedly, almost by default, and they were unable to disengage completely from the transnational forces that repeatedly pulled them together for generations after independence. From very early on, the various cities competed with each other for spatial preeminence and were thus predisposed to dismember jurisdictions and fragment territorial suzerainty, following changes in the structures of authority and rule. At the same time, their geopolitical closeness brought most societies in the isthmus—on both the Pacific and Caribbean sides—into recurrent interactions, transnational connectedness, and various attempts at federal unification and reunification.

Today, Central America is a region comprising several states that share the isthmus: Guatemala, El Salvador, Belize, Honduras, Costa Rica, Nicaragua, and Panama. These distinct nation-state identities crystallized in the course of the nineteenth and twentieth centuries, through a tension-ridden process of interplay with each other, in ways that dictated such construction through the interface of nation-state building and transnationalism. It is this chapter's claim that if the perspective of collective identities and small states is combined with the problématique of transnationalism, a deeper understanding of their paths of development in the last centuries is enabled. On the basis of wider research published in book-length form,[20] I draw attention here to the possibilities opened up through such intertwining of comparative analysis with perspectives anchored in the study of transnationalism and a perspective of connected histories.

Societies construct collective identities in diverse ways, involving a process of symbolic creation and reconstruction crafted to denote the shared experience and orientations that may unite their members and set them apart from others. The images societies construct and the stories they tell about themselves are crucial in representing who they are and in catalyzing feelings and emotions. They are equally crucial in crystallizing the group's consciousness and motivating individuals to identify with collective visions and aims. Condensed in key symbols and artifacts—such as flags, shields, and national anthems—these images acquire a presence of their own and a representational power. Such images are projected over time, shaping collective visions and the memory of future generations, albeit with an enormous variability among and within nations and groups.[21]

Shmuel N. Eisenstadt and Berhard Giesen indicated how, since the eighteenth century, Germany was represented as a *Kulturnation*, the locus of a transcendental realm of sublime essences and forces of history. Germans would come to conceive of their nation as a sublime operator of historical action, in romantic ways that predated the process of state construction and nation building undertaken by Otto von Bismarck in the late nineteenth century. By then the romantic idealization had led to a blood- and soil-related nationality discourse, which later on, under Nazism, assumed extreme primordial overtones, leading to genocide and the Holocaust.[22] Contrastingly, in Japan, elites prioritized primordiality as the basis of the national identity and almost divinized it, although not in terms of a transcendental or universal mission, as was the case in the monotheistic religions and civilizations.[23]

The case of Central America, however, differs from both of these examples. The political and intellectual elites of the isthmus—with the possible exception of Costa Rica—could not easily romanticize their historical origins, which typically involved power competition, domination, and political fragmentation. The elites could not assume primordiality as central to the construction of their collective identity, since their hierarchical social visions predicated cultural subjugation of internal ethnic and cultural groups that were bearers of distinctive primordial identities. Unsurprisingly, the new states in both Central and South America gave priority to civil-political principles, which superseded and often even neglected the ethnic diversity of their populations, sometimes endorsing racial superiority over subaltern sectors. Furthermore, independence was attained without major heroic sacrifices and "hallowed grounds" that could be celebrated in poetry, ballads, holidays, monuments, or pantheons for fallen martyrs. Relying on civic markers, elites found themselves entangled halfway between a pure factionalist contest for power and the need to construct a commitment to new nations with no distinctive origins, primordiality, or historical transcendence.

Overall, states had to develop a sense of their distinctiveness by projecting idiosyncratic narratives, practices, and images as the legitimating basis for their claims. Different societies underwent this process of nation building through varying historical paths and a variety of concrete developments.[24]

Such construction and reconstruction of nation-states' identities, shared in its generic traits by many states worldwide, became convoluted and protracted in

Central America, as the new states could hardly elicit in the population a sense of being part of an "imagined community."[25] Once separate, the nineteenth-century republics faced the dual task of consolidating their territorial control and domination while constructing a sense of collective identity through their policies, practices, and ceremonies. They had to define and create national membership and boundaries, which implied recognizing certain categories of citizenship as paramount, while replacing, ignoring, or denying—without fully eradicating—earlier forms of identification and subsuming more localized and ethnic identities.

The complex and prolonged process of nation building in Central America was a result of many factors. The shared colonial and early postcolonial identity was the most prominent. A strategy stressing the political structuring of the countries and denying distinctive primordial identities to build separate nationalities was also involved. The improvisational character of the states representing cities interested in dominating other urban centers and enlarging the hinterland they controlled also had an impact. Relevant too, as stressed by Robert Holden, was the contested nature of personalistic, factional, and clientelistic politics, which fueled public violence and did not allow the early consolidation of political centers with authority over the inhabitants of each state.[26] For decades after their separation, the states could not consolidate their boundaries and seclude themselves from a dynamic of regional intervention. The interference came from factional armies and clientelistic entourages, which were driven by the prospect of taking power in their own home region or another region and disregarded borders and state jurisdictions. Rebels in one area were supported by allies in the neighboring states, willing to topple those in power and facilitate the rise of political forces sympathetic to their own designs. What in a modern view could be interpreted as "invasions" were at that time considered mere advances of forces willing to change constellations of power and, in some cases, to define state boundaries anew. The wars that ensued were not seen as "national" wars or "anti-imperialist" wars. All political forces shared the understanding that these were internal, fratricidal wars. It would take external threats and interventions to generate a "national" interpretation of the struggle for independence. Yet initially, even the sense of collective self-determination was embedded in a transnational optic of intestine struggles and resistance to external intervention and threats.

The analysis of how Central American societies led Janus-faced dynamics, constructing distinct identities and reconnecting transnationally at times, or wrapping the transnational as national, is fascinating. In this perspective, these societies reflect the complex dynamics of consolidation of distinct nation-state identities intertwined with transnational trends cutting across those distinct entities, yet without fully replacing one another.

The National Packaging of Transnational Processes

The process of constructing distinct collective ("national") identities gained momentum by the mid- to late nineteenth century. At that time, narratives of national identity were projected as explanatory factors for the incomplete development of countries endowed with considerable resources yet undermined by the fractured character of the political and economic elites. The process itself remained intertwined in transnational connections that superseded, and in fact even allowed, such construction.

At the base of such narratives were historical foundations. Much of the systematic analysis of how the various polities of the isthmus managed to construct and reshape the collective identities of their "imagined nations" is yet to be done, even though research has provided illuminating guidelines.[27] An important work in this direction is Consuelo Cruz's seminal comparison of the experiences of Nicaragua and Costa Rica, part of whose populations merged in their resistance to William Walker in the mid-nineteenth century. In her work, undertaken from the perspectives of identity politics and the structuring of collective memory, Cruz drew attention to the distinct processes of these two isthmus societies through an analysis of the rhetorical frames that were constructed, a process that started in colonial times and fully unfolded after independence. These frames presented what—in the anthropological sense—these societies "told themselves about themselves," projecting them as credible stories of collective character that their citizens could rely on as they envisioned their present actions and future endeavors.[28]

These frames constituted, in Clifford Geertz's terms, a model of and a model for society. That is, those narratives constituted concomitantly a description of behavioral patterns and status symbols, as well as a blueprint for action, on which functional roles and institutions could be modeled.[29] Cruz showed that the narratives shaped in colonial times pervaded the historiographies and the sense of self-representation and collective memory of these societies, which in turn affected subsequent policy options, allowing or disallowing strategies of persuasion on the basis of their presumptive realism and normative sway. In this manner,

> [t]he Costa Ricans' frame upheld as truth the claim that they were, both by reputation and in fact, an inherently peaceable and diligent people. This frame, in turn, restricted the intensity and scope of political debate and struggle, creating in the process sufficient space for intra-elite consensus building and, ultimately, the political stability necessary to craft and execute developmental policies. In the case of postcolonial Nicaragua, the argument is exactly the reverse. The rhetorical frame that triumphed there generated a set of negative expectations that

created incentives among political rivals for *preemptive, particularist* bids, thus closing off space for effective developmental leadership. The upshot of all this was the emergence of distinct national identities and equally distinct collective fields of imaginable possibilities—one as "civic" and optimistic as the other was "anarchic" and fatalistic.[30]

While Costa Ricans built a narrative of self-confidence and trust, Nicaraguans became entangled in a logic of mutual distrust and disbelief in themselves, which repeatedly reinforced vicious cycles of internal divisiveness, civil war, and mutual annihilation. This self- perception was projected well into the twentieth century, as illustrated by the writings of cultural critics and authors. Paradigmatic is the renowned nationalist essayist and poet Pablo Antonio Cuadra (1912–2002), who often lamented the deceitful "nature" of Nicaraguan individuals.[31]

These societies faced events that challenged their ability to disengage completely from transnational forces and frameworks of reference, even if each society could package them as "national." A major example developed in the 1850s, as the entire region faced the rise of William Walker and his private army of North American *filibusteros* (freebooters), who began to take control of power in Nicaragua. Walker's intervention led to a war that was fought by what today we would define as a transnational alliance of nationals of various isthmian countries against Walker, while paradoxically—or perhaps not, since it fitted the logic of state claims, advanced in parallel by several of the isthmian states—this war became known in isthmian historiography as "the National War."

The transnational dimension of the struggle was so evident that its symbolic appropriation in terms of the emerging images of nationhood was done in a plural fashion, and the states involved could not completely obliterate the transnational angle as an underlining current of narrative and symbolic representation. In such a manner, the fight against Walker only rekindled once again the tension-ridden process of disengagement of the states and embedded the history of these nations within the persisting transnational dimension of their existence in the isthmus.

In 1853, Walker began to participate in filibustering expeditions in Sonora and, later on, in Central America. After gaining independence, Nicaragua had been involved in endless fighting between liberals, with a stronghold in the city of León, and conservatives, with their center in Granada. Facing a rising tide of conservatism, led by Rafael Carrera in Guatemala, Nicaraguan liberals called in North American adventurers to help their cause, promising them generous land grants.

Under contract with the liberals, Walker and 57 Californians arrived in the region; they were reinforced by 170 locals and about 100 Americans upon landing. Even though initially he suffered defeat by forces led by a conservative commander from Honduras, due to parallel defeats of other liberal commanders, Walker managed to rise as commanding officer and took over the city of Granada. This opened the door to his recognition as chief of the armed forces under Patricio Rivas and eventually led to his becoming the head of state of Nicaragua. By executing and exiling opponents, he controlled the country and was elected president in June 1856. Walker's agents recruited American and European men to sail to the region and fight for the conquest of the other four Central American republics. In a failed attempt to secure his party's nomination for an upcoming reelection, President Franklin Pierce recognized Walker's claim to Nicaraguan power.[32]

This move would trigger a sense of pan-Latin American solidarity and, moreover, galvanize the resistance of Central American states. In addition, Walker aligned himself with railroad and shipping capitalists Cornelius Garrison and Charles Morgan, who were competing with Commodore Cornelius Vanderbilt for control of the company that secured the only major trade route from New York to San Francisco through Nicaragua. In doing so, Walker made an enemy of Vanderbilt, leading Vanderbilt to support the military coalition of Central American states, which was led by Costa Rica. Vanderbilt prevented supplies and men from reaching Walker, pressured the US government to withdraw his recognition as the Nicaraguan power holder, and gave North American defectors from Walker's forces free passage to the United States.

Walker had managed to gain control of Nicaragua, but he was soon thrown out of power in a struggle that would also become immortalized as the "War of Independence" in Nicaraguan and Central American historiography, which served as a substitute for the war of independence that Central America had never experienced.[33] By May 1857, Walker had surrendered to the US Navy and was repatriated. Subsequent attempts by Walker to regain power in Central America failed and led to his imprisonment by the British, who controlled the Caribbean coast of Honduras. The British handed Walker over to the Honduran government, which executed him in September 1860.

The fight to oust Walker became a source of collective pride and was portrayed as a cornerstone of national identity in more than one country of the region. This struggle against Walker also carried transnational connotations that emphasized Central American solidarity and patriotism. The built-in tension between nation building and transnationalism was thus encoded symbolically in the recreation and commemorations of this historical event and would be instrumental in the construction of collective identity.

In Costa Rica, April 11 became one of the key national holidays, commemorating the battle of Rivas in 1856, in which a makeshift army of Costa Rican peasants who were chasing Walker defeated him at Rivas, Nicaragua. This began the decline of Walker's power, culminating in his eventual surrender to the US Navy.

Juan Santamaría, a young drummer from Alajuela, Costa Rica, volunteered to burn down the wooden fort of Rivas where Walker and his men had taken refuge, thereby forcing them outside. Santamaría, who immolated himself to burn the fort, was an overlooked hero at the time. However, beginning in the late 1880s and continuing officially in 1891, this illegitimate mulatto son was made a national hero. A statue of Santamaría depicting a strong and handsome soldier carrying a torch was placed in Alajuela, and Ruben Darío, the great Nicaraguan writer, wrote a poem immortalizing his memory. Today, Santamaría's heroism is taught in schools, and his sacrifice is eulogized and celebrated by the children of Costa Rica in commemorative performances.

Unsurprisingly, the story of the opposition to Walker has been equally central to the construction of an "imagined national community" in Nicaragua. Promoted by historians and politicians, the struggle was portrayed in the country as a war fought by Nicaraguan patriots, joined by the armies of neighboring states. It produces a national interpretation without completely obliterating the themes of Central American solidarity and transnational patriotism.

Many Central American leaders were involved in the struggle against Walker. A look at one such leader, Nicaraguan general José Dolores Estrada, provides insight into the conscious appropriation of symbols and creation of tradition in the service of national imagery and the resulting glorification of the state as the repository of the values of the nation. On September 14, 1856, then colonel Estrada commanded a force of 120 to 160 men that clashed with a force of "more than 200" led by Walker's friend Byron Cole, at the Hacienda San Jacinto. Estrada's forces defeated them, which triggered a reversal in Walker's fortunes and—according to Nicaraguan historiography—diminished his chances of controlling Nicaragua.

After the fight against Walker, Estrada continued to be active in politics and was exiled to Costa Rica from 1863 to 1867. He returned to Nicaragua upon the declaration of an amnesty, but passed away in 1869, at the age of seventy-seven. Estrada had organized private meetings of comrades and friends every September 14 to commemorate the battle of San Jacinto. After he died, his friends continued the tradition. A few years later, state authorities decided to officially adopt the September 14 commemoration and to make it a public celebration. After making a visit to the house of Estrada's sister, the dignitaries would continue to the Palacio Nacional to make a toast in the memory of the deceased hero. They invited all those men who had accompanied Estrada and were still alive to join the president, ministers, heads of the army, and notables for a toast and speeches to eulogize and pay honor to Estrada's memory.

The state officially appropriated the image of Estrada, a person of oligarchic origins, and transformed it into a hero of popular background. Estrada became one of the people, humble and ready to make sacrifices for the fatherland. At the same time, Estrada's background as a son of Granada was downplayed. His home city, Granada, had been involved in the fratricidal wars that led to the involvement of foreign mercenaries such as Walker in the internal affairs of Nicaragua. Estrada was increasingly portrayed as "the notable son of Managua," the city named as capital precisely to overcome the antagonism between Granada and León. The symbolic transformation of Estrada took place less than a generation after the war, as the promulgation of the Constitution of 1858 enabled a decline in internal struggles. Ceremonies commemorating September14 began to be celebrated in all pueblos, cities, and towns, on the eve of the declaration of independence of the Central American republic, as a kind of second independence, this time of the Republic of Nicaragua.

The battle became a timely means of constructing collective—national— identity in a society that until Walker's invasion could not claim to have fought a war of independence. The society had no fallen heroes to mourn in order to claim a line of historical continuity that connected contemporary citizens to the sacrifices of the founding fathers, as in other lands that had fought to gain their independence from the royalists. September 14 thus became the surrogate event for the war of independence lacking in 1821. According to the minister of foreign affairs of Nicaragua, Anselmo H Rivas, in a speech delivered on September 15, 1873, the lack of wars of independence in Central America had hindered the development of a sense of nationality. He further noted:

> The Fatherland has [finally] understood that the powerful weapon to fight these two enemies of its well-being [namely, the lack of heroes and fratricide wars] is the patriotism of his sons; and to promote it, has established this civic occasion [the battle of San Jacinto], so that, while remembering the heroic virtues of the American patriots, the youth should be encouraged to follow in their footsteps.[34]

September 14 (1856) and September 15 (1821) were linked to create a common historical past and to dilute the localisms still lingering at that time. Likewise, and as could be expected, this constructive process glossed over but could not eradicate the tensions existing between national narratives and previous interpretations of the nation as anchored in a transnational realm. These different interpretations and narratives continued to coexist, albeit with changes in their relative saliency in different states and times. Thus, while analyzing the political lexicon of annual addresses by Costa Rican presidents between 1821 and 1949, Víctor Hugo Acuña Ortega found that, until 1847–48, the terms "nation" and "republic" were used to characterize Central America, while the use of "province" and "state" was reserved for Costa Rica. Furthermore, the idea of the unity of Central America as needed and the inevitable result of historical destiny continued to be promulgated repeatedly in presidential addresses from 1861 to 1921, along with the simile of the Central American family.[35] In contrast, Patricia Fumero Vargas found that for Nicaragua during the early 1870s, there was an increase in the mentions of independence in texts alluding to September 14, a similar rise in mentions to the independence of Nicaragua, and a less pronounced growth in mentions of Central American independence in speeches devoted to September 15.[36]

The experience of that war was highly important for the process of construction and reshaping of national and transnational identities in the region. It clearly fits within Eisenstadt and Giesen's analysis of construction of collective identities, Eric Hobsbawn and Terence Ranger's earlier analysis of invented traditions, and Anthony Smith's studies of naturalization of historical events.[37] That experience has the additional aspect of projecting a persistent tension between the redefinition of state boundaries and the reformulation of the meaning of the "national," thus recreating the transnational dimension of politics, now from beyond the crystallization of discrete state boundaries. As indicated, the war was rapidly appropriated symbolically as a "national war." In spite of its label, armies from all over the region waged it across state borders, thus entrenching persisting transnational threads, even as these nations entered new phases of nation-state consolidation. The very character of the confrontation could not erase the transnational dimension projected into later periods. The war could be claimed in parallel by various states, and thus its transnational character was projected into the rhetoric and memory of future generations, even in those cases when state agencies officially discouraged it.

Transnational Social Movements and Interstate Connections

The Janus-faced character of collective identities and political membership in the isthmus determined an intermittent renewal of projects of unification drawn by political elites as well as by social movements, and many processes of transnational spillover from one society to another. Sustaining these attempts at reunification, beyond the specifics of each attempt, was an underlying feeling of disappointment with the current achievements of the separate republics, often seen as "sections" of a more substantive fatherland. The supporters of these initiatives had the conviction that a golden age awaited the strategically located isthmus, provided the countries managed to overcome past divisiveness. In the nineteenth and early twentieth centuries, there were at least ten such major attempts. In the early twentieth century, these attempts were even supported by US interests. Indeed, the General Treaty of Peace and Friendship was signed in Washington, DC, in December 1907, under the sponsorship of the United States.

Efforts to revive a confederation failed, but the delegates signed eight conventions aimed at stopping transnational fighting as countries agreed not to intervene in the affairs of their neighbors through the manipulation of political exiles and other measures. With the opening of the Panama Canal only a few years away, the United States was strongly interested in the political stability of the isthmus. Within the isthmus, the antagonistic position of El Salvador was crucial, since its policy of distrust of Guatemala's striving for regional hegemony assured the parallel projection of Nicaraguan influence until 1908. Likewise, Salvadoran opposition to the increasing dependence of Central America on US financial support led to various early transnational initiatives such as the creation of a Central American bank in 1912.[38]

In what follows, for reasons of space, I analyze here only early twentieth-century initiatives to foster a renewal of the vision of transnational regeneration of the Bolivarian vision, leaving subsequent trends for later chapters. These initiatives were of two types: top-down initiatives, paradigmatically exemplified by the International Central American Office, and a myriad of bottom-up initiatives, such as the Central American Unionist movement; the University Reform movement, spreading from Córdoba in Argentina; the Latin American Union; the Alianza Popular Revolucionaria Americana (APRA), created in Peru; and the Asociación General de Estudiantes Latinoamericanos (AGELA), founded in Paris. Earlier ideas served as inspiration; among them were those of *Ariel*, the work of Uruguayan José Enrique Rodó, and of the modernist writers and vitalist philosophers of the turn of the century. These initiatives and projects influenced later generations. The pan-Latin American and anti-imperialist visions surged again among dependency theorists, theology of liberation priests, and leftist activists in the Cold War era, as well as in the movements that supported the early twenty-first-century Pink Tide governments.

Located in Guatemala, the International Central American Office was established with the express goal of supporting "the peaceful recreation of the Central American Fatherland." The office, which represented delegates of the various states of the isthmus, cooperated with the member governments in promoting the harmonization of constitutional charters, the unification of educational contents and customs tariffs, monies, weights and measures, the adoption of a single shield and flag, and so on. The office published a quarterly journal that promoted the spirit of transnational unity through notes on common history, national heroes, and symbols, in addition to reports on regional treaties and information on the member states. The spirit of transnational mission that pervaded its activities can be illustrated by quoting the opening paragraph of its April–June 1920 issue. It served as a wake-up call to the region, exhorting members to find a sense of unity:

Central America, wake up. The feeling of nationality stands up boldly in each of the five Republics of the Isthmus. Our peoples, melted by misfortune, diminished by animosity, increasingly sense the imperative need of transforming into optimal reality those spiritual ties that, albeit in weak form, have maintained the noble and fertile idea of Central American solidarity during the painful phase of our separation. Tying our fraternity within an indissoluble bond and enabling the emergence of a free, great and prosperous nation in the heart of the new world, constitutes the imperative mandate of our peoples.[39]

The journal sought to promote regional fraternity, overcoming nationalist egotism. Those committed to a Central American fatherland were encouraged by the experience of Italy and Germany, which were united after centuries of fragmentation. Writing about the Italian experience, they imagined the future of their own fatherland. They chose to stress the voluntary, spiritual commitment of those willing to work for "national unity" beyond "sectionalism."

In the 1910s and 1920s, the institutional trend of treaties signed by delegates from the isthmus states was accompanied by renewed transnational activities led from the bottom up by the Unionist Movement, a network committed to the idea of a Great Central American fatherland.[40]

That movement constituted a transnational network of idealistic activists, who tried to recreate the project of a Central American nation. They operated at the grassroots level, promulgating that spirit, convinced that the union of early independence had failed due to a combination of factors. Among these, they singled out the egoistic drive of reactionary elites, their manipulation of the ignorant masses, and their co-optation of intellectuals who otherwise could have opposed the dissolution. Accordingly, they envisioned reunification as being led by a new cohort of committed intellectuals who would spread the word and nourish the latent massive support for the unionist revival. In their eyes, this revival was the "truth of the future," which would soon turn into a reality with many benefits for the well-being and pride of Central Americans, living in liberty, democracy, justice, and the rule of law.[41]

The origins of this movement date back to the 1890s, spearheaded in Guatemala by a group of students led by Salvador Mendieta (1879–1958), a Nicaraguan youngster who arrived in Guatemala in 1892 to study at the Instituto Nacional de Varones. There, he became acquainted with other Central Americans of means who were studying in Guatemala. Expelled from the Guatemalan institute due to his student activism, he moved to El Salvador to complete his secondary education, remaining active in student circles willing to promote a sense of Central American fraternal bonds. In late 1897 he was back in Guatemala, where he started his studies in law at the university, and in 1899—under the government of Manuel Estrada Cabrera—he founded a student association committed to promoting Central American bonds and fighting the dictatorships of the isthmus. Imprisoned and expelled from the country, he completed his studies in Honduras in 1902. Back in Nicaragua, he continued to create unionist associations and afterward became a prolific writer and speaker, defending the regeneration of the Central American societies and the recreation of the union.[42] In the early twentieth century, driven by confrontations with those in power, Mendieta founded the Partido Unionista Centro Americano and relocated serially to Costa Rica, El Salvador, Honduras, and Nicaragua. Later on, as he and others again launched the Partido Unionista de Centro América (PUCA) in 1919, the movement achieved its full impact, benefiting particularly from the support of pro-unionist governments in 1920–21 led by those in Honduras and Guatemala.[43]

Many intellectuals, teachers, and students, most of them from an upper-class background, joined the movement, as they were disillusioned with the liberal, positivist, and materialist projects, and refused to recognize the true republic of their dreams in the states where they lived. According to the unionist creed, being a divided nation, Central America could not prosper. The solution was to unite as a region open to all humankind. Moreover, once Central America was united, both Mexico and South America would be in a stronger position to resist the onslaught of US economic interests. The unionists wanted to regenerate the wider nation, promote the spiritual consciousness of a shared destiny among all the inhabitants of the isthmus, and create a just society. They wished for a society in which individuals should not only be considered abstract citizens with duties, but also concrete persons enjoying basic rights, irrespective of ethnic, gender, or status differences.[44] Aware of the failure of previous projects, they hoped to achieve a bottom-up regeneration. They trusted this would be attainable by promoting a consciousness of common destiny and building a model of equality, social justice, and tolerance that would encourage the union while respecting the autonomy of the various states and regions. They did not exclude other projects, such as continental Bolivarianism, but rather thought that those projects would have better chances of realization with a united isthmus.[45] They were more critical of pan-Americanism, due to its top-down agenda and its connection to imperialist and interventionist schemes, which some of them resisted and revolutionary changes geared to establishing a society "without private property, parasites, autocrats, plutocrats, and religious, national, racial, and male supremacists." Donald Clark Hodges indicated that these ideals were combined with the use of violence as part of a Sorelian legacy transmitted into the Americas by Spanish anarcho-syndicalists, which Augusto César Sandino, the Nicaraguan leader fighting US military forces in the isthmus, eventually incorporated while adopting a spiritualized vision of social justice.[46]

Imbued with the vision of Central American regeneration, especially in the years preceding the one hundredth anniversary of the end of Spanish rule in Central America, many of the unionists wandered through the sister nations of the region. They were either suffering the perils of exile or living as expatriates, trying to promote enthusiasm for the unionist creed in their new environments. They envisioned their wandering as a "pilgrimage" and "apostolic mission." From a transnational perspective, probably the most important long-term contribution of the unionists was the widening of Central American public spheres through many publications that spread their ideas in the struggle for cultural hegemony in the 1920s to 1940s, along with the opening of spaces of sociability accessible beyond distinctions of gender, nationality, and to lesser extent, class and race.[47] This work of diffusion of ideas and creation of spaces of sociability expanded public debate on issues such as the incorporation of indigenous and *mestizo* subaltern sectors and women in full citizenship or the regeneration of society from the bottom up. Through such activism and diffusion of ideas, they influenced conceptual paradigms and impacted the thought of thousands of individuals. Among them were figures like Juan José Arévalo, who would later take an active part in politics, and others, like the daughters and granddaughters of the women who participated in the female circles named after Gabriela Mistral and would achieve recognition of the female rights to vote and stand for elections in Guatemala in 1946.

The unionists were only one of the movements inspired by ideals that could transcend the discrete nation-state horizons of the region. Decades earlier, patriots such as Cuban José Martí and Puerto Rican Ramón Emeterio Betances had agitated and mobilized support against the remnants of Spanish colonialism in the Americas, from their exile in the United States and Paris, respectively. In South America too, the younger generations supported cultural and political projects of transnational significance. The youth "vitalist" generations followed the predicament of intellectuals such as the Uruguayan José Enrique Rodó, author of *Ariel* (1900), or the Dominican-born Pedro Henríquez Ureña.

Outstanding among those bottom-up initiatives was the university reform movement that started at the University of Córdoba in central Argentina. In that stronghold of conservative scholastic learning, students revolted between March and October 1918 and demanded the democratization of higher education. In their statement of purpose of June 1918, the students indicated that "the youth no longer asks. It rather demands the right to be recognized, expressing its own thought at the university bodies, through its representatives. The young people are tired of bearing tyrants. If one has been capable of making a revolution in people's consciences, its ability to intervene in the government of our own house cannot be ignored."[48] After a series of clashes, the movement achieved recognition of autonomy for higher education, the coparticipation of students in running the university, and open competition for *cathedras*. Soon the movement—which had a clear Latin Americanist vocation—spread to Buenos Aires, Mexico, Lima, and La Habana, promoting social justice and preaching the importance of pushing political reforms. Student leaders preached their creed while traveling to the neighboring countries, exchanging letters, or relocating as exiles. They also published over a hundred magazines and publications that triggered interest in the ideal of renewal, building networks committed to social justice and transnational Latin American solidarity.[49]

Their practices became a sounding board for new ideas on a continental scale. Following and reacting to geopolitical developments such as the US occupation of Cuba and Puerto Rico and the interventions in the circum-Caribbean tilted the movement toward explicit anti-imperialist positions. Those developments motivated young people to join forces in a process that soon overflowed the confines of academia. In Peru, the student leader Víctor Raúl Haya de la Torre first felt inspired by the message of Argentine Socialist Alfredo Palacios, who spread the news of university reform while on a visit to Peru. Palacios received recognition as the Master of the Youth of America at the first National Student Congress, chaired by Haya de la Torre, who would soon found the APRA movement. In Argentina, Palacios was part of the circle around physician and essayist José Ingenieros, who in 1923 launched the periodical *Renovación: Boletín de ideas, libros y revistas de América Latina*, a forum to which intellectuals from all over the continent contributed, preaching the ideal of transnational development. The magazine survived Ingenieros's death in 1925 and continued publication until 1930. At the same time, Palacios began to be involved politically, founding the Unión Latinoamericana (ULA), and soon also the Alianza Continental, a coalition of forces that included Argentine radicals and military officers promoting the reelection of Hipólito Yirigoyen in 1928. In 1924, Haya de la Torre created APRA, with the mission of working for Latin American unity and fighting imperialism. Peruvian intellectual José Carlos Mariátegui also promoted the reform movement and projected the idea as part of his renowned "Seven theses of interpretation of the Peruvian reality." Under the influence of Haya de la Torre and Manuel Seoane, founding members of APRA, ULA would soon join forces with that organization to push an anti-imperialist agenda for the Americas.[50]

Likewise, in Bolivia, the visit of Alfredo Palacios in 1919, and especially the arrival in 1925 of Miguel Seoane, an Aprista leader exiled in Argentina, initiated a process that would give rise to Bolivian Marxism and revolutionary nationalism. In Cuba, the ideas of renewal of the reform movement were particularly attractive in the face of the frustrations of the republic, with Julio Antonio Mella (1903–29) as the architect of the reform movement at the University of Havana in 1922. The experience of that period would lead Mella in his short life to be a founding member of the first Communist Party of Cuba, of the José Martí

Popular University, and of several magazines, as well as to suffer imprisonment and exile in Mexico, before the Machado regime assassinated him. Another influential figure was Dominican Pedro Henríquez Ureña (1886–1946), who settled in postrevolutionary Mexico after experiencing the US military occupation of his native country and moving to Argentina in 1924. Henríquez Ureña's humanist ideas and praise of Spanish American language and culture resonated strongly with reformist students. Mexican José Vanconcelos traveled to Argentina in October 1922, linking sociability with the consolidation of an ideological link between the Mexican Revolution and the movement for university reform. In turn, Chilean educator Gabriela Mistral's (1889–1957) affinity with the struggle of young Chilean university students resulted in a visit to Mexico. Arriving at the invitation of Vasconcelos in 1922, she spread reformist ideals at a time when she was gaining continental recognition for her poetry.[51]

The activism of that generation, the generation of the "Centenary," emerging one hundred years after Latin American independences, not only generated mutual recognition in sister countries, but also resulted in expulsions, exile, and expatriation; some of them moved beyond the continent, making Paris a particular center of relocation and activism in exile. Paris, the center of the 1789 Revolution and already idealized as the "city of light" in the nineteenth century, became a center for the networks of defiant pan-Latin American activists. Meeting young people from all over Latin America led to the creation of AGELA, the General Association of Latin American Students, and other activist nuclei in Paris in 1925–28, whose adherents preached the idea of reconstructing the lost Latin American unity. Promoting sociability and spreading pan-Latin American ideals, these encounters allowed activists to rethink Latin America in broader terms than the nation-states, fostering anti-Yankee, anti-imperialist ideas, although, paradoxically (or not), those young activists opted to ignore the parallel phenomenon of French imperialism. In the long term, those networks would forge years later a Third World imaginary, one that would align the Latin American Left with the liberation movements of Asia and Africa, whose countries occupied structurally similar positions in the world system. In later decades, these themes continued to ebb and flow, along with geopolitical shifts and new socioeconomic challenges, as discussed in later chapters.

This chapter has discussed processes shaping collective memories and historical narratives, cross-border practices, social networks, and movements of ideas and peoples. We have followed various aspects interconnecting the states and societies in the Americas within a long-term transnational perspective that existed long before the current stages of globalization and persists beyond the domain of economics. Accordingly, we see that globalization and transnationalism are not coterminous, although they may impinge upon one another. I have focused particularly on the domains of politics, public life, and the construction of collective identities, tracing the tension-ridden interplay between the process of constitution of states and distinctive national identities, on the one hand, and on the other, the lingering presence of alternative projects of reconstruction of broader, transnational commitments and identities. Both processes have been entangled in shifting ebbs and flows at different historical moments. For some sectors, that early experience and failure of Boliviarianism became a source of inspiration for later transnational projects, while for others that memory solidified the will to take a distinctive path of disengagement.

It is important to point out here that other transnational forces have been present in Latin America. For example, as analyzed in detail elsewhere,[52] the circum-Caribbean sea has been the homeland of transnational Afro-Caribbean and ethnically mixed populations like those of the Miskitu and the Garifuna, whose perspective contrasted with the logic of the nation-state.

Bridging the Luso-Hispanic Axis

Brazil and Spanish America had developed their own ways until the late nineteenth century. With the exception of the interregnum of 1580–1640, when all Iberian American territories had been united and the flow of persons, goods, and ideas had been opened, Brazil had become independent under an imperial house and relatively soon stabilized under the prolonged rule of Dom Pedro II, who managed to retain the loyalty of regional elites for decades. Witnessing with disdain the anarchical character of early republican life and *caudillismo* in Spanish America, for decades Brazilian elites were content with their distinct pattern of development.

The War of the Triple Alliance, in which Brazil allied with Argentina and Uruguay against Paraguay, allowed closer connections and a reassessment of perceptions of Brazilian superiority, leading some elite sectors to question the core Brazilian institution of slavery and eventually to challenge imperial rule. In the following decades, there was a growing circulation of people, translations, and information across state borders, that is, an increased connectedness that reshaped the mutual image of these neighboring countries. Brazilian elites increasingly perceived Spanish American countries as developing model states embracing internal peace, mass migration, urban modernization, and insertion in world markets. Spanish America became significant for both republican and monarchist elites, as the so-called Generation of 1870 turned its gaze increasingly to South-South relationships. Ori Preuss, who studied this process, identified that anxieties over European and/or North American imperialism were coupled with increasing self-confidence and respect in the region, noting that "the triple presidential encounters were a transnational celebration of South

American virility, military might, and economic prosperity; a spectacle of *Paz y Administración, Ordem e Progresso.*"[53] *Letrados* and political elites alike used those images to favor or resist change in Brazil, while the abolition of slavery in 1888 and the end of imperial rule in 1889 immediately became transnational events celebrated in the Spanish republics. In the 1880s, elite members added South American stops to their grand tours, until then mostly geared to travel through Europe. In 1888, Brazil joined Argentina, Bolivia, Chile, Paraguay, Peru, and Uruguay in a South American Congress in Montevideo, and in January 1889 these countries signed agreements concerning patents, the protection of literary and artistic property rights, and judicial processes. In the 1890s, exiles like dissident republican Rui Barbosa fled into exile in Argentina, publishing articles for Brazilian readers there, which followed a South American optic, for instance by denouncing a common struggle against authoritarianism and favoring a conservative liberalism. In 1899–1900, the mutual presidential visits of Argentine Julio A. Roca and Brazilian Manuel Ferraz de Campos Sales further cemented state cooperation. Increasingly, this cooperation led to the ABC alliance between Argentina, Brazil, and Chile, which by 1914 tried to mediate between Mexico and the United States in the midst of hostilities during the Mexican Revolution, and which in May 1915 signed a treaty of cooperation, nonaggression, and mediation that lasted to 1930.

A growing maritime flow of ships connected Valparaíso, Buenos Aires, and Montevideo to Brazilian ports and from there with Europe and the United States, carrying Chilean, Argentine, and Uruguayan newspapers, whose articles resonated in Brazilian elite circles and were sometimes translated and published in local periodicals. Intellectuals and statespersons met face to face in congresses, editorial rooms, and coffee shops; exchanged letters and books transnationally; and cited and relied on each other's works. Intellectuals thus played a growing role in journalism, diplomacy, and education, not just in their home nations but also in neighboring countries. Even during the early phases of Brazil's Old Republic, when a resurgence of negative stereotypes focused on the disruptive potential of republican life and the correlated restriction of civil liberties, there was no complete return to isolationism. The recognition of Argentina's novel image and modernizing accomplishments had become part of Brazilian elites' interpretive toolkit, leading in later decades to a no less competitive assertiveness on the part of Brazilian policymakers, but not to isolationism.[54]

By representing both a long-term competitive challenge and a promise of cooperation, Argentina and other Spanish American nations, such as Chile, Mexico, and Venezuela, emerged from an era of unruly *caudillismo* into orderly progress by the late nineteenth and early twentieth centuries, playing a central role in the redefinition of Brazilian identifications, projects, and policies along a transnational perspective. At the state level, Latin American countries often failed to translate those continuing connections into international solidarity, as sociologist José Luis de Imaz recognized in his erudite work *Sobre la identidad iberoamericana*.[55] At other levels, however, both intellectuals and political figures repeatedly established transnational connections and interactions, including creating them while relocating to sister nations as exiles, in recurrent waves of forced displacement and expatriation, as analyzed in later chapters.

This chapter has discussed how collective identities and images have affected the power, meaning, and character of the social, political, and cultural forces shaping societies entwined with one another, rather than as mere discrete units evolving separately. In different periods and under varied circumstances, there have been diverse ways of envisaging the destinies of the region. Some expressed the logic of consolidating nation-states, while others projected transnational connections, as traced in the last two centuries in diverse political initiatives, civil society networks, belligerent actions, cross-border coalitions, and transnational practices. Rather than claiming that the region has existed as an objective entity, I analyzed some of those processes and forces that have promoted transnational commitments or fought them. In a broader compass, this analysis underlines the relevance of focusing attention on the construction of collective identities as an autonomous dimension of social life, connecting visions of history, membership in political communities, and future-oriented projects. As such, this analysis has additional relevance for understanding the geopolitical and cultural history of macro-regions. It is particularly relevant as research demystifies a lineal reading of history that once canonized the hegemony of the nation-state and more recently, seemed to erroneously promulgate the decline of nation-states under the aegis of globalization.

4

The Politics of Exclusion

Exile and Its Transnational Impacts

For many decades and across the Americas, political exile was considered ubiquitous, but no systematic attempts were made to explain its crystallization and development. The phenomenon was seen as a natural correlate of being involved in politics, and as such was taken for granted. Indeed, for a very long time, forced territorial displacement was mostly addressed as a biographical note or, at most, a chapter in the biographies of major political and intellectual figures of nation-states' histories.

In the last twenty years, this has changed, as research began exploring the full macrosociological and political role that exile has played on both national *and* transnational levels. Resulting from the politics of exclusion, exile affected the construction of nation-states, shaped the format of citizenship, and prompted transnational dynamics across the region. Studies of forced migration and expatriation have led to the unavoidable recognition that the very practice of constrained territorial displacement shaped awareness of the emergence of separate nation-states. Additionally, they have revealed that beyond the logic of territorial nation-states, any country that expelled or received exiles was likely to witness long-standing and persistent transnational dynamics. In more than one sense, *the national and the transnational mutually constituted one another.* Thus, beyond their empirical findings, studies of political exile made analytical contributions to the "transnational turn." The far-reaching personal and institutional implications of displacement and exile—many of them of transnational impact—have thus received increasing attention on the part of researchers and policymakers alike.[1]

Essential to this understanding is the role of exile as a key mechanism regulating political struggle in elitist, authoritarian, or limited democratic political systems. As much as the lower classes have traditionally been marginalized in Latin America, the widespread use of exile to deal with political opposition and activists has reflected the attempt of those in power to exclude any contesters from politics and the public spheres of those states, without risking the entire structure of the body politic.

Once used and abused to regulate the political domain, political exile generated complex processes at different levels of articulation, spanning from the

Transnational Perspectives on Latin America. Luis Roniger, Oxford University Press. © Oxford University Press 2022.
DOI: 10.1093/oso/9780197605318.003.0005

local and regional domains to the transnational and global levels. At all those levels, this mechanism of political exclusion projected tensions between the political and social backgrounds of the displaced individuals and the transformative processes that occurred in the places of relocation, where the exiles had to rethink their life projects while adapting to new challenges, lifestyles, and practices. Research has also identified the substantial transformations that exile has undergone in the era of globalization. Recent years have seen the publication of literature that combines the work done by professionals who stayed in the countries of origin and others who had left their countries of origin years ago— moving research toward a global approach to the communities of co-nationals in exile during the latest wave of military dictatorships.[2] Building on a tradition of in-depth studies of sites of exile,[3] researchers achieved progress by bringing together analytical and empirical contributions from academics in the fields of the humanities, history, and the social sciences. This chapter reviews some of these issues, with particular emphasis on the formative and transformative impact of forced territorial displacement in Latin America.

The Empirical and Analytical Significance of Political Exile

After attaining independence in the early nineteenth century, all countries in the region—in spite of following different institutional paths—incorporated forced migration and expatriation as a major political practice. Those in power used and abused exile forms as a major mechanism of institutional exclusion. Territorial ostracism and its counterpart, the possibility of receiving asylum, soon permeated the political cultures and expectations of all these societies.

The historical and cross-national impact of exile can be grasped by looking at its ubiquitous presence in settings as geographically and historically distant as nineteenth-century Argentina and twentieth-century Honduras. Unfolding a century apart and located thousands of miles apart, in both countries exile appears as the key mechanism of institutional exclusion. Referring to the rule of Juan Manuel de Rosas in the Río de la Plata (1829–52), Argentine historian Félix Luna assessed the fate of those who opposed Rosas, the Restorer of the Laws. Most likely their fate would be limited to three very specific alternatives: *encierro, destierro, o entierro*, that is, imprisonment, exile, or burial.[4] Is it mere coincidence that thousands of miles from Argentina, in Central America, one of the victims of political persecution by the government of Tiburcio Carías Andino (1932–49) referred almost identically to the plight of the Honduran dissidents in that period? In the absence of human rights protection, good and evil became blended, with no clear sense of justice and no freedom prevailing: "The Honduran who did not agree with the dictatorship could choose between imprisonment, banishment or burial. Those were the alternatives. No one could resist, protest or even criticize [the ruler]."[5] The ubiquitous use of exile as a major mechanism of exclusion from the body politic in Latin American states did not go unnoticed in these and other countries of the region. Throughout the nineteenth and twentieth centuries, the experience of exile occurred repeatedly to major political and intellectual figures. At the same time, until the mid-twentieth century, with some notable exceptions, exile was not questioned, as elite circles and wider social strata took it for granted as the likely fate of individuals competing for positions of power or falling from the grace of those in power. In addition, until recent times, most historians and social scientists disregarded the role of exile as a mechanism that projects transnational links across the continent, sidelining such impacts in favor of nation-state perspectives and frameworks of analysis.

Such perspectives would be challenged as a result of the rising attention exile received during the Cold War. By the mid-twentieth century, political exile was no longer the fate of a few individuals involved in politics. The transnational aspects of territorial displacement could not be ignored as banishment, exile, and expatriation from South America became massive in the framework of the Cold War. Many of those displaced retained their agency and voice abroad through transnational advocacy networks, while the home South American dictatorships established transnational repressive networks operating together against the remnants of revolutionary and guerrilla activists. In addition, civil wars and international intervention produced considerable waves of transnational displacement in Central America. Amid all these developments, the key importance of exile became evident, as the term was both conflated and in tension with the figure of the refugee, a legal category that starting in 1951 international agencies recognized and made into an object for their assistance. Exile's connection to transnational issues and the format of citizenship in the region became an important focus of analytical inquiry.

The connection of exiles to transnational networks of solidarity and advocacy also contributed to the principled shift in conceptualization. While many personal testimonies and biographical notes had previously called attention to exile, the new waves of forced exile and expatriation created new awareness of the historical depth and contextual width of this phenomenon, as well as new interest in its multiple functionality. In this new stage, research began to trace the profound impact exile had, in parallel manner, on both the countries of origin and residence and the transnational level. To use the terminology of the social sciences, from being merely a dependent variable, exile became significant as an independent variable that, by its very nature, has transnational importance.

At that new stage, researchers started tracing the widespread and recurring presence of exile as a mechanism of institutionalized exclusion since the early nineteenth century, in parallel to the establishment of independent states and bearing historical antecedents in colonial times. Indeed, the roots of the phenomenon go back to colonial times. There is still debate about whether territorial displacement in the colonial period and exile in independent times are one and the same phenomenon. However, it is clear that the expulsion of colonial subjects to the confines of the Portuguese and Spanish realms or the removal of individuals to places where the authorities could control them was widely used in the colonial period in a multiplicity of variants with various names such as, among others, *degredo, destierro, traslado, deportación,* and *expulsión.*[6] During colonial times, such displacement served first as an instrument of control over criminals, outcasts, and rebels, and second to strengthen the defense of imperial frontiers or their expansion.[7]

Yet it was in the early nineteenth century, after independence, that exile developed the political profile that, mutatis mutandis, persisted throughout the subsequent centuries. In the new independent states, exile became widely used and abused in politics and public life, an addition to imprisonment and executions. In the collective imagination and in public areas of the countries of Latin America, exile became a central way of "doing politics."[8] Because of space limitations, here I focus on the historical significance of exile as reflecting the matrix of citizenship in Latin America, its transnational implications, its recurrent presence, and its changing significance.

Exile and the Format of Citizenship in Latin America

Citizenship in elitist-hierarchical societies is problematic due to their tendency to recognize entitlements selectively. It is doubly so when, as in Latin America, the system has supported—in its rhetoric, religious tenets, and ideology—idioms professing to open the political system. As elitist as these political systems have been, republicanism contained utopian elements that were embraced by sectors willing to gain and widen popular political participation. These attempts could be rather anarchical, as in the nineteenth-century civil wars (prolonged into the late twentieth century in Colombia and Central America), or more controlled, such as during populist periods and in settings dominated by clientelism.

In *La formación de las almas,* historian José Murilo de Carvalho discussed Brazilian republican leaders' systemic need to consolidate themselves in government, which led them to project their visions and representations beyond narrow elite circles. In order to do so, they created images, allegories, and rituals, and set up educational programs aimed at generating a common willingness to abide by the new ground rules. When possible, they sought to instill a sense of membership, nationhood, and pride in the fatherland. Individuals became citizens when they realized they were part of both a state and a nation.[9]

And yet, as elites in Brazil or Spanish America undermined their prior status as part of empires or abolished the empire (as in Brazil in 1889), republicans kept the state as a central focus of power. For instance, according to Murilo de Carvalho, in Brazil this was due both to the long étatist tradition inherited from the Portuguese and to the interest of many upwardly mobile sectors in keeping the state as the main provider of employment, especially in the urban areas. Thus, rather than citizenship, what resulted was a situation of "state-ship," a biased perception of citizenship linked to the overwhelming—more or less paternalistic and somehow coercive—power of the state as the provider of partial and selective rights, which hinged on the maintenance of a hierarchical socioeconomic, political, and administrative structure of control. Similarly, in Spanish America most elites made efforts to retain the elitist and hierarchical structure of control throughout the civil wars that characterized the aftermath of independence.

Maintaining such a structure of control through a process of infighting (as in the transition to independence) entailed many perils for the upper sectors of society and the ruling class. This was particularly the case in Spanish America, where the Napoleonic occupation of Spain started a process that led to a sequence of "devolutions" of sovereignty to the *pueblos* throughout the region and subsequent moves toward a reconstitution of administrative hierarchies, but in new ways that ultimately fragmented the Spanish territories of the Americas.[10]

During colonial times, various forms of translocation and displacement had been used within the boundaries of the Spanish and Portuguese empires as part of the administration of justice rather than on the basis of politics, as would be the case later. In colonial times, as historian Tamar Herzog showed for the penal system of Quito in 1650–1750, displacement reinforced an image of swift and efficient colonial administration, achieved with little investment and at low administrative cost. In parallel, the use of displacement reflected a situation in which justice was conditioned by the nature of small and closely knit communities, which were unable to punish their transgressors in situ and found it easier to transfer the "problem" to another, far away area.[11]

Displacement left from the start a wide berth for personal decisions and created a tradition in which local authorities enjoyed the discretion to banish individuals who endangered local stability. The use of translocation was widespread and permeated local culture, and it established a strong precedent for political exile.

In the process of disintegration of the Spanish Empire, the possibility of going into exile remained open to those rebels who were part of the social elites while, interestingly enough, it was often denied to those belonging to the popular classes and non-White ethnic groups.[12] The failed movement Túpac Amaru in 1780 and the Comunero Rebellion of 1780–81 provide good illustrations of the different punishments reserved for individuals of "ethnic" background. In the early 1780s, neither the *mestizo* José Gabriel Condorcanqui (Túpac Amaru) nor the *mestizo*, or perhaps *mulatto*, José Antonio Galán were granted the privilege or "doubt" of exile bestowed on members of the social elite. Both Galán and Túpac Amaru were executed after their rebellions failed in New Granada and Peru, respectively.

As political struggle permeated society during the wars of independence and the ensuing civil strife in Spanish America and from the 1820s to 1840s in Brazil, the option of displacement was projected into the political realm, becoming expatriation and exile. In this transitional period, it was mainly a privilege, granted to—or taken by—rebels of upper-class background and activated through the mediation of networks within the context of local hierarchical lines of distinction. Illustrative are the cases of some of the founding fathers of the Hispanic American states—Simón Bolívar in Venezuela, the Carrera brothers in Chile, Francisco de Paula Santander in Colombia, and Agustín de Iturbide in Mexico— all of whom were given that privilege denied to individuals of lower ethnic or racial background.[13] Many central political actors took the road of expatriation, among them José de San Martín, the liberator of Chile and Peru, who opted to leave and to end his days in Europe, and Bernardo O'Higgins, the founding father of the new Chilean Republic. Facing factionalism, the alternatives were to get involved in strife or leave.

Even though some of the most striking cases of displacement resulted from the will of political actors to avoid the dangers of exacerbated factionalism degenerating into civil war, most exiles were forced to leave their home countries by those in power. The political history of the Andean countries, on the one hand, and the Provincias Unidas del Río de la Plata in the South, on the other, is pervaded by such trends of forced exclusion through exile. Forced exile was the fate of communities such as those who fled to Uruguay and Chile during Juan Manuel de Rosas's rule in Buenos Aires. The same fate befell countrywide leaders such as Gervasio Artigas, José Fructuoso Rivera, Manuel Oribe, and Juan Antonio Lavalleja in Uruguay, as well as Pedro II, the second and last emperor of independent Brazil, who left the country in 1889 and died in exile in Paris in 1891.[14]

Exile's being at first a privilege granted within elite circles can be clearly assessed by following the case of Simón Bolívar. His early exile exemplifies how some of the patriots who rebelled against the established authorities were allowed to leave their countries after defeat, based on status and social hierarchy, instead of facing a more severe punishment. In August 1812, Bolívar managed to meet Captain Domingo Monteverde, the royal authority, through the mediation of Francisco Iturbe, a community member highly respected in loyalist circles and a distant friend of Bolívar. Accordingly, Bolívar was allowed to leave for Curaçao, in spite of conspiring against the Spaniards.[15]

The physical elimination of conspirators was an extreme measure, a step to avoid if possible. Worth mentioning in this connection is Manuel Rodríguez, an uncontrolled guerrilla fighter, who had conspired with the Carreras against Bernardo O'Higgins. When his role in the affair was discovered, he was forced to sign a declaration of repentance. Later he was even nominated to high administrative positions by both José de San Martín and Bernardo O'Higgins. The usual manner of punishing conspirators was prison or translocation to a place from which the conspiring agents could no longer act politically. In contrast, the Afro-Venezuelan general José Padilla of Cartagena was sentenced to death in spite of his many contributions to political independence, due to Bolívar's fear that this emblematic figure could possibly launch a caste war of African Americans against the White leadership of the country.[16]

The tensions between the old aristocratic expectations of displacement and the pressures from the opening of politics to participatory models exploded, breaking the norm inherited from colonial times in many cases and leading to the execution of opponents. Illustrative is the case of the Carrera brothers, who were involved in intense struggles with O'Higgins, and two of them met their deaths following attempts to unseat the latter. Until 1821, when he was executed in front of a firing squad, José Miguel Carrera led a relentless power struggle against O'Higgins and those responsible for the execution of his brothers.[17] Yet exile continued to be widely used even during the bloody period of the early to mid-nineteenth century, as well as in following decades. The death penalty given to leaders of opposing factions and parties could be a stepping stone to a deepening struggle and civil war. Thus, a common mechanism bridging political confrontations and avoiding tragic results was the mediation and intercession of social networks on behalf of a persecuted party. I mentioned earlier the case of Bolívar leaving Venezuela through the intercession of social connections. Around 1827 Bolívar found himself, as president of Colombia, confronting his vice president, Francisco de Paula Santander, and deciding his fate, while social networks interceded on the latter's behalf. The situation reached a point where the vice president feared for his life, and he wrote to Bolívar asking to be allowed to leave Colombia:

> In case the government cannot guarantee my personal rights against certain aggressions, I implore your excellency to give me a passport to exit Colombia with guarantees for me, three servants and my luggage, since the natural law dictates me to seek a safe place, in spite of the law and my destiny as vice-president, rather than expose myself to become a fruitless victim of ill will and vengeance.[18]

After a failed coup d'état in September 1828, Santander, who had not participated in it, was nonetheless sentenced to death, in a clearly political trial. Members of the elite and the church raised their voices to intercede on his behalf.[19] The Council of Ministers deliberated on the issue and issued a statement, advising that Santander's life should be spared and strategically reinforcing exile as opposed to applying the death penalty:

> It will be in the interest of the government to commute the death penalty into the cancellation of employment and the translocation [extrañamiento] from the Republic, prohibiting him from entering back the territory without a special permit from the Supreme Government; under the condition that if he fails to abide by the terms of this prohibition, any judge or military chief could apply him the death penalty in the place of his capture; and that his properties should be kept as deposit, without any possibility of selling or mortgaging them, to function as a security bond so that he will not break the prohibition and to be confiscated in the future, in case he breaks the prohibition. . . .The Council is of the opinion that, by taking this road, the vengeance of justice [sic] will be satisfied, while the government will get the love, admiration and respect of the governed and thus attain the needed peace and trust of the citizens.[20]

Bolívar commuted the death penalty to exile, but Santander was imprisoned again for seven more months in Cartagena. Only after the intercession of José Antonio Páez in Venezuela was Santander able to leave for Europe and the United States.

Exiles could never be sure of being able to return to their homelands. In these highly personalistic polities, much depended on shifts in the balance of power, such as occurred during the dethronement or death of an incumbent ruler. Such shifts could transform exile into a springboard back to power. Santander returned to Colombia in October 1832, after Bolívar's death, as the elected president of the republic, following the restitution of all his military honors.

Return from exile in circumstances in which the political scenario had not changed radically could produce a tragic end. This was the case for Agustín Cosme Damián de Iturbide (1783–1824), the ruler of the short-lived independent empire established in Mexico. Soon after he was nominated emperor in May 1822, Iturbide faced growing opposition from those coveting greater political power. Republican elements led by General Antonio López de Santa Anna and buttressed by federalist forces representing regional interests rebelled. A tug of war ensued as these forces tried to impose new parliamentary elections to force the legal dethronement of the emperor. In March 1823, Iturbide resigned the throne and was allowed to leave Mexico for Europe, with an entourage of twenty-seven members, which included his family, secretary, and servants. He explained that his decision was a way to keep social peace and avoid civil war. Once in the "Old Continent," he was treated as an exiled monarch. In Mexico, rumors abounded about Iturbide planning to come back at the head of an army provided by the Holy Alliance. The republican government enacted regulation allowing the state to send into exile, without trial, any person suspected of conspiring against the republic. As Iturbide traveled from Livorno to England, the Mexican Congress blocked his pension payments and ordered the death penalty if he should return to Mexico. In May 1824, unaware of the latter decision and disregarding José de San Martín's advice not to return since an act of this kind would probably trigger a civil war, Iturbide decided to go back. As soon as he arrived, he was taken prisoner and summarily executed.[21]

Progressively, the return of exiles became linked to policies of amnesty and pardons aimed at achieving "national reconciliation." This trend opened the issue of political and administrative reincorporation of exiles into the home society, sometimes even accepting the returnees into the ruling coalitions and inner circles of power. Outstanding, but far from exceptional, was the case of Chile. There, under conditions of early state consolidation, the government looked for ways to diminish the frictions provoked by civil strife by reinstating the displaced individuals into their formerly abolished privileges, pensions, and ranks.[22]

In that period, exile functioned as a transitional mechanism that regulated tensions in polities in which the presence of strong opposition leaders could lead to a zero-sum political game and civil war almost by default.[23] By sending away those who had led the defeated faction—what would be considered the opposition in a more developed political context—the rulers could claim to be moving in a lenient way toward organic unity, which they claimed to legitimately embody. Exile thus became a major mechanism regulating access to positions of power, built on exclusion but claiming to unite the nation. The opposition was often demonized and stigmatized as a divisive force conspiring to destroy society, while the rulers claimed they were re-establishing the cherished and broken unity of society. As such, a mechanism of political exclusion of elites could be represented as a source of harmony.

All these processes were carried out without opening the way to a more pluralistic vision of politics. While they were in exile, the lives and even the properties of the excluded leaders would be respected. But once the exiled leaders attempted a comeback into the political game, the odds of a zero-sum game were so high that many of them paid with their lives.[24]

In societies with deep social cleavages and relatively narrow elite circles, the rulers preferred political exile over other means of political exclusion. For as long as was possible, elites were interested in avoiding a situation of total war that could weaken the hold they had over the whole social matrix. The latter could become a reality by launching a cycle of mutual retaliation, creating long-term blood feuds, or forcing the elites to open the political game to growing numbers of supporters from the lower strata. These developments could endanger the entire position of the elites in the medium and long range. Because the conditions for imprisonment were seen as unsuitable for members of the elite, a prison sentence was often a harsher measure than exile and as such was used as a threat. Social networks, friendship, family ties, and clientelistic entourages played into the system of power in favor of the nontotalistic solution of political exile.

Transregional Political Dynamics

In early independent Latin America, in a situation of undefined borders, exile was not conceived of in terms of modern political asylum. Rather, individuals forced to move to other regions thought of it as a tactical escape from the sphere of influence of their persecutors, the rulers of their home societies. While staying outside those rulers' sphere of control, the displaced individuals did not perceive themselves as foreigners, but as "patriots" moving within the borders of the Great American fatherland, or as expatriates waiting to return to the homeland.[25]

With the passing of time, the territorial displacement of "political enemies" beyond the areas directly controlled by the new states became related to the effective definition of borders between the newly formed states. An outstanding example of such transregional dynamics is that between Perú, Bolivia, and Chile in the nineteenth century, a dynamic also present within the circuit of Central America and parts of Mexico. Other examples are the Southern Cone, including Argentina, Paraguay, Uruguay, Southern Brazil, and at times Chile, as well as the connected spaces of Venezuela, Colombia, and Ecuador. Decades later, the geographical circuits of displacement would become even wider on a massive scale. As an illustration, I focus here on the first circuit of displacement.[26]

Connections between Peru and Alto Perú (later Bolivia) had existed since Incan and colonial times. Similarly, in the colony, territorial links connected Peru and Chile, with many instances of individuals from Peru being relocated in Chile, which constituted the outer frontier where the Lima authorities sent troublemakers. The links between Peru and Alto Perú were weakened between 1776 and 1809, when Alto Perú was incorporated into the newly created Viceroyalty of the Río de la Plata, with its capital in Buenos Aires, but they became relevant again with independence.[27] In fact, many of the figures who shaped Peruvian history from the 1820s to the 1860s were natives of other regions in what are now Bolivia, Venezuela, and Ecuador. These include Andrés Santa Cruz, Juan José Flores, and José de la Mar, the leading *caudillos* who fought and plotted with each other, expelled each other from power, and ruled Peru during that period.[28] There was a lack of separate national consciousness. In 1828, when Peruvian general Agustín Gamarra invaded Bolivia, claiming it was indivisible from Peru, many Bolivians defected to his camp, making his job easier:

> Since the Bolivian nationality was recently established and there were old ties and sympathies between Lower and Upper Peru, nobody thought with guilt, or considered it treason, to belong to Peru if the invasion eventually had that aim, or to remain in the new Bolivian Republic. The masses in particular ignored the political question stirred by the quarrelling parts.[29]

The political game was dominated by *caudillos* who attempted to unite Bolivia and Peru, to append part of Bolivia to Peru, or the other way around, as seen in the attempt by General Andrés Santa Cruz to establish a Peruvian-Bolivian confederation. The governments of Peru and Bolivia were deeply involved in each other's domestic politics for decades. Many of these "national" leaders expelled each other or fled from Peru or Bolivia, mainly to Ecuador or Chile, and then returned. Once abroad, they sought a temporary stronghold from where they planned a return to power, supported or opposed by the political forces in the host societies. In tandem with internal strife and translocation, those in power defined the rules of the game about exile and return. In general, the sanctuary offered by host countries was respected, while attempts to return would be severely punished, often with the death penalty.[30]

Since the crystallization of the new states did not preclude overlapping territorial claims, the political class of each region continued to exercise extensive influence on the neighboring countries.[31] The case of Peru, Bolivia, and Chile is not unique. Many of the leaders of Uruguayan independence, starting with Artigas, were exiled to Argentina, Brazil, and/or Paraguay. Likewise, during the dictatorship of Rosas in Buenos Aires and as federalist *caudillos* ruled the Provinces of the Río de la Plata (later Argentina) and the Banda Oriental (later Uruguay), individuals favoring centralization and liberalism left for exile in both Uruguay and Chile. Other Rioplatense members of the young intelligentsia fled as far as Lima, Guayaquil, Sucre, and Rio de Janeiro. Similarly, persecuted Chileans fled north, primarily to Lima, or crossed the Andes into Mendoza, Buenos Aires, and Montevideo.[32] More to the north, political exiles moved between Venezuela, Colombia, and Ecuador as well as within the Caribbean area, Central America, and Mexico.[33]

At this stage, exile exhibited *a three-tiered structure*, in which displaced individuals and communities of exiles played an increasingly important role. Political classes intervened in the configuration of other countries' political factions according to their own interests. When the faction they sided with was defeated, they often hastily accepted the vanquished political actors in their territory, hosting them and even supporting their plans of return, still playing regional politics in spite of defeat. They acted in such a manner so as to regain control of the neighboring political scene or at least exercise their influence by strengthening sympathetic political allies. When the defeated faction was inimical to their political script or design, they could still host the expelled individuals and control their freedom of action. Thus, they could curtail the possibilities of plotting against their ally, the ruling government in the neighboring country. In all cases the displaced individuals and communities of exiles played an increasingly important role in this three-tiered structure, both within the plans of regional hegemony of the host countries and within their home countries' strategies and pressures on the states hosting them.

The presence of exiles was tolerated and even fostered as a political tool to be used by the host country in relation to the political scene in the exiles' home countries. This attitude not only impinged on the country of origin of the exile but also contributed to defining the rules of membership in the host political community. Often, while exiles were used in the transregional power games, they were precluded from intervening in the local politics of the host country. Liberal Argentine exiles who settled in Chile lived under a conservative and authoritarian presidential regime without being able to influence local politics according to the ideological visions that they professed upon their arrival. As a rule, exiles were welcome as long as they either sided with the rulers in power or did not interfere in internal politics. When the exiles took positions contrary to the government's, they were usually expelled from the host country.[34]

While abroad, exiles and émigrés continued to be deeply factionalized, all struggling to represent the collective will and seeking to gain the support of the host governments as they drafted plans for the invasion of their home countries. For their part, hosts were willing to support such military campaigns whenever they felt they coincided with their geopolitical interests and supported their control of the exiles' leadership. The exiled leaders were heads of clientelistic networks of followers, who accompanied them outside the home territory. Once back in power, the returning leaders rewarded those who had taken the road of exile with them.[35] Prone to suffer the consequences of deep factionalism, their personal allegiance was expected, reinforcing a Manichean view of politics, which was thought of as divided into friends and foes.

In that formative period, exile became a major feature of political life. When the polities reached higher levels of institutional consolidation, exile was already an institutionalized part of a politics of exclusion. To use the terms of Albert Hirschman, exit was internalized in the political culture, pushing forward a rebellious and contesting form of voice in exile, which prevailed over more open and accommodating politics of voice domestically.[36]

There were other important implications for the structure of inter-American politics and diplomatic relations. As political exile had become a recurrent aspect in their political life, Latin American jurists and representatives debated the right of asylum on a transnational level. In the 1860s and 1870s, delegates from Latin American countries discussed asylum for the first time. And in the late 1880s and 1890s, jurists advanced early drafts of a South American corpus of norms of international private law and international penal law.[37] Thus, the principle that Linda Frey and Marsha Frey identified in the history of diplomatic immunity applies equally to the case of regional exile in the Americas:

> Rooted in necessity, immunity was buttressed by religion, sanctioned by custom, and fortified by reciprocity. The rules and conventions governing diplomatic immunity have been historically shaped and conditioned. . . . Subtly, acquiescence in small changes led unintentionally to the creation of precedent. Courtesies hardened and over time became "rights."[38]

From a comparative perspective, Latin American jurists and diplomats were among the pioneering voices pushing forward multilateral rules and conventions of asylum, as documented by historian Pilar González Bernaldo de Quirós regarding the work of such jurists as Carlos Calvo and Estanislao Zeballos, among others.[39] The first regional document that attempted to regulate asylum was produced at the First South American Conference on International Private Law in Montevideo in 1889. In 1911, the Andean countries reached agreement on extradition at a congress in Caracas. The Central American countries reached a parallel agreement in Guatemala in 1934. Inter-American treaties on asylum and political refuge were signed in La Havana (1928), Montevideo (1933), and Caracas (1954). The 1928 treaty denied the right of asylum to common delinquents, while the 1933 agreement clearly defined the legal framework of political asylum. Most American nations adhered to the treaty and ratified it, with the exception of Venezuela, Bolivia, and the United States. In 1939, these understandings found their way into the most comprehensive regional treaty yet negotiated, accepted in Montevideo by the countries in the region. The 10th Inter-American Conference produced an agreement on political asylum in 1954. The Caracas congress dealt with this aspect explicitly following the renowned case of Víctor Raúl Haya de La Torre, founder of the APRA movement in Peru. After his party was outlawed in 1948, he had spent five years practically imprisoned in the Colombian embassy in Lima.[40] The 1954 convention declared that "every state has a right to concede asylum; but cannot be forced to concede it, neither to explain the reasons why it denies it."[41] Asylum remained a state prerogative, to be granted by individual states as they took into consideration the gravity and nature of the political crime committed.

It is worth emphasizing that asylum was a focus of concern in Latin America even before it reached global attention. In the international arena it was only in the 1960s that concern regarding asylum reached a critical mass. Specifically, in December 1967, the Declaration on Territorial Asylum was adopted by the General Assembly of the UN and enforced Article 14 of the Universal Declaration of Human Rights. The Declaration recognized that the granting of asylum by a state "is a peaceful and humanitarian act and that, as such, it cannot be regarded as unfriendly by any other state."[42] In the 1980s and 1990s, following the displacement of hundreds of thousands of refugees in Central America, a series of Latin American congresses were organized by the United Nations High Commissioner for Refugees (UNHCR or in its Spanish acronym, ACNUR). These congresses brought together government officials, UN agents, professional experts, and NGOs to discuss the humanitarian and legal problems of asylum and refugees.[43]

The Widened Use and Descent of Exile

The Latin American countries were ahead of others in developing mechanisms of asylum in the international arena. The persistent elaboration of these treaties reflected the recognition of exile as a continental and transnational phenomenon. And yet such recognition reflected as well that Latin American nation-states had routinized their role as both expellers and possible hosts of the troublesome oppositions of the sister nations.

By the late nineteenth and early twentieth centuries, the consolidation of nation-states had shaped a situation in which the banner of transnationalism was carried mostly by those activists interested in reclaiming Bolivarian ideas on behalf of anticolonial struggles, as discussed in the previous chapter. The increasing weight of US interests in the region and the reaction of Latin American activists to the pressures derived from the rise of hemispheric hegemony and its impact on local situations of power also took part in shaping this process. Yet these social and political movements cannot be understood except through the optic of people experiencing lives in motion, time in exile, and wandering over a transnational scope.

With major innovations in transportation and communications, networks could move across borders and widen the impact of their ideas and organizational tactics. Historian Barry Carr analyzed how transnationally wandering activists in the greater Caribbean region resisted identification with the nation-states, as they were animated by new radical anti-capitalist ideas including socialism, communism, and anarchism. He indicated that they constructed "networks of revolutionary activism and transnational solidarity [between 1910 and 1940] sustained by expanding transnational capital and fed by labor migration, the proletarianization of agricultural labor, and the emergence

of national and transnational resistance to authoritarian regimes and imperial intervention." Through their organizational work, public demonstrations,
meetings, and publications, they had a diasporic, transnational impact. This impact was reflected in pivotal events such as the Mexican Revolution, the anti-
Machado mobilizations and 1933 Revolution in Cuba, the Sandino movement
in Nicaragua, and the peasant and indigenous mobilizations in El Salvador and
Honduras.[44]

The incorporation of new groups into politics, especially in the twentieth century with the enlargement of the franchise, also diluted the character of exile as
an elite phenomenon and its replacement by territorial displacement as a phenomenon affecting members of all social classes and strata. Eventually, exile
merged with and became blurred within a broader diasporic phenomenon of
other displaced individuals, including economic migrants, sojourners, and the
widespread phenomenon of refugees, who increasingly were recognized by the
international community as deserving special attention and treatment. The older
types of elite expatriates and political exiles persisted, related somehow to their
strife against structures of economic and political power. At the same time, territorial displacement became a life experience for wider groups affected by cycles
of violence, repression, and persecution. Thus they opted to take the road of escape abroad, beyond their home habitats.

One should bear in mind that both exiles and refugees are part of a universe
of individuals forced to migrate; the distinction between them is more a function of social attributes and self-definition and boils down to the willingness of
the displaced individuals to remain independent or make themselves available
for the official recognition and support of international organizations. Retaining
autonomy over one's life is the crux of the exile's decision.[45] Ariel Dorfman perceptively captured this distinction as he reflected on his own experience in his
autobiographical book *Heading South, Looking North*. After he found asylum in
the Argentine embassy in Santiago de Chile in 1973, Dorfman was interviewed
by a United Nations High Commissioner for Refugees (UNHCR) representative, who explained to him the conditions and benefits of the refugee status
he was offered according to the 1951 UN statute. "What I need to know—she
said—is if you intend to avail yourself of refugee status." The advantages were
clear: training and job placement, language courses in the country of asylum,
preferred housing, free medical attention, social security, and no need to renew
visa approval each year from the local immigration authorities. Dorfman recol-
lected clearly the reasons for declining that status: "I was now being offered a future in history as a victim." In contrast, he defined himself as an exile:

> I chose it automatically because I wanted to see my emigration as part of another
> tradition. . . . There was something Byronic, defiant and challenging, about

being an exile, something vastly more romantic and Promethean than the fate embodied in that recently coined word *refugee* that the twentieth century had been forced to officialize as a result of so much mass murder and wandering. . . . [B]y rejecting the passive term and opting for the more active, sophisticated, elegant one, I was projecting my odyssey as something that originated in myself and not in the historical forces seething outside my grasp. Instead of formulating my future in terms of what I was seeking, refuge, I conceived myself as ex-cluded, expelled, ex-iled, as if I had absolute freedom to choose which of the many countries of the world my free person would wander. . . . I was going off into the wilderness like a rebellious, solitary, persecuted angel.[46]

When the political systems widened participation, exile was already an established figure in the political culture, the imaginary, and even the internal and regional legislation of these countries. This widened participation resulted in the massification of the phenomenon of territorial displacement and exile. For central political figures becoming exiles, the widening of politics entailed a proliferation of persecuted activists, union leaders, students, professionals, peasants, workers, and other members of the middle and lower classes, who fled their countries. As thousands of individuals moved abroad to escape political persecution, communities of exiles developed throughout the continent as well as in Europe. Various places became *lieux d'exile*, attracting new waves of politically persecuted individuals and groups.

Political exile radically transformed and intensified. The masses entered into politics and mobilized with populism, and during the Cold War the extent and costs of political polarization were magnified, leading to massive political escape from harsh repression. As polarization increased and the local doctrines of national security were enforced through military dictatorships, the phenomenon of political exile and translocation spread beyond the boundaries of the political class and became a mass phenomenon. In the second half of the twentieth century, tens and sometimes hundreds of thousands of Chileans, Uruguayans, Argentineans, Brazilians, Paraguayans, Guatemalans, Salvadorans, and Cubans, among others, felt forced to leave their home countries as a result of political repression and fear of persecution, in addition to other personal and economic considerations.[47] Once abroad, these larger groups formed communities of exiles and refugees in the host countries.

At that stage, a new dynamic developed as the transnational communities of exiles and expatriates established connections to advocacy networks in their countries of residence and transnational networks of solidarity with NGOs and associations. Through such contacts and networks, the exiles achieved broader resonance with their cause, somehow reversing the original aim of the expelling governments, which was to isolate them and preclude them from having an impact on their home countries. This process then set up a relationship of four factors, in which the traditional triadic dynamics of interaction between the exiles, the countries of origin, and the host countries are transformed by interacting with a fourth tier of transnational networks and international agencies and NGOs, shaping new forms of exile politics of wider projection.[48]

Under such conditions, transnational dynamics are evident in the spread of individual leaders throughout the region and beyond, such as the emergence of political parties in exile, the establishment of cross-national political alliances, and counteralliances and transnational repressive operations targeting the oppositions in exile. On a regional level, the twentieth century witnessed the formation of such *a four-tiered structure* of exile. Beyond the individual countries' preoccupation with their own exiles and the exiles they hosted, they started developing international networks, trying to appeal to international organizations and states beyond the region to affect policies and regain power.

This trend became more pronounced during the last phases of the Cold War, when the fate of persecuted citizens of individual countries became of increasing concern to the international community, debordering the treatment of political exile contained by the nation-state. The coup led by Augusto Pinochet against the constitutional government of Salvador Allende was a major focus of concern, especially driven by the plight of masses of Chileans looking for asylum in Santiago's embassies or escaping abroad. Once relocated throughout the world, the national and transnational networks rekindled the banner of solidarity with the exiles in their fight for the restoration of democracy and against the human rights violations of the dictatorship. No less fundamental in reconstructing the international arena was the effect of the Argentine military administration's policies of forceful abduction, disappearance, and denial of its citizens' rights. Argentine authorities embarked on a policy of systematic disinformation and denial of human rights violations, claiming that the claims were the result of conspiratorial webs linked to international Communism. All the while, the increasing evidence shaped a dense web of critics in the transnational and international arena, which would radically change the discursive and political balance in favor of the exiles.[49]

Many concerned organizations and networks were instrumental in this transformation into a dense organizational scenario defending human rights. Civil associations and committees of solidarity acted in Europe and the United States. With officers in these countries' administrations concerned with flagrant violations, political networks such as the Socialist International supported persecuted political activists, domestic human rights organizations, and transnational organizations like Amnesty International and Americas Watch. These transnational organizations gained heightened profiles and respectability as they contested the dubious explanations of targeted states about their records of humanitarian violations. Powerful representatives of the international media, such as the *Washington Post* and the *New York Times*, were concerned with international commissions such as the Inter-American Commission of Human Rights, centered in San José de Costa Rica, and the UNHCR and its domestic representative agencies that supported the flow of refugees in European and other countries.[50]

The de facto rulers of the last waves of authoritarianism in Latin America were increasingly forced to argue and counterargue issues of human rights, thus paradoxically reinforcing the hold that human rights would have as the normative discourse that was about to supersede the previous hegemonic discourses of national sovereignty, at least on the declarative and normative levels. This transformation, also in effect in the intellectual arena, recreated the terms under which the plight of the exiles would be examined.[51] Exiles would henceforth find greater political space for their long-term activism in favor of the end of authoritarian rule, the restoration of democracy, and a full inquiry into the record of human rights violations by the dictatorships. In the end, the massification of exile backfired, as the international and transnational arenas became cages of resonance for the plight of the exiles and their demands.

While exiles intend to remain true representatives of the people, living abroad and interacting in host societies forces them to learn new practices and deal with new organizational models that transform their daily routines, visions, and behavior, either voluntarily or unconsciously. This poses a dilemma for all those exiled on personal, psychological, family, and community levels: how to appropriately interact with a host society, perhaps even developing hybrid identities and new commitments. Moreover, if exiles settle in what they perceive as a more developed society than the one they came from, a society that for instance pays more attention to the environment or state regulation, they are faced with this dilemma in a more acute manner. The more time passes in exile, the more likely it is that their sojourn will result in a new amalgamation and fragmentation of identities, a diversity of visions, and a living heteroglossia, which some may celebrate and others regret. Experience in exile forced those displaced to reconsider the ideals that they brought from the countries they left behind, and/or act tactically in order to convey their message in terms of new discourses that they once ignored or even denounced as harmful for their political commitment. Paradigmatic examples are their becoming part of transnational networks and the adoption of new discourses. An example is the human rights discourse through which the exiles of the Cold War could denounce the repression that, in terms of revolutionary discourse, was just the price that every fighter had to pay in the struggle for revolution. Once abroad, the exiles from the last wave of mass repression discovered the mobilizing power of the emerging discourse of human rights. They approached such a discourse as a bridge to networks of solidarity in countries such as those of Western Europe or North America, in a tactical way at first. Yet with the passing of time, this approach led many to realize that their old vision of revolutionary struggle should be reformulated, at least in connection to the new discourse of rights. This led to a profound process of redefinition of social and political visions, essential in later changes in their countries of origin.[52] These are just some of several theoretical implications that territorial displacement and exile generated for Latin American states and societies.

Theoretical Implications

Following theoretical developments in the social sciences and history that point out the growing centrality of diasporas and transnational studies, the study of Latin American exile has become an issue of central concern. Studying exile contributes to understanding the connection between the structure of state politics and struggles over the construction of citizenship *in a geopolitical scenario that transcends the boundaries of individual nation-states*. Studies of exile thus become relevant in connection with perspectives stressing transnationalism and cultural transformation, with shifting and hybrid identities. That is, the national and the transnational are realms emerging together, constituting one another. The systematic study of exile thus leads to new approaches to Latin American development, away from traditional readings of national histories and toward a more regional, transnational, or even continental scale of analysis.

On a theoretical level, the ubiquity of exile in Latin American countries highlights the tensions between the principle of national membership and the principle of citizenship. Once people are displaced from their home countries and forced into exile, they may lose citizenship rights. However, at the same time, their displacement can give rise to a deeper adherence to what the individuals perceive and claim to be the "national soul" of their home countries. Judith Shklar stressed in works published posthumously that this situation arises when exile breaks the political obligations of governments toward their citizens. It also leads to the redefinition of the parallel bonds of loyalty, fidelity, and allegiance once the exiles are living outside their countries of origin, the telluric basis of their citizenship. According to Shklar, banishment and displacement thus open a cycle of existential and political reflection, due to the lapsing of obligations of those expelled or forced by their governments to escape abroad:

> Exiles cannot do what most people—accept their obligations and political loyalties as simple habits. Displaced and uprooted, they should make decisions about what kind of life they lead now. As politicians, they should at least reflect

on these decisions and [develop and] different and mutually resolve their political rights, and links.[53]

With the passing of time, states aim to construct a certain sense of collective
identity, which remains latent and implicit—and is assumed without reflection
in daily life by those living in a particular territory. This dimension of collective identity is necessarily reflected upon, recognized, and often challenged
and redefined by those in exile. As a result, many of the displaced have found,
rediscovered, or reinvented abroad the "collective soul" of their nation in primary or spiritual terms. This contrasts with the definitions of that same identity
by those, who holding power, expelled them or forced them to flee the homeland. Although some exiles and transnational migrants disengage themselves
from the territorial and emotional attachments they once had, for many others
living abroad has led them to redefine their ties of solidarity in terms of the collective identity of origin. Yet dialectically, this struggle redefines national identity in terms distinct from and often broader than those dictated by the rulers
who ostracized the exiles. Thus, exile opens up a fascinating field of political and
cultural debate for those societies, particularly during regime changes and especially when they restore democracy and open their public spheres to greater
pluralism and debate.

At the same time, many exiles have established new links with exiles of sister
nations while abroad, strengthening a dynamic of mutual recognition and identification of issues and concerns shared transnationally within the Americas.
In other words, *their collective identity evolved while embedded in transnational
identity and transnational solidarities.* Accordingly, it was not uncommon for
exiles to not only play an important role in the redefinition of a national vision,
but also to have a potent impact on the reconstruction of pan-Latin American
identities.

In modern times, as indicated, territorial displacement brings to the fore the
tensions encoded between the principle of national membership and the principle of citizenship. Once people feel pressured to go into exile, they may lose
the entitlements attached to citizenship, but concurrently they may become even
more attached to the national soul. The "national soul" is a covert, but potent, dimension of collective identity in these societies that often emerges in exile.

A notorious example from before independence is the case of the Jesuits, who,
once they were in exile, wrote chronicles and panoramic descriptions of the home
kingdoms and territories left behind. They embedded their work with a sense of
local patriotism that, once independent, the new states would garner to create
a sense of national identity. In later instances of displacement, national identity
was often displayed transnationally, bringing many exiles to build ties with other
communities of co-nationals in the diaspora, other nationals experiencing the

same fate, and transnational networks of solidarity and advocacy. Significantly, while many of these nationals discover, rediscover, or invent the national soul in primordial or spiritual terms, at the same time their life condition of displacement beyond the "national" territory leads them to identify the transnational connection they share with exiles proceeding from other states in the Americas.

This recreation of a national imagery along with transnational reconnections has taken place in the midst of communities of exiles since the early process of independence in the nineteenth century. That is, while engaging in power struggles, those displaced individuals were unwillingly major actors who also contributed to the tension-ridden twin process of defining both nation-state and transnational identities. This process was closely tied to shaping the boundaries of the emerging states and mental borders in this part of the Americas. While abroad, exiles often rekindled or resented the sense of attachment to sister nations in the Americas. Exiles and expatriates even invented the term "Latin America" in mid-nineteenth-century France. Since then, many exiles have reinforced the recognition that the citizens of various states have shared common problems and interests.

Exiles and expatriates elaborated pan-Latin American ideas after relocating beyond the borders of their home countries. Particularly salient were those who faced broader arenas of discussion and claimed to represent the "true soul" of the home countries on a transnational scope. One of these figures who took pride in the culture and collective identity of Latin America was José María Caicedo, a writer and intellectual who was born in Bogotá in 1830. At the age of seventeen he began a career in political journalism, but he soon discovered the limits of free speech in Colombia. Beginning in mid-1849, he was editor of the newspaper *El Día*, in opposition to the government, which incited a riot that destroyed its machinery. His political stance led to a duel in 1850, in which he was shot. At the age of twenty he left Colombia for Paris, where he intended to recover from his wounds. He became an expatriate who, save for short visits back home, remained abroad until his death in 1889. He came to represent his country in London and Paris, was Venezuelan consul general and chargé d'affaires in France and the Netherlands, and later on was chargé d'affaires for El Salvador in France and Belgium. Yet more significantly, Torres Caicedo developed a continental approach to the countries in the Americas from afar. He was among the first to coin, no later than 1856, the term Latin America as a common denominator for the Hispanic, Portuguese, and French Americas. "We love our native country with passion," he said in 1864, "and yet, we consider the beautiful Latin American land as a common fatherland."[54] As a prolific Latin American writer and literary critic in Paris, he came to play an important role in the International Literary Association, led by Victor Hugo, which was founded there in 1878. There, Caicedo projected the voice of an entire continent. He supported the idea of a

Latin American union, which he first advanced in a book with that title written in 1864, and even founded an association with that purpose in mind.[55]

At certain times, exile led to the emergence of concrete transnational political and cultural projects and experiences. Illustrations abound, such as the case of José Martí and fellow Cubans who befriended Ramón Emeterio Betances. With Betances, a founding father of Puerto Rican nationalism, they organized patriotic clubs aimed at attaining the independence of both Cuba and Puerto Rico from Spain in the late nineteenth century. Another prominent figure was Eugenio María de Hostos y Bonilla, a native of Puerto Rico, educated in Spain and a sort of wandering expatriate educator, who was very influential in the Dominican Republic and Chile. He too campaigned for the independence of Cuba and Puerto Rico, and in favor of a federation of Antillean nations that would include those two islands and the Dominican Republic. These patriots collaborated on that unsuccessful project, partially thought of as a preemptive move aimed at precluding US political hegemony after the envisioned independence.

In Central America, activists moved peripatetically throughout the region in the 1920s, partly due to deportation by state authorities but sometimes motivated by their own transnational agendas. Paradigmatic, though perhaps extreme, is the case of Agustín Farabundo Martí (1893–1932). In 1920, he was deported from El Salvador to Guatemala, where he spent five years, mostly with indigenous or *ladino* laborers, many of whom participated in mass protests and were machine-gunned collectively, while others were shot or hanged by local citizens and military reservists. The memory and legacy of this activism was projected in El Salvador for decades by the Farabundo Martí National Liberation Front (FMLN), which fought US-backed military rule during the Cold War and remained a major political force after democratization.[56] From a transnational perspective, another important long-term contribution of the unionists was the widening of the Central American public spheres through the creation of many publications from the 1920s through the 1940s. These spread their ideas in the struggle for cultural hegemony and also opened spaces of sociability beyond distinctions of gender, nationality, and, to a lesser extent, class and race.[57]

The spirit of reunification that the transnational movement kept alive for some time combined with the sincere attempts of the International Central American Office to work within the framework of pan-Americanism. It publicized efforts at regional coordination and promoted the sense of Central American solidarity. Unsurprisingly, the "confederation of interests" soon broke apart and once again came to nothing. The first major blow to the institutional mechanisms devised by the conventions resulted from the placement of Nicaragua as a protectorate of the United States in the 1910s. Costa Rica, along with El Salvador, Honduras, and Colombia, protested, and eventually Costa Rica brought the case before the Central American Court of Justice. It claimed that the US-Nicaraguan treaties of 1913–16 constituted a violation of territorial rights and of Central American conventions, specifically violating the neutrality of the region. The court accepted these arguments, but Nicaragua withdrew from the court, and it became evident that there was no way to enforce the ruling, as the United States ignored it as well. This led to the discrediting of one of the key Central American institutions. When the court's convention came up for renewal in 1918, Central Americans rejected the opportunity to renew it, mainly due to this incident. There was an attempt to revive the court in 1923, but states and citizens alike were already skeptical, and the pan-Central American hopes of 1907 were gone.[58] Skepticism thus grew out of the recognition that regional interests were subordinated to those of the United States, both by what was later called Big Stick interventionism and by the US presence in the Caribbean and Central America. One should remember, however, that such interventionism was not due exclusively to the expansionist drive of the United States. The weak institutionalization of states generated a situation in which domestic contenders kept calling on the United States to serve as a mediating force that could intervene, supporting them in their transnational power struggles.

The drive toward Central American coordination emerged out of the need to regulate coexistence and the impossibility of remaining isolated from international networks. Still, even the International Central American Office had to recognize that the international treaties signed by the countries of the isthmus were "doctrines" more than "binding laws." Therefore, they lacked the capacity to be implemented except through "moral recognition." In the following decades, such recognition became increasingly marginal. In 1923 a new treaty was signed by the Central American states that reiterated the principles of the 1907 agreements. However, by then the United States was clearly the sole arbiter of interstate tensions and the force behind the possible consolidation of separate nation-states in the isthmus. This became evident in 1927 when tensions almost led to a "banana war" between Guatemala and Honduras, behind which were the United Fruit Company and the Cuyamel Fruit Company, both looking for further land concessions. The United States intervened forcefully to put down the conflict, and two years later the source of tension was eliminated as the Cuyamel Fruit Company was taken over by the United Fruit Company.[30]

From the mid-1920s to the early 1930s, these developments brought university students—especially many studying in Guatemala—to adopt the pan-Central American perspective. They moved beyond unionism, which, according to their understanding, was looking backward, into more radical positions, phrasing their goals in anti-imperialist terms. Inspired by the Mexican Revolution's new ideals, the rising prestige of Marxist ideas, and the potent surge of the university reform movement first launched in Córdoba, Argentina, many of them became fervent supporters of anti-imperialist and pan-Latin American positions.

Standing out in addition to Martí, discussed above, was Augusto César Sandino, who led an armed struggle against international intervention and domestic dictatorships. Starting in 1920, Sandino had experienced life in the economic enclaves of the Atlantic coast of Central America, first in Bluefields (Nicaragua), then in La Ceiba (Honduras), then briefly in Guiriguá (Guatemala), and finally in Tampico (Mexico). In these places he witnessed the diversity of the circum-Caribbean area populated by "British West Indian blacks," Garifunas, US plantation farm managers, and a multinational labor force. That labor force included foreign radicals and adventurers, many of whom led economic struggles and fought against US economic interests and imperialism. Wandering through that part of the Americas, Sandino developed a vision of resistance to international intervention and Bolivarian, transnational commitments. His key officers and some of the rank-and-file soldiers came from all Central American territories, some even from Mexico and the Dominican Republic. Imbued by this vision, he and his transnational cadre resisted the US military presence in Nicaragua from 1927 until his assassination in 1934.[59] Following those decades of interventionism, the United States elaborated a "good neighbor" strategy for containing or controlling political change by leaving behind well-trained local forces to protect the interests of US corporations and the governments and political leaders favored by US policymakers.[60]

In the late twentieth century, the reverberations of the Cold War recreated transnational connections and horizons once again. In the Southern Cone, for example, expulsions and exile, migrations, and relocations had a strong impact on the redefinition of political agendas. That impact took on different forms. Provided there were no major constraints in their choice of destination, a large percentage of individuals forced to flee their home states chose to settle in neighboring countries, hoping to return within a short time. Yet democracies collapsed one after another, and there was justifiable urgency to escape repression. This need was particularly intense for those who came from where repression was harsh and as the circle woven by Operation Condor's transnational repression closed in on activists who defied the established social and political order in an increasingly authoritarian-run South America. Under such circumstances, new relocations took place in a kind of "serial exile," which in the cases of Uruguayans, Argentines, and Chileans led to the emergence of diaspora communities in sites far removed from their countries. In the case of Paraguayans, due to the comparatively early establishment of a huge concentration of co-nationals in Argentina, this phenomenon was less pronounced. Dispersion made communication more difficult, but it granted resonance to the plight of exiles. The extent to which different communities of co-nationals made a proactive commitment to challenge the home dictatorships was crucial to the enactment of that challenge, and they were able to do so in effective ways by cooperating transnationally. The authoritarian governments of Chile and Argentina, followed by that of Uruguay, would soon discover that while in the short run they succeeded in silencing exiles and indoctrinating sectors of domestic public opinion, in the end the use and abuse of political exile backfired. Given the connections that the displaced individuals and networks established with transnational advocacy forces at work in the global arena, their plight received significant resonance.

The practice of territorial displacement and exile has played a vital part in shaping the forms and styles of Latin American politics. At the same time, exile has contributed to (re)shaping collective identities from afar, yet not in the sense that exile is the "mother" of nationality, as often claimed by those who follow Benedict Anderson.[61] Repeatedly, exile has equally recreated transnational bonds, which later on refracted back onto the countries of origin. Unsurprisingly, exile reinforced the transnational concerns of elites and their global outlook. With the passing of time, the structure of exile, originally triadic (i.e., built upon the interaction between the state of origin, the country of relocation, and the exile communities), added an increasingly crucial fourth dimension, that of the transnational networks of solidarity and the international community. Finally, exile contributed to making diasporas not just a long-standing presence in the region, but also a presence that under certain circumstances became a driver of change, spanning both the host country and the country of origin, as in the case of the Paraguayans residing in Argentina.

5

International Wars and Conspiracy Theories

with Leonardo Senkman

Those who adopt a conspiracist worldview interpret the world as the object of sinister machinations, opaque plots, and malevolent forces that operate in the shadows. They usually assume the existence of nefarious underground powers, secret plotters of projects of domination or destruction, including foreign powers and economic interests. As "truthers," that is, truth seekers, they consider it a moral duty to unmask these plots and mobilize to confront the hidden powers, defeating their vicious plans for domination. Only then, they believe, will they be safeguarding the integrity of a collectivity, its spirit, and its material resources.[1]

Crises fueled by wars can be a fertile ground for conspiratorial thought. Faced with the challenges that a war generates and willing to mobilize support for their struggle, those who share a conspiracist stance may make sense of the situation by pointing out the evil machinations of powerful enemies and interests. Incorporating fragmented pieces of information, they assert cherry-picked evidence as proof of subterranean plots planned by malevolent forces.[2] If a lack of trust in institutions, authorities, the media, and even science is added, many people may give credence to conspiracy theories, especially on the losing side of the war.[3]

This chapter discusses the variable development of conspiratorial narratives around international wars in Latin America, trying to assess why in two out of the three cases considered here (the War of the Triple Alliance and the Chaco War), the appeal of conspiracism was high, while in contrast, conspiracism did not play a major role in the War of the Pacific. Organized thematically, the chapter does not follow a chronological sequence. Discussion starts with the case of the War of the Triple Alliance of 1864–70, follows with the Chaco War of 1932–35, and concludes by reviewing the War of the Pacific (1879–83), which preceded the second case by over half a century.

Transnational Perspectives on Latin America. Luis Roniger, Oxford University Press. © Oxford University Press 2022.
DOI: 10.1093/oso/9780197605318.003.0006

The War of the Triple Alliance against Paraguay: A British Plot?

Between December 1864 and March 1870, imperial Brazil allied with republican Argentina and Uruguay to wage war against Paraguay. Known as the War of the Triple Alliance, the conflict started when the coalition of those three countries reacted to Paraguay's president Francisco Solano López's movement of armed forces into Brazilian and Argentine territory on the way to Uruguay. López considered that this move would halt Brazil's intervention in Uruguay, where the empire sided with one of the warring factions, thus tilting the regional balance of power.

Under the rule of Carlos Antonio López (1841–62), Solano López's father, Paraguay had become an economic powerhouse buttressed by the state's monopoly over exportable agricultural products, its metallurgy, and its educational system. Confident of the state's capacity and ability to mobilize the population, Solano López ruled authoritatively, like his predecessors (his father and Dr. José Gaspar Rodríguez de Francia, 1814–40), reinforcing the sense of connection with the Paraguayan people, as he spoke with them in Guaraní, the native language, which reinforced the emotional bond.

In Paraguay, recruitment was universal; following the Triple Alliance invasion of Paraguay's territory, the population mobilized for a total war in a desperate attempt to achieve an unlikely victory. Geopolitically, Solano López went to war expecting to get assistance from Argentina's federalist forces, primarily those led by General Justo José Urquiza, governor of the province of Entre Ríos. This external support, however, did not materialize. Left on their own, Paraguayans sacrificed themselves in the belief that Solano López's decision to go to war would sustain their national independence.

The Paraguay war was the longest and bloodiest international conflict fought in South America up to that time. Mass mobilization interfered with agricultural production, resulting in food scarcity. The war produced hundreds of thousands of casualties, with lives lost in battle or to hunger, disease, sanitary conditions, destitution, forced evacuations, and displacement. Paraguay suffered almost complete destruction, with most of its male population decimated. The Triple Alliance imposed territorial losses and economic indemnities on Paraguay, and after 1870, the liberals came to power. Supported by Argentine liberals, they maintained their supremacy until the rise of the Colorado Party. The Colorados claimed to be following the legacy of the Lópezes, attaining political hegemony for most of the twentieth century and becoming the basis of political support for General Alfredo Stroessner, the supreme ruler of Paraguay between 1954 and 1989.

In Brazil, the war reinforced the power of military officers and the large land-owners' disaffection with the ruling Bragança dynasty, as they resented the forced recruitment of the slave labor force. The full impact of these shifts became evident years later, as republicanism replaced the empire in 1889, and Emperor Pedro II sailed off to exile in Europe. In Uruguay, the fratricidal struggle continued until 1904, when the country finally stabilized. Argentina experienced the confrontation as both an international conflict and a civil war, since its own federalist and "unitarian" coalitions tried to make strategic gains as they drew different lessons from Paraguay's defeat. In the end, the war reinforced the process of political unification underway since the early 1860s, while weakening the liberal faction of President Bartolomé Mitre, the architect of the war against Paraguay.

From its start, the war was highly unpopular across the region, with public debates developing rather early, particularly in Argentina, a country undergoing a process of incomplete national unification around competing visions of federalist autonomy—equally personified in Paraguay's case—versus centralization around the port city of Buenos Aires. Argentines even joined the Paraguayan Army, as in the case of Colonel Telmo López, son of the historical leader of the province of Santa Fe, Estanislao López. Some *caudillos* led armed uprisings against the central government, which reacted by declaring a state of emergency, closing newspapers, and expelling opposition figures to exile. As expected, those opposing Buenos Aires's primacy—for example, Carlos Guido y Spano (1866) and Juan Bautista Alberdi (1869)—saw in the international confrontation a war of aggression against a regional project of autonomous development. From his self-imposed exile in France, Alberdi blamed President Mitre for surrendering Paraguay to Brazilian expansionism: "His writings presented Paraguay as a defender of Latin American republicanism against monarchical despotism. . . . Alberdi's arguments transcended the war period and resurfaced later on in the works of Paraguayan revisionists."4

Those critical of the war rejected the alliance with the Brazilian Empire, a slave-owning society. In addition, Brazil's emperor was the cousin of Emperor Maximilian of Austria, whom Benito Juárez was fighting in Mexico. Also energizing their reaction was the sense of sympathy for the struggle of the Dominican people against a second Spanish occupation and of solidarity with the defensive alliance of the republics on the Pacific littoral against an attempted Spanish military intervention. Several Latin American states tried to mediate in the conflict, and Colombia even contemplated offering citizenship to Paraguayans in the eventual case that the allies would impose the dissolution of Paraguay as a sovereign country.

Among the Paraguayan revisionists was Juan E. O'Leary, who in 1919 portrayed President Solano López as a nationalist leader who had fought for

Paraguay's sovereignty and its model of economic development. Relying on Alberdi's assessment, O'Leary and other critical revisionists viewed the conflict as a grand conspiracy against Paraguayan autonomy. They characterized Paraguay as a modern nation marked by political stability and progress, until the Triple Alliance destroyed it.[5] O'Leary's reading was highly critical of the liberal regime that had assumed power in Paraguay after the defeat. As such, the view that O'Leary disseminated widely among the army and other Paraguayan institutions served to support the empowerment of the Colorados, a party that saw itself as the heir of Solano López's legacy in the twentieth century. That narrative, which had foundations in the past, is still strong among substantial sectors of Paraguayan society.[6]

Ultimately, Paraguay's critical assessment of the war transcended national borders to mark the historiography that emerged transnationally in Latin America after World War II, along with dependency theory and Marxism. In the 1950s and especially the 1960s, the Argentinean Left, under the influence of dependency theory, endorsed the revisionist thesis claiming that the British stood behind the Triple Alliance. According to that thesis, the British intended to destroy Paraguay as an alternative to the British model of free trade with South America. Multiple authors, including León Pomer, Eduardo Galeano, and Vivián Trías, advanced that thesis, suggesting that British commercial designs pressed war on Paraguay.[7] Pomer's *La Guerra del Paraguay: Estado, política y negocios* (1968) resonated in Brazil as much as the publication of *Genocidio americano* by Julio José Chiavenato a decade later. According to that line of argumentation, the British needed to secure sources of cotton in the context of scarcity created by the US Civil War.[8]

Those readings recognized that in the course of the war, Argentina underwent a professionalization of its army, the disciplining and nationalization of its masses, the repression of internal dissent, the assertion of its borders, and the reaffirmation of the political and economic project linked to global markets. On the other hand, the conflict laid the foundations for the increasing dependence of Argentina and all belligerent countries on England, through their connection to international markets as exporters of primary products and importers of manufactured products from the industrialized world.[9] Those accounts tended to downplay the role of Solano López's decisions, as he misread Paraguay's prospects for victory, and once the war started, persisted in fighting to the death, bringing about a tragic, relentless pulverization of his predecessors' achievements.

The conspiratorial thesis was particularly endorsed by leftist intellectuals and writers who lifted the banners of anti-imperialism. Uruguayan Eduardo Galeano, for example, attributed the war to Argentine liberals and Brazilians fulfilling the role that the British Empire had assigned them, namely making Brazil a center for the consumption of British manufactured products all across South America:

Shortly before going to war, the Argentine president had inaugurated a new line of British railways in his country, and had delivered a fiery speech: "What is the driving force behind this progress? Gentlemen, it is the English capital!" Not only the population disappeared in defeated Paraguay, but also the custom tariffs, the smelting furnaces, the rivers closed to free trade, the economic independence and vast areas of its territory. The victors implanted free trade and large estates within the borders reduced by dispossession. Everything was looted and sold; the lands and the forests, the mines, the yerba-mate estates, the school buildings. The foreign occupation forces installed successive puppet governments in Asunción. As soon as the war ended, the first foreign loan in its history fell on the still smoking ruins of Paraguay. It was British, of course.[10]

Likewise, in 1979, coinciding with the Sandinista Revolution in his home country, Nicaraguan José Fornos Peñalba completed a PhD dissertation at the University of California at Los Angeles that reaffirmed the thesis of a grand plan designed by the British. In Vitor Izecksohn's assessment, Fornos Peñalba's thesis understood the war as a mechanism for maintaining British regional control.[11]

Nonetheless, there were pronounced differences in how authors assessed England's role vis-à-vis the role they attributed to regional actors. Argentine essayist Abelardo Ramos saw in the war the final stroke of a persistent British policy aimed at precluding a union of autonomous provinces in Argentina, trying to support the primacy of Buenos Aires as a nodal point of access to international markets. According to Ramos, an intellectual identified with the nationalist Left, the results of the war conveyed its main purpose. Namely, in addition to the loss of life of its people, the Paraguayan state lost its autonomy and became indebted; while large estates dominated the countryside, Paraguayan workers became extremely poor and worked under dismal conditions in the yerba-mate estates.[12]

Contrastingly, for Trotskyist Milcíades Peña, the war was the logical continuation and last stage of attacks by Mitre's oligarchy against the Argentine littoral and interior provinces. In his analysis, which resonates with Alberdi's reading of the situation, the war was not simply an international war but rather a civil war waged transnationally across state borders, linked directly to the needs of Argentine internal politics. In the context of defining nation-state boundaries, the war played a key role in disciplining the Argentine provinces and detaching them from the Paraguayan developmental model, which had become a point of reference for many of those provinces. Another connection was rooted in the support that Mitre received from the Brazilian Empire in its fight against the Argentine Confederation. Looking at Paraguay, especially in his later works, Peña considered that the war represented a break in the model of independent capitalist development led by the Paraguayan state.[13] If for Ramos, the war seemed to be the outcome of the actions of an antinational class submissive to the designs of British imperialism, for Peña England did not play a main role in the war. England's role emerged after the war, not as one of its causes. For him, England did not force the conflict, but on some occasions even tried to prevent it. This does not mean England ignored the advantages the war brought it, including the opening of a new market and the massive debt of the countries that had been involved.[14]

Other analysts have been highly critical of the narrative of a British plot. Brazilian historian Moniz Bandeira portrayed Brazil's expansion in the Río de la Plata basin as a continuation of Portuguese colonial policies and discarded the thesis that the war was a proxy for British imperialism. Rather, he attributed the war to the protracted and violent process of the constitution of nation-states in South America. Countries in the basin lived in a permanent state of war over porous borders after they gained independence. Factional conflicts within countries and clashes between states were equally endemic.[15] Likewise, Ricardo Caballero Aquino saw in the outbreak of the war the product of regional territorial disputes and the "unsolved legacy of Spanish-Lusitanian struggles." In his view, believing otherwise—that is, in hidden conspiracies—"requires an act of faith and a modicum of inferiority complex and delusions of grandeur, both symptoms of incipient paranoia, a frequent companion of authoritarianism."[16] After checking the correspondence of British diplomats in Buenos Aires and Montevideo, Alfredo da Mota Menezes concluded that "there are no indications that England orchestrated the War."[17]

The Chaco War between Bolivia and Paraguay as a "War of the Standard Oil Co."

In 1932–35, Bolivia and Paraguay waged a dreadful war, with over eighty thousand soldiers succumbing to bullets, thirst, malaria, and other diseases, as well as tens of thousands more wounded or taken prisoner. For Paraguay, the outcome was a stimulating victory. It was an energizing push away from catastrophic defeat in the War of the Triple Alliance. Contrastingly, for Bolivia, the bloody defeat in the Chaco War continued the process of territorial loss that began with its defeat in the War of the Pacific and the cession of territory to Brazil in 1867 and 1903.[18]

In Bolivia, the impact was profound, as the war involved thousands of indigenous inhabitants from the highlands to the subtropical front, allowing them as well as the young conscripts from the cities to get to know each other and glimpse the character and problems of Bolivian society. Accordingly, the war was a catalyst for new processes, as it generated unease in both civilian and military circles, increasing popular bitterness toward the ruling elites and the inefficient and corrupt high command of the army. According to historian Herbert Klein, "the veterans who survived the Chaco would become the ferment from which a new political order would emerge in Bolivia."[19] Indeed, the general disenchantment with the outcome of the war generated reformist trends among army officers and led to the rise of the Movimiento Nacional Revolucionario (MNR), which resulted in the Bolivian Revolution in 1952. In Paraguay too, despite its victory, the war generated a period of instability that would develop into the long dictatorship of Stroessner (1954–89), who ruled Paraguay in a forceful and repressive manner under the veneer of an electoral system dominated by the Colorado Party.

From the beginning, observers felt compelled to make sense of this war. One interpretation shared by many, especially on the Left, was that the war had been the product of a conspiracy laid by big foreign oil corporations and their allies in the Bolivian oligarchy and government. According to that interpretation, the war was an "imperialist adventure," a "War of the Standard Oil Co." against the Royal Dutch Shell company operating in Paraguay, bringing the two landlocked nations of South America into a collision with profound consequences. The war emerged as a paradigmatic case of a conflict that many in Latin America—and beyond—interpreted as resulting from the conspiracy maneuvers of foreign oil interests. Without doubt, economic factors played a fundamental role in the outbreak of the war, the major war between South American nations in the twentieth century. Yet what merits exploration at the center of this inquiry is how popular and intellectual imagination tilted toward attributing the war to a conspiracy driven by imperialist economic interests, downplaying the political agency of those involved throughout the region, and how such a narrative was swiftly and widely accredited as truthful, being diffused on a transnational scale. We trace here the transference and reception of this narrative in South American sources from Bolivia, Paraguay, Argentina, and Brazil.

The "War of the Standard Oil Co."

While the war was ongoing, the Bolivian communist leader exiled in Argentina, Tristán Marof, expressed the following conspiracy theory in *La tragedia del altiplano*:

> Why was Bolivia fighting in the Chaco? For the national honor as avowed in the manifesto of the intellectuals of July 30, 1932? No. Bolivia fought to obtain a port and to defend the four million hectares of domain against the interests of the English Royal Dutch Shell.[20]

Similarly, in neighboring Paraguay, Carlos R. Santos published a short book of essays and documents on the imminent Paraguayan-Bolivian conflict, in which he suggested that the Standard Oil Co.

> had verified the existence of very rich deposits in Bolivia, near the Chaco, and reached the conviction that it [the Chaco] also had them [such rich reservoirs]. Standard Oil realized that delivering the product by pipelines through the Pacific would involve unreturned expenses due to the crossing of the Cordillera and considered more practical the exploitation via the Paraguay River. This criterion encouraged Bolivia to launch its senseless campaign against our Chaco territory. [. . .] Very few can ignore, equally, that Bolivia is considered practically a factory of that opulent company.[21]

Marof's analysis was more sophisticated, even if still putting the onus on Standard Oil's pressure. According to him, on the Bolivian side, the war had been the result of an oligarchic power structure allied with Western capital:

> [The war was the work of a] half dozen Bolivians who have it all: millions, servants, the fatherland. And that's why they trample on the republic, they guide the massacre and enrich themselves even more, being allies of the American and British capitalists. [. . .] With the Bolivian economy in ruins . . . the only way out for [Daniel] Salamanca's government was the war in the Chaco, [where] a powerful company, owning more than four and a half millions of oil fields, pressed for that purpose. . . . The dreamed victory over Paraguay and the access to a port on the river of the same name on behalf of the Standard Oil and with the sacrifice of Bolivian weapons was the only possibility that men in the Bolivian government, that is the feudal lords allied to foreign imperialism, had to subsist, thriving and continue dominating over their servants [the citizens of Bolivia].[22]

Marof was forthright, saying that "this is what Salamanca and his clique wanted, smelling the oil and ready to deliver Bolivia, unhindered, definitely to the Yankees, in an alliance to the neck for their loans and investments." According to him, if Bolivia had won the war, the social question would have been completely diverted. Workers would have been dominated, a military dictatorship would have been established, and the aspirations of the masses would have been restrained, "forcing them by force and a paltry salary, to the rough work of the mines and oil wells, under the whip of the foreign foreman, owner of the wealth."[23]

This analysis of the Bolivian political-economic elite known as *la rosca*, which was conducted from exile by the leader of the Túpac Amaru organization, would be transformed into something slightly different due to the ideological bent of the Fourth International—namely, a conspiracy theory according to which the oil companies provoked the fratricidal confrontation of Bolivia with Paraguay:

> On July 31, 1932, the armies of Bolivia and Paraguay began a war pulled by the Yankee oil company Standard Oil and the Anglo-Dutch Shell. It lasted three years, with between 90 and 150 thousand fallen combatants and both peoples bleeding to death. Oil was never found in that region.[24]

Many Latin Americans echoed the conspiracist view, according to which the Standard Oil Co. had maneuvered the Bolivian government into going to war. Thus, in his analysis of British policy in the Río de la Plata, Argentine nationalist essayist Raúl Scalabrini Ortiz echoed that argument about the genesis of the Chaco War, noting the interference of foreign capital interests:

> On the other side are the reckless, aggressive and insolent US capitals of the Standard Oil and General Motors, to whom we owe September 6 [September 6, 1930, the date of the coup d'état of General José Félix Uriburu in Argentina], *the fratricidal Chaco War* [emphasis added], a separatist trend in the Province of Salta, and the shameful oil law currently in force.[25]

The long-lasting impact of this conspiracist interpretation can be traced for decades in the works and writings of respected Latin American intellectuals and political activists. Illustrative are the statements by Argentine investigative journalist Gregorio Selser and Uruguayan writer Eduardo Galeano, who replicated this interpretation as late as the 1980s and 1990s. In his book *Cronología de las intervenciones extranjeras en América Latina 1899–1945*, Selser described events on the date of July 31, 1932, as follows: "The War of El Chaco begins between Paraguay and Bolivia, lashed respectively by England and the United States or, what is the same, by the oil companies Shell and Standard Oil."[26] Likewise, while acutely describing the suffering of those who were the cannon fodder in a ruthless war, Galeano insinuated in *Memoria del fuego* that the interests of the foreign oil corporations were behind the war involving some of the region's poorest people:

> *Hidden between the folds of both flags stand the Standard Oil Company and Royal Dutch Shell, which dispute the possible oil of the Chaco* [emphasis added]. Embedded in war, Paraguayans and Bolivians are bound to hate each other in the name of a land they do not love, that nobody loves. Chaco is a gray desert, inhabited by thorns and snakes, without a songbird or a people's footprint. Everything is thirsty in this world of terror. The butterflies huddle,

desperate, over a few drops of water. The Bolivians arrive from the fridge to the oven: they have been uprooted from the peaks of the Andes and thrown into these scorched bushes. Here they die of bullets, but more die of thirst. Clouds of flies and mosquitoes chase the soldiers, who duck their heads and jog through the tangle, in forced marches, against the enemy lines. On one side and on the other, the barefoot people are the cannon fodder that pays the errors of their officers. The slaves of the feudal patron and the rural priest die in uniform, at the service of imperial greed.[27]

These statements are a testimony to the belief held by many intellectuals and political actors throughout Latin America that the machinations of the oil companies, which they denounced, were behind the impulsive and ineffective war that would cost Bolivia part of that subequatorial desert zone known as Chaco Boreal, that is, Northern Chaco.

The Historical Evidence

Given the superiority of the Bolivian Army at the beginning of the confrontation and the nationalist discourse of President Daniel Salamanca, the outcome of the war came as a devastating surprise to those who intended to expand the Bolivian territorial hold and recover national pride. That national pride had been damaged after losing it access to the sea in the War of the Pacific, in addition to territories ceded to Brazil in 1867 and 1903. The debacle required a review of consciousness, which contributed to the rise of conspiracy theories, a "weapon" of the weak as they tried to make sense of history. Relying on partial facts that were extrapolated and given aggrandized significance, a "mythology of the war for oil" (to use historian Herbert Klein's term) was shaped and given credence as a means of coming to terms with the national tragedy, now interwoven in a narrative of imperialist conspiracy.

While many in Bolivia and across Latin America continued to spread the thesis that the antagonistic interests of foreign oil corporations had motivated the Chaco War, historians discarded its veracity. Even nationalist historians who were militants of the Bolivian MNR recognized the complexity of the political and economic interests that had led to the war and the subsequent military-civilian revolution of 1943. Thus, Manuel Frontaura Argandoña attributed the origin of the confrontation to the push forged by the competitive interests of the plutocracy of the tin barons and much less to the struggle between Shell and Standard Oil, although of course countries such as Argentina and Chile were also involved.[28]

On the one hand, Frontaura Argandoña's analysis left no doubt about the distance between the historical evaluation of a nationalist who recognized that Bolivia had been affected by forces detrimental to its collective interest and the simplistic conspiracy theory of a hypothetical "War of the Standard Oil Co.":

> Broad, serious and dark is the theme of the Chaco War. [. . .] *The Chaco was not an oil war, at least not for Bolivia, because the apparently contending English and American companies just agreed on doing harm to Bolivia* [emphasis added]. [. . .] Both financial and political groups armed a laborious and good country as is Paraguay. They advised it militarily and financially. They gave it assurance of victory, *a autrance* as one says. For those ferocious groups, the victimization of one hundred thousand men meant nothing. The main thing was the riveting of their interests. The war had to happen anyway.[29]

In a detailed history of his country, Bolivian writer and historian Porfirio Díaz Machicao clearly indicated how a context of partisanship and economic crisis of the landlocked country led to the conclusion that the occupation of Chaco would allow a way out of territorial confinement and trigger an economic bonanza. Additionally, he explored how, as of 1931 and perhaps even earlier, Bolivia had plans to move ahead and conquer Chaco, which were prompted by the fear that the Paraguayans would take possession of that territory. Moreover, Machicao highlighted how clashes between the patrols of both countries were interpreted as challenging "Bolivian dignity and decorum" as well as how tactical thought prevailed over strategic thinking. Another point he emphasized was how the divergences of opinion and tensions between the executive branch and the general staff of the army affected the entire development and outcome of the war.[30]

In the late 2010s, Argentine researcher Maximilano Zuccarino summed up the state of the art in research on the thesis of the oil industry pushing for war, stressing its wide reception despite the feeble historical ground. Zuccarino suggested a more reliable appreciation of the role of oil in the plot that led Bolivia and Paraguay to face each other on the battlefields of the inhospitable Chaco. Standard Oil and Royal Dutch Shell were invested in the oil-rich region, but the corporations did not promote the armed conflict to acquire a territory supposedly rich in oil, as suggested by Sergio Almaraz, Julio J. Chiavenato, Arturo Frondizi,[31] and Alfredo Seiferheld. Rather,

> [recent works such Stephen Cote's stress] the growing need on the part of Bolivia to increase its oil production to supply urban consumption and the mining industry and, at the same time, find a fluvial outlet to export the surplus through the Paraguay River until the Atlantic ocean.[32]

Historical research has thus questioned the factual basis for the thesis of the "War of the Standard Oil Co." It invites us to disentangle how nonetheless the conspiracy theory reached such wide reception in Latin America. What were the factual evidence and discursive mechanisms that sustained that narrative? How were factually unconnected events interwoven into a conspiracist worldview claiming to have discovered that the belligerent countries were played by imperialist forces and interests?

Did Standard Oil Finance the Bolivian Army?

The conspiracy narrative of the "War of the Standard Oil Co." gained credibility because it seemed to be backed by Bolivia's huge contractual concessions to the company and the lack of an official agreement on the part of Paraguay and Argentina to allow Bolivian oil to be transported through the Paraguay River. In addition, to provide a more factual basis, those sustaining the conspiracy theory argued that Bolivian soldiers were transported from the Altiplano to the battlefield in Standard Oil trucks.[33] Such "factual" information is easily challenged when considering that the Bolivian government maintained a conflictual relationship with Standard Oil for years. The company did not produce at the levels it was supposed to according to the terms of the territorial concession and even resisted paying taxes as demanded. In addition, Salamanca's government confiscated the trucks of the North American company for use in the transportation of soldiers from the Altiplano.[34]

The narrative suggesting that Bolivia was coerced or persuaded by the Standard Oil Co. into entering the war concealed the lack of cooperation and the tensions that prevailed between the Bolivian government and Standard Oil. Already in 1970, based on archival documentation and secondary sources, researcher Leslie B. Rout Jr. had clearly indicated in a book on the policy of the peace conference on Chaco the series of factors that had led to the unsolvable relations between Bolivia and the company.[35] In the first place, Bolivia had granted vast monopolistic land concessions to Standard Oil aimed at making a huge profit by enlarging revenues for the public treasury. Yet until 1927, the oil company had concentrated oil production in only four wells (Bermejo, Sanandita, Camiri, and Catamindi), from which it produced only a small volume, given the lack of a clear outlet to the petroleum markets. In addition, between 1919 and 1928 Standard Oil conducted a legal battle against the Argentine province of Salta over oil concessions, which generated in Argentina a wave of nationalist reactions. In 1922 this led to the creation of Yacimientos Petrolíferos Fiscales (YPF), the national Argentine oil company, with Standard Oil moving part of its operations to Bolivia.[36] In 1925, the Argentine government denied a request from Standard Oil to build an oil pipeline from Bolivia to a deepwater port on the Paraná River through which it could export oil, while in 1927 it imposed exorbitant tax increases on Bolivian oil. The popular belief that by taking possession of Chaco, the company would gain access to a deepwater port that allowed the navigation of cargo ships, did not have any real support, due to the nature of the fluvial basin and routes. In addition, the idea of transporting oil in small boats was equally unreal in practical terms. This in turn explains the decision by Standard Oil to reduce oil production in Bolivia to levels of domestic demand, withholding concessions, even if that contradicted the expectations of the Bolivian authorities.

This confluence of factors undermined friendly relations between Bolivia and Standard Oil. In 1928 tensions reached a point where, upon learning that the company had covertly moved oil to Argentina in 1925, President Hernán Siles demanded the payment of taxes for undeclared profits, giving Standard Oil a deadline of January 1, 1930, to deliver the payments. The company challenged the order in Bolivian courts. In addition, in 1928 Bolivian Army officers had taken possession of Standard Oil trucks without compensation. Siles's successor, Salamanca—already immersed in the war—tried to overcome the company's policy of not producing oil in accordance with its maximum capacity by nationalizing the refineries until the cessation of hostilities.[37] After the war, in March 1937, the government of President David Toro canceled the concessions and seized possession of the company, nationalizing it without any compensation, claiming that in 1925–27 Standard Oil had secretly produced more oil than it declared and had exported it through private oil pipelines to Argentina.[38]

In other words, the relations between Bolivia and the oil company were already tense before the armed conflict, making it unlikely that there was a joint secret plan for the capture of the eastern part of El Chaco, wherein no oil deposits would be found. Nonetheless, this feeble factual support did not deter the formation of a conspiracy theory that gathered credibility in political and intellectual circles, in Bolivia and throughout Latin America.

Decoding the Transnational Diffusion of the Conspiracy Theory

According to different analysts, in 1932 the Argentine and Paraguayan press— probably beginning with the Argentine anti-imperialist publisher Claridad— argued that Standard Oil was financing the Bolivian aggressor and supplied the needs of that invading army in the Chaco, so as to gain territory for a pipeline to the Paraguay River.[39]

Nationalists energized by the dispute between the Standard Oil Co. and the province of Salta motivated these accusations, projected by the Argentine press. That narrative served to convince Paraguayans that the hostilities had opened at the initiative of Bolivia, being supported by the capitalist interests of Standard Oil and the apparatus of the United States. In that context, they argued, Paraguay had entered the war with the sole desire to defend its national territory. On January 26, 1933, Standard Oil denied these accusations in the pages of the *New York Times*, declaring its neutrality in the conflict between Bolivia and Paraguay. The newspaper also reported that the company would initiate a legal suit against Bolivia for confiscating its automotive park and cargo animals, again highlighting the tensions and lack of cooperation between the oil company and Bolivia at war.[40]

In a second phase, US senator Huey Long, who was preparing to launch his presidential campaign in 1936, echoed the conspiracist argument. Long, a populist, used the conspiracy theory to attack Standard Oil, an emblematic capitalist corporation which he had fought with and been attacked by as governor of Louisiana (1928–32). A few years later, when Long had been elected to the US Senate, he found the argument beneficial in denouncing the alleged dark maneuvers of the Standard Oil Co. On May 30, 1934, Senator Long delivered an energetic speech denouncing Standard Oil for provoking the Chaco War and financing the Bolivian Army to seize the oil-rich Paraguayan Chaco, which would enable building an oil pipeline from Bolivia to the Paraguay River.[41]

Given the political prominence of Long, the US press immediately echoed the conspiracy argument and projected it to national public opinion, from where it was again refracted into Paraguay. It thus gained international credence. Even those who, like Juan Stefanich (the journalist and future chancellor of Paraguay), clearly attributed the war to "belligerent dreams, the cult of force, the chimera of Bolivia's military potential," at the same time echoed Long's assertions about the interference of Standard Oil.[42]

Once the Bolivian advance of military forces stalled and there were sharp defeats, with around sixty-five thousand soldiers fallen, captured, or deserting the ranks, in addition to tens of thousands of wounded, the conspiracy argument spread widely in Bolivia as well. In Bolivia, the claim was used by sectors who wanted to attack "reckless President Salamanca," the oligarch allied with Standard Oil and the high military command responsible for the defeat and a likely loss of national territory.[43]

While serving in the US Senate, Long continued to have great power and influence in Louisiana, where he developed various projects. When Judge Henry Pavy opposed some of his initiatives for legal reasons, Long tried to dismiss him. Pavy's son-in-law, a physician by the name of Carl Weiss, went to the Louisiana state legislature building in Baton Rouge during Long's visit in September 1935, allegedly to ask him to reconsider the decision. When he was rejected by Long and his bodyguards, he opened fire, killing Long just days after he had announced his decision to run for the US presidency.[44] Long's bodyguards then killed Weiss. For many in Latin America, Long's death had been clearly orchestrated by the American oil company. According to Scalabrini Ortiz, Long's "passionate attack on Standard Oil, for his intervention in the Chaco war, cost him his life," when he was "killed a few weeks after voicing his complaint."[45]

In Latin America, Long's assassination reaffirmed the narrative according to which Standard Oil and Shell, motivated by their competing desires to obtain the Chaco's oil deposits, had coerced the two landlocked countries of South America to go to war. The theory convinced many in the region, even though geologically the central Chaco had no oil reserve indicators, and oil does not exist in the area.[46] Even Spruille Braden, an American businessperson who had strong interests in Standard Oil, doubted that there were important oil reserves in the disputed Chaco region.[47] Moreover, even those who attributed the war to the conspiracy of oil interests and the rivalry between the American oil company and the Anglo-Dutch oil company recognized that Standard Oil dominated the Bolivian deposits "with the purpose of keeping them as part of its world reserves." For that reason, the oil company had concentrated more on the exploration and drilling of wells than on production, "as it lacked the intention of exploiting them until an eventuality arose that could prevent the supply of the Latin American and European markets from their ordinary sources of production."[48]

The Weight of Historical Animosities Leading to the War

The confrontation between Bolivia and Paraguay had started decades earlier, due to the lack of certainty about which right of colonial boundaries (*uti possidetis*) should prevail to set the border between the wo countries. Bolivia claimed rights over the territory that extended to the Paraguay and Pilcomayo Rivers, based on titles of the Audiencia of Charcas. At the same time, Paraguay claimed rights based on ordinances of the Spanish Crown, dating back to sixteenth-century Capitulaciones and the Ordinances of the Intendance of 1782, sustained by their continued territorial possession even after 1810. Paraguayan politician and historian Efraím Cardozo offered the following evaluation of the situation on the eve of the war:

> Discrepancies were fundamental. The two countries did not even agree on what was the subject of the litigation. According to Bolivia, it was mainly about the Chaco [in its entirety], yet according to Paraguay, only about its limits. But as things were in 1932, the problem was no longer a confrontation over territorial

entitlements, but of contrasting policies phrased in terms not reducible to legal solutions.[49]

From the 1880s to the 1920s, the countries held futile negotiations over the sovereignty of that territory. For Paraguay, the Pinilla-Soler protocol of 1907, which had divided the Chaco between a Paraguayan zone and another to be arbitrated by Argentina, was considered binding. While Paraguay ratified it, Bolivia delayed its acceptance, until it was rejected in 1910, ignoring the status quo line and placing pillboxes in the territory to stop any Paraguayan advance, whether for cattle grazing, *quebracho* extraction, or settlement by Mennonites. In the 1920s, nationalist fervor had spread in both countries, impeding diplomatic talks about the Chaco. Attempts at arbitration by the International Conference of American States on Conciliation and Arbitration, and by Argentina, the United States, and the League of Nations, did not produce any results, thus giving rise to the bloody confrontation.[50]

The historical weight of these differences seems to have been at work. Bolivia had, as President Salamanca stated, "a history of international disasters that we must counteract with a victorious war." That war would open for the country a way out to the sea after having been cut off from it, and in this manner Bolivia would also regain national pride. Paraguayans would resist being removed from a region that constituted more than half of their national territory and an important base of their economy, over which the United States had recognized Paraguayan rule. Between June and July 1935, through the mediation of representatives of a group of American countries, a ceasefire was agreed upon. This ended the hostilities based on the positions the belligerent countries had reached and on a peace conference that, by direct agreement or arbitration, was expected to end the litigation that had led to the war.

The outbreak of the Chaco War was fundamentally fueled by unresolved border disputes between the belligerents and historical dreams of renewed national grandeur. After the cessation of hostilities, Argentina began to work diplomatically against Bolivia, while Brazil worked against Paraguay, fed by geopolitical considerations, vested economic interests (landowning and fluvial transportation by Argentines in Paraguay), and still-prevailing false ideas of access to the—nonexistent—oil reserves in the subequatorial Chaco. The Chaco War had exacerbated conspiracy theories in Brazil as well, targeting its historical rival and potential enemy of the Río de la Plata, which supposedly was allied with Paraguay and Royal Dutch Shell, fearing a victorious advance of the Paraguayan Army with Argentine support during the war. From the Brazilian perspective, the most salient threat was the possibility that the Paraguayan Army could achieve the old secessionist project of separating Santa Cruz de la Sierra from Bolivia, thus leaving the Amazon valley open to "Argentine infiltration." In addition, Brazil feared that the Guaraní troops, while descending via the Mamoré River, would seize the region of Cochabamba, where—it fantasized—there were oil reserves.[51] Unsurprisingly, at the peace negotiations Brazil sided with Bolivia. On July 21, 1938, Paraguay and Bolivia signed a definitive peace treaty of Peace, Friendship and Boundaries in Buenos Aires. Paraguay did not retain all the territory that its armies had occupied. It did not manage to set the border on the banks of the Parapití River, as was its maximalist aspiration, but there is no doubt that it retained most of the territory in dispute, also reaffirming its sovereignty over Bahia Negra on the Paraguay River. As for Bolivia, achieving a free port over the Paraguay River and possession of the entire Parapití River basin did not conceal the enormous territorial loss it suffered. A new frustration was beating heavily over the nation of the Altiplano that prompted radical political changes in the following decades.[52]

The War of the Pacific: Historiographic and Popular Assessments

In the War of the Pacific (1879–83), Chile defeated Bolivia and Peru and occupied territories that had been part of both countries.[53] On February 14, 1879, Chilean troops landed in Antofagasta and occupied the Bolivian coast, where an absolute majority of the population was already Chilean. Peru sent a plenipotentiary minister to avoid a military confrontation, but being aware of the Bolivian-Peruvian Treaty, on April 5, Chile declared war on both Bolivia and Peru, using armored ships, rifles, and uniforms of English production, and acquired domain over sea routes by October. In May 1880, the Bolivian-Peruvian troops clashed with the Chilean troops in the Peruvian province of Tacna but suffered defeat. The Bolivian troops then withdrew toward the Altiplano, where they hoped to resist a possible attack from the Chileans. The Chilean Army did not advance eastward but rather to the north, where it defeated the Peruvian troops defending Arica at the beginning of June 1880. Landing in Pisco and Chilca, the Chilean Army continued the war campaign and ended it after occupying Lima, the Peruvian capital, in January 1881.

The capture of Lima demoralized and divided Peruvians. After that, some remnants of Peruvian forces waged a guerrilla war, but at the same time, the defeat and resistance generated disorder and indigenous rebellions. That is to say, a period of uncertainty ensued, until October 1883, when Chile and Peru signed the Treaty of Ancón, which set the terms for concluding armed hostilities. Under the terms of that treaty, in addition to paying compensation, Peru ceded the province of Tarapacá to Chile and granted it possession of Tacna and Arica for ten years, at the end of which it committed to hold a plebiscite or popular consultation to decide the final sovereignty of both provinces. The war left profound marks on the three countries. Peru lost 36,000 square kilometers and Bolivia some 158,000, including 480 kilometers of coastline, which closed off Bolivia's access to the sea.

As in the case of the War of the Triple Alliance and the later war over Chaco, some analysts projected the thesis that the war had resulted from a conspiratorial plan concocted by foreign powers, in this case the British. In Bolivia, there were those who upheld the thesis that the war—as much as the cession of Acre to Brazil—was the product of "the Machiavellian work of Anglo-Yankee imperialism," as Alberto Mendoza López put it after the Chaco War.[54] Likewise, Peruvian Enrique Amayo stated in a PhD thesis at the University of Pittsburgh (later published) that the War of the Pacific was—as the secretary of state of the United States, James Blaine, had declared before a congressional foreign relations committee—"an English war against Peru with Chile as an instrument." In support of that argument, Amayo indicated that the defense of free trade established a common interest of Chile and Great Britain against Peru, "a country that opted for the opposed and almost unprecedented [doctrine] in Latin America, that of nationalization [of the nitrate monopoly] as an essential instrument to reorganize its economy."[55]

Based on the statements of Blaine, who served as US secretary of state in 1882, during the negotiations that led to the signing of the Bolivian-Chilean treaty of 1883, many people in Latin America still project the vision that it was "an English war against Bolivia and Peru, with Chile as an instrument." The following comment on the Bolivian lawsuit at the International Court in The Hague is clear-cut, stressing that the structure of command and impetus for the war had all been coordinated by the British:

> The War of the Pacific responded to the interests of the British and Chilean oligarchy, alluding to investments in the nitrate industry. [It] was planned by England. Chile received very comfortable economic facilities to acquire British weapons, the Chilean uniforms were made of English cloth, and the Chilean soldiers carried English rifles on their shoulders. Chilean Rear Admiral Patricio Lynch, general Chief of the invading troops of Peru, fought in China and India as an English soldier.[56]

Similarly, Peruvian Luis Ernesto Vásquez Medina's *La verdad detrás de la Guerra del Pacífico: El Imperio británico contra el sistema americano de economía en Sudamérica*, published in 2012, reaffirmed that historical interpretation and projected it in a conspiratorial tone.[57] Vásquez Medina claimed that the war was not merely "a regional confrontation between Chile, Peru and Bolivia, as is commonly believed." It was rather part of a strategic plan launched by the British imperial system to destroy the autarkic process of Peruvian industrialization and seize Peruvian and Bolivian resources.[58] The narrative suggested the existence of a conspiracy articulated by the British Empire long before the war, using the financial capacity of the City of London, the resources of the Admiralty, the intelligence services, and the British Chancellery, aimed at destroying the Peruvian project of emancipatory development. In this framework, Vásquez Medina claimed that the assassination of US president James Garfield was actually part of a conspiracy to prevent him from continuing to support Peru in the peace negotiations after the Chilean occupation of Lima.[59]

The conspiratorial thesis failed to influence a wide audience. Most analysts, as well as Bolivian and Peruvian citizens, refrained from conferring too much credibility in this case on the thesis of a hidden master plan that conspiracy theorists like Vásquez Medina fancifully denounced. Historians such as V. G. Kiernan, Jorge Basadre, and Heraclio Bonilla ruled out the conspiratorial interpretation. For instance, Peruvian historian Bonilla argued that the role of investors and shareholders linked to the ownership of guano and nitrate sediments was limited to requiring each of the parties to protect its interests. According to Bonilla, the hegemony achieved by Great Britain would have been a consequence "of the successful negotiations of the guano and nitrate shareholders (as if that were not a test of economic imperialism) who obtained the recognition of the debts in exchange for an implicit British support for the territorial annexations of the Tarapacá and Antofagasta provinces."[60]

We should thus ask, without underestimating the importance of international financial capital and the British Empire in the second half of the nineteenth century, what factors operated in this case against embracing a conspiratorial thesis, as opposed to the acceptance of conspiracy theories about the other two wars. We should start by checking the developments on the ground that led to the war.

An English War against Peru with Chile as an Instrument?

During the first six decades of the nineteenth century, the Atacama area witnessed innumerable armed confrontations in the wars of independence, including guerrilla warfare, civil wars, and attacks by armed bands and international forces. In the 1870s, a developmental "rush" cycle for guano and saltpeter emerged, similar to the California gold rush a few decades earlier.[61]

Following its independence from Spain, Bolivia extended its sovereignty over a territory with significant resources, coveted by both Peruvian and Chilean-English economic forces interested in positioning themselves in the international markets. Indeed, as Alonso Barros affirms, "during the second industrial revolution and the new phase of capitalist globalization, the war was materially linked to the expansion of agriculture and the arms industry in Europe, the United States and Japan. The nitrates of the desert were their fertilizer and gunpowder."[62]

Chapter 3 discussed how the CSFA company of nitrates and railroads of Antofagasta (Bolivia), with joint Chilean-British capital, and the massive conglomerate of Chilean *rotos* played a decisive role in the confrontation with Bolivia leading to the outbreak of the war. Completing the tensions was the prominent reporting of the daily clashes between the Chilean workers and residents and the Bolivian police, which convinced the Chilean public of the need to annex the Bolivian littoral territories. According to the press, led by Edwards's *El Mercurio*, the occupation of the northern coastline was justified by the arbitrariness and humiliation that the Chilean workers and residents suffered at the hands of Bolivian forces of order, whose *cuicos*—a derogatory epithet used for poor Bolivians of indigenous and *mestizo* stock—abused their authority, while the authorities ignored the formal commitments of the 1874 treaty. This narrative differed radically from the Bolivian perspective. Bolivians believed they had the right to impose order among the Chilean *rotos*, whom they despised. In this context of misgivings, conflicting interests, and local violence, the racialized caricature of the enemy in a stereotyped way served to provide an emotionally charged ground for an international confrontation, instrumental as each state was trying to justify the legitimacy and honor of taking steps that led to war.

Bolivia and Peru had signed in 1873 a secret treaty of mutual support and protection against Chile, thus creating the background for a triadic confrontation:

> Chile, for its part, had also repeatedly offered to sign with Peru, Bolivia and/ or Argentina, warrior alliances against one or the other, always with territorial prizes involved in the deal. All were pressing to redraw the South American limits of *uti possidetis* [the possession of territories at the time of independence], as occurred in the War of the Triple Alliance.[63]

There is no doubt that Peruvian nationalists had led a process of economic development that the war truncated. Until then, Peru had increased its use of energy, imported coal, and steam machinery and promoted the laying of railway lines for future development. It is also clear that the Chilean port of Valparaíso and the Peruvian port of El Callao were competing for the same maritime markets. The tension between Chile and Peru was also accentuated around the markets for guano and saltpeter, in addition to the control of the silver mines in the early 1870s. Finally, no one questions that England and the United States, until the assassination of President Garfield and the assumption of power by Vice President Chester Arthur, supported different interests in the South Pacific. From this, conspiracists such as Vásquez Medina reached the conclusion that the British imperial authorities meticulously orchestrated the war from the beginning to divest Peru of its developmental assets:

> With no natural resources to sell and indebted to the British banking system, the Chilean oligarchy of the Edwards and the Montt, only had to sell their complicity against Peru, the way that the Rothschilds wanted: a war of prey and destruction against Peru. England had been preparing for war since 1875, the year in which Manuel Pardo nationalized nitrate, the strategic element, whose world monopoly was shared by Peru and Bolivia.[64]

The problem with this thesis is that the supporting information was biased, for instance the role that Vásquez Medina claimed the "English Admiral Patricio Lynch" played in the war and the claim that the United States had decided to intervene in the war in favor of Peru, a move interrupted by the assassination of President Garfield, perpetrated by an agent of the British Empire.[65]

Lynch was the officer who commanded the Chilean forces during the invasion of Peru and who was responsible for a "punitive expedition" that destroyed the town of Chimbote in late 1880.[66] During the northern occupation, he repressed the owners of the haciendas—whose resources paid for the Peruvian resistance—with extreme severity. Additionally, he imposed exactions and war tributes on them, set fire to haciendas, broke machinery, recruited the Chinese local labor into his army, and sowed destruction in the face of any resistance. Lynch (1824–86) was Chilean, the son of an Argentine military officer and a Chilean citizen. At the age of fourteen, he joined the Chilean Navy and served as a cadet during the war between Chile and the Peruvian-Bolivian Confederation in 1836–39. In 1840 he joined the British Navy and participated in various military campaigns, including the First Opium War against China. He reached the rank of first lieutenant, a rank that Chile recognized when he returned in 1847, after the Chilean government requested his relief and return. His role in the repression of the Chilean Revolution of 1851 earned him a promotion to the rank of frigate captain. While in retirement, Lynch moved to Peru in 1864 to volunteer along with 152 other Chileans willing to defend Peruvian sovereignty against the threat of a Spanish colonial *reconquista* in the Spanish-South American War, where he joined the Chilean Navy, after Chile also declared war on Spain. In 1867, he was appointed maritime governor of Valparaíso, and from then on and throughout the War of the Pacific he played a crucial role in defending Chilean interests by holding high positions such as that of vice admiral of the Chilean Navy and general in chief of the Chilean Army of occupation. His performance was that of an authoritarian officer in a war situation. A decade earlier, however, under other circumstances, he had fought with the same determination in the defense of Peruvian sovereignty against Spain.

Likewise, the argument that the United States was willing to enter the war in defense of Peruvian territorial integrity relied on some facts while ignoring others, a key element in the construction of conspiracy narratives, as it selectively included all those geared to strengthen the theory of the hidden agenda behind the war. Lawrence A. Clayton's exhaustive research on US-Peruvian relationships shows clearly the role that US interests played in the war and its outcome in the peace negotiations between Chile and Peru.[67]

The modernizing development of Chile and Peru brought with it both a rivalry in the South Pacific—already evident in the war of the 1830s—and an arms race during the 1860s and 1870s, which intensified the friction between the two states. That tension increased in the 1870s under the presidency of Manuel Prado, as Peru acquired its railway network, considered to be the engine that spearheaded development and civilization. Behind that accomplishment was Henry (Enrique) Meiggs, a native of New York, who arrived in Chile after trying his fortune in the California gold rush and escaping from creditors and the law. In California, Meiggs got experience constructing rail networks, while he led a notorious nouveau riche life, womanizing and bribing politicians. Between 1868 and 1871 he did the same in Peru, managing to attract European capital through bonds issued in exchange for the income generated by guano reserves. Meiggs became a generous philanthropist, patron of letters and the arts, and a source of relief in the face of natural disasters such as the 1868 earthquake. Likewise, he was an active contributor to politicians and journalists, not only in Peru but also in Chile and Bolivia. Clayton considers that Meiggs was a "man of the times," a dreamer and catalyst for the Peruvian elites and political class who believed in the transformative power of industrial modernity. Peruvians admired him, yet he was equally active in Chile and Bolivia until his death in September 1877.

Historian Jorge Basadre criticized the excessive expectations and credulity of Peruvians regarding the projects, some of them spectacular, that Meiggs conceived. Basadre reproached them for having generated an excessively adventurous spirit and undertaking works beyond the capacity of the state, creating growing indebtedness and financial speculation.[68] This assertion places responsibility on Peruvians, who, in their excessive optimism, did not moderate and channel some of the plans proposed by Meiggs.

The commercial interests of US firms connected with Europeans and Peruvians in the Peruvian provinces of Tarapacá, Tacna, and Arica, and personal contacts such as those established by Meiggs and Grace, tilted the sympathies of the United States toward Peru in the war with Chile. In parallel, the interests of Chilean and English investors in the Bolivian province of Antofagasta inclined English sympathies toward Chile.[69] But the question arises of whether England or the United States instigated a fratricidal war to try to displace the other maritime power from the South Pacific. Both countries, as well as France, followed the war closely. Wars have always proved to be the testing ground for new weapons and devices. The War of the Pacific prompted the United States to dispense of its wooden ships and transform its navy by building iron ships. The United States also tested torpedoes in the War of the Pacific. However, Clayton points out that Stephen Chester, the expert whom Charles Flynt, an associate of William Grace, hired in the United States to handle the torpedoes in Peru, almost sank the *Huáscar* with a torpedo in the port of Callao.

The United States did not intervene in the war, even if some veterans from both sides of the US Civil War agreed to be recruited and participated on the Peruvian side. Rather, in the crucial years of the war, the United States wavered in its policy between Peru and Chile. The Chilean invasion of and advance on Peruvian soil coincided with the last two years of President Rutherford Hayes's administration. The president and Secretary of State William Evarts decided to maintain neutrality, unsuccessfully trying to mediate between the belligerents. In March 1881, when Garfield assumed the presidency with Blaine as secretary of state, Chile had already defeated the Bolivians and Peruvians and had occupied Lima.

At the diplomatic level, the United States was ineffective and "laughable" in the eyes of North American observers, so it disappointed the immense expectations that it had created among Peruvians through its mediation attempts in favor of Peru. The United States only entered the conflict effectively with the appointment of Blaine, who was staunchly pro-Irish and had antipathy toward England. He felt that he could stop or mitigate the impact of the Chilean victory and occupation of Peru, behind which both the president and Blaine saw English interference. Faced with criticism from members of Congress, Blaine defended the administration's pro-Peruvian position by claiming that the War of the Pacific had actually been "an English war against Bolivia and Peru, with Chile as an instrument." Since its mention by historians like Kiernan,[70] this statement was repeated over and over again in the popular media and reproduced as irrefutable proof by those who, like Vásquez Medina, attributed the outbreak of war to the British Empire.[71] However, as shown by Clayton, Blaine had set contradictory objectives for the US diplomatic representatives to the belligerent countries: to maintain the territorial integrity of Peru and to achieve peace as soon as possible even if that goal implied a territorial loss on the part of Peru.[72] The new secretary of state Frederick Theodore Frelinghuysen acceded to a demand by the US Congress to make public Blaine's instructions; Blaine's enemies in Congress accused him of supporting Peru for monetary gain. Chilean foreign minister José Balmaceda heard about the change of direction in US diplomacy and expressly affirmed that Tarapacá was irrevocably Chilean territory and that, if the United States wanted it to remain Peruvian, they would have to fight for it. By then the United States had reverted to neutrality, and Peru was left to its own devices, and thus was forced to negotiate peace with the Chileans on the terms dictated by them.[73]

Divergent Narratives

Another major factor in curtailing the popular appeal of conspiracy theories in this case has been that each of the belligerent countries developed its own narrative to explain to itself the outcome of the war and justify it to others. Bolivia and Peru, the countries facing defeat, blamed one another as much as they harbored animosity toward Chile, the victorious side. Each country had to promote a politics of memory to maintain its divergent claims and organize them as much as possible according to factual evidence that could support what they considered their legitimate rights over the disputed territories.

After the tragic outcome of the war, with both Bolivia and Peru losing parts of their territories to Chile, the defeated nations developed divergent historiographic and popular narratives. In *El Mostrador*, a Chilean digital newspaper, filmmaker Hernán Dinamarca, who co-directed the documentary *Epitafio a una guerra* (2010) with Bolivian Armado de Urioste and Peruvian Jorge Delgado, reflected on the "different emotions, sometimes irreconcilable, with which each people lives and remembers the conflict." According to Dinamarca, while Bolivians live the emotion of loss of territories and their access to the Pacific Ocean, Peruvians are trapped in resentment both against Bolivians who failed to live up to the terms of their alliance and against Chile for taking away their territories and deeply humiliating them by occupying Lima. Chileans, on their part, do not give up their sense of victory, thus moving in a completely different direction:

> The coexistence of these emotions that are culturally dominant in each country (although, as in everything, there have been exceptions) has been a constant for more than a century. Little has changed and little has been done to bring change, with those feelings remaining the main obstacle search of solutions.[74]

In an interview with Patricio Rivera Olguín, a Peruvian teacher gave testimony about the official memory of the war in his country:

> In 1879, Bolivia and Chile had strong disputes over the Atacama nitrate region. Bolivia had threatened the Chileans with expropriating their nitrate fields if they did not pay a ten-cent tax for the quintals [of nitrate] that Antofagasta produced. To avoid this, Chile invaded that port on February 14, 1879. Peru tried to mediate in the conflict and Chile declared war on Peru for not declaring itself

neutral. Immediately afterwards, several campaigns and guerrillas developed, followed by agreements and treaties.[75]

The teacher highlighted the existence of the Peruvian-Chilean conflict over the control of nitrates. From the Peruvian perspective, the war was Bolivia's fault. Peru entered the war, investing resources and human lives, out of loyalty toward Bolivia, in compliance with the Treaty of Mutual Defense of 1873. Bolivia, on its part, did not respond energetically to the threat, ending its effective participation in the war in 1880, when it withdrew its forces in the direction of the Altiplano, abandoning Peru to its fate and leaving it to continue fighting against the Chileans without Bolivian assistance.

In contrast, Bolivians espoused other narratives about the war. E. Jorge Abastoflor Frey has written a thorough assessment of the war from the Bolivian perspective, which contradicts the Peruvian narrative. According to Abastoflor Frey, Bolivian thinking has been circular and has gone from defeat, via loss and domination, to anger, rage, and frustration. In his view, the Peruvian narrative against his country is flawed and relies on fallacies. The Bolivian author aimed to discard that narrative, suggesting the following contrasting historical assessment:

(i)   While Peruvians tend to blame Bolivia for the war, in reality the objective of the war would have been Peru transforming Valparaíso into the key port of the region instead of Callao, since Chile wanted to neutralize Peruvian maritime supremacy in the South Pacific. As proof, he mentions that the guano and saltpeter resources of Peru were five times greater than in the Bolivian coastal zone, and the war ended with the occupation of Lima and not with the occupation of La Paz, which is a clear testimony of the Chilean objectives;

(ii) About the assertion that Peru entered the war out of loyalty to Bolivia, in reality Peru became involved since Chile declared war on Peru on April 5, 1879, after it tried unsuccessfully to mediate between Bolivia and Chile, instead of sending troops to the defense of Bolivia;

(iii) On the resources for the war, in reality Bolivia transferred the resources that Peru requested to enter the war. When Chile invaded Peru, the Peruvian president sent a telegram requesting the sister country to send troops, with Bolivia complying, participating in the defense of the Peruvian territory, while "the allied commanders, who were Peruvians, refused to carry out a campaign to recover Bolivian territory." Accordingly, "all the blood spilled and the resources invested by Bolivia were for the good of Peru, although Peruvian historians do not recognize it";

(iv)   Bolivia did not abandon Peru. After the Battle of Alto de la Alianza in 1880, Bolivian troops withdrew to Bolivia awaiting a Chilean attack. By then, Bolivia had concluded its effective participation in the war, but for the next three years it provided Peru with supplies, equipment and weapons;

(v)   The alliance between Peru and Bolivia stipulated that peace with Chile should be signed jointly by both countries. However, Peru signed a separate peace with Chile in 1883 and Bolivia only signed a truce pact with Chile in 1884 and peace only in 1904, a clear indication that Peru did not defend Bolivian interests, betraying expectations and not the other way around.[76]

That is to say, the narrative of each defeated country maintained a dialogue with the recriminatory arguments of the other defeated country, while rejecting them. However, there is a difference between the two. In Bolivia, many still licked the national wounds and attributed their country's backwardness to the result of the War of the Pacific, which took away their access to the seas. Contrastingly, Peru and Chile agreed on their border between 1883 and 1929–31, and although for decades they disagreed on their Pacific maritime border, they projected the defeat in the War of the Pacific onto Bolivia. According to their interpretation, Bolivia took irresponsible steps, beginning with President Hilarión Daza Groselle's starting the war without contemplating Peruvian interests, which would have required coordinating a joint direction on the eve of the war. In August 2015, the Chilean press reproduced Peruvian journalist Jaime Bayly's harsh criticism of the Bolivian position, in which he reminded President Evo Morales that Bolivia had declared the war, a move that also produced territorial losses to Peru, without repeating the litany of complaints that Bolivia continued to voice for generations:

> It is true that Bolivia had access to the sea [and lost it]. . . . Yet, who declared the war? . . . If Bolivians were so reckless that they declared war on a neighbor that crushed them militarily. . . . What do you [Evo] want now, to get back what went lost more than a century ago?[77]

Bayly was alluding to an unsettled issue that disturbed the Bolivian collective memory. The loss of the littoral province and access to the sea has been taken up repeatedly by Bolivian heads of government, from the left-wing military government of the 1930s, through the revolutionaries in the 1950s, to the military administration in the 1970s, and then by Gonzalo Sánchez de Lozada in the 1990s to 2000s.[78]

In Chile, the victor's narrative demands that the defeated should assume their responsibility and accept that their country has rightly paid the price of the war. Without any remorse, the Chilean authorities expect closure. They do not tolerate the symbolic acts of resistance that continue to take place in the territories annexed in the war, such as the beheading of the busts of Chilean heroes of the war in Arica, once in Peruvian territory, or the erection of a Bolivian flag in the city of Antofagasta.[79] In March 2017, the Chilean foreign minister, Heraldo Muñoz, warned the Bolivian government not to bring up the issue for political gain. "Muñoz described the claims of Bolivian President Morales as a provocation, who this Thursday protested because the Chilean police forced the removal of a Bolivian flag placed on a building in the city of Antofagasta, in northern Chile."[80] From time to time, the media reflect the existence of deep-rooted xenophobic prejudices toward sister nations. A case causing particular consternation occurred in February 2013, when a group of Chilean sailors were filmed, in a video later uploaded to the internet, as they jogged through the streets of Viña del Mar singing a warmongering stanza: "I'll kill Argentines, I'll shoot Bolivians, I'll cut the throats of Peruvians."[81] The video created a scandal in Chile, resulting in an inquiry and the promise to "prevent these situations from happening again."[82]

The narratives of the three countries, which contain such disparate emphases, are replicated in the educational programs of those South American nations. In recent years, under the aegis of the Andean Pact, incipient attempts have taken place to iron out the differences. Various historians, filmmakers, and intellectuals from the three countries have tried to find meeting points. Thus, for example, around the new millennium, Chilean and Peruvian historians tried to articulate a shared vision. In 2005, historians Eduardo Cavieres and Cristóbal Aljovín—members of the Universidad Católica de Valparaíso and the Universidad Mayor de San Marcos del Peru, respectively—drew up a common history textbook for both countries. Carrying the title *Chile-Perú Perú-Chile, 1820–1920: Reflexiones para un análisis histórico de Chile-Perú en el siglo XIX y la Guerra del Pacífico*, it highlighted facts that departed from the warlike narratives, stressing instead the common humanity of the combatants and some of their compassionate acts toward enemy combatants during the war.[83]

The effects of the war have continued to reverberate into the twenty-first century. Bolivia has tried to project among its citizens and those abroad the image of continuing to be a country that boasts a naval force and has not renounced its intention to overthrow the Mediterranean geography that the War of the Pacific imposed on it. In March 2017, thousands of citizens—among them students, military and police personnel, state employees, and citizens' organizations—participated in a massive street mobilization, organized by the Bolivian Navy in support of the case opened before the International Court of Justice (ICJ). "Dressed in blue and white T-shirts, some with drawings of paper boats or the phrase 'Sea for Bolivia,' the participants toured the center of La Paz singing the naval march, which is a vindication of the Bolivian claim for the reintegration of an access on the Pacific coast."[84] On April 5, 2017, on the 138th anniversary of the official declaration of the War of the Pacific, President Morales published on his Twitter account (@evoespueblo) a message related to Bolivia's maritime aspirations: "On today's date, in 1879 Chile declared war on Bolivia after 50 days of invasion. In the purpose of justice, truth and reason, we will return to the Pacific." Through this and other means, the Bolivian government promoted a campaign on social networks and in the media to promote the hashtag #MarParaBolivia during April, while the navy commemorated the 191 years of its existence with a naval operation in the waters of Lake Titicaca in November 2017.[85]

For its part, Peru filed a lawsuit before the ICJ at The Hague regarding the border dispute over a 28,350-square-kilometer triangle, which is rich in marine resources, on the platform of the Pacific Ocean between the two countries. In a 275-page report with 89 annexes that was submitted to the court in 2009 in support of its claim, Peru indicated the historical antecedents of the confrontation between the Peruvian-Bolivian Confederation and Chile in the 1830s. However, it attributed the maritime dispute to its defeat in the War of the Pacific, which led to a settlement over land but left the maritime border undefined. Indeed, Peru recognized Chilean sovereignty over the coastal area of Tarapacá, which is rich in natural resources, by signing the Treaty of Ancón in 1883. Under the same treaty, Chile was to convene a plebiscite on the fate of two other areas, the former Peruvian provinces of Tacna and Arica. However, it delayed its convocation and began a process of "Chileanization" of that region. Only in 1929, under the Treaty of Lima and mediated by the United States, did both countries reestablish diplomatic relations and solomonically divide the disputed territory. Tacna returned to Peru, and Chile retained Arica. According to the Chilean press, "[In its lawsuit before the ICJ, Peru stated] that none of these agreements [established] a maritime boundary between the two countries and that a provisional line has been used for issues related to fishing, but this was not an international maritime border. According to Lima, the Chilean government [had] recognized the right of both countries to an exclusive maritime domain including soil and subsoil and now Santiago [had denied] that right to Peru."[86]

The ICJ issued its verdict in January 2014. It recognized the Chilean argument that the maritime platform should be drawn according to the line agreed between the two countries at the beginning of the twentieth century. However, it concluded that the line should be drawn in a diagonal-south line starting at 80 nautical miles, by means of which Peru was granted a marine area of one-third of the 68,819 square kilometers that it had claimed. Chile obtained international recognition of its sovereign jurisdiction over the sea platform and over two-thirds of the economic zone, an unalterable recognition since the ICJ's decision is not appealable.[87]

The Transnational Appeal of Conspiratorial Narratives

To conclude, we return to the initial riddle: Why did a conspiratorial interpretation not become the master narrative in the case of the Pacific War, while it dominated the discourse on the Chaco War and the War of the Triple Alliance?

We can apply several factors. In the first place, giving credence to the thesis of a British imperialist scheme pulling the strings of Chilean aggression would ignore the protagonism of localized interests and social forces in triggering the conflict. Moreover, those who supported the conspiracy narrative about an imperialist master plan behind the War of the Pacific have been at an analytical disadvantage in claiming that the British Empire would gain much by fueling a war whose opening balance did not necessarily favor the Chileans. Likewise, historical evidence does not support the thesis that the United States intended to intervene in defense of Peru, based on a statement by Secretary of State Blaine. We have seen that economic activities were not limited to just one side of the border. Likewise, we have indicated that the United States maintained neutrality and tried to mediate in the conflict without succeeding in preventing the Chilean invasion of the littoral. The United States supported Peru in the peace negotiations with Chile and had an interest in contesting British regional hegemony, something it achieved in the twentieth century, but did not intervene on the ground forcefully in the 1880s. We have registered the ambivalent directives under which US diplomats worked even under Blaine. Conspiracists failed to consider the multiple and often contrasting interests within the US administration. Furthermore, Blaine became secretary of state only in 1881, when the Peruvian defeat was already evident. The assassination of President Garfield merely entailed a return to the previous neutrality, which reinforced the loss of Peruvian territories to Chile in 1883.

Not only did the reliance on partial evidence weaken the conspiracy thesis compared to the narratives wielded by the societies defeated in the war, but our analysis indicates that even more decisive was the variance in the accounts and the politics of memory that crystallized after the war in Bolivia and Peru. Primarily Bolivia but also Peru had a stake in keeping the historical account open to sustain irredentist demands over the territory lost to Chile in the war. For Bolivia, this implied recovering its access to the sea. For Peru, it meant gaining international recognition of a broader oceanic platform. These concrete goals determined the defeated nations' strategic need to retain a credible reality check, relying on historical evidence that, if presented internationally, could have some chance of success in litigation. In turn, this need reinforced the drive to postpone closing the book on the past. Hence, Bolivia and Peru encouraged use of the politics of memory tuned to historical narratives, which they projected onto the new generations through the educational system, official ceremonies, and *lieux de memoire*.

Complicating the scenario was the gap in the narrative of the defeated nations. The interpretive distance between Bolivians and Peruvians led to mutual recriminations that citizens of those defeated nations throw at each other when describing the other nation's participation in the war, trends that enlightened sectors in each country have tried to overcome in recent decades.

Both countries suffered territorial losses to Chile, yet they tried to hide the gap in the paths that they adopted to pursue their interests and conduct the war with Chile.[88]

All of this marginalized the conspiratorial narratives vis-à-vis the claims, litigation, and ancestral prejudices between the nations involved. The complexity of regional history seems to indicate that in this case, the considerations, motivations, and internal actions of social, economic, and political actors in South America had a determining weight equal to or even greater than geopolitical intrigues supposedly concocted in Britain or the United States. Overcoming the discord of the past, without forcing the historical plot and without hiding responsibilities or evading the protagonism of both local and transnational factors alike, was more instrumental than raising the notion of an alleged conspiratorial master plan to explain defeat in the War of the Pacific. That path is also healthier in the long term for any society, as it does not deny social actors their agency and role in shaping history.

In the twentieth century, conspiracism changed focus yet continued to prevail as a major way of interpreting geopolitics in the region. Latin American countries could not ignore their position at the periphery and semiperiphery of the world system, as they were subject to the impact of geopolitical and economic forces beyond their control.[89] In addition, plots were launched repeatedly throughout the region aimed at removing power holders or at defeating opposition forces, some of which were successful.[90] As many heads of government were deposed, sent to prison, or forced into exile,[91] political actors in Central and South America developed a "sixth sense" about suspected intrigues, investing energy in finding out who could be plotting against them and the national interest, both domestically and in the international arena.[92]

Conspiracism is a mode of analysis, a logic of interpreting and thinking about reality in terms of hidden threats and malevolent plots, the product of secret nefarious activities. The theories that such a worldview suggests are an episteme that conditions and interprets the world as the object of sinister machinations.[93] It is then rational for those who think and imagine reality in such a manner to unmask, expose, and punish those who "in the darkness" have planned to affect the integrity of a nation, a society, or the whole of humanity. The Chaco War highlights the likelihood of that general trend, as sectors of Latin American public opinion gave credence to conspiracy theories claiming to disclose geopolitical machinations by British and subsequently Yankee imperialism. Such views were sustained by the very real impact of international forces in hemispheric affairs, foremost being the increasingly hegemonic role played by the United States and its policies aimed at controlling access to resources deemed strategic for US investments in the Americas. The alignment of most Latin American elites and armed forces with the United States from the late 1930s and their multilateral and bilateral military cooperation would eventually lead to the US backing of dictatorships and training of counterinsurgency forces fighting the revolutionary movements in many South American and Central American countries from the 1960s to the late 1980s and early 1990s.[94] As historian Felipe Fernández-Armesto put it colorfully, by the early twentieth century and for many decades, the "United States would not tolerate in the Americas any imperialism but its own."[95] In 1982, in his Nobel Laureate address, Colombian writer Gabriel García Márquez incisively asked why the powerful nations of the Global North "applaud Latin American innovations in the arts while checking, even sabotaging, its experiments in politics and economics."[96]

Geopolitical considerations conferred credibility on suspicion of the intimate connection of US economic interests and its foreign policy in the Americas. Still, US intervention was not uniform, but shifted across time, something often glossed over by those denouncing US imperialism. The agency of domestic political actors was also frequently underestimated, as clearly shown in the tensions developing between Latin American right-wing governments and the US administrations during the 1970s and 1980s. Ignoring such nuances, in the context of the Cold War, the hegemonic role of the United States in the Americas generated polarized alignments, with intellectuals elaborating cultural visions defying the hegemon. Outstanding among them were dependency theory[97] and theories on the "development of underdevelopment,"[98] which sustained countervailing political projects of decolonization and solidarity among Third World nations affected by corporate capitalism and hegemonic Western powers. Accordingly, a major cultural divide and confrontation shaped the political perceptions of Latin America during the Cold War years, as increasingly recognized in contemporary historiography.[99] In later decades, such recognition also led IR scholars to develop an approach of peripheral realism, inspired by the dependent global status of Latin America.[100]

Against this background, for many Latin Americans who theorized the geopolitical marginality of their nations, it became only natural to embrace conspiracy theories of covert imperialist strategies of domination, even when, as in the case of the Chaco War, geopolitics had operated in ways that were more complex. Equally worthy of attention is the transnational path of reception of such conspiracy theories, as analyzed in this chapter. What is certainly ironic, and perhaps tragic, is that many Latin Americans enmeshed in the confrontational logics of the Cold War period aggrandized their attribution of US and UK imperial might to the point of depleting and sidelining their own political agency, making themselves only victims while flattening historical complexities into narratives driven by conspiracism. Relying on conspiracy discourse and theorization to claim victimhood, flattening historical complexities, and depleting historical players of agency over the destinies of their society carry a danger. While defeat in war and policy failure, along with a sense of geopolitical marginality, may explain why conspiratorial narratives have been appealing in some constellations—such as two of the three cases analyzed here—these tendencies may be detrimental to societies in need of a truthful assessment of long-lasting disputes and historical claims.

6

The Cold War and Its Transnational
Imprint in the Americas

Geopolitics is a major conditioning factor of national and transnational dynamics. At the core of this chapter is an analysis of the process of "Latin-Americanization" of the Cold War antinomies. Throughout the twentieth century, regional geopolitics was overdetermined by the rising dominance and pretended hegemony of the United States, which displaced previous European powers such as Spain, Great Britain, and Germany. Such power was felt for decades in the region, such as when the US Marines occupied Central American countries in the 1910s and 1920s and trained national guards to retain power; when it operated coups d'état, as in Guatemala in 1954; and when it invaded the Dominican Republic in 1965 and Grenada in 1981. Naturally, while addressing the Cold War in Latin America, research first focused attention on the US role and projected the master narrative of regional interventionism supporting the authoritarian turn of that period. Increasingly, recent works, particularly by historians and IR academics, have recognized the agency of local forces in Cold War developments, including the transnational spread of revolutionary movements and the effects of counterinsurgency measures by dictatorial governments practicing state terrorism transnationally, in South America and Central America from the 1960s to the early 1990s. The interface of these two layers explains how the multistate region experienced the dire consequences of the Cold War on the lives, dignity, and bodily integrity of millions of Latin American people.

Hemispheric Hegemony and Cold War Geopolitics

The Spanish-American War of 1898 marked the definitive rise of US geopolitical dominance in the Western Hemisphere. The United States occupied Cuba and Puerto Rico, which until then were part of the Spanish Empire. In a few years, Cuba accepted the terms of the Platt Amendment, which conditioned its sovereignty until the early 1930s, while Puerto Rico remained dependent on and associated with the United States. In the late 1890s, the United States also managed to curtail or contain German and French inroads in Central America and the Caribbean. By 1901, Britain tacitly accepted—in the Hay-Pauncefote Treaty

Transnational Perspectives on Latin America. Luis Roniger, Oxford University Press. © Oxford University Press 2022.
DOI: 10.1093/oso/9780197605318.003.0007

signed with the United States—that Central America was within the US sphere of influence. By 1903, the United States supported Panama's independence from Colombia, in return for the exclusive rights to build the Panama Canal and control the Canal Zone.[1]

The following decades witnessed further reinforcement of US hemispheric hegemony, which was sustained by policies aimed at controlling access to resources deemed strategic for US investment in the Americas. The United States took an active role in the "liberation" of Panama from Colombia and established control through pacts and military occupations. The pursuit of US commercial interests and investment often implied influencing or controlling the destinies of other states and nations in the hemisphere, initially those of Central America and the Caribbean. As Jan Knippers Black put it colorfully, "[G]unboat and dollar diplomacy helped to keep other Central American states submissive, and the owners of United Fruit and other companies openly boasted of buying and selling presidents."[2] Increasingly, this strategy unfolded also in the Andean region and the Southern Cone.

The first three decades of the twentieth century were characterized by the recurrent, and in some cases permanent, US presence in the Caribbean and Central America. This presence has come to be known as Big Stick interventionism, which was practiced in Cuba, in Puerto Rico, and for years by marines occupying Nicaragua, Haiti, and the Dominican Republic. Such interventionism cannot be attributed exclusively to the expansionist drive of the United States. The weak institutionalization of national states generated a situation in which domestic contenders called the United States to serve as the transnational actor that could intervene, supporting them in their power struggles. As Robert H. Holden indicates, under such situations of hollow legitimacy and fragmented authority, the United States easily became

> a kind of transnational *patrón* who distributed favors and bought clients by playing on divisions within and among the governments of Central America. As early as 1911, Adolfo Díaz, the U.S.-installed president of Nicaragua, offered the U.S. *chargé* in Managua a treaty that would permit Washington "to intervene in our internal affairs in order to maintain peace."[3]

It was this complementary nature of these interests that brought about the recurrent direct regional intervention of US forces in the early twentieth century. On a deeper level, US and Latin American legal figures interacted in multiple and tension-ridden ways, defending norms of nonintervention in inter-American organizations such as the American Institute of International Law starting in 1912, much as decades earlier they had participated with European colleagues in the Institut de Droit International.[4]

Following those decades of direct intervention, the United States elaborated a strategy for containing or controlling political change by leaving behind well-trained local forces to protect the claims of US corporations and the governments and political leaders favored by US policymakers.[5]

The 1930s and early 1940s were a hiatus from direct intervention, dictated by Franklin D. Roosevelt's "Good Neighbor" policy. That model paradoxically contributed to the growth of US trade and direct investments in the region as well as the alignment of most Latin American elites and armed forces with the United States. The principle of nonintervention was strongly supported by the inter-American system, which saw in it a delayed recognition of the Bolivarian principles of a Latin American international normative regime. Promulgated by Simón Bolívar in the early 1820s, Bolivarianism implied the equal standing of states whatever their size and power, the nonrecognition of territorial gains following wars, the peaceful settlement of international disputes by mechanisms of arbitration, and a system of collective security, which would include mutual defense and neutrality. Since the 1820s, Bolivarianism had represented an ideal of peaceful coexistence among Latin American states, somehow superseded after 1889 by pan-Americanism, a movement that recognized the leading role of the US agenda in establishing the continent's common norms.[6] While the new US policy did not obliterate the memory of earlier interventions, it was perceived as a more egalitarian recognition of Latin American nation-state sovereignty.

In the 1930s, sympathy for Germany and the Axis countries was still widespread, along with distrust of the United States. However, soon the influence of Great Britain, France, Germany, and other European countries diminished. Even in Mexico, a country that enshrined in its collective memory the loss of a third of its territory in a war with the "colossus of the North," a process of alignment with the United States took place on the eve of and during World War II.[7] Throughout the region, cooperation grew during the war, as reflected in the Inter-American Defense Board (1942). Countries in the Western Hemisphere granted air and naval bases to the United States. The process accelerated in Brazil, which sent soldiers to fight alongside the American Fourth Army in Italy during World War II and received US support in the form of equipment, military training, and the establishment of military academies. World War II put aside the former pattern linking Latin American armed forces to European armies. By the end of the war, the United States had established strong bilateral military ties and acquired a near monopoly of training and equipping of Latin American armed forces. Beginning in 1951, the countries signed a series of bilateral agreements for US military assistance. Those agreements defined grants and credits for the acquisition of US military equipment, the stationing of US military missions in Latin America, and the training of Latin American officers in military schools both in the United States and in the Panama Canal Zone.

The cooperation during the war also led to multilateral cooperation and optimism, as expressed in the Inter-American Treaty of Reciprocal Assistance, signed in Rio de Janeiro in 1947, and the launching of the multistate, regional Organization of American States (OAS) in Bogotá, Colombia, the following year. Still, under the Truman administration (1945–53), US interests remained focused on Eurasia, particularly on Germany and Eastern Europe, Greece, Turkey, Iran, and China, and considered Latin American issues to be less urgent. As the countries met in Bogotá, it was not the United States but rather Chile—under the presidency of Gabriel González Videla (1946–52) carrying out a staunch policy of anti-Communism, reflected in the Law for the Permanent Defense of Democracy (1948)—that wanted to align the inter-American community into a common front against the Communist threat.

According to historian James Lockhart, who researched the Chilean interface of domestic and foreign policy during those years, the Cuban, Dominican, Panamanian, Brazilian, and Paraguayan delegations backed González Videla's proposal, while the Mexican, Ecuadorian, Bolivian, and Argentine delegations opposed it. The United States mediated the process, being aware that Latin American conservatives were using the exaggerated narrative of the Communist threat to suppress all opposition. While the delegations were gathered in Bogotá, however, the Colombian populist leader Jorge Eliécer Gaitán was murdered, leading to major riots. González Videla suggested the murder had been motivated by the USSR directing Colombian Communists, to disrupt the OAS meeting and possible passage of an anti-Communist resolution in solidarity with Chile. Finally, the Chilean, US, and Brazilian delegations jointly proposed a moderated anti-Communist resolution that declared Communism "incompatible with the concept of American freedom." González Videla's Chile and the United States also attempted to promote such anti-Communist policies at the United Nations (UN), failing to do so. Neither superpower intervened in Chile or the Southern Cone in the late 1940s. [8]

By the early to mid-1950s, the Cold War superpowers had established spheres of influence, and early nationalist attempts at agrarian reform were met with a coup in Jacobo Arbenz's Guatemala in 1954, orchestrated and backed by the US Central Intelligence Agency (CIA). By then, Latin American states had firmly connected with the US camp, and as democratically elected presidents faced the contrasting pressures of political polarization, they favored a multilateral, developmental-statist, and reformist approach, soon to be tested under the growing confrontations of the Cold War. In Chile at that time, anti-Communism resonated particularly with the professional officer corps, thus shaping a long-term bias among many officers, including Augusto Pinochet, against the Left. Those officers learned then that Chilean Communists and Marxist-Leninists were internal enemies threatening Chilean security, and much later they would resort to drastic actions against the government of Salvador Allende, whose economic policies polarized society and threatened the military chain of command.[9] Moreover, by then, major sectors of Latin American societies endorsed the cultural underpinnings of the American way of life, as Benedetta Calandra and others studying the Cold War from a cultural perspective have emphasized.[10]

The "Latin-Americanization" of Cold War Antinomies

In the 1960s, the Cuban Revolution became a major pole of attraction for young people growing up in authoritarian and unequal environments throughout Latin America. Spearheading the ideas of anti-imperialism, anti-capitalism, national liberation, and armed struggle, the revolution resonated with many middle-class youth, born in the 1930s or early 1940s, often college students or dissidents from Communist parties, who in the post-Stalinist era disengaged from blind support of the USSR. Resenting the existing political and economic structures backed by the United States, revolutionary leftist groups emerged in Paraguay, Argentina, Brazil, Colombia, the Dominican Republic, Guatemala, Mexico, Nicaragua, Peru, and Venezuela. These groups advocated following the Cuban model of *foquismo*, a revolutionary vanguard leading an assault that would mobilize massive support toward radical change. While the Communists supported broadening coalitions with bourgeois organizations so as to create the future "necessary" conditions for radical change, the new groups proclaimed revolutionary violence as the anti-imperialist strategy to reach social liberation on a continental and even global scale. Cubans offered support and training to insurgent groups throughout Latin America. International meetings such as the Tricontinental in 1966 and OLAS, the Latin American Solidarity Organization, in 1967, lifted the banner of Third Worldism and fortified cross-continental ties as well, particularly with Africa, as seen in support for the Front de Libération Nationale of Algeria in its struggle against imperial France and for those fighting in Guinea-Bissau, Congo Brazzaville, and Angola.[11]

For its part, the United States placed increasing emphasis on ties with the Latin American military, police, and national guards. As the Cuban Revolution of 1959 radicalized its regional impact, the concerns of the US and its allied Latin American countries deepened and accelerated the process. By 1960, nearly seven thousand officers had been assigned to military assistance advisory groups in Latin America, and police forces were trained in counterinsurgency methods. In the early 1970s, military grants and credit sales more than tripled, to over $218 million. Simultaneously, the size of the Latin American armed forces grew exponentially, especially in those countries in which the military seized power.[12]

The agreements for military cooperation were originally set within the framework of the multilateral arrangements. Accordingly, the United States had reassured Latin American countries that the format of assistance neither was intended to trigger an arms race between countries nor would it lead to US intervention, such as in the form of entrenching dictatorships. Respecting the national sensibility of the armed forces was key to enabling such an increase in military relationships. Latin American military professionals saw themselves as the heirs of the founding fathers of their states, similarly engaged in solidifying national identity. Like many officers elsewhere—and most civilian leaders in their societies—they believed in their vocation for leadership. In some countries, perhaps most notably Brazil, Argentina, Peru, and Panama, they felt committed by vocation to fight against their societies' underdevelopment, illiteracy, poverty, and national fragmentation.[13]

In the context of the Cold War, the vision of focusing on their society's unity and development became an increasing concern, focusing on national security and a need to fight internal insurgency and enemies. Gradually, Latin American armed forces identified leftist groups as the enemy who, with their revolutionary discourse and activities, were destabilizing the political arena and colonizing public spaces and culture in a detrimental and anomic way. They saw that influence as inimical to the "true" values of their nations. Their professional training added corporate consciousness and alienated them from the disorderly civilian political class, unable to deal with their countries' challenges and vulnerable to agitators pushing Marxist and other leftist "foreign ideologies."

In conjunction with military cooperation, various Latin American leaders and policymakers, such as Raúl Prebisch, head of the Economic Commission for Latin America (ECLA), devised developmental projects geared to bolster democracy by tackling socioeconomic development. Brazilian president Juscelino Kubitschek was particularly instrumental in understanding that unless countries promoted economic change, reduced inequality, and brought about literacy, they could face a revolutionary upheaval. A study by Christopher Darnton reconstructed how, despite the Eisenhower administration's initial reserve, Kubitschek had already enunciated in 1958—months before Castro took over power in Cuba—a developmental project, the Operation Pan-America (OPA), and mustered transnational support for the idea. That vision, pushed through the meetings of the OAS, became a core model for the Alliance for Progress (AFP), the cornerstone of US foreign policy in the Western Hemisphere from March 1961, when President John F. Kennedy announced it, to at least the March 1964 coup in Brazil or perhaps the 1965 intervention in the Dominican Republic. Conceived as a program of US assistance for the promotion of democracy in the Americas, it followed the precedents of the Truman Doctrine and the Marshall Plan. In this case, as Darnton showed, the transnational understandings between

Kubitschek and other Latin American presidents, primarily Argentina's Arturo Frondizi and Colombia's Lleras Camargo, laid the ground for effective agenda setting at the discussions taking place at the OAS. The Cuban Revolution soon became a wake-up call for the United States, and unsurprisingly,

> [b]y the time Kennedy was elected and U.S. leaders decided that the threats posed by the Cuban revolution demanded a major response, the deck of options was stacked in favor of a multilateral, developmental-statist, reformist, democratic approach (as opposed to a bilateral, private capital–driven, conservative, and militarized arrangement).[14]

The US perception of the threat that followed the Cuban Revolution combined with Kennedy's support of modernization theory to articulate the AFP as a program of international assistance. Yet the ground was laid by "the construction of regional solidarity in support of Kubitschek's proposals through the access points provided by the [OAS] CECE meetings in Washington, Buenos Aires, and Bogotá, as well as Brazilian diplomacy outside these meetings, and subsequently [. . .] the repercussions of this Latin American consensus for the Kennedy campaign, the U.S. State Department, and the U.S. Congress."[15]

Nonetheless, President Kennedy still increased US support for the hemispheric security forces in parallel to the AFP, and President Lyndon B. Johnson continued that orientation. Bolivia stood out among the countries where the AFP model was attempted. As stressed by Kenneth Lehman, Bolivia had been a favorable place to test those premises. In the April 1952 revolution, the MNR managed to bring to power leaders who, in spite of their rhetoric, were genuinely interested in modernization along capitalist lines. Motivated by ideological visions that were more liberal than Marxist, the new elites sought US assistance as the driving force of this change. Increasingly, the United States provided the desired assistance on conditional terms, demanding that Bolivia become open to private initiative, foreign investment, and the logic of free markets. Unable to deliver the promised results in the short term, neither in Bolivia nor elsewhere, both Latin Americans and the United States became disappointed with the reformist option.[16]

As the revolutionary option gained momentum, the strategy of counterinsurgency spearheaded by the United States became the main mechanism of confronting Communism. Following the Cuban Revolution and Cuba's efforts to export that revolution—creating "as many Vietnams as possible"—the United States moved to condone and support authoritarian rule in the name of national security.[17] If Latin American countries were unfit to follow the US model of development and, in the context of the Cold War, were on the brink of political breakdown and the threat of revolution, perhaps it was time to make room for a renewed domestic model of "order and progress." Such a model resembled that which, in the late nineteenth and early twentieth centuries, had been successfully adopted by the followers of positivism in Latin America.

From a geopolitical perspective and in terms of resources, small countries depended heavily on US decisions. Partnerships were rather lopsided. While it is true that in the early 1960s leaders such as Victor Paz Estenssoro of Bolivia used their connections with Washington to try to maneuver domestic political forces, the United States weighed in on local power constellations struggling to dominate the public arena. In some cases, confrontations occurred between fractions of the armed forces, foreshadowing the rise to power through coups d'état led by the military. An example can be seen in the confrontations in Argentina in the early 1960s, which eventually led to two cycles of military dictatorship, spanning 1966–73 and 1976–83.

In 1964, the United States supported the Brazilian coup that deposed President João Goulart on March 31. Paradigmatic of the US shift to support military options is the case in neighboring Bolivia on the eve of General René Barrientos deposing Bolivian president Paz Estenssoro in November 1964. Both the US embassy and the State Department moved to support military intervention, motivated by fears that Paz could be assassinated and Vice President Juan Lechín, a leftist, be made president.[18]

So came to an end a period in which the United States had supported the reformist option, which—despite idealistic perceptions—failed to produce the expected twin of democracy and capitalism. In the case of Bolivia, the shift to military rule and the provision of US military training paid off, at least in the short term. General Barrientos, through the use of populist and paternalist means, built broad support among Bolivian peasants and succeeded in isolating Che Guevara's guerrilla forces. This led to the capture and execution of the revolutionary leader in October 1967, in a joint CIA-Bolivian operation.

Starting in the 1960s, the impact of US hemispheric policy converged with domestic trends, primarily increasing socioeconomic mobilization, to create polarized political arenas. Latin American governments had the supportive vision of being on the front line of defense of Western civilization, as led by the United States and encoded in doctrines of national security. As a result, these governments slipped into a renewed use of regimes of exception, military intervention in public life, and suspension of constitutional freedoms and guarantees, with severe consequences in the realm of human rights across the region.

Against the backdrop of the Cold War and the inability of ruling elites to lead their countries to peaceful coexistence and development geared to benefit all social classes, a growing sense of support for radical change dominated intellectual circles and the younger generations. Many supported the feeling that Latin American societies should be radically transformed, if necessary by force. In one of the most widely read essays in that period, Eduardo Galeano proposed the overthrowing of landlords throughout the region, suggesting that the will of the people would be sufficient to generate change: "There is much rottenness to throw to the sea in the way to the reconstruction of Latin America. The deprived, the humiliated, the damned, they have this task in their hands. The Latin American national cause is, before anything else, a social cause."[19] The potential for violence was imbued in the ideological polarization that prevailed across public spheres. As Ana Pizarro observed, for the Left, the 1960s and early 1970s were years of practicing "criteria" in the social sciences. This included discussing dependency theory as opposed to developmental approaches, criticism and countercriticism, launching a dialogue with Africans who were emerging from decolonization processes, and assessing the significance of the Cuban Revolution and the prospects of Caribbean and Latin American integration.[20]

Influencing the political climate during this period were leftist anti-imperialist feelings, the spread of liberation theology, and demands to protect the rights of minorities. The messages contained in the elaborations of the Left were rejected by others who held diametrically opposed visions of their society, and who were no less passionate in their own views and positions.[21] The very principled positions of these circles and the semisacredness with which they cognitively structured and evaluated the forces of society contributed to the clash that tore apart these societies in the period leading up to the military takeovers.

Formal democracy broke down and was replaced by military rule, in a domino effect that started in Brazil in 1964 and would involve all Southern Cone countries in a wave of authoritarianism. To a large extent, the coups d'état signaled the defeat of the legacy of populist mobilization and leftist radicalization that the region had experienced recurrently for several decades.

For Brazil, historian José Murilo de Carvalho's research showed that, contrary to accepted wisdom, two factors were detrimental to sustaining democracy. First, the breakdown of civilian rule was not the result of a lack of democratic support by the citizens, as reflected in voting patterns, but rather of a lack of democratic conviction among the elites. The elite were undermining democracy by precluding any compromise and negotiating arrangements in Congress and in the parties. Second, the lack of communication between the masses and the politicians failed to capture the popular mood. That is, the elitist and hierarchical character of political articulation in these societies was detrimental to the health and continuity of democracy during this period.[22]

After the coup against President João Goulart, many Brazilians crossed the country's porous borders into Uruguay, either fleeing or being banished from the national territory. Among the deposed were Goulart, the former governor of Rio Grande do Sul, and the "Red" admiral Candido Aragão, along with about two hundred core activists and other exiles. Following a long tradition of asylum being granted to citizens of neighboring sister nations, the democratic government of Uruguay welcomed the newcomers, particularly those arriving from Rio Grande do Sul, a Brazilian state with which it shared many friendships as well as economic and social connections. However, even if it was not hostile, the Uruguay civilian government resented the Brazilian coup that had broken down democracy across the border. For Brazil, the relocation of those exiles was a source of concern, as it turned Montevideo into a sanctuary of resistance to the dictatorship, which caught the attention of Brazilian intelligence and espionage services:

> Through exile control and monitoring schemes, the intelligence services prepared numerous reports and gathered information on Brazilian citizens who contacted the exiles, the detection of routes used by those contacts, the support infrastructure in the border area, and the probable return of the "subversives" to Brazil.[23]

Brazilian diplomats and officers also approached Uruguayan sectors that could be sympathetic to those operations of surveillance and control. In his memoirs, Brazil's ambassador, Manoel Pio Corrêa, described how he operated, stressing his relentless efforts to visit departments near the border, forming connections with officials there: "In each Department, I zealously visited the president of the Departmental Board and the members of the Board, the Chief of Police, sometimes the Bishop, and always the main political chiefs, the local notables and the most powerful *fazendeiros*."[24] By attaining such cooperation across territorial borders, the intelligence services and civilian right-wing sectors reshaped ideological frontiers on a transnational scope. State sovereignty came to be superseded by ideological frontiers, preceding a decade of what, following the 1973 coup against Salvador Allende in Chile, would develop into a bloody transnational operation of extermination of leftist activists, which became known as Operation Condor.[25]

Meanwhile, revolutionary organizations mushroomed, along with increased mass mobilization and support. The death of Che Guevara in 1967 had marked a shift of emphasis from rural guerrillas to urban groups. Armed actions relied on wider support and mobilization of students, workers, and middle-class individuals, who lifted banners calling for individual freedoms and social justice and confronted the policies of newly installed authoritarian administrations. Among other organizations created in this period were Brazil's PRT (Partido Revolucionario dos Trabalhadores) and the Revolutionary Communist PCBR; the ERP (Ejército Revolucionario del Pueblo) in El Salvador; the FAL-Fuerzas Armadas de Liberación, FAR-Fuerzas Armadas Revolucionarias, and Montoneros in Argentina; the Tupamaros in Uruguay; and the Communist

League in Mexico. The transnational connections many of these groups sought to establish deepened contrasting hopes and concerns over the possible replication of a revolutionary takeover in any corner of the Americas.

State Terrorism, Transnational Insurgency, and Counterinsurgency

When Allende was elected president of Chile, he launched a "peaceful road to Socialism," radicalizing Eduardo Frei Montalva's previous slogan of "revolution in liberty." Allende attempted what turned out to be impossible in the framework of the Cold War: to move a country in the Western Hemisphere toward socialism by constitutional and legal means, while letting some of its radicalized supporters push economic policies that affected private interests. Radical leftists such as Castro thought it ridiculous, and the United States found it unacceptable, thus opening the region to geopolitical intrigues and counterintrigues. In 1970, following Chilean elections and foreseeing the Chilean Congress's probable election of Allende as president, the United States attempted to prevent the latter by supporting military plotters who eventually assassinated General René Schneider, the top commander of the Chilean armed forces.

During Allende's administration, the United States, under the leadership of Henry Kissinger, who served first as President Richard Nixon's national security adviser and later as secretary of state, encouraged and supported destabilizing maneuvers by parties opposed to Allende's Popular Unity (UP) coalition. This policy also applied to the military plotters led by General Pinochet, who shortly after being charged with the top command of the armed forces, ended the unique experience of the Chilean move toward socialism, on September 11, 1973.

After decades of research, thousands of declassified documents, and countless studies, there is consensus that after the failed initial plans to overthrow Castro, Richard Nixon and Henry Kissinger were forced to accept the existence of a socialist Cuba. However, that recognition did not obviate the fact that, once the Socialist senator Allende was elected president of Chile in 1970, they tried to crush that experience, investing millions of dollars to attain such a result. Among other things, in mid-September 1970, they invited Lieutenant General Alejandro Agustín Lanusse, commandant in chief of the Argentine Army and soon to be the de facto president of the country, to the CIA headquarters in Langley, Virginia. Richard Helmsd, the CIA director, tried in vain to convince him of the need to conspire against Allende. Lanusse did not join the plot, faithful to his belief in national self-determination and the respect of popularly elected governments in neighboring countries, including Chile. Lanusse would meet amicably with Allende in July 1971 and again in May 1973 for the assumption of the presidency by a democratically elected Peronist candidate, civilian Héctor Cámpora, in Argentina.[26]

In 1975, the commission of inquiry onto the covert operations of the US intelligence services in Chile (1963--73), chaired by Democratic senator Frank Church, handed in its report. According to its findings, "the Central Intelligence Agency spent three million dollars in an effort to influence the outcome of the 1964 Chilean presidential elections. Eight million dollars was spent, covertly, in the three years between 1970 and the military coup in September 1973, with over three million dollars expended in fiscal year 1972 alone."[27]

For both the United States and the Communist countries, the Chilean path to socialism had become an exemplary case in the global confrontation between the opposed geopolitical camps. As recognized by Chile's National Truth and Reconciliation Commission in its official report in 1991:

> The Cuban Revolution and the "Cold War" once again contributed, indirectly, to accelerate our crisis. In their context, the victory of Popular Unity and President Allende in 1970 was seen as a triumph for one of the superpowers in conflict, the USSR, and as a defeat for the other, the United States of America. This explains why the US government immediately planned and executed a policy of intervention in the internal affairs of Chile. Its purpose was twofold: to prevent the rise of Salvador Allende to power in October 1970 (the so-called *track one* or first path); and later on, after they failed in preventing it, a policy of economic destabilization of the new government (the *truck two* or second path). This is directly related to the devastating economic crisis of 1972, which was an integral and transcendental part of the broader crisis that ended in September 1973. They characterized inflation in terms never before known, [evident in] the productive breakdown and the acute shortage of essential items; the collapse of foreign trade, and a progressive paralysis of the entire economy.[28]

Peter Kornbluh, a scholar at the National Security Archive of George Washington University, reinforced that reading by citing one of the thousands of declassified documents from the archives of the US State Department, a 1974 US embassy strategy paper stamped "secret":

> Chile [. . .] has become something of a cause célèbre in both the Western and Communist worlds. What happens in Chile is thus a matter of rather special significance to the United States. Distant and small though it is, Chile has long been viewed universally as a demonstration area for economic and social experimentation. Now it is in a sense in the frontline of world ideological conflict.[29]

In another work, Kornbluh highlighted the obstacles that Allende faced due to the US maneuvers contributing to his truncated mandate, including a blockade of loans requested by Chile at the World Bank and a discontinuation of credits and guarantees to Chile at the Export-Import Bank. Kornbluh summed up that "the mix of economic sabotage, political propaganda and army prodding worked. Allende found himself confronted by growing disorder and soaring inflation. At every turn, his policies encountered well-funded adversaries."[30]

The evidence to that end seems irrefutable. As indicated, as early as 1975, the Church Commission of the US Senate recognized the US motivation to derail Allende's experiment in the Western Hemisphere and limit its attractiveness as a model of development.[31] In addition to the US interest and interference in Chile, there was parallel interest and interference by Cuba, as well as the ambivalence and intermittent support of the Soviet Union for the Chilean experience of advancing toward socialism through democratic means.

Such consensus exists, even if researchers do not always agree about the attribution of responsibilities for the coup of September 11, 1973. In the popular imagination and some academic works, the bloody coup of September 11, 1973, was typified as a paradigmatic case of US intervention in Latin America. Some works did not hesitate to characterize the fall and death of President Allende as a typical case of imperialist conspiracy. This line of analysis is reflected in the work of Luis Corvalán Marquéz and Kristian Gustafson.[32] Various works denounced several intrigues between the CIA and Chilean military and civilian conspirators, such as the kidnapping attempt that culminated in the death of the commander in chief of the Chilean Army, René Schneider, as well as Nixon's and Kissinger's role in the design to prevent the consolidation of Allende's administration.[33] Likewise, the Hinchey Report (2000) clearly recognized a US strategy, as it had engineered the idea of a 1964 coup in Brazil, encouraging the Chilean plotters to topple Allende. The same report, however, highlights that the CIA learned the exact date of the coup shortly before it took place. According to the CIA, the agency "was aware of coup-plotting by the military, had ongoing intelligence collection relationships with some plotters, and—because CIA did not discourage the takeover and had sought to instigate a coup in 1970—probably appeared to condone it."[34]

Investigations such as those conducted by Arturo Fontaine, Joaquín Fermandois, Tanya Harmer, and James Lockhart have recognized the geopolitical constellation, yet they stressed the agency of Chilean actors and the role of historical contingency.[35] For example, while the United States sought ways to undermine Allende, his administration adopted indecisive measures that galvanized the opposition. These studies also underlined the limitations of US power, something that became evident as Pinochet took power and unleashed a brutal and bloody repressive policy, ignoring US expectations that he would follow the Brazilian military model. Years later, Pinochet even criticized the United States for not leading the fight against global Communism more assertively. These works also provided documentary evidence from primary sources in the United States and other countries, stressing the role played by local actors and highlighting, for example, the fear and uncertainties fueled by the Chilean political and civil sectors. On the one hand, there were well-founded fears of a conspiracy by the Right and its allies. On the other hand, the opposition's concerns for the future of Chilean liberal democracy faced a more radical left turn.

Tanya Harmer's work also questioned simplistic approaches claiming the coup was just the product of a US conspiracy. Without ignoring the covert operations of the Nixon administration to destabilize Allende's government, Harmer argued that the Cold War in Latin America had a complex dynamic of its own, since in the years of the Popular Unity, relations between the Global South and the Global North did not exactly correspond to the global ideological conflict between a liberal West and Communism. During Allende's presidency, while the existing relationship between the US government and China (and subsequently the US and the Soviet Union) would shift to détente and engagement, a different logics operated at the inter-American system. On the contrary, the ideological confrontation led Chile to be in the eye of the hurricane of a global ideological confrontation, refracting the divide internally. Harmer pointed out that "Chileans were the determining factor of their country's international relations and future, not just passive spectators who watch, and are affected by outside actions."[36] Consequently, when characterizing the military intervention of September 11, 1973, Harmer indicated that "it was the Chilean military, not Washington, who ultimately decided to act and, despite Cuba's preparations to face a coup, it was also Allende and the Chilean left who were unable to defend the revolutionary process that they had initiated."[37]

Without forgetting the destabilization of Chile through sabotage campaigns, psychological propaganda, and US funding of the opposition, simultaneously Harmer helped readers understand the role of protagonist played by Chilean actors in the context of inter-American relationships. This is fundamental to reading the Chilean drama.[38] On the one hand, Harmer restored the operational autonomy of Chilean political and civil forces, questioning the univocal interpretation of those who considered them passive subordinates of global dictates during the Cold War, which was an easy hook for those "fishing in the Chilean troubled waters." Harmer also took into account the transnational input of other actors such as Brazil under the military president Emílio Garrastazú Médici, comparing the experience of the Popular Unity government with that of deposed João Goulart in Brazil. She mentioned that Brazil's cooperation with the US effort to destabilize Chile resulted in an exchange of officers and support of its intelligence service in the weeks leading up to Allende's fall.

The other regional actor with a transnational impact was Castro's Cuba. Just as Allende understood the need to ease the tension and confrontation between Chile and the United States in order to achieve economic and geopolitical goals, at the same time he sought Castro's understanding for his project of building socialism in a peaceful way. Although there was a certain overlap, since "both shared a series of common values and a vision of the world that united them at a critical moment in the history of Latin America," their experiences and methods were at opposite poles.[39] According to Harmer, Castro's acceptance of Allende's path despite their dissimilar political approaches could break Cuban isolation in the Americas. Departing from just an ideological vision allowed Harmer to avoid any fatalistic reading highlighting imperialist plots or Communist maneuvers. On the one hand, if the provision of arms and military training also characterized the relationship between Allende's Chile and Cuba, on the other hand the tactical differences between the countries about the appropriate path toward socialism increasingly alienated them. Harmer pointed out that "even if the military apparatus of the Socialist Party had received three deliveries of weapons from Cuba, beyond the GAP the Cubans also separately trained and armed sectors of the MIR, the PS, the CCP and the MAPU while Allende was in office."[40]

Nonetheless, at the fatal hour of the September 1973 coup, the Chilean revolutionaries faced the coup plotters alone, without the assistance of those transnational currents and outside actors, and were defeated. This more complex reading of the Chilean political scene and the inter-American scene helps readers avoid an interpretation limited by the terms of an external imperialist conspiracy in the middle of the Cold War.

The coup in Chile gave credence to the claim by the revolutionary Left that only violence would open the door to socialism in Latin America. With the election of Juan D. Perón as president, Argentina became a haven for political exiles and revolutionary organizations. Uruguayan Tupamaros, Bolivian ELN (National Liberation Army), Paraguayan groups within the Colorados party, and the Chilean MIR (Revolutionary Left Movement) joined the Argentinean Montoneros and ERP, as they were convinced that they would trigger a process leading to an irreversible path toward Socialism.

With mass mobilizations at their peak, these groups thought they could galvanize public opinion and bring about a mass insurrection following their vanguard actions. They engaged in a partially successful series of kidnappings of corporate CEOs for huge ransoms and some military actions in remote areas, such as the rural hinterlands of Tucumán in Argentina, as well as terrorist attacks on military personnel. In doing so, the revolutionary groups passed from an initial phase of euphoria to decimation by paramilitary networks and later by the military in power. By August 1973 they had devised a plan to coordinate their actions transnationally and provide mutual logistical, financial, and military support across borders through a revolutionary coordinating junta (JCR). Knowledge of this augmented the concern in military circles and enabled them to taint the nonviolent opposition with the violent tactics of the guerrilla groups.[41]

The military in Brazil, Paraguay, and the various countries of the Southern Cone managed rather early on to marginalize the radical Left, after launching their own network of counterintelligence coordination and following the capture of some key Southern Cone activists in Paraguay. However, they continued to use the actions of the radical revolutionary Left as central to their own narrative of being instrumental to redeeming their nations from the threat of international Communism. As such, they operated a network of transnational repression of those groups and their sympathizers in the framework of Operation Condor.[42]

Certainly each country underwent a breakdown of democracy and entered the authoritarian period in a different way, discussion of which is beyond the purview of this chapter. Many factors influenced the breakdown of democratic rule, with the foremost being the character of political struggle and polarization and the variable levels of mass political mobilization. Other factors involved were the degree of political violence and the perceived menace of leftist onslaught, the prevailing doctrines of national security diffused during the Cold War, and the relative incapacity of the political classes to confront the ongoing crises.[43] All these factors affected the specific timing and road to authoritarianism, as they were played out against the background of distinct political paths and patterns of civil-military relationships. These factors would affect the patterns of repression and massive human rights violations committed by the various governments as well.

Yet beyond those differences, there was coordination in the war against "subversion," most significantly spearheaded by Operation Condor, which was launched by Colonel Manuel Contreras of the Dirección Nacional de Inteligencia (DINA), Chile's state security agency. While preparing this move, Contreras traveled to the United States to ask for training; subsequently, the Chileans benefited from the help of US military advisers in counterintelligence. Secluded from the public eye, Operation Condor was designed to coordinate the exchange of intelligence and the launching of combined operations against political activists in exile, many of whom were abducted, assassinated, or transferred for interrogation from one country to another and later disappeared, in the most complete secrecy and lack of accountability.[44]

It may be claimed that, in the short term, some top US officials and agencies welcomed the initiative of Chile and its partners in Operation Condor. They overlooked the genocidal policies adopted, at least before its agents struck in Washington, DC, assassinating former Chilean foreign minister Orlando Letelier and his secretary, Ronni Moffitt, a US citizen. Yet in the view of several Latin American high-level officers, the United States was passive and not aggressive enough in the fight against Communism during the Cold War. I would accordingly claim that, even taking into account the training and support of the United States, one should look for a no less fundamental source of conviction of the military commands in their shared, albeit nuanced, belief in doctrines of national security.

Doctrines of National Security and the Genocidal Turn

These societies, which in the 1960s and 1970s had experienced processes of massive popular mobilization and increased (disordered and almost "anarchical") participation, were forcefully demobilized under civilian-military rule. In many cases, political parties were banned from existing, or their activities were frozen by decree. Educational systems were regimented and disciplined after major military interventions in universities and school programs were reshaped according to the new ideological parameters. Heavy censorship was imposed upon the media, and cultural expression was "purified" of any leftist orientations; trade unions were attacked, with many of their activists jailed and assassinated. Professional and entrepreneurial associations were co-opted, "cleansed" of hostile elements. Self-censorship crystallized as the result of a highly repressive situation. Policies of annihilation of the radical Left and its supporters were carried out both domestically and beyond national borders.[45]

Because of their functional role, their formation, and their professional training, the military saw themselves as guardians of the nation's values and traditions, especially in times of crisis. The national security doctrines, shared by the military establishments of the Latin American countries in the framework of the Cold War, posited a link between the concepts of nation and state and the central role of the armed forces in connection to both. Military leadership considered itself the most qualified and perhaps the only capable institutional actor for achieving the defense and promotion of national interests. The military responded to the political and institutional challenges posed by the generation dreaming of accomplishing a socialist revolution with groups of armed radical leftist guerrillas using violent means to bring about a revolution. The armed forces believed they had the right and obligation to redefine and organize their nations according to the guidelines of the doctrines of national security.[46]

According to that doctrine, the basic values of a nation are anchored organically within Western civilization (interpreted in terms of Christian values), the defense of private property and initiative, and opposition to Communist and Marxist ideas. As Manuel Antonio Garretón indicated, national unity was sought and came to be interpreted in terms of a tradition or "soul," consisting of "freezing certain historical facts or universalizing particular features that are defined outside the freely expressed collective will."[47] The military leaders thought they were most qualified to channel the "true" national spirit through the state machinery, safeguarding the nation. Paradoxically enough, this trans-nationally shared vision that centralized the role of the state in shaping the direction of society was also held by the revolutionary Left.[48]

The organic conception of the nation implied a binary view of the world that resembled the categories of the Cold War. Eliminating the enemy was the only option, since these individuals were considered to be beyond redemption due to their irreparably ideological and flawed political views (a concept denoted in Spanish as *irrecuperabilidad*). By exterminating these "contaminated" cells or organs, both physically and ideologically, society could manage to retain its basic parameters of national values and traditions. If necessary, the armed forces would extirpate the threat. They followed the ideological visions they had incorporated from the French theorists of counterinsurgence developed in the Algerian war, reinforced by the strong anti-Communist visions taught in the School of the Americas and other US training centers of anti-guerrilla warfare attended by Latin American officers. The local idioms of organicism gave further credibility to national security doctrines that stressed the primacy of the collectivity over individual rights. According to this logic, whenever necessary, individual rights, including the most basic human rights, had to be subordinate to national aims and goals.[49] In Argentina, for example, that conception guided the physical elimination of thousands of individuals considered to be enemies of the nation; the terms used were organic in nature and projected a medical discourse that demanded the "extirpation of ill tissues" from the national body. This hinted at the genocidal practices adopted to decimate an entire generation and its dreams of radical political change, as indicated by writer Ricardo Piglia.[50]

Based on those doctrines of national security, the commanders of the armed forces thought that their societies were being penetrated by a secluded enemy that aimed at destroying the moral values of the nation. Accordingly, they developed a systematic technology of terror and repression aimed not only at the physical destruction of the enemy, but also at eradicating its memory from the annals of the nation. This led to a descent into the dehumanization of those detained or abducted and the eventual assassination of thousands of them and the hidden disposal of their remains. Brutally torturing these individuals and denying them the most basic human dignity, the military proceeded to summarily execute and "disappear" thousands of them. In almost contradictory terms, the enemy was defined ambiguously so that the targets could be elastically broadened to include not only active supporters, but also sympathizers or citizens who promoted issues related to social justice, agrarian reform, healthcare, education, or improved working conditions. The military governor of the Buenos Aires province during the first junta regime, Ibérico Saint-Jean, expressed this approach most clearly: "First we kill the subversives; then we kill their collaborators; then . . . their sympathizers; then those who remain indifferent; and finally we kill the timid." [51] In a binary world, such as the one envisioned by the military, there was no room for indecision or lack of full commitment.[52] In such an extreme definition of the situation, all means were deemed legitimate for fighting "subversion." Flagrant human rights violations were ignored, while the armed forces claimed to be saving their countries from being destroyed from within.[53]

In Argentina, between 9,000 and 30,000 persons were abducted and later vanished without a trace. Chile has officially recognized a death toll of over 3,000 as the result of state and politically motivated violence. Other countries in the Southern Cone made use of long-term imprisonment, torture, and forced exile, as was typical of Uruguay and Brazil. In Paraguay, the most conservative assessment put the number of victims around 128,000, including 18,792 tortured, 59 summarily executed, 336 disappeared, and 3,460 deported. The suffering and carnage were paramount elsewhere as well. In Peru, according to official data from the Truth and Reconciliation Commission in its 2003 report, 69,000 citizens lost their lives during the conflict between the Shining Path and the Túpac Amaru Revolutionary Movement and the armed forces and police that the civilian government used to fight guerrilla groups. In Colombia, there were 1,982 massacres between 1980 and 2012, with a toll of 177,307 dead, 25,000 disappeared, 30,000 kidnapped, and more than 5,000,000 individuals displaced. In Nicaragua, the National Guard was responsible for some 40,000–50,000 murders before the fall of Anastasio Somoza Debayle in 1979. In El Salvador, state forces were responsible for killing 75,000 civilians, more than 1 percent of the total population during the civil war. In Guatemala, where the guerrillas had surged in 1960, the civil war lasted for thirty-six years, with more than 250,000 dead, among them more than 50,000 disappeared and hundreds of thousands displaced by force at the hands of the armed forces or militarized civilian units known as the Civilian Self-Defense Patrols.[54]

In the cases of Chile and Argentina, however, the United States discovered, to its own dismay, the limits of its power. During the Nixon and Ford terms, the administration refrained from joining those countries who criticized Pinochet. It maintained cordial relations with the military regime, while circumventing the US Congress's limitations on economic assistance by ordering its delegates to support loans from international banks to Chile. In late 1976, when the Chilean repression and blatant abuse of civil rights gained awareness in US public opinion, the United States tried to pressure Pinochet to change the country's domestic policies, to no avail.[55]

The image of the Pinochet regime was seriously tarnished following international campaigns of denunciation led by a strong transnational network of Chilean activists and committees of solidarity. These campaigns led to the disclosure of international terrorist actions led by DINA agents in cooperation with the intelligence and security units of sister countries against the democratic opposition in exile. Among these were the assassination of General (retired) Carlos Prats and his wife in Buenos Aires; the attempted assassination of Bernardo Leighton, a prominent Christian Democratic exile, in Rome; and last but not least the murder of Allende's former ambassador to the United States and minister of defense, Orlando Letelier, in Washington, DC. These events had a progressive impact on the United States. In the words of Peter Kornbluh:

> In the United States, Chile joined Vietnam as a catalyst for national debate over the corruption of American values in the making and exercise of U.S. foreign policy. During the mid-1970s, events in Chile generated a major political reevaluation of human rights, covert action, and the proper place for both in America's conduct abroad. The Kissingerian disregard for Pinochet's mounting atrocities prompted an outraged Congress to pass precedent-setting legislation curtailing foreign aid to his regime, and to mandate human rights criteria for all U.S. economic and military assistance. Public revulsion of Washington's ongoing association with Pinochet's brutality prompted a widespread political effort to return U.S. foreign policy to the moral precepts of American society—creating a groundswell that helped elect Jimmy Carter as the "human rights president."[56]

For the Southern Cone, the ascent of President Jimmy Carter in 1977 led to the elevation of human rights to a centerpiece of US foreign policy. Carter supported various UN declarations condemning Chile for its curtailment of human rights, the State Department invited many of General Pinochet's foes for briefings, and the United States accepted a large number of political exiles. Once in the country, the exiles energized public opinion against their repressive home governments. Following the latter actions, Carter temporarily withdrew his ambassador and reduced the embassy's staff. Military assistance was stopped, and the Chilean Navy was not allowed to participate in maneuvers with the US fleet. The United States canceled credits destined for Chile, refused to insure private investments there, and vetoed Chilean loan applications. The pressure led to some cosmetic concessions, such as the release of a few political prisoners, and the promise to return Chile to democracy by 1991. While this was a major step, Pinochet planned his exit in a way that would institutionalize core aspects of his regime. In 1980 Chilean citizens approved a new constitution devised by Pinochet's legal advisers, which created a series of authoritarian mechanisms that ensured the irreversibility of some of the main institutional and structural transformations established under the military regime. Moreover, US pressure had its own limitations, as William Sater stressed, since General Pinochet proved to be capable of sidestepping Carter's human rights stance. Moreover, Washington's efforts to isolate Chile achieved the goal of antagonizing General Pinochet. After a while, the Pinochet regime criticized Washington for "not taking the lead in a world crusade against communism."[57]

In the case of Argentina, the pressure from the Carter administration in the 1970s only marginally impacted the junta's genocidal practices. First, Kissinger gave his support to the goals and methods of the dirty war, without criticizing its repressive methods, at the very same time that the US administration was praising the economic direction of the de facto government. Second, the military junta moved to project a false international image of respect for human rights in Argentina, in the belief that it could overcome its critics, that Cold War optics would prevail, and that Carter meant only a temporary shift in US policy. Third, while Argentina supported the United States on disarmament issues, it reinforced international relationships with Cuba, Yugoslavia, and other nonaligned states. The Cubans claimed to understand the need for military intervention in Argentina, and the Soviets did not put pressure on Argentina due to their own human rights record. A series of miscalculations—the last of which was the Malvinas-Falkland war—served to undermine the capacity of the Argentine regime to institutionalize itself on lines resembling the Chilean success story. It is unclear, however, whether the end of US military training programs for Argentina and of the sales of military equipment by the United States, which occurred in 1977, had a serious impact on Argentina's policies. Although the numbers of vanished individuals declined by 1978, it was also clear by then that the radical Left had been annihilated. The Argentinean junta continued to pursue its repressive policies, including the mission of military advisers training counterinsurgency forces in El Salvador and Central America between 1978 and 1982.[58]

Under President Ronald Reagan, many of Carter's actions were annulled, as Reagan advocated a quiet diplomacy toward Chile. As the FSLN (Frente Sandinista de Liberación Nacional) defeated the Somoza dynasty in 1979, the Nicaraguan Revolution recreated the ghosts of earlier decades, as it combined with major revolutionary challenges across Central America, bringing the hard line back in the Washington administration. By the late 1980s, the domestic and international pressure against Pinochet contributed to the acceleration of the protracted yet planned transition back to democracy, but under the constitutional terms of the 1980 charter that secured authoritarian enclaves and the maintenance of the economic model in the democratic period starting in 1990.

Due to the mounting pressure in international and transnational fora in Europe and North America, the actions of the military governments came under scrutiny starting in 1976 and increasingly so under Carter's administration. Yet the pendulum shifted again to counterinsurgency support when Reagan came into office in 1981. With Communist Cuba just to the south and the 1979 triumph of the Sandinistas in Nicaragua, Reagan's administration envisioned a Soviet-Cuban campaign aimed at generating a domino effect throughout Central America and the Caribbean. Accordingly, they moved to destabilize the Sandinista government in Nicaragua and consolidate the anti-Communist political forces in El Salvador. In that country, the entrenched elites were unwilling to compromise with the moderate opposition, and the rebels challenged the authoritarian regime. In El Salvador, the Reagan administration introduced a military and economic assistance program that would prevent the Communist rebels from seizing power as they had in Nicaragua. The second part of Reagan's plan involved removing the Sandinistas from power. He terminated all economic aid to Nicaragua and supported the formation of counterrevolutionary guerrilla groups, the Contras, with a base of logistic support in neighboring Honduras. Reagan initially rationalized the use of such groups as a means of preventing arms shipments to El Salvador and later promoted their image as a pro-democracy force that sought to topple the Sandinista regime.

Reagan's Cold War policies toward El Salvador and Nicaragua resulted in massive violence and violations of human rights in both countries. In El Salvador, the United States funneled hundreds of millions of dollars in military aid to fund a repressive military government's bloody war against Communism; in Nicaragua, the Contra guerrillas engaged the government in a war that cost thousands of lives and ruined the country's infrastructure. In El Salvador, during the civil war state forces were responsible for killing an estimated 75,000 civilians, or well over 1 percent of the total population. The conflict spilled over into Guatemala, where guerrillas had been in existence since the 1950s. The civil war lasted until 1996, with over 250,000 persons assassinated, including up to 50,000 *desaparecidos*, and hundreds of thousands of displaced individuals, either at the hands of the armed forces or of the militarized civilian units known as the Patrullas de Autodefensa Civil (Patrols of Civilian Self Defense or PACs).[59]

Since many of those responsible for launching these genocidal practices and massive human rights violations had some training at US academies, we need to address the issue of US influence and responsibility in such atrocities against humanity. The issue of direct influence is rather clear for the case of Central America under the Reagan administration. However, the picture is more complex when assessing the US impact on the genocidal practices carried out in the Southern Cone and reflecting on the impact of US military training. Of course the US had economic, military, and diplomatic leverage over many of the countries of the Americas and was also confident of its capacity to dictate the course of history south of the Rio Grande. Steven Volk mentioned a paradigmatic instance of such self-perceptions among policymakers in the United States: "Henry Kissinger once famously lectured Gabriel Valdés, Chile's Minister of Foreign Relations to the United States, on the direction of history. 'You come here speaking of Latin America', he chided Valdés, 'but this is not important. Nothing important can come from the South. History has never been produced in the South.' "⁶⁰

Equally important to consider is the training received by Latin American high-level officers and soldiers at the School of the Americas (SOA). The school was originally established in the Panama Canal Zone by the United States in 1946 and catered to Latin American personnel beginning in 1949. Students of international relations have observed with perplexity that during the Cold War period, US leaders were "trying to reconcile the irreconcilable by embracing repressive and corrupt elites while simultaneously attempting to foster democracy and social justice."⁶¹ This was not a story of deceit. It rather reflected a crucial contradiction in US policy during the Cold War. Interested in curtailing the advance of the revolutionary Left and radical insurgency in the Americas, the US interest was to find allies interested in supporting the same liberal democratic principles dear to American citizens, starting with the rule of law and individual rights. However, US policies of backing, training, and strengthening the armed forces in Latin America encouraged the forceful takeover of power and the adoption of counterinsurgency methods that tore apart these societies, undermined the rule of law, and produced some of the most atrocious records of crimes against humanity.

The United States opened the door to Latin American alliances by modernizing outdated military equipment and offering courses on US weaponry. As a result, Latin American militaries became dependent on replacing and purchasing weapons from the United States, guaranteeing Latin American allies as well as an increased market for the US weapons industry. The objectives of the SOA included the discouragement of any type of leftist power in Latin America, particularly those inspired by the Soviets or the Cubans. Officially, the school was attempting to "create professional soldiers" while encouraging Latin Americans to learn from the modern, professional US forces. Similarly, the SOA taught courses that encouraged values such as a free democracy and a stable economy in a "well organized society."⁶² In practice, the SOA indoctrinated the military members studying there to repress left-leaning civilians who were supposed Communist threats. Accordingly, the curriculum of the SOA centered on counterinsurgency operations. A review of training manuals prepared by the US military and used between 1987 and 1991 for intelligence training courses in Latin America and at the SOA revealed, according to a firsthand analysis, that they advocated "tactics such as executing guerrillas, blackmail, false imprisonment, physical abuse, use of truth serum to obtain information and payment of bounties for enemy dead. Counterintelligence agents [were] advised that one of their functions [was] 'recommending targets for neutralization,'" a term that is defined in one manual as "detaining or discrediting" but that "was commonly used at the time as a euphemism for execution or destruction," according to a Pentagon official.[63] What is *not* included in these excerpts, however, is the larger context. "The seven army manuals train[ed] Latin American militaries to infiltrate and spy upon civilians, including student groups, unions, charitable organizations and political parties; to confuse armed insurgencies with legal political opposition; and to disregard or get around any laws regarding due process, arrest and detention."[64] The training manuals did not differentiate between guerrilla insurgents and peaceful civilian protestors. Ambiguity was ensconced in the SOA training manuals, according to which a target was "someone that could be hostile or not." Furthermore, there was explicit instruction on the art of "wheedling," the SOA term for an inhumane set of interrogation techniques. Other torture mechanisms recommended by the manuals were "prolonged constraint, prolonged exertion, extremes of heat, cold, or moisture, deprivation of food or sleep, disrupting routines, solitary confinement, threats of pain, deprivation of sensory stimuli, hypnosis, and use of drugs or placebos."[65]

Graduates of the SOA have been implicated in massive human rights violations. In El Salvador, more than half of all officers cited for human rights violations in a major massacre were graduates of the SOA, including 83 percent of those implicated in the massacre of El Mozote. The UN Truth Commission report of March 1993 found that two of the three assassins of Archbishop Oscar Romero—who were also implicated in other human rights abuses, including the organization of death squads—had been graduates of the SOA. In Nicaragua, Father Fernando Cardenal indicted twenty-six members of the Nicaraguan Guardia for human rights violations including torture, the use of electric shock, and rape. Of the accused, twenty-five were graduates of the SOA. Among renowned graduates of SOA were General Hugo Banzer, who ruled Bolivia between 1971 and 1978; and Colombian general Hernán José Guzmán Rodríguez, about whom it is claimed that he protected and aided a paramilitary death squad "MAS" between 1987 and 1990, responsible for the deaths of nearly 150 individuals, as well as Omar Torrijos and Manuel Noriega of Panama; Rafael Videla, Roberto Viola, and Leopoldo Galtieri of Argentina; Humberto Regalado Hernández of Honduras; and Manuel Antonio Callejas of Guatemala. Some of these graduates and others were inscribed in the Hall of Fame of SOA, thus leading critics of the school to claim that "if the SOA held an alumni meeting, it would bring together some of the most unsavory thugs in the hemisphere."[66] Members of the Latin American armed forces were attracted to the SOA for various reasons. Many considered it a valued perk for traveling abroad or a sine qua non for rising in the ranks once back in the home country. Students did not attend the SOA because of their desire to further human rights or promote democracy in their home nations. In fact, students had a poor understanding and lack of regard for human rights, considering it a nuisance or material for jokes.[67] It should be remembered that the counterinsurgency strategies had started much earlier, with the translation of German manuals on waging a total war, such as Erich von Ludendorff's, and the arrival of veteran French officers with experience in the War of Algiers at Brazil's military academies, who from there went on to Argentina. However, due to the experiences shared with fellow military officers from other Latin American countries, a process of transnational reinforcement of attitudes predicating the use of violent means was reinforced. The SOA experience probably increased the likelihood of human rights violations being committed by its graduates as part of the campaign against the radical Left and its supporters. That experience defused conscious resistance as Cold War antinomies shaped genocidal practices in Latin America, thus creating a grim and long-lasting transnational legacy of human rights violations in the region.[68]

7

Democratizing Societies Confront Their Past

The Interface of Domestic and Transnational Factors

When approaching democratization from a comparative perspective, one wonders whether utilizing the transnational perspective is instrumental. On their face, contrary to conventional images of democratization occurring in clear-cut waves (usually identified, following Samuel Huntington, as the first, second, and third waves of such transformation), the cycles of democratization have been uneven. In some cases, these cycles have spanned many ups and downs and uneven timing, even within regions and of course, cross-regionally.[1] Indeed, the interface of path dependence and contingency seems to have shaped the uneven timing of democratization more than any transnational influence. Thus, for instance, as a new wave of democratization started in Ecuador and the Dominican Republic in 1978, other countries—Argentina, Bolivia, and Chile—were in the early stages of a new authoritarian cycle, and Brazil continued to be under authoritarian rule for over two decades, until 1985.[2]

Still, looking at democracy becoming the "only game in town" in Latin America—or at how the Arab Spring movements spread throughout North Africa and the Middle East in the 2010s—one cannot but wonder about transnational impacts and demonstration effects. In the case of Latin America, after suffering long periods of authoritarianism, military takeovers, and state repression, societies emerged as fervent supporters of the democratic credo in the changed global environment of the post–Cold War era. In the late 1980s and early 1990s, these societies enthusiastically resumed democratic discourse and institutions.[3] Representative democracy was heralded as the harbinger of a new age, to differ from previous waves of democratization, as it resulted from the growing role of social movements and civil society, which were instrumental both in dismantling dictatorial rule and replacing earlier strong étatist trends. Linked to international forces and transnational trends, primarily the work of exiles and their advocacy and solidarity networks, the process of democratization in Latin America—as in southern Europe—was modulated to a large extent by pressures generated internally or through internal-external links in order to liberalize politics in these societies due to the erosion of support for authoritarian rule.[4]

Transnational Perspectives on Latin America. Luis Roniger, Oxford University Press. © Oxford University Press 2022.
DOI: 10.1093/oso/9780197605318.003.0008

While there was no clear-cut "contagion through proximity" effect, as Laurence Whitehead colorfully characterized the process developing in Eastern Europe or in the Caribbean—Jamaica, Trinidad, Barbados, Bahamas, Dominica, St. Lucia, St. Vincent, Antigua, St. Kitts, Grenada, and Belize[5]—the triumph of democracy was heralded throughout the region. In Latin America, the macroeconomic policies of neoliberalism that were adopted led to disappointment and soon alternative models were tested. Yet, democracy survived, developing a multiplicity of patterns, ranging from fully representative to participatory and populist.

In the late 1980s and 1990s, researchers devoted efforts to the study of emerging democracies, focusing their attention on the conditions triggering democratization in a changed global context. At that stage, the previous format of the authoritarian regimes and the mode of transition (e.g., whether negotiated, the product of breakdown, or by imposition) seemed crucial in determining institutional continuities and changes. Naturally enough, the balance of political forces and coalitions appeared to mediate the policy path undertaken.[6]

It soon became clear that there was another transnational dynamic at work in the region as well. Transitioning to democracy, the countries that were leaving behind state terrorism and mass repression had to confront the scars of those policies, which were conceptualized anew in this stage as crimes against humanity and legacies of human rights violations, forcing a wide range of issues under the umbrella notion of *transitional justice*. Undergoing periods of civil unrest, repression, and human rights violations, societies faced a tortuous process of coming to terms with that experience, without an easy way to close the book on the past. The repressive cycle forced a lasting confrontation with a widespread spectrum of issues, from the construction of truth and a recurrent search for justice, through acknowledgment and the construction of collective memory, to psychological healing and reparations. The grim legacies of systematic civilian repression continued to weigh not only on the victims and their relatives, friends, and peers, but also on the cultural setup and the prospects of moving beyond this dark history. Confronting contrasting views of what happened, societies found it difficult to reconstruct consensus while ascertaining how to make those responsible accountable for their past deeds and bring them to justice. Furthermore, the public had to decide whether to push for justice, ask forgiveness from the victims or expect expiation from the perpetrators, select policies of compensation and reparation, introduce plans to reform institutions, honor the memory of the dead, and perhaps eventually reach a stage of reconciliation.[7]

The literature on transitional justice came to acknowledge the holistic character of such processes, that is, the fact that "no single measure is as effective on its own as when combined with the others."[8] Research also stressed the protracted process of coming to terms with the past, characterized by constant tensions between demands for accountability and the pragmatic needs of post-conflict and post-authoritarian institutional stability, between normative expectations and political contingency.[9] Less emphasized in the literature was how, beyond influencing the global context of democratic transition, transnational factors also affected policy assessment and brought societies to take those factors into account as they decided on a convenient policy of transitional justice that could address the recent experience of massive human rights violations without destabilizing the system. This chapter suggests a corrective to that lacuna by focusing on how the process advanced in the Southern Cone.

Democratization and the Agenda of Transitional Justice

In the Southern Cone, Argentina transitioned to democracy first, before neighboring Uruguay, Brazil, Paraguay, or Chile.[10] There, the military junta lost popular support and power as its economic policies failed, and the 1982 invasion of the Malvinas-Falkland Islands led to a disastrous defeat. Following evidence of military inefficiency and the public disclosure of corruption, the armed forces lost legitimacy and the battle over the national soul. The organicist vision of the doctrine of national security, put into practice in its Process of National Reorganization (PRN) since 1976, was bankrupt. The military commands, divided among themselves, could not agree on an orderly transition that would preserve elements of their ideological and institutional model upon returning to democracy. Those circumstances provided the framework for the political agenda of the transition, from June 1982 to December 1983, creating the possibility of reshaping Argentina's public sphere completely, while forcing society to confront the crisis immediately. Unsurprisingly, a public acknowledgment of the extent of systematic human rights violations became a major theme in the agenda of the transition.

The legacy of human rights violations disclosed during the transition was of such unprecedented magnitude that it enabled the adoption of decisive policies upon restoring democracy. Historically, Argentina had known many waves of violence, political upheavals, and military dictatorships, as well as socioeconomic crises. However, the violations committed by the armed forces during the PRN exceeded past experience by far. The democratically elected administration of Raúl Alfonsín also used the awareness of recent genocidal practices as a political tool in reshaping the traditional format of civil-military relationships, in which the armed forces had played a major role by intervening in politics for decades.

The promulgation of a law of self-amnesty by the military government on September 1983, shortly before handing over power, was an implicit recognition that members of the armed forces had committed acts that were punishable and could, in principle, be judged. While willing to prevent any opening of debate about repression, the armed forces could not find political sectors willing to make a commitment in that direction. The surprisingly strong support for Alfonsín, the presidential candidate of the Unión Cívica Radical (UCR), when he defeated Italo A. Luder, the candidate of Peronism, was seen as resulting from his commitment not to leave human rights violations unpunished.

As Alfonsín assumed the presidency in December 1983, his administration almost immediately adopted a bold policy of truth and justice, professing to adhere to normative principles such as the rule of law and equality before the law. Under the strong pressure of associations of relatives of victims and human rights NGOs, with the armed forces retreating in disgrace, the government initiated a series of actions both substantial and symbolic in character. Days after assuming power, Alfonsín issued decrees ordering the arrest and prosecution of the members of the three military juntas as well as that of former leaders of the Montoneros underground movement. Also targeted by these decrees was General Ramón Camps, the former chief of police of Buenos Aires province, under whose command a considerable number of victims had been abducted, tortured, and murdered. Likewise, only days after taking office, Alfonsín decreed the formation of a national commission of inquiry on the disappearance of persons (CONADEP), charged with clarifying the fate of the victims of military repression. The truth commission comprised some of the country's most prominent human rights activists, journalists, and well-known public figures, and was chaired by renowned writer Ernesto Sabato. The inquiries, and especially the commission's final report, became central for placing human rights at the center of the agenda in an attempted effort at reshaping Argentine public institutions.

Argentina's return to democratic rule, after one of the most turbulent decades in its history (ending with the military PRN), was perceived as a "foundational" moment in the history of that country. This government's attempts to confront its violent and repressive experience shaped the perception—not just in Argentina, but also across the region—of the beginning of a qualitatively different era by adopting radically new patterns of truth and accountability, soon to be contemplated in many other nations. In three to four years, however, the snowballing of trials of military officers led to the recomposition of the armed forces' resistance and to armed uprisings that, under critical economic circumstances, threatened to destabilize democracy. This led Alfonsín to backtrack on the initial bold policies, introducing legislation that temporarily ended the quest for accountability for past violations. In the early 1990s, in a bid to stabilize society and the troubled economy, another president, Carlos Menem, issued pardons, liberating convicted perpetrators of human rights violations who were serving time in prison. Only after 2003 did Argentina resume innovative mechanisms of transitional justice.

Next to transition back to democracy were Uruguay and Brazil, in 1985. In both, the military commands negotiated the transition with parts of the political class, which agreed to embrace policies of closure on the past. That pattern stood in sharp contrast to the policies that had initially launched in Argentina. Uruguay closely resembled Brazil, where during the transition a 1979 law of amnesty safeguarded legal immunity for members of the security forces, although originally geared to cover political opponents. In both Brazil and Uruguay, unlike Argentina or Chile, years passed before the democratic governments launched official truth commissions with a mandate to elaborate an authoritative and agreed-upon version of human rights crimes committed under the dictatorship. In Uruguay, an NGO, the Servicio de Paz y Justicia (SERPAJ), published a partial report of human rights violations in 1989. In Brazil, the Archdiocese of São Paulo issued a report covering abuses from 1964 to 1979, which was made public in 1998 in book-length form. Decades later, both countries moved ahead and established official commissions of truth, whose reports were released in 2003 and 2014, respectively.[11]

Uruguay's transitional path stemmed from the political class's decision to negotiate the process of redemocratization with the armed forces command and accept moving ahead without addressing expectations of truth and accountability. Due to the negotiated character of democratization, the Uruguayan "solution" was to sanction a law of amnesty for most political prisoners in March 1985, which also aimed at restitution for loss of property and financial losses. In parallel, parliament also promulgated the Law of Expiry (*Ley de caducidad de la pretensión punitiva del Estado*), which granted principled immunity to individuals possibly implicated in recent human rights violations. Additional measures included the establishment of the National Commission of Repatriation, charged with assisting exiles wishing to return to the homeland, which operated until 1989. A law for the reinstatement of state officials fired by the dictatorship was also enacted. Symmetry was supposedly thus established, which would lead to closure. The Law of Expiry, promulgated in December 1986, was challenged twice, once in a referendum on April 16, 1989, and again via a plebiscite on October 25, 2009. Both efforts failed to annul the law and undo the blanket immunity that the restored democracy had granted to military repressors. Unlike in Brazil, the legal framework of lack of accountability eventually broke down in Uruguay, in a protracted process with many social, political, and cultural implications that occurred over years, until it unraveled in October 2011, as discussed in detail in other publications.[12]

In 1989, Paraguay started one of the longest and most incomplete democratic transitions in South America. The uniqueness of the transition in Paraguay, initiated by a coup led by a close associate of General Alfredo Stroessner, the supreme ruler for thirty-five years, indicated that it would take years to achieve a profound change in the legacy of authoritarianism and the construction of historical memory. The Colorado Party, which provided political support for Stroessner's dictatorship, continued to dominate the electoral scene in Paraguay for two more decades.

Chile was the last nation to transition back to democracy, and did so only after Augusto Pinochet secured the continuity of a conservative constitutional framework and a developmental model that would constrain the restored democracy with a series of authoritarian enclaves, including his own senatorial status and immunity for years. Nonetheless, by the late 1980s, seventeen parties had formed a broad coalition to confront Pinochet politically within the constitutional constraints imposed by the military, and it won the electoral contest under the leadership of a single presidential candidate, Patricio Aylwin. That coalition, the Concertación de Partidos por la Democracia, included such varied parties as the Christian Democrats, the Christian Left, MAPU, the Party for Democracy, the Radical Party, the Social Democracy, and two sections of the Socialist Party. Due to the harsh repression and the active work of the exile community and their networks of solidarity, human rights became a central issue for the political forces that led the process of democratization. The experiences of the years spent under dictatorship, especially the persecution of political activists from the Left, along with the links between the human rights organizations and political parties, contributed to the progressive diffusion of the human rights discourse as a cornerstone of the return to democracy since the 1980s.

Nonetheless, the scope of transitional justice opened in the Chilean process of restoring democracy was limited. The Concertación forces were conscious of the dangers of political polarization and had to deal with the legacy of human rights violations from a position of constraint. They lacked the necessary parliamentary majority for changing the legislation that had granted impunity to most of those who had committed those abuses. In addition, the legal framework inherited from Pinochet—the 1980 constitution and the organic laws—as well as a judiciary that had cooperated with the dictatorship, precluded adopting a bold policy of judicial accountability against the repressive apparatus of the dictatorship. Furthermore, in order to clarify the truth about the victims' fate, the cooperation of the armed forces was vital, but it was difficult to obtain.

The path adopted consisted of respecting the impositions of limited democracy and balancing power between the military and the civilian authorities. Within these limits, Aylwin's administration followed a policy of obtaining "all the truth and as much justice as possible." By revealing a truthful account of what happened and by transferring individual cases for judicial prosecution whenever possible, the public sphere remained open to pending institutional crises. Although trials focused on individual responsibility, without demanding general accountability from the branches of the armed forces, their prosecution generated the closing of ranks around the accused. The possibility also existed of individual trials raising the question of commanders' responsibility in a way that would eventually implicate the higher ranks. The plight of the victims and their supporting networks continued to reverberate and divide society for years to come. The seeds of future crises around the memory and treatment of past human rights violations mounted in Chile just as much as in the other Southern Cone countries.[13]

The protracted way in which these societies dealt with the actions of the dictatorships reveals both a long-term concern with institutional destabilization and the achievements in addressing many such issues, in spite of early reticence or ambiguity. Such reticence to deal comprehensively with that grim legacy of repression could be due to unwillingness (as in Uruguay or Brazil), to institutional limits and hesitation (as in Chile), or to successive cycles of policy assertiveness and regression (in the case of Argentina). While each case was different, in all of them several building blocks could converge to open the possibility of moving the agenda toward more resolute policies of transitional justice. First, there were continued pressures from both new and existing networks and organizations that demanded truth and accountability for past crimes against humanity. Public debate opened recurrently after periods of oblivion. The publication of works alluding to or promoting historical memory triggered debates about the past. In part, emblematic cases of searching for the whereabouts of children of forcefully disappeared individuals and for victims' remains reopened those debates. Additionally, generational and political shifts brought forces more committed to the plight of victims and their relatives to positions of power. In addition, the revelations of human rights violations perpetrated under the transnational umbrella of the Condor Operation had most important effects, along with pressures stemming from cases presented in the Inter-American System of human rights.

The agenda setting reflected—even if at first hesitantly and subject to the criticisms of human rights organizations—the weight of these factors. Particularly, the state agenda responded to internal developments, such as persistent demands for accountability within each country. Operating pressures from beyond state borders were transnational assessments affecting the agenda setting, human rights crises with a transnational spillover, and cases presented to the Inter-American System.[14] I discuss these transnational aspects next.

Transnational Assessments and Policy Calibration

In each of these countries, the respective key political and social actors took into account the parallel patterns adopted in the neighboring countries for dealing with the legacy of human rights violations. During the cycle of authoritarian dictatorship, the governments and security apparatuses of the various countries had cooperated across borders in tracking, abducting, or killing members of radical leftist groups and opposition political exiles. They had carried out repression not just within their national jurisdictions, but also transnationally, as evident in the actions of the Chilean DINA and the international counterinsurgency teams coordinated as part of a counterintelligence network known as the Condor Operation. Tied together by these actions while under authoritarian rule, countries remained tied to one another even following democratization.

As they tried to assess which policies of transitional justice they could adopt, the new democratic administrations learned from their neighbors' experiences about the possible consequences of daring to engage in courageous policies of accountability, truth, and justice, or sometimes opting instead to close the book on the past without taking action, thus enshrining impunity. Moreover, as they had cooperated with one another, whenever a human rights crisis developed in their midst, it reverberated in the neighboring countries.

All this opened space for a transnational refraction of policy dilemmas and change of political positions, according to regional shifts. For example, the April 1987 military uprising in Argentina, which protested trials against those officers implicated in human rights violations, and especially the concessions made to the military in the aftermath of the rebellion, produced a radical shift in how different Uruguayan political forces viewed possible courses of action to be followed in their country. Before that date, the Uruguayan Left had considered the Argentine path as a model for their own country, while most of the more conservative forces claimed that Uruguay was a case apart and no inference could be drawn from Argentina or other cases. According to the latter, the path of Uruguayan civility set their country apart. General Hugo Medina expressed the view of Uruguayan exceptionalism, arguing that

> the Uruguayan armed forces permitted a bloodless way out, which is an example for all [Latin] American countries. To this, we should add the fact that military rule allowed us to save many from death. We do not to have to repent for any drop of blood shed in the country.[15]

Following the 1987 rebellion on the other bank of the River Plate, the forces trying to close the book on the past in Uruguay saw a foreshadowing of what could happen in their own country if attempts were made to bring the military to trial over those events. As perceptively noted by journalist Carlos María Gutiérrez, Argentina had completed a full cycle, leaving behind its initial assertive path of convicting members of the juntas and reaching the same political equation as Uruguay; namely, that social peace equals impunity:

From a comparative point of view, it can be argued that, on the issue of military impunity, Alfonsín has finally chosen a Uruguayan solution . . . . Now the Colorados and Blancos that voted or supported the Law of Expiry . . . praise what they call the democratic courage of the neighboring ruler.[16]

On their part, the Uruguayan political forces that rejected compromises with the military shifted their earlier view of Argentina in the other direction. According to them, the Uruguayans should not hesitate in adopting decisive policies because of the example of the neighboring nation, since Argentina had a peculiar tradition of violence and military intervention in politics, which set it apart in the Southern Cone:

These are complex events, not yet clear, which require rigor and avoiding at all costs the risk of abusive analogies. . . . This is not the first time that people tend to simplify realities. [Let us be cautious when addressing proposals aimed at] granting impunity to the war crimes of the Uruguayan dictatorship.[17]

In 1995, Captain Adolfo Scilingo, an ex-navy officer, made a series of public appearances and confessed to having participated in the operations leading up to the "disappearance" of political prisoners. According to Scilingo, the victims were sedated, flown in navy planes to the ocean, and thrown alive into the sea with heavy weights so that their bodies would not be recovered and brought ashore. The declarations he made to human rights activist and writer Horacio Verbitsky resulted in a book, *El vuelo* (The flight), which immediately sold thousands of copies.[18] Following the debates and crisis around Scilingo's revelations in Argentina, the Uruguayan political leadership returned to the thesis of the uniqueness of their country. President Julio María Sanguinetti stressed, in a talk with the high command of the armed forces, that "happily, there is no point of comparison" between the paths of the two nations. In Uruguay, the question of not prosecuting the military was solved by the popular vote that ratified the Law of Expiry in April 1989.[19]

Conversely, in Argentina, once the results of the Uruguayan referendum of April 1989 that confirmed the Law of Expiry became known, the candidate for the vice presidency of Alfonsín's party, the UCR, Juan Manuel Casella, had no doubt that a plebiscite in Argentina would bring about "the support of the People for the decisions of Congress taken in 1983, 1987 and 1988"—that is, the trend toward increasing impunity for members of the armed forces. The Communist leader Eduardo Barcecat, of the leftist Izquierda Unida, considered that "this defeat will be important in all Latin America and especially in Brazil, Argentina and Chile, where it serves as a model for the right-wing regimes and their allies."[20]

Similarly, according to Jorge Correa's evaluation, the recent Argentine experience showed Chileans that the confrontation with the armed forces could destabilize democracy:

> Aylwin was influenced by the Uruguayan and Argentine experiences. [In Argentina], even in the most favorable circumstances, President Alfonsín had to abandon some of his goals due to military resistance. The new Chilean President also took note of the Uruguayan experience, where military officers resisted testifying in court.[21]

A close collaborator of President Aylwin and member of the Rettig Commission, José Zalaquett, suggested that the Argentine case was telling for Chileans, as it showed the crucial importance of revealing the truth about human rights violations and yet, "it also showed the extent to which a government can lose authority when it raises expectations it cannot fulfill." In a converse way, Uruguay also provided a lesson for Chile:

> In Uruguay, the government took a too cautious approach, avoiding not only trials for past state crimes but also any significant official disclosure about past violations. Citizens' opposition then led to a nationwide campaign. . . . Taking these lessons into account, the Aylwin government decided to follow a course it could sustain.[22]

In the mid-1990s, in the midst of the Contreras crisis, others also reflected on the paths of Argentina and Uruguay and their applicability to Chile. In Verbitsky's view, there were no beneficial conclusions from Chile, only mistakes to be avoided, such as that of "worsening even further a situation with extremely rapid measures (Argentina) or extremely cautious measures (Uruguay) that generated military and civilian upheavals [even when] it not only abstained from making the names of the guilty public, but also abstained from investigating."[23] The distinct historical timing of the mechanisms of transitional justice that countries adopted enabled latecomers to infer the significance of those experiences and their possible implications for political calibration in their own countries. In this sense, Argentina had to elaborate the institutional and informal ways of treating the legacy of its previous military government without any previous South American reference, relying only on the more remote precedents of the Nuremberg and Tokyo trials. As Uruguay restored full civilian democracy, it could already look to the other side of the Río de la Plata in elaborating its own path of transitional justice. The Uruguayans could perceive that even in Argentina, where the new democracy incorporated a defeated and divided military, it was extremely difficult—if not impossible—to bring the security forces to cooperate in uncovering the past. Later on, as the Uruguayan political class began to legislate the closure of the human rights violations issue, they looked toward the Argentine regressive trend leading to the Law of Punto Final (Final Point) in December 1986 as a landmark that guided the enactment of their own Law of Expiry. Following extremely different paths, Argentina and Uruguay arrived almost at the same time at legislation intended to put an end to the divisive issue of truth and accountability over legacies of human rights violations.

The protest of concerned sectors of civil society led to different institutional results in Argentina and Uruguay. In Uruguay, concerned civilian sectors articulated a wide mobilization that was framed within the 1967 constitutional provision that allowed civil society to challenge parliamentary legislation, through a referendum in April 1989, a plebiscite in 2009, and several legal moves until it reached success in circumventing the limitations of the 1986 Law of Expiry. The protest in Argentina was as massive as in Uruguay, but was channeled through street demonstrations and legal suits, which met the time limits established by the Law of Punto Final. In this case, the pressures generated by civil society tended to recreate polarization through massive judicial demands against the military, precipitating military rebellions and eventually forcing a regressive trend in the treatment of past human rights violations.

Uruguayans were able to assess the Argentine experience of the dangers of disarticulated polarization, which may help explain the consensual acceptance of the April 1989 referendum results by the victors and defeated alike. The final stages of the transition from military rule to democracy in Chile coincided with the most acute point in the regressive trend of the cycle in Argentina and with the closure brought about by the referendum in Uruguay. For all sectors in Chile, the results evolving in the neighboring societies were interpreted as unacceptable. For the Chilean military and their supporters at that point in time, the trials and resulting humiliation suffered by their counterparts in Argentina had to be rejected, and the kind of popular mobilization they witnessed in Uruguay had to be avoided. For the Concertación, the regression of human rights policies in Argentina indicated the need to follow a cautious path in Chile, and the closure without truth and justice embedded in the Uruguayan path was antithetical to Chilean principles. It was then logical to embrace a piecemeal approach of seeking all truth and as much justice as possible, moving to reform the system while trying to avoid major social earthquakes, something that new transnational crises in the 1990s would prove ephemeral.

Human Rights Crises: The Transnational Angle

The existence of a transnational spillover was apparent by the 1990s.[24] A major development of the transnational impact happened in Paraguay, where a coup ended the thirty-five-year dictatorship of General Stroessner in 1989. Three years later, the country promulgated a new constitution involving a process that was unprecedented in modern Paraguayan history. Not only did political parties draft constitutional drafts, but various social sectors, including indigenous groups, women's associations, and some environmentalists and trade union sectors, took part in the process and suggested concrete proposals, while they lobbied intensely for them. All this reflected a greater openness to citizen participation. The new constitution introduced important changes aimed at democratizing republican powers, removing presidential discretion to legislate by decree-laws, dissolving Congress, or declaring a state of siege or emergency, which in Paraguay had lasted thirty years.

A most important consequence of the new constitution, which carried enormous transnational impact, was its recognition of the right of *habeas data* or access to public information. One of the victims of state terrorism, Dr. Martín Almada, requested this right, which led to the unexpected discovery in late December 1992 of a hidden reservoir of thousands of files, soon known as the Archive of Terror. The discovery of those files is described in detail on the website of the Supreme Court of Paraguay, which operates the archive, whose documentation would support legal cases, both in Paraguay as well as in the other countries involved in Operation Condor.[25]

There is no other such rich reservoir of data on authoritarian surveillance and transnational repression in the region. It is exceptional in terms of the amount of documentation recovered (over 700,000 documents); the detailed information provided on victims, collaborators, and methodologies of surveillance and repression; and the extensive time span, covering the entire period of Stroessner's rule (1954–89) and even the period starting in the 1930s. When the first inquiry was presented, the police denied that they had preserved any such files, while in fact, law enforcement officers continued to work under the supposition that the information they collected would still be used for political purposes in spite of the fall of the dictator, and without any criminal consequences. Paradoxically, the lack of a radical break with the past and lack of apprehension on the part of the Paraguayan security agencies brought them to preserve those files and even continue filing information on suspects for over two more years, until the "discovery" of the archive in November–December 1992.[26]

Finding the Archivo del Terror, now part of the Museum of Memory, produced a chain reaction. Alfredo Boccia Paz, a hematologist who published key books on the systematic violations of human rights perpetrated by the authoritarian regime, recalled that after the fall of the dictator there was little willingness or public interest to deal with that record. According to Boccia Paz, the discovery of the archive induced people to bring the knowledge of the repression to the wide public, so as to "resignify the memory of Stroessnerism in Paraguayan society."[27] The fact that Paraguay, unlike Argentina or Chile, did not promulgate an amnesty law for repressors, implied that those responsible for human rights violations could be brought to trial and convicted. The archival documentation served as evidence in prosecutions of individuals implicated in repression both in Paraguay and across the Southern Cone countries.[28]

The issue of past human rights violations moved in the mid-1990s to the center of the public agenda in all Southern Cone countries more or less simultaneously, despite their having restored democracy at different points in time, including at least a decade earlier. The developments involved scandals and crises, different in their details due to the varied policies adopted for tackling the legacy of human rights violations, yet always involving a generalized sense that there was some unfinished business and that had much to do with the regional nature of the problem. Several major cases started confirming rumors about the "Plan Cóndor," an interstate counterinsurgency cooperative mechanism predicated on the elimination of left-wing activists across the region.

A decade had passed since the release of the report of the truth commission and the trials against the commanders of the armed forces. A new generation, which came of age after the dictatorships, confronted a vivid confession of the lack of regard for human life and dignity, with some hearing for the first time about those events. The news shocked them as just as the older cohort had been shocked years earlier. The revelations, amplified in media interviews and reproduced in the press, precipitated an agitated debate over the legacy of human rights violations and the fate of the disappeared. However, the impact was short-lived and did not change the outcome of an ongoing presidential election, which was conducted mainly around concerns for macroeconomic stability.

Following Scilingo's public declarations in the media and the publication of The Flight, President Menem and the navy's commanders defamed him as a petty and deceitful criminal. Still, General Martín Balza, commander in chief of the army, recognized that human rights violations had been committed under the military government and declared that in the future, the armed forces would act within constitutional limits and moral precepts.[29] That position was criticized by Admiral Emilio Massera, a member of the first military junta in 1976, who declared that no crimes had been committed, nor was anyone illegally killed. Likewise, General Mario C. Díaz, commander of the joint staff, and several retired officers also were critical of Blaza's statement.[30] The debate increasingly widened to include other sectors, such as the police and the Catholic Church. The latter was particularly under fire, since its role under the military governments was questionable. Bishop Miguel Hesayne, well known for his exceptional defense of the persecuted, condemned the official attitude of the church in supporting the armed forces. In a document issued on April 30, 1995, the Catholic Church of Argentina publicly and officially recognized its "past mistakes."

The most active human rights NGOs reacted to General Balza's and others' late declarations of remorse with disapproval, rejection, or scorn. Members of various political parties, the military, concerned NGOs, intellectuals, the church, and the public at large joined the discussion. Balza's declarations won significant civilian support, although some human rights activists demanded a more radical condemnation.[31] Controversy deepened as Argentina was about to mark the twentieth anniversary of the military coup, thus producing a wave of condemnations of the security forces' past policies. In an act commemorating the anniversary of the Argentine military landing in the Malvinas-Falkland Islands, General Díaz declared that he rejected each and every criticism directed against the armed forces, one of the "fundamental institutions of the fatherland." The statement was a source of unease in government circles, as it added fire to the debate.[32] Civilians carried out acts of public censure, and several violent attacks took place against former members of the security forces known for their involvement in the repression.

The reaction spread transnationally. In Uruguay, Scilingo's confession reopened the wounds of old times, as most Uruguayan *desaparecidos* suffered their fate after being detained by joint Uruguayan-Argentine task forces in Argentina. The marking of the twentieth anniversary of the coup in Argentina was widely reported in Uruguay, with more than a passing reference to the local lack of political will to follow the lead of Argentina in dealing with the past. Unlike those in Argentina, the Uruguayan armed forces had maintained a united front until 1996. Nonetheless, in the aftermath of Scilingo's confession, members of the battalion of Naval Riflers anonymously declared that they had committed human rights violations, and in May 1996, Navy captain (ret.) Jorge Tróccoli, who was a student of anthropology at the time, recognized that the armed forces "treated their enemies inhumanly." Although he claimed that he did not participate in the worst acts of torture and assassination, he had fought that war and wanted to come clean.[33] His statement led the student assembly of the Faculty of Anthropology of UDELAR University to expel him. Also, in May 1996 Senator Rafael Michelini accused the armed forces of the assassination of his father. He was the son of Senator Zelmar Michelini, who had been abducted and murdered twenty years earlier while in exile in Argentina, together with Héctor Gutiérrez Ruiz, the former speaker of the lower house of the Uruguayan Parliament, and two other exiles. Calling for an inquiry into the strategy of transnational repression, on May 20, 1996, Rafael Michelini organized a march in remembrance of the disappeared. The initiative, supported by politicians, union leaders, religious and social organizations, human rights groups, and the families of the disappeared and the victims of military repression, was attended by as many as fifty thousand people. Planned to occur in total solemn silence, the march involved some incidents led by radical participants, called to keep silence, and by supporters of the armed forces, buffeted by the multitudes. The Uruguayan parliament also organized an act honoring the memory of the killed parliamentarians. The president ignored the date, unwilling to reopen the debate supposedly closed by the 1989 referendum. For many more years, May 20 was a day of remembrance, with a massive annual march of citizens taking place in demand of truth and accountability.

There were multiple indications of the regional character of the problem and the inability of individual states to confine developments to their own national territory in order to avoid a transnational spillover. The Letelier case in particular called attention to the activities of the Chilean intelligence agency (DINA) outside Chile. In mid-1995, the Chilean courts issued the final verdict in the case, condemning the founder and commander of the DINA, retired General Manuel Contreras, and his secondin-command, Brigadier Pedro Espinoza, to seven and six years of imprisonment, respectively. The DINA had assassinated Orlando Letelier and his secretary by planting a bomb in Washington, DC, in the mid-1970s. Due to US pressure, Chile's 1978 preemptive amnesty law had left that case beyond its purview. Contreras's refusal to comply with the country's Supreme Court's final verdict and gracefully enter prison to serve his time generated a crisis involving the armed forces, solved only after five months of resistance.

One particular case revealed that post-dictatorial collaboration between the Chilean and the Uruguayan security forces continued behind the backs of the democratically elected governments. Chemical engineer Eugenio Berríos Segafredo, an agent of Chilean intelligence, was requested by Chilean courts to testify on the assassination of Letelier. Berríos disappeared from Chile in late 1992. A year later, a man claiming to be Berríos complained in a police station in Uruguay that he was being held against his will in a nearby house by Uruguayan and Chilean personnel. After leaving the station, the man was never seen again. Four years later, in March 1995, a forensic doctor identified the remains of a body on the Uruguayan coast as Berríos. Soon thereafter, a statement by a former DINA officer, Enrique Arancibia, around the forthcoming twentieth anniversary of the military takeover in Argentina, added tensions. Arancibia declared that he was the perpetrator of the 1974 bombing that killed the exiled former commander of the Chilean armed forces, retired General Carlos Prats, and his wife in Buenos Aires. The admission implicated Chilean officers, precipitated a judicial inquiry in Argentina, and generated pressures against amnesty in Chile.

Debates also ensued over the disappearance and probable assassination of more than one hundred members of the Uruguayan opposition residing in

Argentina, and the disappearance and assassination of Argentine members of the opposition by the military in Uruguay. Since the annihilation of the victims was a common feature of the pattern of transnational repressive coordination during the dictatorships and was carried out regardless of national borders and jurisdictions, whenever the issue of the disappearances, tortures, and assassinations became a focus of attention and debate in one of these countries, it emerged in the other societies as well. Almost immediately, revelations in one society reverberated in the others also, since they could put pressure on the armed and security forces, which maintained a wall of silence and refused to provide civilians with the knowledge they requested on the fate of the disappeared. The high commands had rejected the possibility of opening their records and systematically denied having any information about the disappeared. In the context of the post-authoritarian transition, the members of the security establishments found themselves partners in an unwritten pact of silence. Yet at the same time, once fractures appeared in that formidable wall of military silence in one country, the issue spread to the others, thus reopening pressures until new mechanisms of transitional justice would eventually be adopted years after the resumption of civilian democratic rule.

The End of Impunity: Domestic and Transnational Factors

The interface of domestic and transnational factors continued to reverberate as these societies moved hesitantly and in tortuous ways to end the halo of impunity that laws promulgated during the dictatorships or in the transition had enshrined. In Paraguay, for example, it took until 2003 to establish a truth commission. Since 1989, political and social sectors, as well as human rights organizations and victims of the dictatorship, have attempted to convince authorities of the need to establish such a commission, as done in neighboring countries that suffered similar legacies of human rights violations. In 1992, several members of Congress put forward a project-law in that sense, but it stalled for three years, until its approval in November 1995. Then, President Juan Carlos Wasmosy suspended its implementation and appealed its constitutionality before the Supreme Court, which blocked it in July 1998.[34] The initiative regained momentum years later, when human rights organizations coordinated their actions in the Mesa Iniciativa Memoria y Archivo de la Represión, composed mainly of multiple NGOs, with the cooperation of the Ministry of Justice and the Archive of Terror.[35] As they joined forces, these organizations prepared a draft that enabled a short legislative process toward the establishment of the Comisión de Verdad y Justicia (CVJ), whose members were nominated by President Nicanor Duarte in October 2003.

The truth commission was entrusted with the mandate to investigate human rights violations from 1954 to 2003, covering primarily, but not only, execution, extrajudicial imprisonment, torture, exile, and "other serious violations." The period to be covered comprised both the thirty-five years of Stroessner's rule as well as the first fifteen years of the transition. What enabled the CVJ to carry out an effective investigation was its composition, which consisted of a representative of the executive, a member of Parliament, four delegates nominated by the Committee of Victims of the Dictatorship, and three members nominated by human rights NGOs. A marked preponderance of civil society organizations and representatives of the victims gave them an absolute two-thirds majority of votes in decision-making, in marked contrast to many other truth commissions worldwide. Launched in August 2004, its mandate was extended until it prepared an extensive final report in 2008. Under the slogan "whoever forgets is doomed to re-enact the past" (*quien olvida, repite*), the CVJ organized several public audiences "as spaces of awareness, information and recovery of collective memory" in Paraguay and also abroad, primarily in San Juan Bautista de las Misiones, Posadas, and Buenos Aires, Argentina, where a massive community of Paraguayans resided. The hearing held in Buenos Aires took place at the federal Congress, where exiled Paraguayans, as well as Argentines, Uruguayans, and Chileans, who had been persecuted in the framework of Operation Condor gave testimony.[36]

The report of the CVJ identified 20,862 direct victims, 19,862 of whom suffered arbitrary arrest and were illegally kept in prison. Unlike neighboring Argentina, Paraguay did not intend to hide that it had repressive detention centers. Of the individuals arrested, 18,772 were tortured, 59 were subjected to extrajudicial execution, 336 were "disappeared," and 3,460 were exiled. Of those disappeared, 220 people were disappeared in Paraguay, 102 in Argentina, and 7 in Brazil. In addition, the commission documented 41 executions in Paraguay, 17 in Argentine territory, and 1 in Uruguay.[37] The report devoted a special section to political exile, characterizing it as part of "state policy for reducing and eliminating political opponents" and stressing the lack of legal protection for Paraguayan exiles in the neighboring countries "that did not welcome them as refugees or grant them asylum." Indeed, unlike in other destinations, most Paraguayan exiles in Argentina did not enjoy the protection of the UNHCR.[38]

Another case of protracted truth and accountability, in which domestic and transnational factors converged to bring about the change, was Uruguay. Uruguay stands out among the various cases as it managed, through ongoing debates and demands by sectors of society, to come to grips with the legacy of authoritarianism in a way that restored legal accountability, truth, and justice as basic to core national principles.

As Uruguayan citizens participated in the presidential elections of October 25, 2009, they were also called to vote on a plebiscite on the possible cancellation of the Law of Expiry (1986). The plebiscite, which took place more than twenty years after the initial referendum of April 1989, could have ended the legal immunity of members of the armed forces who were responsible for human rights violations and disappearances during the days of the Cold War. In 2006, human rights lawyers, legislators, and judges established the National Coordinating Council for the Invalidation of the Law of Expiry. To collect the needed 251,847 signatures to try to force the plebiscite, the council launched a high-profile campaign in Montevideo in September 2007. The campaign needed to add the signatures of at least 10 percent of the voters and present the request at the High Electoral Tribunal before May 24, 2009. In February 2009, amid an intense debate, the Congress, with a majority of MPs from the leftist Frente Amplio, gave a boost to the campaign by declaring that the law was unconstitutional. The National Party, in particular the Herrera faction led by former President Luis Lacalle, accused the government of being antidemocratic for its decision to ignore the validity of the popular referendum of April 1989.[39] Having received the support of popular artists and public cultural figures, the council managed to collect more than 361,000 signatures. With the required number ratified, the launching of the plebiscite was held with the presidential elections. Days before, the Supreme Court had also declared the Law of Expiry unconstitutional as applied in a specific case,[40] providing a new boost to the demand for everlasting justice. The 2009 proposal to annul the immunity law failed to pass, receiving 48 percent of the vote and producing a result similar to that of the referendum convened twenty years earlier. While these figures revealed once again that society was still divided on the issue, the sense of legal closure was ephemeral and unraveled shortly thereafter.

This was a moment of sad awakening, yet a new push started transnationally and eventually brought the ruling coalition of the Frente Amplio to abide by the demands of some of its popular base and attempt once more to derogate the Law of Expiry through parliamentarian means. The move was attempted in May 2011, when a project-law declaring its unconstitutionality was planned to be passed by both chambers of Parliament. Such a move by the ruling coalition was designed to find a legal formula to undo the Law of Expiry, in a rather last-minute attempt to perhaps avoid condemnation by the Inter-American Court of Justice (IACJ).

These pressures derived from a protest filed by Juan Gelman and his granddaughter, María Macarena, with the Inter-American Commission of Human Rights (CIDH) in 2006. Their protest came after failed attempts in Uruguayan courts to force the state to investigate the events and find those responsible for the abduction and disappearance of Gelman's son Marcelo and daughter-in-law, María Claudia Iruretagoyena. Both had been abducted in Argentina in 1976 and transferred to Uruguay, where they were assassinated, María Claudia after giving birth. The Law of Expiry, claimed by the plaintiffs to be the main obstacle to making progress in the case, was called into question due to its incompatibility with the legal principles of the Inter-American System, which had been recognized and ratified by the Uruguayan state.[41] Asked to explain this contradiction, the Uruguayan government challenged the idea of retroactively applying legal standards and advocated for the sovereignty of Uruguayans' decision to uphold the Law of Expiry twice in popular votes called upon according to the constitution. Due to what the CIDH considered the lack of satisfactory answers by the Uruguayan government over the course of four years on the issue of congruity of the Law of Expiry with the international legal provisions of the Inter-American System, the CIDH passed the case to the IACJ.

By 2010, the IACJ had already condemned Brazil for its lack of progress in the investigation and legal prosecution of those responsible for the assassinations and the disappearances of the remains of the members of the guerrillas of Araguaia, an armed Communist group whose members were killed in 1972–75 and whose remains were disposed of without a trace.[42] Perhaps foreseeing a similar condemnation by the IACJ, the Uruguayan minister of foreign affairs drove the government and its ruling coalition to attempt a parliamentarian derogation of the Law of Expiry through the mechanism of an interpretive law. The lower chamber of deputies approved the project, with the support of fifty out of eighty representatives, in November 2010. Yet the project seemed stalled in the Senate, due to the Frente Amplio only having a slight majority in the chamber and the reluctance of three of its senators, among them Eleuterio Fernández Huidobro, to overturn popular decisions by parliamentary votes.[43] After the Frente Amplio coalition decided to force its internal factions to abide by the decision of its plenary in March 2011, the project-law drafted by former Socialist senator José Korzeniak was approved almost unanimously. Nonetheless, the Uruguayan Senate and Chamber of Deputies failed to approve the project-law declaring the unconstitutionality of the Law of Expiry in May 2011, nearly a quarter century after its original promulgation. A political conundrum was generated that indicated a lose-lose situation for the ruling coalition. Approving the project-law would have implied a disregard for the decisions the Uruguayan people taken in 1989 and 2009, decisions the Frente Amplio had traditionally cherished, for example during popular votes that prevented policies of privatization in 1992 and 2003. Yet failing to approve it in spite of heavy pressures was a clear sign of the unraveling of consensus and lack of binding leadership on this issue within the ruling coalition, which observers presumed might involve a political price to be paid by the Frente Amplio.[44]

All these societies have been unable to avoid confrontation with their past legacies of human rights violations. Often that confrontation has involved a decades-long process of unraveling the original pattern of transitional justice adopted to steer the return to democracy. The intense and yet intermittent progress toward an elaboration of historical truth and accountability for past wrongs involved overcoming fears that the agenda of transitional justice might threaten institutional stability. It also implied discarding the early ideological visions of political activists who had endured prison abuse and torture as the price paid for their political struggle, while the security forces claimed their actions were performed in efforts to safeguard their country's institutions and "national soul." Much changed after the return of democracy. Reparations and compensation were granted; the issue of the return of exiles was undertaken; missing children were located, and some of them assumed the identity of their biological parents, who were killed or forcibly disappeared during the dictatorship; civil lawsuits were opened against the state for its failure to protect citizens; many human rights NGOs and associations of victims and relatives of victims pursued protests and put forward demands for truth and justice; official commissions of truth were established; spaces were claimed as sites of memory; and finally, criminal trials were opened against some of the most notorious repressors and prominent civilian officials who held key state positions during the dictatorship.

Progress has resulted from the combined effects of multiple factors. First are the promoters and agents of remembrance, including the children and relatives of victims, human rights organizations, and intellectuals. Next are the rising pressures of transnational networks committed to the protection of human rights and appealing to the inter-American bodies. Shifts in the political coalitions acceding to power, which are no longer prisoners of past agreements, have been crucial. Revelations about the transnational coordination of the repression, as the crises that reverberated in the neighboring countries loomed large. These converging forces could react in stronger ways to the demands of truth and accountability projected repeatedly by various sectors of civil society through national and transnational networks and international organizations.

One of the crucial issues that restored democracies must address is how to reconcile citizens' personal security and public coexistence with respect for human rights. It seems that the greater the tensions generated around the socioeconomic gap and the larger the unmet needs of the population, along with the growth in crime and everyday violence, the more difficult it is to solve the dilemmas and ambiguities generated in this domain of human rights. Under such circumstances, social sectors concerned with criminality and public insecurity expect police forces to protect them with the same tough hand and expectations of order that prevailed in the period of authoritarian repression, albeit now targeting marginal and criminal sectors rather than political activists. Dealing with these dilemmas and ambiguities may be easier if a society can rely on strong mechanisms to prevent and condemn acts of abuse of authority. It is in this context that head-on confrontation with the legacy of authoritarianism can be assumed to help reduce the danger of impunity in contemporary society, in opposition to providing excuses for those who may commit crimes against humanity for the sake of social control. Some of these societies have taken important steps toward reshaping collective memory and overcoming attempts to move unconsciously into the future. Overall, progress has been made in overcoming the deadlock on the demands for truth and justice and dealing with the heinous human rights violations committed in the name of the social and political order. Moreover, the multiplicity of avenues opened while promoting such recognition seems to have contributed a wide understanding of the relevance of institutional accountability and the importance of human rights.

8

The Crystallization and Erosion
of Transnational Solidarity

Chavismo and the Nuestramerican Rhetoric and Practice

with Daniel F. Wajner

The election of Hugo Chávez to the Venezuelan presidency in 1998 initiated the Pink Tide, a fifteen-year-turn toward center-Left and eft-wing governments along with social and political movements that strayed from the neoliberal model adopted by Latin American democracies in the 1990s. Under the impact of Chavismo, a transnational notion once again came to play an aggregative and mobilizing role in many Latin American societies. Known as Nuestramérica or Our America, the narrative has alluded to major parts of the Americas taking ownership of themselves, in defiance of Global North forces and interests. The notion soon became part of the political vocabulary of presidents, trade union activists, artists, intellectuals, journalists, teachers, and others committed to the idea of a Great Fatherland or Patria Grande. There were calls for "the peoples of Our America" to mobilize and for "the governments of Our America" to take action.[1] Likewise, acclaim abounded for Hugo Chávez, the Commander of Nuestramérica, the defender of the "integrity of Nuestramerican territory," and the leader who planned its future and worked to strengthen its unity.[2] Cultural centers, foundations, literary and artistic contests, radio and television programs, blogs, Facebook sites, and massive hashtags on Twitter, carried the name "NuestrAmérica."

This massive and systematic use of the concept of Our America as a discursive strategy that legitimized political positioning and policymaking grew exponentially with the crystallization of Chavismo.[3] It reached strategic salience at the extraordinary Summit of Maracay in July 2009, when the regional organization until then called the Bolivarian Alternative for the Americas (ALBA) was renamed the Alianza Bolivariana para los Pueblos de Nuestra América— Tratado de Comercio de los Pueblos (Bolivarian Alliance for the Peoples of Our America-People's Trade Treaty [ALBA-TCP]).[4] Given the existence of the multiple national and regionalist agendas, the call for unity and solidarity of all Latin Americans conceived of the subsuming of many disparate ideological,

Transnational Perspectives on Latin America. Luis Roniger, Oxford University Press. © Oxford University Press 2022.
DOI: 10.1093/oso/9780197605318.003.0009

geographic, or cultural identities under one conceptual umbrella and organizational framework. Still, despite the rhetoric of social inclusivity and regional integration, the project remained a top-down enterprise premised on the convergence of interstate preferences. After the charismatic Chávez passed away and Venezuela could no longer pull together its transnational commitments, the project faltered, with unforeseen consequences for its promoters, as some of these movements turned against the Chavista governments themselves, demanding greater rights and protesting the lack of autonomy with respect to the centers of power.

The Pink Tide in Latin America

The cycle of democratization in the 1980s coincided with a protracted recession and an economic downturn, a trend that received the label "Lost Decade" for South American societies. Economic stagnation, foreign indebtedness, and a drop in the prices of commodities led to crises, the discrediting of previous economic models, and willingness to adopt the neoliberal policies advised by the Washington Consensus. These policies were set as "conditionalities" by the global financial organizations—primarily the IMF and the World Bank—to renegotiate the huge debt of the South American countries. Among the policy directions were the need to control inflation, attain monetary stability, liberalize the markets, and restrain economic demands on the state, for example on the part of labor movements. The means were privatization; the reduction of the state's role in regulation of the markets; the reduction of state employment and social welfare; and in cases such as Argentina in the 1990s, pegging the local currency to the dollar, thus attaining short-term stability and a bonanza, even if the long-term consequences would be a major economic disaster, as seen there in 2001.

The wave of structural adjustment, deregulation, liberalization, and privatization of state companies produced modest growth in 1990–97, but it also resulted in a steep rise in unemployment, exponential growth in the informal sectors of the economy, and the deepening of the already wide inequality gap. Deregulation of the economy brought some release of bureaucratic controls that was beneficial in areas such as telecommunications, although it resulted in major failings in other domains, such as the quality of maintenance, the rising cost of utilities, and a decline in food standards and health safety.[5]

These problems would soon result in major social and economic crises that would prove to be explosive politically. The growing socioeconomic gaps were felt as far as Mexico, when the country was about to join NAFTA, the North American Free Trade Agreement, and the Zapatista movement made its initial public appearance to challenge the agreement on January 1, 1994. The state of Chiapas challenged the neoliberal notion of trickling down of wealth, as it was then one of the richest Mexican states in the federation in term of its resources yet one of the most unequal in term of income distribution. At that time, on the eve of a presidential election, the Mexican political system was also discredited by the assassinations of two key figures of the ruling Partido Revolucionario Institucional, known as the PRI party: its presidential candidate, Luis Donaldo Colosio, and its secretary general, José Francisco Ruiz Massieu.[6] These homicides were indications of the deep internal crisis of the Mexican economic and political system. Indeed, the election of Vicente Fox, the candidate of the Partido Acción Nacional (PAN) as president in 2000 ended seven decades of PRI's one-party dominant regime.

In Venezuela, too, by the 1990s failing economic policies and perceived state corruption brought the two-party political system into crisis. A 1992 coup led by Colonel Hugo Chávez against the administration of veteran president Carlos Andrés Pérez of the Acción Democrática party failed, landing Chávez in prison. Yet by 1997 Chávez had created a new movement, the Fifth Republic Movement, which helped him be elected to the presidency a year later; he led the country until his death in 2013.

Chávez's rise to power in Venezuela was followed by a series of electoral victories of center-Left and leftist candidates in many South and Central American countries. Among these victorious candidates were Luiz Inácio Lula da Silva (2003–10) in Brazil, followed by Dilma Rousseff of the same PT (Partido dos Trabalhadores) party until her impeachment in August 2016; Néstor Kirchner (2003–07) and Cristina Fernández de Kirchner (2007–15) in Argentina; Tabaré Vazquez (2005–10) and José Pepe Mujica (2010–15) in Uruguay; Evo Morales (2006–19) in Bolivia; Rafael Correa (2007–17) in Ecuador; Daniel Ortega, who returned to power in Nicaragua in 2007 and consolidated his rule after two more successful campaigns in 2011 and 2016; and Mauricio Funes (2009–14) of the FMLN, ending twenty years of ARENA (Alianza Republicana Nacionalista) rule in El Salvador.[7]

With this regional shift, a process of reorganizing the existing regional integration frameworks started, complemented by the creation of new regional organizations that adopted the discourse of Nuestramerican solidarity. In parallel to the intergovernmental cooperation that was destined to strengthen or co-opt political and ideological allies, both the remodeling of the integration frameworks and the emergence of new organizations responded to Chávez's interest in reaching a transnational power of convocation. More than the idea of an idyllic future, Chávez constantly appealed to the re-edition of a visionary past, evident in his ample references to the figure of Simón Bolívar and his legacy, shaped in the early nineteenth century yet retaining its actuality in the twenty-first century.[8] Thus, Chavista media espoused the idea of revolutionary solidarity and the vision of the Americas becoming independent of foreign control as the center of the Chavista project, the so-called Bolivarian Revolution.[9]

In a sense, Chavismo enacted a preexisting transnational identity to attain legitimacy at the continental level. It recreated and transnationally reproduced a series of narratives, practices, and political demands that had waned after the 1960s and 1970s from the center of political agendas and public spheres, or at least did not keep their earlier momentum. The Chavista discourse proclaimed a renewed commitment to shared transnational bonds and attempted to mobilize them at the popular level, leading for instance to the strengthening of indigenous and African American movements as well as global ties within the framework of networks linked around notions such as "Global South," "the Third World," and "twenty-first-century socialism."

Such a strategy relied on historical legacies with deep popular appeal. Moreover, Chavismo combined a strong transnational discursive impetus with the use of oil revenues to sustain social and political movements that would support it. The influence of Chavismo was due not just to its discursive rhetoric, but also to its altruistic promotion of regional integration. Assuming a revisionist attitude toward the neoliberal policies dictated by the Washington Consensus that prevailed in the 1990s, and under the cover of a narrative with strong emphasis on transnational unity, Chávez made available some of the profits from the sale of oil crude—popularly known as "petrodollars"—for regional targets. In this sense, Chavismo not only called for the implementation of a vision of regional integration; it was also willing to assume the costs that such a project implied. Specifically, one of the main criticisms of pivot countries (Brazil, Argentina, and Mexico) was their inability or unwillingness to translate their potential regional leadership into initiatives supported by substantive resources.[10] The perception that, unlike those countries or the United States and the European Union, Venezuela was certainly willing to give up resources in a direct and flexible way, was a powerful incentive for other forces in the Americas to join, or at least tolerate, the advance of Chavismo. Thus, regardless of whether the allied movements endorsed transnational solidarity based on ideological convictions or as a tactical tool, its use generated and reinforced a community of meaning and a shared imaginary among broad sectors, affecting political dynamics on a regional scale.[11]

Chavismo and Nuestramerican Regionalism

Breaking with the foundations of cooperation within the framework of the so-called open regionalism, Chavismo influenced previously existing regionalist logics by conceiving of ALBA in 2001 and officially creating it in 2004.[12] It is worth mentioning that until the mid-2000s, Venezuela continued to be part of the free trade area known as the Andean Community of Nations (CAN). Only in April 2006 did it withdraw from CAN, in tandem with the consolidation of the "turn to the left" that started in 2003.[13]

Claiming that the Free Trade Area of the Americas (FTAA; Área de Libre Comercio de las Américas, more widely known by its acronym, ALCA) would be a revamped version of a pan-Americanist project geared to retaining US hemispheric hegemony and profits, Chavismo created imbued ALBA with a different transnational vision. ALBA was thus born as an alliance of countries with ideological affinity under a clear program opposing the ALCA project promoted by the United States. Years later that alliance included Bolivia, Cuba, Ecuador, Nicaragua, and various Caribbean island states. Politics took center stage, and the commercial component was relegated to a subsidiary role.[14] ALBA attempted to operate a transition from an agenda of neoliberal integration guided by free markets to an alternative project, in which countries conceive of regional cooperation under the aegis of states and the mobilization of social support networks. The transition aimed to lead to new practices and institutions, in a process that different academics have called posthegemonic or postliberal regionalism.[15]

The key event that consecrated Chavista leadership in regional politics occurred at the Fourth Summit of the Americas in Mar del Plata on November 4–5, 2005. There, Chávez achieved a diplomatic success in preventing the summit from reaching a regional agreement on the free trade agreement (ALCA). To do this, Chavista leaders and activists issued calls to save Nuestramérica. Mobilizing on a massive scale and launching powerful media campaigns, they convinced many people of the need to halt the US plan, which they identified with a plot of the Global North and its domestic allies.[16] Unsurprisingly, with public opinion tilted against the FTAA, once at the negotiating table in Mar del Plata, only the United States, Mexico, Panama, and Trinidad and Tobago showed a clear disposition to advance toward the agreement, while Venezuela, along with the four members of MERCOSUR (Mercado Común del Sur, i.e. Southern Common Market), exerted strong opposition. The attempt to isolate the Venezuelan government failed, and the tone imposed by the anti-FTAA coalition generated deterrence in many other countries in the region that, even if they might be interested in the free trade agreement (FTA), chose to remain silent. Although the issue remained on the agenda for future meetings when "the necessary conditions" would be in place, in practice the lack of concrete deadlines signaled the death of the FTAA.[17] In the words of Chávez himself, "[E]ach of us came here with a shovel, yes sir, a shovel for the gravedigger, because Mar del Plata is the grave of the FTAA."[18]

Furthermore, Mar del Plata impressed the popular imagination with the idea of the victory of resistance by the Americas "against the Empire" and that the FTAA did not go through due to "the strong will of the Peoples." In short, the famous slogan of Chávez, within the framework of the anti-summit, of throwing "the FTAA . . . to hell!,"[19] represented the closure of one stage and the beginning of a new one. Chavismo viewed the defeat of ALCA as a sign that Venezuela was no longer isolated at international summits, as had previously been the case. Hence, the anniversary of the defeat of that agreement became a commemorative anniversary for the movements associated with the Chavista project.[20]

The Chavista strategy then moved to a second stage of attempting to transform the existing integration frameworks of South America, and, if that were not possible, to create new regional frameworks allowing a convergence with other regional powers such as Brazil, Argentina, and then Mexico. In other words, Chávez conceived a mosaic of regional, subregional, bilateral, and interregional projects, a conglomerate made "to measure" that would allow a reconfiguration of Nuestramérica through multiple alliances.[21] Chavismo was able to try this strategy because it benefited from the coming to power of related political forces in the other Latin American states. In 2006 Evo Morales became Bolivia's president, followed a year later by Daniel Ortega in Nicaragua and Rafael Correa in Ecuador. Those countries would then join ALBA, along with several Caribbean islands such as Dominica, Antigua and Barbuda, and Saint Vincent and the Grenadines.

Given their inability to transform the CAN, where they met fierce opposition from governments that supported pan-Americanism and the signing of FTAs with the United States, in April 2006 Colombia and Peru announced their withdrawal from CAN and their intention to join MERCOSUR.[22] Venezuela also confirmed that it was withdrawing from the G3, which starting in 1989 had brought together Venezuela, Mexico, and Colombia. In July 2006, Venezuela signed the protocol for accession to MERCOSUR, although the cumbersome ratification process was only completed in 2012, a result of Venezuela's estrangement from Paraguay due to the overthrow of President Fernando Lugo.[23] The Venezuelan presence in MERCOSUR fundamentally strengthened the discourse of social and cultural integration in the region, as well as the projection of a block of nations supporting a model of "productive integration."[24]

The second strategy, that of creating new regional frameworks, was launched at the III South American Summit in Cuzco in December 2004, with the creation of the South American Community of Nations. The impetus came from Brazil, with Venezuelan collaboration. Initially launched under the acronym CSN, changed later to CASA, the regional organization would refound itself as UNASUR at the summits of Isla de Margarita (2007) and Brasilia (2008). Intended to accentuate subregional integration, the project focused mainly on infrastructure, financing, and energy. At the same time, it sought to assume importance in the realms of politics and security, domains that until then had remained within the OAS, whereas UNASUR shifted to exclude the United States and Canada.[25]

The external reaction to the domino effect of this organizational explosion was not long in coming, warning of possible Venezuelan hegemony at the transnational level, which to a certain extent fired back the Chavista discourse. After the failure of the FTAA in 2005, the United States tried to counterattack through the selection of Latin American countries with which it would deepen its bilateral cooperation through FTAs, trying to create a circle of countries that would weaken Chavismo.[26] This strategy was called "ALCA light," or *alquitas*, in the words of Chávez himself. In South America, this strategy was successful with Colombia, Panama, Costa Rica, and Peru; in other cases, however, the United States would lose the battle.

Uruguay's case is paradigmatic of a widespread reaction to the possibility of reaching an FTA with the United States. Throughout 2006, there was a deep ideological debate in the country about the eventual signing of an FTA. In 2005, the Frente Amplio, an umbrella coalition of leftist parties, came to power for the first time. Some of its leaders, such as the president and the minister of economy, adhered to a moderate Left, while others were closer to a more radical Left. The former considered that there was popular consensus for supporting an FTA, because in their opinion, an FTA could improve conditions for Uruguayan products to access global markets. For others, however, negotiating an FTA with the United States would have represented a betrayal of Latin American integration and a surrender of the anti-imperialist struggle.[27] In this situation, sectors of civil society that were collaborating with Chavista platforms put great pressure on the ruling coalition. Finally, the Uruguayan government rejected the FTA, although it accepted the possibility of signing a Framework Agreement for Trade and Investment (TIFA; Acuerdo Marco de Comercio e Inversión). As this was a purely economic agreement that did not address the political dimension of the FTA, the government of the Frente Amplio estimated that it would carry lower political costs and not entail losing legitimacy among the party bases and the intellectual class. This maneuver by Chávez and his supporters highlighted the limitations of the US capacity to implement an effective counterstrategy of foreign policy.[28]

As leader of the Iberoamerican project, Spain collided with Chavismo. With the strengthening of the Iberoamerican Community of Nations (Comunidad Iberoamericana de Naciones), relying on the Iberoamerican Summits, held since 1991, and on an active Iberoamerican General Secretariat (SEGIB) since 2005, Spain sought to exert renewed influence in Latin America. Seeking to strengthen an alternate transnational discourse, SEGIB promoted Iberoamericanism, a vision close to Hispanic Americanism but also including Portugal and Brazil.[29]

The frontal collision became most visible when King Juan Carlos I intervened in the XVII Iberoamerican Summit of Heads of States in November 2007, telling Chávez to "shut up" in a resounding way. The wave of reactions, messages, and countermessages generated by that acrimonious exchange revealed that many defended Chávez and censured Spain as the carrier of a colonialist vision of leadership.

In any case, toward the end of the first decade of the twenty-first century, Chávez decided to pursue his own strategic path of regionally organizing beyond ALBA, a framework that had not managed to expand its membership in a notable way. Chávez could not assume a leading role through existing organizations such as the OAS or the Iberoamerican Community of Nations, sponsored and led by extraregional powers, or through MERCOSUR or UNASUR, which were more limited geographically and where from the beginning there had been contesting regional leaderships such as Brazil's. He then decided to establish a new framework of regional integration.[30]

In this third stage, Chavismo launched the Community of Latin American and Caribbean States (Comunidad de Estados Latinoamericanos y Caribeños; CELAC), as heir to the Rio Group and the Summit of Latin America and the Caribbean (CALC). CELAC was designed to promote regional integration and development, projecting its voice at the highest political level and incorporating strong social bases. The control that the Venezuelan leader had over the Caribbean Community (CARICOM), where he had half the votes, assured Chavismo a greater weight in the decisions adopted in that framework.[31] He also projected the regionalist boom through thematic interstate projects, generally linked to development areas promoted by UNASUR. The emblematic projects included the Banco del Alba and Banco del Sur, as well as the Trans-Caribbean Gas Pipeline, the Gasoducto del Sur, and new overlapping cooperation frameworks for gas and oil issues such as the Group of 10 (G-10), all of which were organizational efforts aimed at achieving financial and energy autonomy in the region.

However, the initiative began to show the costs of all these overlapping regionalist offensives. Soon there would be a progressive return to focusing on regional and interregional trade agreements.[32] Beginning in April 2011, the Pacific Alliance (Alianza del Pacífico) developed as a bloc that grouped Chile, Colombia, Peru, and Mexico, all countries that had signed FTAs with the United States. For Chavismo, that initiative was a conspiratorial counterweight that originated with the neoliberal bloc. The Chavistas saw it as a conservative counteroffensive that appealed to the recomposition of the hegemonic presence of the United States.[33] Another sign of a decline in Chávez's momentum was the growing calls to resume negotiations with the European Union, from both CAN and SICA (Sistema de la Integración Centroamericana, i.e. Centroamerican Integration System) in 2012, and repeated by MERCOSUR in multiple instances.[34] In 2014–15 the two lines approached a collision, as electoral shifts to the center-Right took place in Guatemala, Argentina, Panama, and Honduras, and as serious institutional and economic crises emerged in Brazil, Venezuela, and Nicaragua, countries ruled by the Left.

Particularly salient signs of erosion were the massive protests against Daniel Ortega in his fourth presidential term. The government had increasingly concentrated political and economic power, led by Rosario Murillo, his wife and vice president, their family, close allies, and supporters. With the elimination of single five-year presidential terms by the Supreme Court of Nicaragua in 2009, the elimination of Ortega's main political opponents by rulings of the courts staffed by his supporters, and his control of public funds, Ortega had won a third consecutive election in 2016, but his policies were being hotly contested by April 2018. Unwilling to accommodate demands of systemic liberalization for weeks, the regime reacted by forcefully repressing protestors, leaving more than two hundred dead and many more wounded. Social sectors that had once supported the FSLN's revolutionary leader became disenchanted with the revamped Ortega's authoritarian rule and probusiness policies. As these sectors joined the protest, the government branded them as terrorists willing to destroy Nicaraguan society and resorted to employing paramilitary groups, progovernment mobs, and police, who used live ammunition and mass imprisonment to quell the protest. Since then, the intercession of the Catholic Church has enabled some negotiations, but these have not diminished the contradictions of the regime allied to Chavismo in the Americas, which has clung to power by any means despite major citizen disenchantment.[35]

Subaltern Sectors, Ethnodevelopment, and Shifts in the Identity Agenda

Another important aspect of Chavismo's rise and erosion was the strengthening of the identity agenda of subaltern sectors. On many occasions, the question arose of to what extent Chavismo opened an agenda for the empowerment of ethnic and racial identities and whether the strengthening of ideological-cultural dynamics led to a recognition of subaltern sectors at the state and transnational levels. That is to say, did Chavismo function as a promoter of new norms, or at least as the resonator of such identities? Likewise, even if Chavismo promoted the process, we must ask ourselves about the results of such empowerment once the governments that at first sponsored a politics of identity then tried to control and even curtail the process.

The idea of "popular power" was at the center of Chavismo's earlier pronouncements and became even more pronounced after the middle classes abandoned Chávez and he resorted to mobilizing the Venezuelan popular sectors.[36] The important role that Chavismo entrusted to the Bolivarian Circles, not only for organizational and electoral purposes, but also around the construction of collective identities and agglutination of popular interests, also extrapolated them abroad with the promotion of grassroots activism in local communities. Hence the Chavista experience generated a certain common denominator with other popular mobilizations such as that of the Mexican Zapatistas, the Bolivian *cocaleros*, the Brazilian landless, and the Argentine *piqueteros*. Chávez's charismatic and defiant leadership played a key role in inspiring these varied mobilizations, based on mass protest and a range of heterodox and often zigzagging discourses.[37] Likewise, the exaltation by Chávez of the "will of the people" against the "oligarchy," of national interests against foreigners, and of a moral community facing a conspiracy, reproduced and enhanced the same discursive patterns.[38]

Chavismo centralized a call for the peoples of the Americas to mobilize regionally against the FTAs. As it galvanized the opposition to the creation of the FTAA, it shaped a transnational coalition of civil society organizations, which included unions, social and indigenous movements, environmental organizations, and others, coordinated and mobilized under the umbrella of a hemispheric social alliance. From that moment, Chavismo stressed that the social response to the FTAA summit—what became known as the "Anti-Summit"—was an emblematic victory of *los pueblos* of the Americas. Along with Chávez and Kirchner, Evo Morales, then still an indigenous leader, also participated in early November 2005 at the event at the Mar del Plata World Cup Stadium. The final demonstration was massive and supported by key popular figures, including, among others, soccer player Diego Armando Maradona; Nobel Prize winner Adolfo Pérez Esquivel; leaders of the Mothers of Plaza de Mayo; famous artists such as Silvio Rodríguez and Manu Chao; and hundreds of members of social, union, and student movements in the region. This kind of social mobilization was a recurring aspect of gatherings in Uruguay, Ecuador, Costa Rica, Colombia, and Peru. The fight against the FTAA and the FTAs produced regional joint work to prevent "domination over our lands" and support the hope that a new "integration of the peoples of Our America" would be possible. The fight against FTAs continued in later meetings such as the Anti-imperialist Summit of July 2013 and the massive 17th Latin American and Caribbean Student Congress in Nicaragua in August 2014.[39] On the other hand, as we have seen, Chavismo constantly appealed to Latin American unity and used references to the revolutionary and moral legacy of historically marginalized ethnic groups.[40]

For nearly five hundred years, markers of indigenous and Black ethnicity were subsumed under other collective identities, mainly social class and status. Ethnicity and race were continuously present, evident in daily encounters and in Native American and Afro-American rebellions, which instilled fear and met with repression. Whereas in the late nineteenth century, the extermination of indigenous populations was still the rule in reaction to mobilized subaltern populations, by the early twentieth century new strategies emerged to deal corporatively with the indigenous populations, primarily *indigenismo* and co-optation, in addition to continuing mechanisms of containment and repression.[41]

Decades later, starting in the late 1970s, both international and local forces pushed a new recognition of race and ethnicity. On the global scene, international conferences took place, among them a 1977 Geneva conference on indigenous populations in the Americas and a conference on ethnocide and ethnodevelopment in Latin America, held in Costa Rica in 1981, where delegates adopted a declaration on the inalienable right of indigenous peoples to self-determination. Around the same time, a UN working group on indigenous populations was established, and the UN appointed special rapporteurs, whose reports were discussed at the international body. Latin American countries also became major proponents and signatories of the International Labor Organization Convention 169 on the Rights of the Indigenous and Tribal Peoples (ILO C169 of 1989). Six years later, the UN declared its first indigenous decade. Moreover, a new recognition of the multicultural and pluri-ethnic character of states crystallized in the 1980s and the 1990s, as several Latin American countries drafted new constitutions, dismantling the uniform concept of citizenship that states expected to prevail until then.

This trend accelerated under the impact of several processes. One was the way localized struggles contributed to the emergence of a broader sense of ethnic identity. One examples is that of the Kayapó people and their allies, who opposed in 1989 a proposed hydroelectric project in Altamira, Brazil. Their campaign was so successful that they generated an international outcry that brought the World Bank to withdraw the planned funding of the dam project. This successful outcome energized many other indigenous communities in Brazil, particularly in the Amazonian basin. Most important was the impact on creating a sense of broader Indian identity, built on top of the more parochial identities that had separated one group from another. Activists from the Wauja, an Arawak-speaking group in the Xingu National Park of Northern Mato Grosso, created a cross-ethnic network of supporting representatives of Indian groups that in the past had fought against each other.[42] In Ecuador, cross-ethnic mobilization changed how indigenous identity was perceived, allowing it to become a tool for collective action. While in the past, self-identity had been severely stigmatized, once the Indians of the Ecuadorian highlands had protested the deterioration of agrarian conditions in the early 1990s and developmental projects that threatened their territories in the 2000s, a strong sense of self-value, solidarity, and purpose colored their ethnic identity. Ethnicity became a viable channel for advancing demands and gaining public recognition to an extent unknown in the past, as they confidently protested, stopped the delivery of produce to the towns, blocked highways, marched, and occupied metropolitan areas.[43]

Following the transitions to democracy in the 1980s and early 1990s, grievances by indigenous groups such as the Mapuche in Chile and various Maya communities in Mexico and Guatemala could no longer be treated as a matter of expediency and became a public issue in need of strategic treatment and intervention. The empowerment of marginal strata and groups in peripheral locations could thus become feasible in the framework of the principles of the new citizenship regimes and civil society politics. The full change was precipitated by a growth in the organizational capacity of the subaltern groups. The concrete paths of formation of such leadership differed from case to case. In Ecuador, for instance, , the state ,committed itself to bilingual education and approached the Indian communities with developmental programs in the 1980s, suggesting its willingness to negotiate some degree of territorial autonomy for the groups in the Amazonian region. In this way, the state granted legitimacy to the representatives of the indigenous peoples and recognized ethnicity as a viable focus for advancing demands in the public arena to an extent unknown in the past. In the 1990s and 2000s such official recognition generated forceful mobilizations to resist the neoliberal policies of privatization of public lands and forests that the new administrations moved to implement. In Bolivia, a political movement, the Kataristas, generated a new type of leadership able to transform ethnicity into a channel of popular mobilization and a source of pride and organizational strength. Beyond the concrete forms of such developments, ethnicity became a major force of collective mobilization throughout the region. Its importance derived from the radical critique it made of earlier models that for long had dominated the imagery of societies and public strategy of states.[44]

The process of ethnodevelopment and flourishing of ethnic consciousness was buttressed by a network of international organizations connected to ethnic entrepreneurs within the region. In some cases, Catholic organizations and networks were instrumental, as in the case of the Guaraníes of Bolivia, who organized themselves with the help of Jesuit priests. In others, exiled professionals were most active in providing international guidance and support, as in the case of the Guatemalans. International agencies such as the Inter-American Development Bank supported various projects launched by groups engaged in the reduction of poverty and the expansion of literacy. Human rights organizations were most instrumental during military repression and the civil wars. Following redemocratization the focus turned to, in addition to the defense of human rights, cultural survival and the protection of the environment. In this endeavor a wide gamut of NGOs and foundations in Europe, the United States, and Canada provided the financial means and organizational and symbolic influence that helped bring local groups to the attention of the media. In countries relying heavily on Western models of development and legitimacy, this global advocacy network granted support, respectability, and a sense of protection to groups that in the past had been defenseless and at the mercy of the repressive apparatus of the various national states.

Transnational organizations became increasingly involved with the problems facing Native American populations, among them the Indigenous People's Biodiversity Network, the Indigenous Knowledge Program, the Catholic Church, the World Council of Churches, the Amazon Coalition, the Legal Defense Fund, and Cultural Survival. A number of formal and informal regional networks have also developed, such as the Coordinating Body for Indigenous Organizations of the Amazonian Basin (COICA), the South American and Mesoamerican Indian Rights Center (SAIIC), Consejo Nacional Indio de Venezuela (CONIVE), and the Confederation of Indigenous Nationalities of Ecuador (CONAIE), to name just a few. The transnational indigenous advocacy network brought together indigenous and nonindigenous voices such as scholars, government officials, and environmentalist and other advocacy movement leaders.[45] The intersectionality of the issues buttressed such dynamics, as aptly described by historian Erick Langer regarding the environmental groups, which intertwined with indigenous groups in the 1990s, particularly at the 1992 Earth Summit in Rio de Janeiro on environmental issues:

> For environmental groups, the best way to call attention to the loss of wilderness in the Americas was to bring in Indians who represented the pristine way of life that was in congruence with the ecology of the forest where deforestation, mining and invasion by settlers created crisis conditions.[46]

Langer and other social scientists registered how NGOs concerned with environmental issues, such as the World Wildlife Foundation, the Sierra Club, Greenpeace, and similar preservation of forest environments, found logical allies among the indigenous peoples and at the same time supported the conservation of the culture and way of life of Native American groups. No less fundamental in bringing about these alliances was the parallel raising of consciousness triggered by the commemorations of the 500th anniversary of 1492 and the codification of indigenous rights in international law and the region's constitutional charters.[47]

Whereas most previous frameworks of regional integration and coordination, such as pan-Americanism, Iberoamericanism, and the South American project, had hitherto rather overlooked this dimension, with exceptions such as APRA and Katarismo, Chavismo allowed these groups to be involved in an organic way as part of its vision of Nuestramérica. That notion at the center of the Chavista program avoided significant identity contradictions while it highlighted the component of broad collective membership in a region where the populations of indigenous and Afro-American descent could feel part of it. In other words, Chávez knew how to create a message that incorporated inclusive identity allusions, linking social, transnational, regional, and global levels. The combined use of multiple, mutually reinforcing legacies was evident in Chávez's famous speech of September 11, 2008, when—following a crisis in US-Bolivian relations—he expelled the US ambassador from Venezuela. In that address, Chávez made explicit reference to Guaicaipurú and Túpac Amaru, indigenous figures of colonial times and symbols of resistance, along with mentions of Simón Bolívar, the Creole Liberator of Hispanic roots.[48]

In this, Chávez was consistent from the beginning of his rule. The "Bolivarian" Constitution, promulgated in 1999, recognized the rights of the indigenous peoples. In 2001, the ceremony of transferring Bolivar's remains to the national pantheon mentioned indigenous leaders of popular resistance. The figure of Guaicapurú also stood out in 2002 as the administration announced its decision to rename the celebration of October 12 the "Day of Indigenous Resistance" instead of the "Day of the [Hispanic] Race." Likewise, one of the so-called Bolivarian missions of Venezuela, whose expansion I expand on later, was named after Guaicaipurú.

References to Túpac Amaru abound among political movements, including those connected to Chavismo. At the center is the figure of Túpac Amaru II, a *mestizo* leader who led an indigenous mass uprising in the then Viceroyalty of Peru in the 1780s. Reverential remembrance of him has included recent and contemporary movements being named after him, such as Uruguayan Tupamaros, the Peruvian MRTA, and the Tupamaro Movement of Venezuela. In addition, the Túpac Amaru Neighborhood Organization (Organización Barrial Túpac Amaru; OBTA), has operated in the Argentine province of Jujuy since 2001. That organization is part of the indigenous movement that expanded its presence to seventeen provinces, with the support of the governments of Néstor and Cristina Kirchner in addition to Chavista funds. Together with other social organizations, the OBTA decided shortly after Chávez's death in 2013 to form a campaign command to support the presidential candidacy and term of Nicolás Maduro from Argentina.[49]

Chávez was not the only one to make use of a discourse that appealed to the indigenous sectors as part of a transnational Nuestramerican identity. Allies in Bolivia, Ecuador, and Nicaragua placed even more emphasis on indigenous identities, largely due to the high indigenous makeup of their countries. A few months after assuming the presidency, Morales gave a speech to a large crowd in which he proposed an indigenous refoundation of Bolivia within the framework of American regionalism: "The Latin American indigenous movements are advancing not only to liberate ourselves but to walk alongside other peoples and free them. We are not exclusive or vengeful, that is why we have reached the Bolivian presidency, to solve everyone's problems. [. . .] Solidarity between our peoples is above all, and in Latin America, the indigenous peoples and peoples in general are one big family."[50] A statement by Ecuadorian president Rafael Correa is also illustrative of such identity appeals: "Along these paths of the great home-land, our Simón Bolívar is walking, with all the songs and profound changes, Manuelita Sáenz walks the streets with the workers, and the squares are colorful [in celebration]. The cry of Túpac Catari is heard throughout Latin America, res-onating by the millions long after Catari's death. [Also present is the cry] of Túpac Amaru, who stands up and calls for the ancestral peoples to break the silence of centuries and become a substantial part of these processes of liberation."[51]

Translating such expressions into practical acts, Morales refounded the Bolivian state in 2009 under the name the Plurinational State of Bolivia. Following the introduction of the 1999 Venezuelan constitution, which rec-ognized the indigenous languages spoken in the country, Bolivia also granted official recognition to indigenous languages, just as Nicaragua did in its 2003 constitution,[52] and Ecuador would do in its 2008 constitution.[53] The Ecuadorian constitution also includes concepts drawn from indigenous traditions and used profusely in Chavista discourse: "Celebrating nature, Pacha Mama, of which we are part and which is vital for our existence [. . .] we decided to build a new way of citizenship coexistence, in diversity and harmony with nature, to achieve good living, the sumak kawsay."[54]

Consequently, political legitimation through indigenous claims has become central, especially in the Andean countries. Something similar has happened in the Caribbean countries and those in the north part of South America, and to a lesser extent in Brazil, in relation to the legitimation by means of African American claims, although historically they had less weight.[55] In demographic terms, the Afro-descendants represent a population of weight in eight Latin American countries, calculated at no less than eighty-five million according to national censuses.[56]

In the last two decades, the regional articulation of organizations of Afro-descendants in the region has strengthened greatly. Estimates indicate that re-gional frameworks had already integrated more than a hundred organizations of Afro-descendants in 2008. Among those networks are ONECA (Red de Organizaciones Negras Centroamericanas or Network of Central American Black Organizations), the Alianza Estratégica de Afrodescendientes de América Latina y el Caribe (Strategic Alliance of People of African Descent in Latin America and the Caribbean), and the Network of Afro-Caribbean Women. These networks are bolstered by national articulations, which are responsible for the coordination of almost two hundred organizations.[57] This process also involved changes in national legislation. Recognizing the ethnic and cultural diversity in their countries, governments reformed old or promulgated new laws and created institutions in charge of addressing the demands of Afro-descendants concerning their autonomy, development, identity, equality, and nondiscrimination.[58]

Also in the area of regional integration, the impact of this discursive change has been substantial, as the various regional organizations have further developed their spaces for citizen participation.[59] In MERCOSUR, the shift from the 1990s has been impressive, when the concern for indigenous and Afro-descendant issues was on the sidelines.[60] Under Kirchner and Lula and with the Venezuelan influence in the mid-2000s, MERCOSUR underwent a shift toward social and identity issues. The organization deepened its social and cultural dimension and adopted it in its official speeches. It launched the program "Somos MERCOSUR," aimed at achieving civil participation, organized the First Meeting of the Social and Productive MERCOSUR and its First Social Summit, and developed cultural policies, among other projects that put indigenous and ethnic peoples on the agenda.[61]

A peak occurred on October 11, 2013, with the formation of the Indigenous Mercosur, under the pro tempore presidency of Venezuela and within the framework of celebration of the Day of Indigenous Resistance. Addressing a public in which indigenous delegations from twelve countries participated, the Venezuelan foreign minister, Elías Jaua, greeted them and reminded them that Chávez

> taught us to claim ourselves as Indians and as Afro-descendants that we are the children of this Latin American land and Caribbean. [. . .] We are also Indians and we have to recognize it, and we are proud of that. Indigenous comrades, [he said], be assured that the Bolivarian Revolution led by President Maduro, that between landowners and indigenous people, this revolution has a clear and defined option, [favoring] indigenous peoples.[62]

Likewise, the Venezuelan minister for indigenous peoples, Aloha Núñez, recalled that her government had recently processed 108 applications, delivering 80 land titles for 2,800,000 hectares to indigenous communities, and that they would continue to manage demands in the future. Other Venezuelan officials, such as one vice minister at the Ministry of Popular Power for Education and one vice minister of communal territories at the Ministry of Popular Power for Indigenous Peoples, also highlighted legislative efforts of linguistic recognition and educational modalities, as well as the adoption of indigenous technology in the health system and the promotion of healthy eating. A year later, the presidents of the member states of MERCOSUR declared that they welcomed the creation of the Meeting of Indigenous Authorities of the organization, known as RAPIM.[63]

The case of UNASUR is perhaps the most peculiar in its relationship with the Chavista discourse and the inclusion of indigenous claims in its documents. Various Chavista sites referring to this organization note that, starting with its founding documents, UNASUR highlighted the legacy of the indigenous peoples.[64] UNASUR's documentation shows a more ambiguous scenario. In December 2004, in the founding declaration of Cuzco for the then South American Community of Nations (CSN), mainly supported by Brazil, there was no mention of indigenous peoples or leaders.[65] Nor did any such mention appear in the statements of September 2005 at the First Meeting of the CSN Heads of State.[66] It was only at the Second Meeting of CSN's Heads of State in December 2006, in the so-called Declaration of Cochabamba, Bolivia, that the issue took center stage as part of the construction of a South American Union. The location of the meeting, hosted by the Bolivian government, was decisive. In the Declaration of Cochabamba, the founding states indicated that the CSN "recognizes the multi-ethnic, multicultural and multilingual character of our peoples. This community [of nations] is based on historical bases, recognizing the role played by the indigenous peoples, the Afro-descendants and the con-tract labor migrants in the social struggles of the region." Likewise, it affirmed the need for a democratic and plural system respectful of indigenous peoples as part of CSN's guiding principles.[67] Similarly, in Cochabamba, the participants is-sued a declaration in support of the UN Declaration of the Rights of Indigenous Peoples, adopted in June of that year.[68] The initial meeting (Taypi-Jenecherú in the native languages) was held at the Félix Carriles stadium, celebrating the oc-casion with social movements and delegates from indigenous peoples, while the closing event of the summit converged with the "Counter-Summit," in which thousands of people from social movements in the region participated, with Chavismo having a central symbolic influence.[69]

Just before the Cochabamba summit, the indigenous organizations had issued a strong statement addressing the presidents of the attending countries, in which they reminded them of their own civilizational existence preceding that of the nation-states and asking them to endorse the concrete proposals they had put forward to promote a South American integration different from that of neolib-eralism.[70] Still, much of what delegates proclaimed at the Cochabamba meeting was diluted in the "Constitutive Treaty of the Union of South American Nations," at a meeting in Brasilia in May 2008. In it, the shared declaration highlighted that UNASUR was "supported by the shared and solidary history of our multi-ethnic, multilingual and multicultural nations, which have fought for emancipation and South American unity, honoring the thinking of those who forged our indepen-dence and freedom in favor of that union and the construction of a Common future."[71] In that version, written under the pro tempore presidency of Brazil, and which entered into force in March 2011, the references to native peoples and indigenous rights had been removed in favor of the notions of South American countries being multiethnic, multilingual, and multicultural nations.

In the case of CELAC, the member states elaborated a "Strategic Agenda for Regional Coordination" on social policy that included consideration of the indigenous and Afro-American populations. At first there was some dissatisfaction and criticism due to the exclusion of native languages from "American" languages in the constitutive charter, which failed to fulfill initial expectations.[72] In its Second Summit in Havana (January 2014), greater attention was given to the role of such communities in socioeconomic and environmental development, as well as their valuable local and cultural practices. Since then, CELAC has taken substantive steps, including demonstrating emphatic support for indigenous rights.[73] CELAC also placed the promotion of collective and individual rights of indigenous populations, Afro-descendants, and diasporas at the center of its cultural action plan for 2015–20. Accordingly, it suggested the holding of congresses, colloquia, workshops, and festivals, as well as the issuing of publications and audiovisual productions devoted to these sectors.[74] Likewise, it has also created a working group focusing on Afro-descendants and charged with the implementation of a Decade of Latin American and Caribbean Afro-descendants.[75]

In 2007, beyond the intergovernmental dimension, ALBA created the Council of Social Movements, charged with deepening the process of identity strengthening with the purpose of mobilizing organized popular sectors within the framework of an "anti-imperialist space" and the integration of social movements in transnational governance.[76]

Finally, another regional body that has been active has been the so-called Parlatino, within which the Permanent Commission of Indigenous Peoples and Ethnic Groups meets periodically, and which approved the Legal Framework for Rescuing, Preserving and Promoting National Indigenous Languages.[77] Another substantive example at the regional level was the creation of the Black Parliament of the Americas in 2005, with the objective of bringing together Afro-American legislators and ex-legislators to develop an inclusive development agenda for the Afro-descendant population, a task it has embraced actively.[78]

The institutional discourse favorable to the ethnic groups was also reproduced in social movements, as seen in the massive 17th Latin American and Caribbean Student Congress, held in Nicaragua in August 2014. Another example is the Third International Meeting for the Integration of Peoples, held in April 2013 in Olmué, Chile, which was organized by Casa Bolívar de Chile and Casa del ALBA Bolivia; its stated objective was "to strengthen the construction of the Patria Grande and the restoration of Abya Yala, within the framework of ALBA-TCP."[79]

Beyond the design of a homogeneous discourse and the impetus for social mobilization, the role of the media was central in transmitting the Chavista lens of information to the peoples of the Americas. The model of direct communication that Chávez established in Venezuela via his weekly program *Aló Presidente* and the network of television channels, radio stations, and press agencies was replicated regionally through the TeleSur network, initiated by Venezuela, Cuba, Argentina, and Uruguay in 2005.[80] TeleSur was postulated as an alternative to regional satellite channels and global satellite channels like CNN, with the intention of breaking the paradigms of domination that, in TeleSur's view, hided the marginalization of the poor; the work of social movements; and the devastating effects of globalization, Northern imperialism, and US hegemony.[81] In the words of the TeleSur cofounder, however, TeleSur intended to end the "permanent conspiracy against Venezuela for 15 years . . . the censorship that exists abroad in relation to Venezuela."[82] While launching his own media, Chávez led delegitimation campaigns and harassed opposition media, an action emulated by the various pro-Chavista governments.

Indeed, beyond their legitimizing use by Chavismo, such emphases produced an empowerment of transnational minorities. Dozens of indigenous and Afro-descendant associations not only received funding, but perhaps more importantly, found a broader political scenario, practical support for identity discourse, and the progressive empowerment of the politicization process of indigenous ethnicity that had begun in the 1970s. They also collaborated in further empowering global support networks, which endowed their leaders with new experiences and resources in different global meetings, as part of an internationalization process of these minorities that had already begun in the 1980s and 1990s.[83]

The Identitarian Boomerang: Regional Challenges

On occasions, the recognition of the cultural and political rights of indigenous and Afro-American populations—framed in the idea of self-determination of the peoples pushed forward by the transnational movements—put excessive pressure on Chavista governments that were willing to control such demands yet unable to do it effectively.[84] By 2011, the commodity boom that had started around 2004 with the rise of Chinese demand was coming to an end, and with it, the capacity of redistribution of state resources was severely reduced. As the cycle ended, the gap between the state's claims and the citizens' corresponding expectations, on the one hand, and the state's actual performance, on the other, was particularly visible in Venezuela, contributing to what one can label a "collective identity boomerang."

Examples of this phenomenon of identity politics "boomerang" have abounded since the rise of Chavismo and greatly increased as the economic crises deepened and the credibility of the Chavista governments decreased. Already in the framework of the debate on a draft of the constitution for the Bolivarian Republic of Venezuela in 1999, expectations had not materialized. The political class did not want to recognize that there was racial discrimination in Venezuela, while Afro-Venezuelans considered declaring that the country was "multiethnic and multicultural" insufficient, and they demanded an explicit recognition of the rights of Afro-Venezuelan communities in the same way that it had been done for the indigenous communities.[85]

Starting in mid-2011, strong clashes took place in Bolivia between the police and the indigenous groups during marches, strikes, and work stoppages. Everything exploded following the repression of a native march that started in the Amazon and was heading toward La Paz. The march was focused on rejection of a 300 km highway financed by Brazil that would cross the TIPNIS indigenous territory (also known as the Isiboro Secure National Park Indigenous Territory).[86] Trying to legitimize his actions, President Morales finally ended up asking for forgiveness; promised to stop the project; and then called for UNASUR, the OAS, and the UN to investigate and oversee the case,[87] although they had little success despite initial enthusiasm.[88] The mobilizations following the debate on legislating the "prior consultation" with the indigenous communities, among other disputed issues, continued until late 2015, when they were met with brutal repression by the government.[89]

During Cristina Fernández de Kirchner's presidency, within the framework of the celebrated bicentennial of independence, more than fifteen thousand members of native communities held the March of Native Peoples leading to the central Plaza de Mayo square, the seat of government, to submit a request to Kirchner demanding the recognition of the territorial rights of indigenous peoples.[90] After the leader of the Qom community set up an encampment opposing the government, with major media coverage, on the central 9 de Julio Avenue, the authorities refused to receive the indigenous leader or consider the group's demands.[91]

In Ecuador, starting in August 2013, Rafael Correa began to face massive protests from the main indigenous confederations and strikes by the workers' unions, demanding that the government rectify its policies and laws on land, oil, and mining exploitation, as well as on water, transit, foreign trade, and indigenous education. Correa claimed that the people did not support such actions and that behind the protests were sectors that wanted to destabilize the country.[92]

One should recognize, however, that indigenous mobilization and empowerment were certainly not limited to countries dominated by Chavista coalitions, but were also on the rise in Chile, Peru, and Colombia.[93]

The demands of the native and Afro-descendant peoples were also reinforced at the regional level, even against the regional organizations that at first had hosted the calls for creation of transnational commitments. For example, in 2009 the Coordinadora Andina de Organizaciones Indígenas (the Andean Coordination of Indigenous Organizations), which brought together the indigenous peoples of Bolivia, Ecuador, Peru, Colombia, Chile, and Argentina, exerted strong pressure on the Inter-American Commission on Human Rights (IACHR). This was the result of the strategic restructuring of the Initiative for South American Regional Integration (Iniciativa para la Integración Regional Sudamericana; IIRSA), a UNASUR project under local, national, and regional indigenous surveillance that included 510 megaprojects financed with $70 billion.[94] Mobilizing discontent, the Andean Coordination of Indigenous Organizations started demanding greater participation in UNASUR, proposing the creation of a council of indigenous peoples at UNASUR, in order to promote the full development of indigenous participation, the prior regional consultation requirement, and dialogue on the climate change agenda.

In any case, Chavismo articulated regional influence, as evident in the widespread support that the Venezuelan government received during the massive protests of 2014, which followed the declared suspension of guarantees and civil rights, shortage of products, and an increase in violence. Shortly after the protest started, more than a hundred socialist, Communist, revolutionary, and popular political movements from thirty-nine countries signed a declaration in support of President Nicolás Maduro and the Bolivarian Revolution.[95] They also organized marches in various countries,[96] and delegations visited Venezuela to express solidarity with its leadership.[97] Regional social movements such as the Latin American and Caribbean Continental Student Organization (OCLAE) provided strong support during those protests in Venezuela. For its part, the Argentine group Quebracho called on the UNASUR governments to speak out "as a regional bloc, to demonstrate to imperialism that Venezuela is not alone. To the state response, we must add the predisposition of the popular organizations on the continent to confront the coup right wing and imperialism."[98]

At the macro-regional level, it took time for the regional consultation forums of the American continent—UNASUR, CELAC, MERCOSUR, ALBA, and even the OAS—to censor the Venezuelan government for its repression of the massive demonstrations, which, starting in February 2014, left hundreds of citizens wounded, many dead, and thousands detained. Initially the forums encouraged efforts to promote dialogue; offered advisory services; and expressed "concern about the violence," calling on "all actors to avoid further confrontations,"[99] yet without making value judgments. In other words, they accepted the narrative of Venezuela's claim that it faced a fascist destabilization campaign, organized by the United States and destined to "hinder the process of regional integration" led by Venezuela.[100] A few countries, among them Panama, Mexico, Colombia, and Peru, expressed some criticism for the use of force. Yet the Venezuelan government constantly stressed the importance of "Latin American solidarity" and continued to call for the "unity of the Peoples."[101]

Given the emphasis Chavismo placed on the legitimizing role of "the people," that vision eventually became a double-edged sword with the parliamentary victory of the opposition. In November 2015, the OAS began to lead a campaign criticizing the Maduro regime, and both UNASUR and CELAC have shown an increased distance from the Venezuelan positions, as countries have started questioning the Chavista record of human rights and clean elections.[102] With the institutional crisis of March 2017 and the political, media, and armed battles that spread throughout 2019, regional and international action has definitely moved into a phase of sanction and isolation, on the one hand, and support and assistance, on the other. The debate has been ongoing since 2014. While some have insisted on announcing the "slow death of Chavismo," others continue to predict it will have a long life.[103]

Public opinion surveys conducted in 2008 and 2013 by Latinobarómetro showed enormous gaps between rhetoric and reality in relation to membership in regional organizations and the strength of transnational ties. Furthermore, they revealed differences between the different countries of the region, especially between those of the north and the south, both in their supranational identification and in their positions toward the external environment.[104] By 2011, a study on "the Americas and the world" registered a significant sector of interviewees in Mexico, Colombia, Ecuador, and Peru who identified themselves as Latin Americans (51, 49, 41, and 34 percent, respectively), while subregional identities—such as the Andean, North American, or Central American—had moved to second or a marginal place, with single-digit percentages in Mexico (7 percent), Colombia (3 percent), and Ecuador (2 percent).[105] The Latin American transnational dimension went hand in hand with a strong national identity and pride, which exceeded 90 percent. In other words, respondents did not perceive transnational identifications as antithetical to national identities, but neither did they support the transfer of sovereignty in pursuit of political integration. Rather, they expressed a confluence of the national with the "grand-national" or transnational project, particularly at the level of cultural affinity and in terms of principles such as solidarity, reciprocity, and the transfer of resources. Equally significant was that identification with Latin America went hand in hand with a relative lack of knowledge of the neighboring nations, since, apart from exiles and labor migrants, only a minority had traveled outside their countries, and there was notorious resistance to accepting foreigners in their states. MERCOSUR, SICA, UNASUR, the recently created CELAC, and even the controversial Pacific Alliance have obtained immense political capital and support among the youth of the region.[106]

Undoubtedly, for some time Chavismo and the Chavista movements tilted public discourse toward a politics of identity and a horizon of transnational solidarity. However, more recently Chavismo entered a crisis with the deterioration of its operational effectiveness within Venezuela and the discrediting of its authoritarian turn. Social inclusion is still a major theme on a Latin American agenda and likewise, indigenous and Afro-American identities remain a powerful mobilizing basis on the continent, even if they are already disconnected from the specific political movement that gave rise to them.[107] Some of these movements turned against the Chavista governments themselves, protesting authoritarian controls and the lack of autonomy with respect to the centers of power. The Pink Tide projects of regional cooperation, predicated on a rhetoric of transnational solidarity and assistance, had remained premised on intergovernmental preferences that were affected by changes in leadership and by the actions of governments unwilling to give up control. Unsurprisingly, with partial exceptions such as Bolivia's supporting the return of Morales and the narrow electoral victory of Pedro Castillo in the July 2021 presidential elections in Peru, their assertive legitimacy has eroded, as their standing has been challenged by the very social bases that years earlier had supported their rise.

9

Diasporas, Transnational Ties, and Ethnic-Religious Minorities

Jewish and Muslim Latin Americans

This chapter explores situations affecting citizens whose ethnic or religious diaspora identities and transnational contacts either gain them recognition or delegitimize their standing in the eyes of authorities and sectors of public opinion. The analysis reviews the Jewish presence in the Americas before diving deeper into the case of Jewish Venezuelans, followed by comparative notes on Muslims and Arabs living in the Triborder area (TBA) where the jurisdictions of Brazil, Argentina, and Paraguay meet. As Latin America has been primarily a continent of Christians, these case studies explore the meeting ground between the states' geopolitics and cultural premises and their implications for those whose intersectional identity may open grounds for sectors challenging their legitimate standing as citizens.

For both Jews and Muslims living in the Americas, as for other communities—for example, for Irish, Germans, or Italians—one can trace histories of voluntary or forced displacement, dispersion in multiple diaspora locations, and diversity of forms of identification with ethnonational, religious, and other identity frames. Depending on circumstances, their ethnic or religious ties have been a source of either increased pride and social capital or shame and decreased public presence. This chapter traces two such situations in which shifting geopolitical constellations prompted the threat of delegitimation for citizens who claimed to hold transnational ties and, as such, personified a threat to society and the nation-state.

Jewish Latin Americans: Diversity and Multiple Homelands

The history of the Jewish people is one of multiple homelands and ancestral birthplaces and diverse forms of construction and negotiation with regard to the boundaries of identity, religion, and civilization, while interacting with other societies, cultures, and civilizations. The multiple waves of Jewish translocation generated varied forms of identity and subidentities and several Jewish

Transnational Perspectives on Latin America. Luis Roniger, Oxford University Press. © Oxford University Press 2022.
DOI: 10.1093/oso/9780197605318.003.0010

languages and dialects, in addition to Hebrew, which serves as the shared ancestral language.[1]

Among the first to settle in the Americas were *conversos* or New Christians, who had been forced to convert to Catholicism or face expulsion from Spain and a few years later, from Portugal. Those who did not accept conversion were expelled from Spain in 1492, settling in Portugal, Morocco, and the Ottoman Empire, including Turkey, Bulgaria, Greece, and the Balkans. As with any conglomerate of people migrating, theirs is also a story of resilience, disengagement, and reconstruction of communal commitments. Tracing their roots back to Spain (*Sepharad* in Hebrew), their descendants became known as Sephardim. For centuries they continued to speak Spanish in a late-fifteenth-century modulation, incorporating terms and expressions from Hebrew, Turkish, and later also French, Italian, and Balkan dialects, which became a distinctive Jewish language known as Ladino or *djudeo-espanyol (judeo-español)*.

Some of those expelled from Spain settled in the Middle East and North Africa, and many adopted the Arabic language. They thus became undistinguishable from the local communities whose ancestors had settled there many centuries earlier as exiles arriving from the Kingdom of Israel, which fell to the Assyrians in 722 BCE. The latter set of Jews, comprising some Egyptians, Syrians, Iraqis, Iranians, and perhaps even Yemenites and Ethiopians—along with the Moroccans who became acculturated to the Arabic and Berber cultures—are known as Mizrahim ("Oriental" Jews), another umbrella category that was coined in modern Israel. With the weakening of the Ottoman Empire in the late nineteenth and early twentieth centuries, many of them also arrived in the Americas. In that same period, the alluvial influx of migrants encouraged by the ruling positivist elites also included Ashkenazis ("Occidental" Jews) arriving from European countries, ranging from Central and Western Europe to Russia, Poland, and other Eastern European societies. The Ashkenazis' defining language was Yiddish, a distinctive language evolving from German in medieval times and written in Hebrew letters, and they have also differed from the other Jewish communities in religious customs and doctrinal authorities.[2]

Sephardic Jews have been part of the demographic mosaic of the Americas since the beginning of Iberian colonization. The heterogeneous character of Sephardic communities has prevailed in Spanish and Portuguese America, where *conversos* and crypto-Jews had already settled in colonial times. During the union of the Portuguese and Spanish Crowns (1580–1640), Sephardis from Portugal and Holland reached Pernambuco and from there moved to the Spanish territories. Others settled in territories under English and Dutch control, such as Curaçao, Jamaica, and the Guyanas, where they could practice their religion freely.

New Christians of Spanish and Portuguese descent who sailed across the Atlantic lived in a marginal situation, as even those who had reached the upper layers of colonial society and the Atlantic trade faced limits due to the possibility of becoming targets of suspicion and accusations. Once the enforcers of orthodoxy had started the machinery of the Inquisition in the late sixteenth century, loss of freedom and resources, deteriorating health, and even loss of life were potentially the lot of those under its review.

Following political independence, Sephardis settled in the Caribbean port cities of Venezuela and Colombia, marrying Christians and assimilating within their surroundings. Moroccan Jews from Tétouan and Tangier, attracted by the rubber boom, arrived later in the Brazilian Amazonas, moving on to Rio de Janeiro and São Paulo following the decline of the industry, yet also leaving behind locals of Moroccan descent, who have recently started reclaiming their Jewish identity. In the early twentieth century, the decline of the Ottoman Empire and the emergence of Turkey as a nation-state, coupled with Muslim unrest in Syria and Lebanon under the French mandate, created new waves of Sephardi and Oriental Jews leaving those countries and the Balkans. As many in those centuries-old communities started to migrate and settle elsewhere, the complexities of identity and identification in the New World became evident once again. A huge inner diversity unfolded between *turcos*—who self-identified in multiple ways as Moroccans, Damascenes, or Shamis, Alepines, or Halebis— and Ladino-speaking Sephardis. All these groups interacted with each other in the diaspora as well as with the Russian, Polish, German, and Austrian Jews and other immigrant newcomers and longtime residents in the Americas.[3] Margalit Bejarano and Edna Aizenberg have called attention to the singular position of the Sephardic Jews in the Americas:

> The Sephardic population in the Americas is formed by many small groups, divided according to communities of origin in the Iberian Peninsula, the Middle East, and North Africa, and dispersed among English-, Spanish-, Portuguese-, and French-speaking societies. From a local perspective, the presence of the Sephardim in each Jewish community was overshadowed by the presence of dominant groups of Ashkenazim from Eastern Europe, creating the Sephardic image as "a minority within a minority." Seen from a global perspective, however, we may view the Sephardic diaspora as a mosaic of identities that together form the largest concentration of Sephardim outside the State of Israel.[4]

During the alluvial period between the 1860s and 1920s, Latin American elites encouraged mass migration to their countries, conceiving it as an important mechanism for developing and "civilizing" their societies. However, seventeen Latin American countries had national-origin preferences in their laws, and many used ethnic preferences, often framed in cultural terms that hid racial discrimination. Northwestern and Iberian Europeans were preferred over central and eastern Europeans, Middle Easterners, Japanese, Romas, Chinese, or Africans. The idea was to encourage the flow of "assimilable" immigrants and ban those that were "unassimilable." Governments used negative barriers to deter the latter and positive means such as free passage and higher quotas to lure the immigrants they wanted.[5] Jews constituted a small minority (less than 3 percent) of the approximately eleven million immigrants who reached Latin America in that period. In Latin America, they became known as "Russians," that is, Ashkenazi or European Jews, and as "Turks," that is, Jews (and non-Jews) who arrived from the Ottoman Empire. Ashkenazi Jews arrived during the alluvial era to escape extreme poverty, overpopulation, and pogroms in Russia and Eastern Europe, crossing the Atlantic in search of livelihoods. Major waves arrived in the 1920s and 1930s, the two decades before the Holocaust. The percentage of Jews who came from the Ottoman Empire was much smaller.[6]

In contrast to colonial discrimination, in this period the region was open to Jews, who arrived mainly in the period from the 1880s to the mid-1920s, when the monopoly of the Roman Catholic Church, as the predominant legally recognized faith, was loosened in most countries. Whether reflexively or not, migrants congregated mostly in Argentina, Brazil, Uruguay, Mexico, Chile, and Venezuela. Countries that offered a refuge to Jews fleeing the Nazis in the 1930s, such as Bolivia and the Dominican Republic, saw the number of Jews reduced in the aftermath of World War II.[7] The states encouraged assimilation of immigrants into the national culture as the only legitimate path toward integration, and thus some of the newly established Jewish communities encountered initial difficulties in striving to preserve their Jewish identity while adapting to society, which they had done in Eastern Europe. The precedence of many in Russia, a country undergoing revolutionary upheaval in the late 1910s and 1920s, created prejudice and antagonism. In some cases, as in Argentina, police and paramilitary forces targeted and attacked both activists and hard-working Jews during the Tragic Week of January 1919. Presuming all Russian Jews were "maximalist" agitators (radical revolutionaries and anarchists), the attackers killed and wounded many of them, and the authorities arrested or expelled many from the country.

Newcomers combined strong communal commitments with transnational sensibilities toward Jewish relatives and friends living in other diaspora locations, while they also maintained in part an active participation in social organizations and movements such as Zionism, Communism, Bundism, and territorialism, linking with fellow activists in other countries. The internal diversity of the Jewish communities was immense, with some stressing their religious identity and others their cultural or ethnodiasporic allegiances. Such inner diversity also characterized Venezuela, where Jews had fifteen synagogues, several community centers, and several schools. In 1966, five major organizations created the Confederation of Jewish Associations of Venezuela (CAIV), which integrated the Sephardic Jewish Association of Venezuela (many of whose members were from Morocco, including former Spanish Morocco), the Ashkenazi Jewish Union of Caracas, the Venezuelan Zionist Federation, B'nai B'rith of Venezuela, and the Federation of Venezuelan Jewish Women. Jewish youth movements and smaller communities also joined the CAIV. Other organizations included the Orthodox congregations of Shomrei Shabbat and Jabad Lubavitch and the Jewish Rabbinate of Venezuela.

In various Latin American societies, the children and grandchildren of Jewish immigrants were able to move upward in terms of socioeconomic mobility, yet they continued to be exposed to grassroots anti-Semitism promoted by small nationalistic groups. Prejudices were particularly reinforced in Argentina, Brazil, or Chile, under the impact of xenophobic ideas projected by Nazi propaganda, which was particularly prominent among German communities. In the case of Argentina, the abduction in 1960 of Adolf Eichmann to bring him to justice in Israel generated anti-Semitic waves. These attitudes produced concern in periods of high social and political unrest, when both Right and Left forces alleged that the Jews' loyalty to their countries of residence was compromised by their attachment to Israel. In some extreme cases, that suspicion was exploited for political reasons, either by fringe elements or during the escalation of repression. Such a case occurred in Argentina under the military juntas of 1976–83, when Jewish prisoners and suspects were particularly subject to repression by members of the security forces imbued with social prejudice. In Venezuela, these trends were less visible until the mid-1990s, although there too, assimilation was expected, and social suspicion existed along with the possibility of organizing communal institutions freely. This trend was far from universal and was less obvious in Brazil or Panama. In some countries, such as Chile, members of the Palestinian community who were highly critical of Israel's policies added other sources of friction and stereotypical prejudice toward local Jewish citizens. In several countries, including Venezuela under Chavista governments, the demonization of Israel served as a potent discursive mechanism for social movements and state coalitions that supported a confrontational approach toward the United States and its allies.

Diaspora Ties and Their Transnational Significance

Following the Holocaust, Israel and the United States became the nations with the largest Jewish congregations. The genocide of Central and Eastern European Jews centralized the place of Israel for Jews worldwide, as the newly established state claimed the role of protector of Jews anywhere and called for an "ingathering of exiles," welcoming Jewish migrants as full citizens. In the United States, a redefinition of religious affiliations took place, shifting the balance from Orthodox Jews toward Conservative and Reform denominations. The post–World War II period also saw the cultural "creolization" of Jews in Latin America, that is, an increasing shift away from Yiddish, Ladino, or Jewish-Arabic dialects to the vernacular languages of the larger society—Spanish in Mexico, Central, and most of South America, and Portuguese in Brazil—a process that was fully under way by the late 1960s and early 1970s.[8]

The Six-Day War in 1967 marked a peak in the identification of local Jews with Israel, as its victory in the war became a source of pride, public recognition, and legitimacy, which would soon be contrasted with the US trauma in Vietnam. The war created a sense of relief and triggered belated feelings of Jewish solidarity in the face of adversity and encouraged a move toward Zionism. Israel resumed a new centrality, even for those Jews not identified with Zionism.[9] Through their identification with Israel, communities reaffirmed the legitimacy of their activities and their place in the diaspora. Thus, Israel became a focus of identity and Zionist activities for growing circles beyond core activists. In the longer run, however, the continued occupation of the West Bank and the Gaza Strip and the growing plight of the Palestinians changed Israel's image. Even when taken in the framework of considerations of realpolitik, as in the case of Mexico, UN General Assembly Resolution 3379 of November 1975, which deemed Zionism to be a form of racism, tilted public opinion against Israel. In turn, this started a process that led to a narrower space for a legitimate public presence for Jews, at least for those who proudly displayed their transnational connections and who were not joining the chorus of condemners.[10] For many, Israel continued to be a source of identification, but a process of disengagement increasingly took place. Latin American Jewish communities were exposed to claims and suspicions of dual loyalty. This phase led to the fragmentation of the community, the distancing of many from Zionism, and the renewed importance of other axes of identity, primarily religion.

In the Cold War context, young Jewish activists also moved away from Zionism, increasingly joining general leftist organizations. The prospects of carrying out a revolution that promised to erase structural inequality and promulgate universal social justice appealed to young Jewish activists. Many then discovered the prevalent authoritarian prejudices and discrimination in revolutionary leftist circles. Others confronted anti-Semitism when they were abducted and tortured, and many disappeared in the framework of the repression launched by military regimes throughout South America. Particularly acute was the case of Argentina, where the armed forces carried out a comprehensive policy of repression of ever-expanding circles of "internal enemies" following the coup in

March 1976.[11] Under the de-facto military governments that ruled Argentina until late 1983, individuals with Jewish names and background were overrepresented, with 1,300 victims; many more suffered persecution and torture or went into exile. Among those who escaped were between 350 and 400 individuals who fled to Israel, partially with the help of Israeli diplomats and representatives stationed in Argentina and the neighboring countries. Israeli representatives in Argentina did not have any legal or diplomatic grounds to assist local individuals of Jewish background, since they were Argentine citizens. In addition, the victims of repression, whether Jewish or not, did not have any special motivation to ask for Israeli help when they sought to escape, since they identified Israel with the very international forces they were fighting against. Many Argentines of Jewish background had, at that time, only a distant or partial connection with Judaism, and at times they were even hostile toward Israel and Zionism due to their leftist ideological beliefs. Still, concerned with the fate of fellow Jews, several Israeli representatives and diplomats relied on the overall cooperation between the two countries and used the lack of semantic clarity between their Israeli identity and that of local Israelitas (Jews) to help several hundred Jews escape who had been detained or whose lives were under threat. The projection of the image of Israel as the Jewish state, ideologically and morally endowed with the mission of helping persecuted Jews, overcame even the initial reluctance of young activists to relate and to settle, at least temporarily, in Israel.[12]

These complex transnational connections changed in the transformed environment during the return to democracy of the 1980s and 1990s, as the region underwent a series of profound and contradictory transformations that affected Jewish life. At that time there was an increasing process of global integration, including economic policies of deregulation, a retreat of the state, and privatization of public companies and services. These policies were part of the standard neoliberal reforms promoted by Washington, DC–based institutions such as the World Bank, the IMF, and the US Treasury, known as the Washington Consensus. From the perspective of citizenship, this period witnessed a diminished emphasis on nation-state regulation and a correlated increased recognition of cultural diversity and the legitimate public presence of ethnic and religious minorities. These trends affected the ways in which Jews participated in public life and expressed their transnational ties, which led to growing diversification. Although the process had started decades earlier, it now became a watershed, with more restricted ethnic and religious identities in some Jewish communities—for example, of Halabi vs. Shami identities among Syrian Jews in Panama or Mexico—and the recentralization of other Jewish themes, such as history and values. With the passing of time, the return to religion occurred even in the Latin American communities that had once been rather secular, like those of Argentina and Uruguay. Shifts occurred in the direction of disengagement from the communal organizations and toward stressing religious piety, with Orthodox and ultra-Orthodox groups becoming more prominent.

In some countries, notably Argentina, Brazil, Chile, Mexico, Colombia, and Panama, Jews increasingly enjoyed windows of opportunity to become fully integrated in the public realm, occupying key positions in politics, culture, and economics.[13] This integration reflected a profound change in the nature of many Latin American societies, many of which have left monolithic definitions of citizenship behind to adopt pluralistic definitions of their societies. Such a transformation was evident in a series of constitutional reforms promulgated in the region (discussed elsewhere in this book). Laws were also enacted that penalized discrimination, for instance in Brazil and Mexico, where anti-Semitism was criminalized and deemed a crime that, once proven in court, carried a mandatory sentence.

Starting in the late 1990s, a backlash took place against the policies of structural adjustment, privatization, and retreat of the state, reformulating again, in some cases, the basic tenets of citizenship.[14] In various situations, the system almost broke down. This was the case in Argentina in the early 2000s, which led to the crystallization of major shifts in the public's self-understanding of citizenship and displaced the neoliberal, market-centered conception based on property rights and consumer sovereignty that had been dominant for nearly two decades, in favor of various forms of civic-centered citizenship rooted in social rights and visions of the common good.[15] In other cases, as in Ecuador, a process of political delegitimation by street protest took place, in which demands for social accountability led to popular impeachments and the replacement of power holders.[16] In Bolivia and Venezuela, new elites moved to redefine the very foundations of republican life. Democracy shifted away from procedural forms toward placing a greater emphasis on plebiscitarian and direct democracy, led by populist leaders who organized social movements and adopted major policy changes.[17] Those leaders started implementing alternative political projects and socioeconomic policies and established new transnational alliances with a confrontational approach to the United States, its allies, and their worldwide policies.

Trends of delegitimation of Israel and symbolic violence against Jews proliferated again in the early 1990s, as events in the Middle East such as the Lebanon War and the First Gulf War produced an atmosphere in which Israel was censured and accused of perpetrating war crimes against the Palestinians. Even when not negating the Holocaust, as would later become fashionable, some conspiratorial narratives spoke of the fabled power of an international Jewish lobby. Often explicit anti-Semitic overtones were linked to the delegitimation of Zionism and Israel. For instance, in Mexico some of the intellectuals who had opposed Mexican support in 1975 for equating Zionism with racism were moved to question Israel and Zionism by 1991. Both the traditional Left and anti-Semitic circles anchored in the Right participated in this process of censuring and delegitimization in Mexico.[18] In Chile, the strong community of descendants of Palestinians cultivated prejudices and preached a delegitimation of Jews sympathetic to Israel, as some German immigrant sectors that identified with Nazism had done in the past. Likewise, in Argentina, domestic forces unconcerned with the loss of Jewish lives cooperated in carrying out the terrorist attacks on the Israeli embassy and on the AMIA Jewish Community Center in 1992 and 1994, respectively. This trend has become more critical in the past decade, in parallel with developments in the Middle East, including military measures and operations led by Israel—primarily the lack of progress in the peace process, the building of the Wall and not giving up the territories, and the wars against Hezbollah in Lebanon and Hamas in Gaza. There have been new waves of condemnation of Israel in Latin America. These shifts have led to a delegitimation of Israel and symbolic aggressiveness against individuals identified with transnational Jewish links in Israel and the United States. The trend of public delegitimation has been the strongest in Venezuela, where the demonization of Israel spilled over onto the organized Jewish community, suspected of disloyalty to the Chavista regime because of their transnational ties with fellow Jews abroad, including in Israel and the United States.

Public Legitimation and Delegitimation in Venezuela

The Bolivarian Revolution redefined Venezuela's international alliances, including its relationship with Iran, and radically transformed the public environment of Jewish Venezuelans. Until Hugo Chávez's rise, the organized Jewish community had open access to the leadership of the two political parties that ruled the country for decades. Acción Democrática and COPEI had maintained an open line of dialogue with the community and provided an institutional context adverse to anti-Semitism. from the perspective of Jewish Venezuelans, the experience of popular anti-Semitism that had existed for instance in some Argentine circles, seemed alien to Venezuela's tolerant society.

The polarized political arena of the 2000s, Chávez's emphatic rhetoric, and his strategic choice of international alliances changed all of that, creating an almost complete block of access for the Jewish community leadership to national decision-makers. Reflecting the new international position of the Chavista government on events in the Middle East, parts of the movement in power launched explicit anti-Semitic attacks on national media. The transnational connections of Jews with Israel and fellow Jews in the United States affected their legitimate image as Venezuelan citizens.

Opinions full of hatred and anti-Semitic overtones started appearing in pro-Chavista publications and digital media, such as the website aporrea, a pro-Chavista forum that received the National Prize for Alternative Journalism in 2006, influencing circles of Chávez's supporters. Defined as a space and forum for "popular communication for the construction of Socialism in the XXI century," in its official statement the website claimed to reject "any racist, sexist or homophobic declarations" and welcomed "respectful criticism . . . but not sabotage." In spite of such professed moderation, the site contained messages demonizing Jews and even clear incitements to violence.

Following is a short selection of such highly emotional expressions, colored by events in the Middle East and relying on traditional stereotypes and demonizing slurs.[19] In a post claiming that Israel had committed a "palpable and real" Palestinian Holocaust, worse than the one "said to have been committed" against the Jews by Nazism, a Chavista activist denounced Jews as members of "an evil demonic sect." He went on to characterize Jews as

insensitive beasts and slaves of cursed money, feeling supported by the demon of the largest and most vicious criminal nation on earth, of all times. . . . You managed to fabricate a lie, with which to deceive the world to create a state serving a mercantilist religion.[20]

Another post revealed the extent of confusion, conspiratorial thought, and hatred expressed toward Israel and the Jews in some Chavista circles. Denouncing the Holocaust as a lie created by "fake propagators of crematories," its author claims that the Jews are a "sect" that infiltrated the Christian people, bringing them to apostasy:

Among those phony murderers, [stand out] the Hebrew "school" of greed, sustained by the sect of Judaism and its ramifications of dissimulation, including the Sadducees of Nero, the Russian Bundists-Stalinists, and in the last five centuries, the Witnesses of "Jehovah." The latter "testified" about the false "holocaust" suffered by the Jews.[21]

The following post also shows how widely present was the demonization of the Jews. What is striking is the contradiction between claiming to advocate a universalism of love while it projects a demonic vision of Jews as being beyond the pale of humanity:

Hunting Jews should be a task of peace and love. As you manage to hunt any Jew, catch him with a net of love and affection. Tell him that we humans know that they too can become human, [feeling] respect, love, solidarity [. . .] these feelings exist and are characteristic of some humans.[22]

The process of increasing stigmatization and demonization narrowed the options for Jews participating in public life. The case of Venezuelan general Raúl Isaías Baduel, the commander in chief of the Venezuelan Army from January 2004 to June 2006 and minister of defense from June 2006 to July 2007, is paradigmatic. Once General Baduel broke ranks with Chávez in July 2007 and spoke out against the constitutional reform promoted by Chávez and the National Assembly, the connections he had maintained with Jews for years made the latter suspected plotters against Chávez. Baduel had developed those contacts as an advocate of interreligious dialogue, but once he turned against the president, all the Jews became suspected enemies. The delegitimation of Jewish Venezuelans had consequences for the quality of life and security of Jewish institutions. These reached the point of a security forces operation being launched in the Jewish community school of Caracas, which was inspected for hidden weapons, while children were on their way to class.[23]

Seen in a comparative context, the contrast with Argentina and Cuba is striking. In the aftermath of the terrorist attack on the AMIA community complex in Buenos Aires, Jewish activists and institutions led recurrent demonstrations to demand justice and criticize the ineffective judicial process. The more those activists protested, the greater the public support and recognition they had as Jewish Argentines who shared a concern for democracy with other citizens and expressed their outrage against the lack of institutional accountability.[24] The case of Jewish Cubans is even more remarkable, as Cuba shared with Venezuela a similar geopolitical standing. In Cuba, Jews occupied positions of trust in the state, the Communist Party, the diplomatic service, and the army. Even after Cuba broke off diplomatic relations with Israel in 1973 as part of the nonaligned and revolutionary movement, choosing to align with the Soviet Union and to be in open confrontation with the United States, Israel's supporter and ally, Cuban policies and treatment of Jewish citizens were not affected.[25]

The Cuban state broke with Israel at that time, but that did not radically affect Jews on the island. Cuban researcher Maritza Corrales Capestany attributed the persisting amiable attitude of the Cuban government to several factors, including the participation of Jews at multiple historical crossroads. According to her, Fidel Castro and other leaders kept in mind that Jews had participated alongside other Cubans in the early nineteenth-century struggle, had supported José Martí in the 1890s, were among those who founded the Communist Party in 1925 and who fell fighting Machado's dictatorship, and had been part of the July 26 movement. Jews such as Fabio Grobart and Ricardo Subirana Lobo had access to top Cuban leaders and old-time Communists, who were aware of their personal trajectories and revolutionary commitment. Their shared experiences and activities created a special relationship that endured even the breakdown of diplomatic relationships at the interstate level. Even if it complicated relationships by affecting communitarian "ethnic organization," the rupture with Israel did not translate into negative treatment of the Jewish community:

> The historic absence of antisemitism, the imprint of a Martí-like and anti-Fascist thought, and the presence of Jews with access to the upper echelons of leadership, together with the scarce population, created conditions for a "preferential" treatment and allowed their placement in important positions in all spheres of the society.[26]

In 1992–95, even the ethnic organizational aspect of Jewish communitarian life was restored. With the help of foreign Jewish organizations and the solidarity of other groups, Jews in Cuba established commercial and transnational cultural relations with Jews living abroad. This culminated in a friendly visit by Fidel Castro to the Jewish community in 1998, another sharp contrast with Hugo Chávez in Venezuela.

Another lens through which to view this issue is that of Venezuelans of Italian background. Jewish Venezuelans experienced a reflection of the official delegitimation of Israel and suspicion of their maintenance of transnational ties with Jews elsewhere. Such transnational connections led to censure and penalization, which led many Jewish Venezuelans to feel a sense of exclusion from the body politic. Denied access to the political realm and unable to defend themselves publicly without relinquishing their transnational ties, they saw their dignity, respect, and social capital affected. The politics of identity clearly targeted them. The alternative explanation, that they were being targeted due to their accommodated socioeconomic position and opposition to the regime, crumbles when comparing their situation to that of Italian Venezuelans. The Italian Venezuelan community shared with the Jewish community a similar socioeconomic status and transnational ties with the mother country and diaspora, yet the Chavista circles and leadership did not target them for censure, as they did the Jews. Moreover, Jewish Venezuelans opted to avoid confrontation and declined, as long as possible, to support open critics of Chavismo. Only much later, as attacks became unbearable, did they move to reassert their claim for respect as full citizens of Venezuela.

Comparative Notes on Muslim Latin Americans in the Triborder Area

Another comparative angle is that of Muslim Latin Americans, who like Jews have contributed to the economy, politics, and culture of the societies where they have been received and yet have traditionally been a focus of curiosity, prejudice, and suspicion. As in the case of the Venezuelan Jews, I assess here whether the reverberations of Middle Eastern conflicts in the form of terrorist attacks affected the public image and positioning of these communities in Latin America. As indicated earlier, depending on circumstances, transnational diaspora ties can be a source of either increased pride and social capital or shame and decreased public presence.

Since transnational ties have also functioned as a major symbolic marker of identity for Arab and other Muslim diaspora groups, I trace the trade-offs of legitimation and delegitimation affecting them. After a short characterization of the intricacies of the collective identities of these populations in the Americas, this section focuses particularly on the effects of the radical Islamic terrorist attacks of the 1990s and early 2000s on the communities living in the border area where the territorial jurisdictions of Brazil, Argentina, and Paraguay meet. This region is usually called the "Triborder area" or, in the vernaculars, the *tríplice fronteira* (Portuguese) and the *triple frontera* (Spanish).

In this area, the borders of Brazil, Argentina, and Paraguay intersect at the convergence of the Paraná and the Iguazú Rivers, connecting Foz do Iguaçu (Brazil), Ciudad de Este (Paraguay; founded as Ciudad Stroessner in 1956 and renamed after the fall of the dictator in 1989), and Puerto Iguazú (Argentina). Close to the magnificent Iguazú Falls, the three cities attracted millions of tourists, while the region's interconnectedness and low regulation made it an economic powerhouse. Underdeveloped customs controls and free trade zones made cross-border commerce attractive for locals and many migrants, many of them of Syrian, Lebanese, and Taiwanese descent. Some analysts have estimated that billions of dollars were also generated from money laundering, arms trading, drug trafficking, the production of fake documents, and counterfeiting. These illicit and illegal activities prompted counterintelligence inquiries about the suspected role of local Shi'ite networks funding and recruiting for Iran and its proxy, Hezbollah.[27]

The intersectionality of descent, language, and religion complicates analysis in this case, much as in the Jewish case. Not all Muslims are Arabs, and not all Arabs are Muslim. A majority of those migrating to Latin America, particularly in the first few waves of transatlantic migration from the Ottoman Empire, were Christians, many of them Maronites yet some also Christian Orthodox or Latins, and some were Jews and Druzes. The first waves of arrival from Ottoman lands—primarily from Syria and Lebanon—were nonetheless labeled "Turks," much as Jews arriving from the former tsarist empire and other European lands were known popularly as "Russians" for generations to come. Moreover, while most of the migrating Muslims were Sunnis, a minority were Shi'ites arriving mainly from Lebanon, whose religious centers, however, are in Iran and neighboring Iraq, thus adding complexity to the construction of collective ties and identifications in Latin America.[28]

In the early 2010s, Ella Shohat and Evelyn Alsultany painted the following picture of Arab Latin Americans at large:

> Arabs in Venezuela, Argentina, Brazil, and many other countries are largely of Christian-Lebanese descent, although some are of Jewish and Muslim backgrounds. While statitics indicate that 8.5 percent of the population in Argentina is Arab, only approximately 1.5–2.1 percent are Muslim. Roughly a quarter of a million Colombians are of Arab descent, the majority of whom live in Barranquilla and Cartagena, and about 400,000 Arabs live in Venezuela. Approximately 1 percent of the Mexican population is of Arab descent, and an estimated 0.28 percent are Muslim. In Brazil, there are approximately nine million people (5 percent of the population) of Middle Eastern descent, and 1.5 million of them are Muslim. Many Arab-Brazilians have attained high status as finance ministers (Ibrahim Abi-Ackel), novelists (Milton Hatoum, Raduan Nassar), filmmakers (Karim Ainouz), theatre directors (Antônio Abujamra), and media producers (Ali Kamel). It is often said in Brazil that there are more Lebanese there than in Lebanon, and although most Arab-Brazilians are Christian, there are also fifty-five mosques and Muslim religious centers throughout the country.[29]

Paradoxically, even though there has been little direct Iranian immigration to Latin America, Iran's radical vein of Islam has impacted the life images of Muslims and even those of Arabs in Latin America. Nowhere has this transnational impact been more clear than in the Triborder area. Those living in the area are almost exclusively Muslim (estimated in over ten thousand Sunnis and Shi'ites), with about three hundred Druze and a few dozen Christians. Unlike other places in Latin America, this area was pioneered by Muslims, not Christian Arabs, with inhabitants tracking their descent from several Syrian, Lebanese, and Palestinian waves of migration. The earliest wave arrived there in the late nineteenth and early twentieth centuries, followed by Sunni Muslims arriving after World War II, then by Shi'ites from southern Lebanese villages who began arriving in the late 1970s and more heavily in the 1980s and 1990s, fleeing the Israeli occupation of Lebanon. John Tofik Karam, who studied the Triborder area characterized the composition of its population as follows:

> Today an equal number of [mostly Lebanese] Sunnis and Shiites compose an estimated 90 percent of the twenty thousand Arabs who live and work between Foz do Iguaçu [Brazil] and Ciudad del Este [Paraguay]. . . . There are,

in addition, Arabs who [are] Druze, Catholic, Evangelical, Maronite, and Orthodox Christian.[30]

Although others may identify them as "Arabs," most of the residents consider themselves Brazilian or Paraguayan citizens. This self-identification persists even while they experience transnational lives as they reside in Foz and their children study in Brazilian schools, cross daily to Ciudad del Este, and share feelings of solidarity with fellow believers and members of their diaspora worldwide. After a terrorist attack on the Israeli embassy in Asunción in May 1970 that left one diplomatic secretary dead, Brazilian authorities suspected that the Arab and Muslim communities of Foz do Iguaçu and Ciudad del Este were behind the attack, and the media reflected that sentiment. This assumption about a terrorist local cell soon proved to be false and was relegated to oblivion.[31]

However, two events revived a politics of collective delegitimation: the March 17, 1992, bombing of the Israeli embassy in Buenos Aires and the July 18, 1994, terrorist attack on the AMIA Jewish Community Center in the same city. The terrorist attack against the Israeli embassy, which caused 22 deaths and 242 injuries, remained impune. Similarly, the investigation of the AMIA attack in 1994, which caused the collapse of the building and 85 deaths, more than 300 injuries, and material damage of varying intensity in various surrounding blocks, has not borne substantive results. The investigation into who was responsible for the 1994 massacre soon produced two leads. The first lead, which occupied the AMIA court case for several years, was the so-called local connection. The second lead was an "international connection" that held that either Syria or most likely Iran and its proxy force, the Lebanese Hezbollah movement, had been responsible for sponsoring, financing, and launching the attack. From the beginning of the AMIA inquiry, both leads were at the center of the judicial decision to prosecute former agents of the police of the Province of Buenos Aires and the request from Interpol for the international capture of several diplomats and leading officials of the Islamic Republic of Iran, holding them accountable for the terrorist actions. As a byproduct of those inquiries, the media and government reports, based on skewed journalistic sources, stated that the TBA's Muslim and Arab communities were likely involved in terrorism, profiling them as supporters and operatives of terrorism, or at least as their money launderers, and victimizing them collectively as such.[32]

Since then, the judicial system has conducted several inquiries, prosecutorial decisions, and trials, with little result. The proceedings, trials, and revoked convictions led to a surge in conspiracy theories, which boomed due to the suspicion of cover-ups and interference by political interests, intelligence and counterintelligence services, and suspected geopolitical interests and pressures. The ups and downs of the investigation seemed to run parallel to the geopolitical positioning of Argentina vis-à-vis the United States and Iran, making advances whenever the administrations sided with the United States—especially after the September 11, 2001, terrorist attacks on US soil—and retreating when the country looked to establish alternative international alliances, including one with Iran. The shift in position in international politics under President Cristina Fernández de Kirchner and Chancellor Héctor Timerman led them to approach Iran within a general reconfiguration of Argentina in search of alternative allies and new markets, which influenced the Iran-Hezbollah track.[33]

In the framework of Argentine international repositioning, the signing in 2013 of a memorandum of understanding between Argentina and Iran led to an offensive by prosecutor Alberto Nisman, denouncing the alleged complicity of the president and her chancellor in negotiating with and not criminalizing the Iranian administration, which according to Nisman was behind the 1994 attack on Argentine soil. Nisman denounced the president, her chancellor, and other figures in national and local politics, accusing them of trying to cover up what happened and impede the progress of the investigation. According to the prosecutor, the signing of the memorandum with Iran would have made it easier for Iranian officials responsible for the attack against the headquarters of the Jewish Community Center to testify in their own country without appearing before the Argentine courts, in exchange for raising the "red alerts" agreed with Interpol. When he died in January 2015, Nisman was about to appear before the National Congress, where he planned to declare that the memorandum with Iran had been concocted to reap economic benefits, including the importation of Iranian oil in exchange for the export of Argentine grain. It is evident that the Iran-Hezbollah conspiracy plot would not have played its vertiginous role without dramatic changes in Kirchner's international policy from those of previous administrations. The memorandum was approved by the Argentine Congress but never went into effect, as the Federal Criminal Cassation Chamber declared it unconstitutional in December 2015. However, the wide media echoes of Nisman's accusations and his presumed assassination on the eve of his testimony before Congress brought the conspiracy plot to its highest boiling point.[34]

The terrorist attacks in Argentina had no clear-cut connections to the Triborder area. Yet as Omri Elmaleh has indicated, "[O]ver the years, intelligence agencies and local and international media were convinced that some of the culprits [of the targeted attacks in Buenos Aires] and their supporters could be located some 1,300 kilometers away within the Muslim (mostly Lebanese) diaspora in the Triple Frontier of Argentina, Brazil and Paraguay." With some media outlets casting doubt on the "national" loyalties of the TBA Muslim transmigrants, the states conducted arrests and raids, even when they lacked substantive leads. The lack of institutional Muslim unity weakened the capacity of the triple frontier Muslims to deflect their profiling as terrorist supporters or operatives.[35] The 9/11

attacks on US soil reinforced the fears surrounding presumed international terrorist networks that were operating cross-nationally, perhaps with the support
of local cells in the communities in the Arab and Muslim diaspora, and tilted
the balance toward their delegitimation. Indeed, as soon as the narrative of terrorist allegiances took center stage in the media and imagination of both popular
and academic circles following those attacks, the international media projected
images of transnational connections of the Muslim community in the TBA to
Hezbollah and Iran. Furthermore, this surge in reports—many of them with
only partial supporting evidence—exacerbated suspicions that through their
transmigratory economic activities across borders, Arab and Muslim networks
in the Triborder area TBA were not just involved in smuggling activities and in
avoiding true taxation, but also were engaged in money laundering and active
support of the terrorist networks.[36] These images built upon dated stereotypes
that depicted Middle Eastern people as committed to networking among themselves and inclined to bargaining, greed, and even malevolent actions.

Such interpretations started before the 9/11 attacks on US soil, yet following those attacks, the demonization of the local community of Arab and
Muslim backgrounds was exacerbated. Armed forces periodicals sponsored
by the Research Division of the US Congress similarly made unfounded
allegations concerning the existence of some type of terrorist connection in the
"Triborder area." While ignoring World Bank reports and Brazilian government
investigations that contradicted their assertions, these texts "cited the press as
the source." CNN recycled the news story of terrorist cells in the tri-border region in November 2002, and the top-shelf US magazine the New Yorker likewise
alleged that "terrorist groups from the Middle East"—including al-Qaeda—had
organizational and financial bases in Foz do Iguaçu and Ciudad del Este. Jeffrey
Goldberg, the author of the article, did not cite trusted and verifiable sources but
nonetheless repositioned the triple border region more centrally within the US
storyline of the war on terror. In 2003, the rumors multiplied in US and South
American media. Bin Laden himself, several news agencies reported, had passed
some time in the tri-border region in the mid-1990s. The New York Times, the
Washington Post, Veja, O Estado de São Paulo, and other media outlets across the
Americas gave substantial coverage to the rumor. This conspiracy theory seemed
to gain legitimacy through CNN's previous allegation that a photograph of the
Iguaçu waterfall was found at an al-Qaeda training camp in Afghanistan.[37]

Reacting to these accusations, local Muslims, together with other Brazilians,
Paraguayans, and Argentines of diverse backgrounds, created the movement
Peace without Frontiers. In November 2001, gatherings of approximately
forty-five thousand people professed their commitment to peaceful coexist-
ence. Participating in the events were "national representatives" from Brazil,
Argentina, Paraguay, and the United States, alongside "religious representatives"

of Islam, Christianity, Judaism, spiritism, and Buddhism; many read messages of peace and fraternity. Naturally the event was covered by the local media, but mostly it was downplayed compared with the greater coverage given to the more "serious" suspicions of terrorist activities in the TBA. It may be true that sectors of the local communities had supported Hezbollah financially, but there is little evidence to support the accusations of active recruitment and support of terrorist activities. Nonetheless, the association by faith has generated a persistent trend of delegitimation of the local Arab/Muslim community. As recently as December 2019, August Treppel, the executive secretary of the Inter-American Committee against Terrorism (CICTE) of the OAS, conveyed a sense of certainty about the TBA being not just a place of persistent illicit activities such as smuggling of goods and trade in pirated goods, but also a hub for terrorist groups. According to Treppel, such groups "take advantage of the vulnerabilities of the local public institutions," aided by local money laundering, counterfeited documentation, and arms and drug trafficking. He mentioned that in November 2019, CICTE brought together high-level officials from the three countries to discuss a new counterterrorism initiative, "strengthening operational capabilities for preventing and combating ML/FT in the Triborder area." "CICTE also aims to provide capacity building for the prevention, detection and investigation of money laundering and terrorism financing operations; training for law enforcement personnel on special investigative techniques; and information on common methods and typologies for the identification of emerging threats in the TBA."[38] Such generalizations ignored what social researchers and historians of the region have consistently shown; namely, the inner diversity of the TBA communities tracing their ancestry to the Middle East. Such inner diversity would easily disclose the existence of terrorist networks. Moreover, the reaction of wide sectors of the local populations to the demonizing reports following the 9/11 attacks indicate that those reports snowballed partial evidence that manipulated stereotypes and predicated delegitimation on the service of geopolitical positions, much as Jewish citizens were targeted by radical elements in Chávez's ruling coalition in Venezuela.

In the two cases analyzed in this chapter, transnational ties functioned as a major marker of identity for diaspora groups. Even though probably more pronounced in the case of Venezuelan Jews, this process of delegitimation was also present in the case of Brazilian and Paraguayan Muslims. To approach such trends analytically, it may be useful to review some of the political and sociological theories that cover the politics of identity and the practice of dialogue and negotiation inherent in democratic citizenship. The classical liberal view of citizenship in procedural democracy that predicates neutrality over citizens' collective identities has been criticized as unrealistic.[39] Shmuel Noah Eisenstadt and Will Kymlicka, among others, have stressed that states embed in their citizenship a cultural program that integrates universal principles along with particular identities and premises. While many individuals and groups accept systemic assumptions and take them for granted without further reflection, their implications are made explicit during times of crisis or when under contestation.[40] Likewise, Nancy Fraser and others have emphasized recognition as part of the dynamics of justice, distribution, and equal citizen access, stressing how groups struggle and seek to be recognized.[41] In the case of Venezuela, this approach may explain some of the background and motives for social forces joining Chavismo, but is less relevant in explaining the process of delegitimation of Israel and its reflection on Jewish citizens. Specifically, theories of recognition cannot explain processes of delegitimation that also involve moral injury and humiliation. Under such conditions, practices of dialogue and negotiation are missing, and analysts such as James Tully and Michael Kenny have identified these practices as crucial for the generation of social and political capital and as conditions for the confident participation of individuals as full-fledged members of society, with a voice and a sense of belonging.[42]

I have traced processes of diaspora communities that have been impacted by international realignments and global articulations that have led to their delegitimation. Constructing the transnational component of Jewish or Muslim/Arab identities as problematic contrasts with a wider trend of multicultural recognition and legitimation of plural identities, which allowed for the full integration of Jewish or Muslim citizens—a trend that various Latin American societies have engaged in recent decades. It should be clear at this point that the two cases analyzed here, in which citizens' transnational ties became a source of public delegitimation, diverged from the general trend in the region.

A final comparative angle is that of French and other European Jews and Muslims, which allows us to ask whether such individuals have similarly been affected by the refraction of geopolitical developments in the Middle East and North Africa. In Europe, there have been growing fears and concerns within the Jewish communities, and increasing attacks on individual Jews and Jewish institutions, related to the violence in the Middle East and concerns with Muslim alienation and radicalism. Attacks were launched, including on Jewish targets, mainly by Muslim youths, in what some observers have assumed was a communal conflict that extended the Israeli-Palestinian conflict into Western Europe. Beyond the similarities, the unfolding of tensions revealed different circumstances. In the case of France, intercommunal acts of aggression reflected the lack of full integration of some second-generation Muslim immigrants, mainly from North Africa. Radical leftist groups, which advanced strong and violent anti-Zionist positions often cast in anti-Semitic terms, joined in.[43] Thus, as in the Venezuelan case, some social and political activists pursued their own agendas by encouraging hatred and transnational delegitimation.

On their part, the Muslim youth felt disenfranchised, marginalized by the dominant culture and the state's *laïcité*, particularly in France. Beyond this shared aspect, two differences could be traced between the situations in Western Europe and in Venezuela. First, while the French government tried to contain communal tensions proactively in order to save the bases of the state principles of citizenship after 2002, in Venezuela the president and his ministers contributed to the polarized rhetoric that weakened the public position of Jewish citizens. Second, some of the Muslim clerics and radical political activists promoting those agendas in France or Belgium have been unrelated to the seats of power, while in Venezuela, the circles promoting such attitudes have been close to state authorities. These observations call attention to the need for a systematic comparative analysis of the various articulations of local, national, and transnational forces at work affecting ethnic and religious diaspora communities in Latin America, much as elsewhere.

10

Transnational Challenges and Twenty-First-Century Dilemmas

This book moves analysis from traditional emphases on nation-states and global insertion to an assessment of transnational dimensions, linkages, and horizons in the region. In two centuries of independent history, the idea of belonging to a region of sister nations did not disappear, even if it assumed multiple forms and underwent changes. As territories fragmented into multiple states constructing nations, over sometimes undefined and always porous borders, at times transnational horizons receded, but they did not vanish. From time to time, cultural carriers and political activists attempted to reconnect those American societies transnationally. By the twentieth century, nation-states seemed to have consolidated their primacy, yet intellectuals and artists, exile communities, and movements of resistance lifted the banner of transnational solidarity as they confronted dictatorships that often carried out repression across territorial boundaries. Our analysis has tracked such linkages through exile networks that crossed borders and reformulated political projects, the transnational struggle against external intervention, the process of democratization, the emergence of transnational movements, and various processes of legitimation and delegitimation of minorities with transnational connections.

The strength of these transnational moments has undergone ups and downs. Transnational nonstate actors such as the exiles and their advocacy networks influenced the processes of democratization and set agendas of transitional justice, even though the resulting equation depended on domestic balances of power and the specific calibration of policy options against structural constrains. Multinational corporations thrived under the cycle of neoliberal policies and underwent tactical losses under Pink Tide governments. For some time, the Pink Tide governments predicated and enacted policies of regional solidarity and postliberal assistance, creating new and often overlapping intergovernmental organizations (IGOs). At the same time, in various countries, civil society organizations and political parties put pressure on power holders to adopt new constitutions that professed recognition of a plethora of human and environmental rights. However, their implementation was not effective, which led to continued attacks on activists or media professionals who were critical of state officials and powerful interests. With the assistance of the international

Transnational Perspectives on Latin America. Luis Roniger, Oxford University Press. © Oxford University Press 2022.
DOI: 10.1093/oso/9780197605318.003.0011

community, several countries created mixed transnational agencies to overcome and curtail corruption in state administrations, with substantive achievements in the short term, although they lacked permanent standing. All these processes have taken place in a context of multiple challenges, including the recent Covid-19 pandemic.

This chapter aims to assess where the region stands in the early twenty-first century, as Latin American democracies exhibit a tug of war between executive policies and strong participatory trends, with countries joining multiple yet segmented IGOs that failed to reach institutional integration and express a voice in unison. These tensions have never been as poignant as in the current scenario, as the region faces transnational challenges and dilemmas, exacerbated by the health pandemic and economic contraction.

Transnational Horizons and Segmented Regional Integration

The spirit of Latin American solidarity has shown great vitality as it has emerged from the bottom up, resuming strength particularly in moments of hardship, such as foreign invasions or during repressive cycles and forced territorial displacements, notably as experienced in the Cold War. At that time, Latin American activists, intellectuals, creators, and musicians projected a regional perspective, as exiles and "insiles" from multiple states that confronted dictatorships and struggled to recover their lost freedoms, working to get their nations to resume civilian democracy. The music and lyrics of groups like the Chilean Quilapayún and Inti Illimani were key to keeping resistance alive on a worldwide scale, energizing not just the struggle against Pinochet in their homeland, but also the fight against all other dictatorships in the region. José "Pepe" Guerra and Braulio López, the Olimareños, who left Uruguay in 1974 when the civilian-military government prohibited their songs and public performances, became a voice that kept the flame of resistance of Uruguayans and other South Americans alive. When they returned to Uruguay after a ten-year absence, thousands welcomed them, and an estimated fifty thousand people attended their performance in Montevideo under heavy rain.

Equally influential was Argentine interpreter Mercedes Sosa, who energized resistance moments and conveyed the longing for freedom and Latin American solidarity both in exile and after returning home. After the March 1976 coup, Sosa dared to include in her public performance protest poems, among them some written by Communist Pablo Neruda, a decision that landed her on the dictatorship's blacklist. While attempting to remain in Argentina, she toured Europe, North Africa, and Brazil, and in 1979 she left for Paris and then Madrid, having been detained and harassed in her home country. While Sosa's work was censored within Argentina, it boomed abroad. She produced several albums, such as *Serenata para la tierra de uno* (1979), which included the song "Porque me duele si me quedo, pero me muero si me voy" (It hurts if I stay, but I die if I leave), by María Elena Walsh. Sosa also performed Brazilian songs on her own and with Brazilian interpreters such as Chico Buarque and Fernando Brant, which bridged Spanish and Portuguese American music. Her continental perspective was reflected in overt references to forced displacement, such as on the album *A quién doy* (France, 1981), which was marked by a sense of loss and nostalgia. Sosa returned to Argentina in 1982, a short time before the Malvinas-Falkland War, and appeared in recitals that turned into massive shows of repudiation of the dictatorship. Due to her public impact, she received new threats on her life and had to leave again. Only in 1984, after the restoration of democracy, was she able to return permanently. That same year she released the album *¿Será posible el Sur?* (Will the South be possible?), which included songs of great impact by Argentine Víctor Heredia and Chilean Julio Numhauser. Her Latin American repertoire was the mainstay on albums such as *Corazón americano* (American heart, 1985), which reproduced her recital with Brazilian Milton Nascimento and Argentine León Gieco. In a 1988 recital under the banner *Sin Fronteras* (Without Borders), she sang with Argentine Silvina Garré and Teresa Parodi (later Cristina Fernández de Kirchner's minister of culture), Colombian Leonor González Mina, Venezuelan Lilia Vera, Brazilian Beth Carvalho, and Mexican Amparo Ochoa. Her pan-Latin American solidarity led her also to try to be part of the Campaign for the *No*, which opened the transition to democracy in Chile, singing with Joan Baez, although the Chilean authorities prohibited her from entering the country. In a PhD dissertation on the resignification of the reception of the *canto popular* and *nueva canción latinoamericana* in Mexico, Cuba, and France, Caio de Souza Gomes shows that these cases were part of a wide phenomenon of transnational resistance and struggle against the dictatorships. The music became the cage of resonance that consolidated a sense of pan-Latin American identity and solidarity with the plight of an entire continent in search of liberation from dictatorships.[1]

Participatory citizenship grew stronger during the Cold War and especially in its aftermath. Citizen mobilization sustained the struggle for democratization against tyrannical rulers and remained in favor of dismantling authoritarian enclaves, getting rid of institutional exclusions, and reducing socioeconomic inequalities. Activists in exile, advocacy networks, and transnational organizations demanded recognition, accountability, and *the right to have rights*. Anchored in civil society, nonstate actors "spoke rights to power," to use Alison Brysk's felicitous term,[2] expressing the aspiration of major sectors of the population to attain a solid respect for the rule of law, greater social justice, and effective and responsible governance from those in power. Several decades later, political democratization has spread across the region, and intergovernmental organizations have multiplied. Representative democracy has become the paramount political system throughout the region, with recurring elections taking place for decades now and shifting balances of power between center–right-wing and center–left-wing governments.

Certainly the political systems have evinced a continuing primacy of executive power, and populist temptations have persisted. Various leaders have sustained themselves in power by whatever means necessary, believing that they express the common will of society. Still, what is striking when considering the citizenship regimes is how interest groups, political parties, social organizations, and unstructured networks have mobilized to contest the terms of membership, the spectrum of recognized rights, and the patterns of popular representation.

What has been salient in recent history is the participatory vitality of citizen participation and mobilization. Eighteen Latin American presidents could not serve out their terms due to massive protests, congressional impeachments, and other procedural coups, all of which are reflections of the mounting pressures and imbalances of power that have developed in the region. Popular mobilizations have abounded, which, although sometimes they have supported power holders, in many other situations they have challenged heads of state, criticized their policies, and brought them down.

In part, political imbalances have been the result of global economic downturns, neoliberal policies of structural adjustment and "flexibilization" of labor markets, and most recently, a pandemic that triggered economic contraction and border closures. All these trends have brought citizens to face an uphill struggle and repeated challenges to their life prospects and expectations. The pandemic has also exacerbated structural imbalances, producing great suffering throughout the region. As I approach these imbalances in the following sections, let me stress again that this analysis aims to look at Latin American realities as they are, not to contrast them with a stylized ideal of Western societies, but also not to downplay the dynamics that these societies face today.

The Vitality and Limits of Citizenship Regimes

In the last wave of democratization, Latin American democracies developed a major tension between political systems that professed to endorse widely inclusive citizenship regimes yet left the economic domain open to market inequalities and substantial socioeconomic gaps. That is, on the one hand, the political realm opened substantially and impressively. Increasingly, countries moved to reject some of their authoritarian legacies. Whether by their own volition or pressured by social movements, many of the new administrations adopted policies of transitional justice and professed to promote civil and political rights. Increasingly, social movements used the expansive language of citizenship in their struggle to deepen democracy, fight corruption, and put forward claims and demands of recognition and greater equality. Particularly potent was, among others, the mobilization of indigenous movements in Colombia, Ecuador, and Guatemala; the Afro-American movements in Brazil and the Nicaraguan-Honduran coast; and gender-diverse movements in countries such as Argentina and Mexico. In some cases, such as the Andean countries and some countries in Central America, states have come to recognize the demands of those movements that were pursuing a politics of identity, promulgating new constitutions that replaced monolithic visions of nationhood with a plural, intercultural, or multiethnic conception of the nation. Thus, it is instructive to see the constitutions promulgated or reformed in the Andean and surrounding areas, starting with Colombia (1991, 2001), Peru (1993), Bolivia (1994, 2009), Venezuela (1999), and Ecuador (2008). All these constitutions involved a recognition of indigenous peoples' collective rights, including rights over lands; rights to administer and conserve natural resources; rights to culture, identity, and education; rights to autonomous decision-making; rights jurisdiction; and in some of countries, recognition of juridical personhood and consultation rights.[3]

The struggle for social and civil rights also led to major innovations, such as participatory budgeting, adopted in several Brazilian cities; the popular assemblies in Argentina and Mexico; the peace roundtables and public consultations in Peru, Chile, Uruguay, and Colombia; and participatory laws in Bolivia, Venezuela, Colombia, El Salvador, and Paraguay. All these mechanisms and innovative measures furthered the popular understanding of the meaning of citizenship, moving beyond electoral democracy toward a growing recognition of *the right to have rights* and, most importantly, the expectation of an effective implementation of human rights as well as an increase in governments' responsiveness and accountability. Massive popular mobilizations took place, with civil society organizations and networks pressing demands from the bottom up. Civil societies have moved countries to introduce innovations into their legal codes, and in some cases—such as Ecuador and Bolivia—to promulgate new and inclusive constitutional charters that recognize the intercultural and plurinational character of the states.

On the other hand, structural economic inequalities deepened. Informal and dual labor markets developed, while illicit and criminal networks intensified their national and transnational operations. In Mexico, for example, the 2000 presidential ballot ended the Partido Revolucionario Institucional (PRI)'s seventy-one-year one-party rule with the election of Vicente Fox from the center-right Partido de Acción Nacional (PAN). While a new political era started, releasing regional and local politics from federal government control, the public spheres remained vulnerable under the impact of inequality and violence, corruption, and cartel activities.

In the last few decades, Latin American democracies have experienced a proliferation of mass protests, often in reaction to economic policies or the accumulation of power by heads of state. This includes protests not just against right-wing administrations, but also against those gaining power on a program of increased democratization and social justice, such as some leaders of the so-called Pink Tide. Starting in the 1990s and into the late 2010s, the region experienced numerous "popular impeachments" and procedural coups, which led to the resignation or toppling of democratically elected presidents.[4] Forced by massive citizen protests rejecting state policies, or by parliamentary and judicial actions, democratically elected presidents had to leave power before the end of their terms. For instance, Argentina's deep economic crisis led to the resignation of President Fernando De la Rúa in December 2001, after just two years in power. Likewise, from the mid-1990s to the mid-2000s, no Ecuadorian administration lasted more than three years, with three presidents brought down by mass protests: Abdala Bucaram in February 1997, Jamil Mahuad in January 2000, and Lucio Gutiérrez in April 2005. Massive popular mobilizations led by students, indigenous women, and labor activists started again in October 2019.

The willingness of heads of state to cling to power also generated citizen reactions and, sometimes, loss of power. Honduran president Manuel Zelaya efforts to change legal provisions and decision to run for re-election prompted a constitutional crisis that led to his losing power in June 2009. Similarly, the 2019 controversial bid for re-election of Bolivian president Evo Morales prompted mass protests by common citizens joined by police forces, forcing the president to resign and seek asylum in Mexico. In between these events were parliamentary impeachments deposing Paraguayan president Fernando Lugo in June 2012 and Brazilian president Dilma Rousseff in August 2016. Lugo's impeachment occurred without much citizen involvement, which greatly contrasts with the experience of Rousseff, whose impeachment was preceded by massive protests against the administration's policies and signs of public corruption. Rousseff's impeachment and fall from power was the result of a loss of coalition support, as well as the massive demonstrations of young people who for two years had taken to the streets protesting against the PT (Partido dos Trabalhadores) government, its policies, and it performance. Protesters had been galvanized by the news of public corruption, the Oderbrecht scandal, and federal overspending on international sport events in 2014 and 2016. Conducting such events at a high cost ignored the already visible signs of economic contraction that soon forced a reduction in governmental subsidies, deeply resented not just by students but also by major sectors of the population.

Structural problems have affected countries led by center-Right administrations as much as those led by center-Left governments. In both cases, massive dissatisfaction with policy decisions generated mass protests, as exemplified by those erupting in Chile and Venezuela, two states with very dissimilar political orientations. These tensions were particularly salient under neoliberal policies of structural adjustment, state deregulation, privatization of public services, and "flexibilization" of labor markets. In some cases, such as Peru under the presidency of APRA's Alan García, the government adopted a neoliberal agenda that prescribed the opening of national reserves and subsoil resources to foreign investment, for logging and mineral extraction. Soon after being re-elected to a second nonconsecutive presidential term in 2006, Alan García issued a series of decrees, and he signed a bilateral free trade agreement with the United States in 2008. All of these actions were geared to attract multinational companies to exploit the Amazon region, disregarding constitutionally recognized protections of that habitat. These policies soon generated major resistance from indigenous peoples under the leadership of the Interethnic Association for the Development of the Peruvian Jungle (AIDESEP), an organization combining over a hundred indigenous federations. The protests, which consisted of massive rallies, marches, and blockades of major roads, were intended to force the government to backtrack, but instead led to violent clashes and loss of life after the government sent troops to disband protesters and "restore order." After encountering strong public criticism and loss of face in Parliament, the executive agreed to undo some of the decrees that had allowed the projected deforestation of Native American territories in the Amazon, albeit without rescinding the FTA and its long-term policies favorable to foreign investment.[5]

Likewise, in Chile, the return to democracy in 1990 left the neoliberal, free-market model and the 1980 Constitution with its authoritarian enclaves intact, both of which had been adopted under the rule of General Augusto Pinochet (1973–90). With the passing of time, many of the constraining constitutional articles underwent reform, yet even then, the neoliberal model of development remained in place. For years, Chile projected an image of being a country that had a successful model of macroeconomic development, which enabled it to accumulate national reserves and register a high per capita income. Nonetheless, that development model relied on a very unequal distribution of national income, with stark differences in the livelihood of the wealthy and the poor sectors of the population and deep demographic and geographic disparities. The origins of this lopsided distribution of national wealth can be traced back for centuries. However, in 1974 Pinochet's dictatorship adopted—even before Margaret Thatcher or Ronald Reagan—a neoliberal economic model, inspired by the Chicago school, and imposed it under repressive controls, thus undermining the possibility of protest and resistance.[6]

The imposition of drastic economic reforms enabled Chile to overcome the economic crisis of the early 1980s and created what many from afar considered a "Chilean miracle." The free-market model predicated diversification, industrialization, and a reduction of organized labor power, under the promise that private initiative would create the conditions for a trickling down of riches. The state ended agrarian reform, capitalized upon the countryside, made labor contracts more "flexible," and privatized public enterprises (with the exception of CODELCO, the state copper corporation); all of these measures were intended to promote growth. That free-market revolution, however, involved an increased socioeconomic inequality and prompted the concentration of wealth and a persisting pauperization of major working sectors, whose power of collective bargaining was nullified. The regime anchored those reforms legally and promulgated a new constitution in 1980, which imposed authoritarian enclaves that, even with the return of democracy in 1990, took years to unravel. The retreat of the state from many of its earlier economic and social functions has remained in place since then.[7]

Even as democratization led to the restoration of civil and political rights, the economic policies of the dictatorship were maintained and boosted through a privatized healthcare system, a costly educational system that pushed low-attaining students from modest backgrounds into a mushrooming network of private for-profit colleges and universities, and a pension system that resulted in fragmented public spheres and wide inequality. While there has been some increase in government spending in essential areas like pensions, healthcare, and education, the costs have kept going up, magnifying public debt and consolidating systemic poverty for major sectors, even for those who have employment.[8] Moreover, remaining highly focused on commodity exports of copper and agricultural produce, and under pressure to find sources of energy, Chile has remained vulnerable to global market fluctuations affecting the population, with a median income just above the poverty line.[9]

Signs of disenchantment with the policies of the democratically elected governments began to appear under the center-Left administrations of the Concertación, led by Mapuche indigenous demands and soon joined by student demands. Since 2011, these has become manifest in the recurrent occupation of educational buildings and public spaces by high school and university students protesting the inequities and rising costs of education. In the case of Chile, the mass protests began in October 2018, unraveling the country's imbalance between macroeconomic performance and the profound socioeconomic gaps that had been tearing society apart. By 2019, major mass protests confronted the policies of Sebastián Piñera's administration. They started as indignation about the state's decision to raise the cost of public transportation. In response to worldwide price increases in fuel and transportation, the government raised the fare for subway transit in metropolitan Santiago in early October 2019. Barely able to afford the cost of living, Chilean high school and university students vehemently protested the measure. The initial rage soon attracted other citizen sectors that felt that their low wages, combined with the costs of privatized education, healthcare, and the pension system, put a heavy burden on their livelihoods, and they resented seeing the political system serving only the wealthy sectors. The Chilean government's initial response was to declare a state of emergency and deploy security forces to restore public order forcefully, while characterizing protestors as criminals. The inability to incorporate citizen protest reminded many of Pinochet's dictatorship. The feeling of being subject to praetorian state measures resonated widely, and the protests spread to working sectors, who joined them. Soon the initial defiance against the public transportation's price hike grew into a large-scale social movement that called for institutional reform, opening the possibility of achieving the promulgation of a new constitution.[10]

The lack of capacity to incorporate protest has been even more flagrant in some of the democracies that professed to advance an agenda of social justice, as had been typical of the leaderships of the Pink Tide. In Venezuela, the golden age of democracy and the oil bonanza remained a dream of the remote past, as an overcontrolling yet highly ineffective administration took over. The result was the expropriation of private enterprises, using clientelism to selectively favor supporters, bringing the country into downward-spiraling scarcity and hunger, and displacing millions of inhabitants beyond its borders as they searched for a better or even basic livelihood. In Nicaragua too, the return of Daniel Ortega to power in 2007 coincided with a cycle of prosperity. For almost a decade, the country enjoyed access to external sources of revenue in the form of multilateral loans and access to Venezuelan oil, which was delivered without demanding immediate payment. Having returned to power after seventeen years in the opposition, Ortega, the former FMLN revolutionary leader, implemented populist policies with those resources, favoring supporters, for example in the form of targeted infrastructural projects or by providing zinc roofs for peasant houses. While prosperity lasted, the authoritarian controls over various institutions and the concentration of power led by Rosario Murillo, Ortega's spouse and the vice president, went relatively uncontested based on a sense of citizen empowerment. The country had also benefited for years from a sense of public security, different from that of several neighboring Central American nations, which were beleaguered by drug trafficking cartels and gangs or *maras*. However, when an economic downturn started in 2016, the model of populist redistribution reached its limits, and the system entered a state of crisis.

At that point, the Ortega-Murillo administration demonized the opposition and used the police and supporting paramilitary groups to repress protesters. Soon, confrontations resulted in several hundred casualties and many more political prisoners, even as the protest continued. With the intervention of the Catholic Church and a representative of the OAS, in May 2018 negotiations were started, with the opposition demanding the liberation of prisoners; the respect of all human rights, including the freedoms of expression and assembly; and justice for those affected by the repression. Some decompression occurred following these negotiations, even though not a single member of the paramilitary forces responsible for the loss of lives faced trial, and hundreds of political prisoners remained in prison awaiting trial.

Thus, even if citizenship set the foundations for the effective recognition of the principles of universal human rights, Latin American democracies continued suffering from a gap between entitlements as recognized by law and the actual life conditions of the population. This citizenship gap persisted due to many states' inability or unwillingness to provide sound conditions of work, food security, and peaceful coexistence. The citizen gap resulted from policies—both neoliberal and socialist—that led to deepening poverty and the deterioration of basic livelihoods for major sectors of the population, due to macroeconomic state decisions or to a corrupt political system. These issues produced contradictory processes; for instance, even countries whose civil societies had recovered from a grim period of repressive policies turned to harsh measures toward marginal sectors whenever they perceived criminality to be on the rise, yet in parallel with the release of authoritarian controls and the opening of public spheres.[11] Against this scenario of massive protests and popular impeachments, the mushrooming of IGOs failed to reconcile their profession of nonintervention in the affairs of member states with their mandate of promoting democracy.

Regional IGOs: Promoting Both Democracy and Nonintervention

Regional intergovernmental organizations have had a growing presence in recent decades. Beyond subregional IGOs such as the Organization of Central American States (ODECA), the Andean Community of Nations (CAN), and MERCOSUR, the 2000s witnessed the creation of such macroregional IGOs as ALBA, UNASUR, and CELAC. Thus, a multiple regional organizational matrix emerged, in parallel to the veteran OAS, which was created in April 1948 and continues to play an important role in the Western Hemisphere through its IACHR and Court of Human Rights, which assist citizens in holding states accountable, as discussed in chapter 7.

In general, Latin American regionalism has sprung from interstate cooperation. For example, in Central America, the 1960s witnessed the creation of the

Central American Common Market (CACM), while in the following decades the region became a major backyard for military confrontation between East and West during the last phase of the Cold War. Following that interregnum, with its sequel of massive violence and civil and transnational wars, there has been momentum for a renewed endorsement of regional coordination. The area has witnessed the creation of many institutions, including a Central American parliament and a Central American bank, and various mechanisms for coordinating policies and confronting shared problems of governance and public security. Yet regionalism has remained under the aegis of nation-state priorities, and as such continues to be segmented.

The multiple overlapping organizations are not integrated, and the initiatives of some to move beyond high-level meetings and reach a transnational social density have been only partially successful. Facing regional challenges and dilemmas, their success has been at best partial and limited. Along with the drive for transnational coordination, a certain fatigue emerged in various academic and intellectual sectors and in public opinion regarding the multiplication and overlapping of regional organizations. That is to say, the broad discursive resonance had limited effectiveness when combined with the proliferation of regional memberships.[12] The allegation of *cumbritis*—the inclination to repeatedly convene summit after summit—has generated a clamor, demanding passage from formal coordination to a level of effective regionalization.[13] Even among leaders of the Chavista wave there were expressions of this sensation, such as when Rafael Correa warned of the danger that "people get tired of these summits [when] they do not see concrete events."[14] Similarly, in Uruguay's then president José "Pepe" Mujica stressed in 2014 the need for substantial transformation beyond rhetoric.[15]

In 2013, shortly before Hugo Chávez passed away and as the Pink Tide was approaching its nadir, Andrés Malamud and Gian Luca Gardini described the twin processes of proliferation and the overlapping nature of multiple intergovernmental organizations, which they correctly viewed as lacking a common core or political center. They noted the lack of comprehensiveness across regional organizations; the OAS includes North American nations, the Ibero-American Community incorporates the Iberian Peninsula, and ALADI encompasses only twelve Latin American states. Furthermore, they added,

> the inchoate Community of Latin American and Caribbean States (CELAC) messily brings together 20 Latin American and 13 Caribbean countries; the Union of South American Nations (UNASUR) unites ten of them together with Guyana and Surinam; and the processes of subregional integration (Mecorsur, the Andean Community, the Central American Integration System) are even less encompassing as regards membership. For its part, the Bolivarian Alliance

for the Americas (ALBA) unites only five Latin American countries with three Caribbean microstates.[16]

According to this assessment, the multiplicity of overlapping and segmented regional organizations reflected intergovernmental connections that remained highly dependent on national agendas and priorities, and thus they were unable to overcome state divergence and push common developmental strategies. Sociologically, politically, and culturally, the region has faced increasing pressures from transnational illicit networks, social violence, and immense socioeconomic gaps. Corruption and administrative inefficiency have generated public distrust, while public insecurity has led to citizens' retreating from public spheres, widespread reliance on private security services, and a growing fragmentation of civil society. In various countries, many fled to escape the vicious circle of unemployment, poverty, and lack of prospects of life improvement. Many more had dreamt of taking the road of migration too, at least until the economic crisis hit the United States and Mexico in the late 2000s.

These challenges have affected the region as a whole and demand decisions that consider the transnational dimensions of state and network interactions across the region. Treaties and agreements have been signed that have newly defined the need to coordinate actions and achieve higher forms of economic integration, harmonization, and regulation. The question is whether nonstate civil networks and multilevel governance can be achieved. There are structural constraints that lend credibility to the idea of supporting regional coordination and transnational cooperation. Small countries face particularly difficult problems such as limitations on internal markets; the threat posed by transnational criminal networks; and the lack of resources needed to redefine the public arena in terms of alternative models of developments, public confidence, and the emergence of civic accountability and diminishing corruption. Thus, pooling resources and easing the formation of regional transnational strengths makes sense. The question is whether the current layer of public agencies at the regional level is working to generate the institutional trust needed to support any further move in the direction of coordinated strategies. Particularly now, these strategies cannot be reduced to economic and trade integration but, to be effective, require addressing a broader range of transnational issues in order to support an ethos of increasing democratization, citizen participation, and multilevel governance in the region. Public opinion sees regional organizations as detached from people's everyday challenges and unable to address the main challenges and dilemmas these societies have faced in recent years. While states seem to be under growing pressures even as democracy has become the 'only game in town," regional organizations have found it difficult to safeguard democracies and citizenship regimes while promoting the principle of nonintervention in the sister nations.[17]

The IGOs have faced this key dilemma, as they have been forced to confront political destabilization, popular impeachments, and procedural coups d'état. The challenge has been to balance their professed adherence to and upholding of democratic systems with the equally cherished principle of nonintervention, which is grounded in decades-long treaties and conventions. Indeed, during the nineteenth and into the early twentieth centuries, Latin American states faced external interventions as a major threat to their sovereignty. Whereas in Europe the main threat to states came from other European states' expansionism, the Latin American experience included territorial fragmentation and foreign interventions, primarily on behalf of Spain, France, and later the United States. Accordingly, these states proclaimed their normative adherence to the idea of equality of states regardless of their size and strength and to the rejection of territorial gains through war. Likewise, Latin American jurists, diplomats, and intellectuals, such as Estanislao Zeballos, Carlos Calvo, Luis María Drago, and Genaro Estrada, elaborated doctrines of international relations based on the principles of nonintervention and inviolability of state sovereignty. In parallel, in 1991 the OAS declared representative democracy to be "an indispensable condition for the stability, peace, and development of the region." It then pointed out the steps to be taken to address "a sudden or irregular interruption of the democratic political institutional process or of the legitimate exercise of power by the democratically elected government in any of the Organization's member states." The organization also created the Unit for the Promotion of Democracy, and in 1992 agreed on a protocol authorizing the suspension of a member country in cases of the overthrow of a democratically elected government. Finally, in September 2001, the OAS adopted the Inter-American Democratic Charter (IADC).[18]

Likewise, the member states of MERCOSUR, the economic and political agreement between Uruguay, Paraguay, Argentina, and Brazil, signed the Protocol of Ushuaia in 1998. The protocol affirms the democratic commitment of its member states and allows MERCOSUR to suspend a member if there is a rupture in the democratic process in that state. UNASUR also passed a democracy clause in 2010, authorizing the suspension of any country experiencing a "rupture or threat of a rupture to the democratic order, a violation of the constitutional order, or to any situation which presents a risk to the legitimate exercise of power and the validity of democratic values and principles." Finally, in December 2012, CELAC issued a special declaration about the defense of democracy and constitutional order. The document outlines the expectations of democracy in the member states and describes the steps to follow if there is a "rupture or alteration of the democratic order that affects it [the constitutional government of a member state] substantially." Of note is that the declaration puts the onus on the government undergoing the crisis to reach out to CELAC for assistance. Not authorizing the organization to respond on its own to the rupture or alternation of the balance of power without a country's request does undermine CELAC's capacity as a functioning regional organization in this realm.[19]

The two parallel principles have shaped a basic ambivalence in how the OAS and the other regional and subregional IGOs have reacted to multiple instances of mass protests, procedural coups, and the ambiguous removal of presidents from power, as well as in situations of overreach and abuse of presidential power and interbranch conflict in the Americas.

Starting in the 1990s, the reaction of the regional IGOs was rather limited and hesitant; it became more assertive with the passing of time, as can be seen in the OAS's reactions to the sequence of loss of presidential power in Ecuador. Three democratically elected heads of state were removed from power in Ecuador between 1997 and 2005: Abdala Bucaram, Jamil Mahuad, and Lucio Gutiérrez. The circumstances of their presidential loss of power were somewhat different. In the cases of Bucaram and Mahuad, the protests were oriented toward bringing down economic policy initiatives. In the midst of an economic crisis, Congress declared Bucaram unfit to continue his term. The vote, accomplished with a simple majority, did not meet the constitutional requisite of two-thirds, prompting Congress to use the military to remove Bucaram and confirm his replacement as president. In the case of Mahuad, the decision to dollarize the economy deepened the economic crisis, leading to an uprising led by the Confederation of Indigenous Nationalities of Ecuador, joined by oil workers, labor unions, and student activists, all calling for Mahuad's resignation. As the protestors began to occupy government buildings, Mahuad fled, and the military command, then led by Lucio Gutiérrez, took control. In 2005, after Gutiérrez had been democratically elected as president, protest erupted again, motivated by the president's abuse of power. The social groups involved in the protests varied from one case to another. While Bucaram faced a broad array of popular sectors and organizations, in Mahuad's removal the protesters were indigenous activists supported and assisted by young military officers. In Gutiérrez's expulsion, the main street protagonists were the urban middle classes of Quito.

Still, in all three cases of popular impeachment, as analyzed by Leon Zamosc, the president's unpopular economic policies, abuse of power, or denounced corruption prompted massive popular protest and produced acute political crises. Most importantly, though, democracy survived. As the presidents fell and were replaced by the vice presidents or by congressionally appointed caretakers, those shifts were presented to the nation as reaffirmations of the democratic constitutional order. As Zamosc indicated,

> the use of sanctions from below is a matter of routine in Latin America, and we do not have to go to the extreme of presidential ousters to see it at work.

When people protest in the streets against this or that particular measure, they are not just expressing opposition in the hope of activating the horizontal mechanisms of accountability. What they are trying to do is force the government to rectify, often using public disruption as a sanction that they will only lift when the authorities reconsider or agree to negotiate. Since their goal is to pressure the government into taking their preferences into account, what we are seeing is the use of strong, direct sanctions in an exercise of societal political accountability.[20]

The question is whether at the regional level, with the proliferation of IGOs, there have been transnational measures to calibrate the crises and sustain democracy, or the parallel commitment to nonintervention has prevailed. In response to the removal of Bucaram from office in 1997, the OAS was notably silent, choosing not to invoke the Inter-American Charter in defense of democracy. Neither did the government of Ecuador choose to invoke that Democratic Charter. In 2000, following Mahuad's loss of power, the OAS took action. On the day of the coup, the government of Ecuador requested the assistance of the OAS in notifying the other member states about the events that had unfolded and called for their help in upholding democratic order. In its first meeting following the crisis, the OAS condemned the attack on the democratic order and vowed to monitor the situation. When the military took over, Mahuad had not yet resigned, but Gustavo Noboa had been voted in by Congress to replace him. This led to a second meeting of OAS's Permanent Council, at which Resolution 764 was passed, which supported the constitutional transfer of power to Noboa but condemned the events that threatened democratic continuity. Though the OAS was more involved in 2000 than in 1997, its meetings did not exert a profound effect on the protection of democracy. Rather, domestic initiatives led to the preservation of democratic practices independently of the OAS's positioning. In 2005, after a review of Ecuador's crisis, the Permanent Council decided to send a special mission to oversee the fair selection of members to the Supreme Court. While this instance of intervention clearly illustrates a more assertive measure upholding democracy, it was adopted after the removal of Gutiérrez, not while the crisis was unfolding. On the whole, however, in ensuring the democratic reinstitution of the Supreme Court, the OAS took one of its most direct actions upholding democracy at the member-state level.[21]

In a 2015 PhD dissertation, Betsy Montgomery-Smith tracked the record of the OAS in thirty-one major cases of threats to the executive and of presidential overreach of power from 1990 to 2012, six of them in the 1990s and twenty-five during 2000–12. Montgomery-Smith agreed with researchers such as Craig Arceneaux and David Pion-Berlin, who pointed out that issues related to democratic vitality, human rights, and the environment have been considered areas of low concern for regional IGOs, as distinct from concerns related to macro-economic performance and regional security.[22] Montgomery-Smith added new insight, explaining the variance in regional IGOs' reactions to the different instances of breakdown of the rules of the democratic game. She argued that the specific responses were the result of three key factors: the clarity of the crisis (whether the crisis violated the explicit democracy clauses of the regional IGOs), the severity of the crisis (the extent to which the crisis threatened the funda-mental democratic foundation of a state), and whether the crisis was a threat to the seating executive or was an instance of presidential overreach. Moreover, OAS and other regional IGOs found it easier to react swiftly and persuasively in situations that threatened a head of state than in situations of executive over-reach. These findings led Montgomery-Smith to conclude that the regional IGOs in Latin America have exhibited a bias toward protecting presidents, especially when a president explicitly requests assistance, regardless of the severity of a crisis, rather than toward cases of overreach of power.[23]

The reaction to recent cases of overreach of power offer a mixed scenario, although overall they seem to validate the statistical analysis. Indeed, the re-gional IGOs seem to have been rather ineffective in the cases of Daniel Ortega in Nicaragua and Nicolás Maduro and Juan Guaidó in Venezuela. In both cases, they practiced restraint and respect for the principle of noninterven-tion, although they did express concern about the toll on citizens. The crises in Honduras in June 2009 and in Bolivia a decade later present a more complex scenario.

When Honduran president Manuel Zelaya decided to call a national ref-erendum to change the constitution, his opponents denounced the move as a mechanism to get rid of a constitutional clause banning presidential re-election and to continue his tenure in office by changing term limits. When the president decided to move on with his agenda in spite of protests and a judicial decision declaring the unconstitutionality of the move, the military decided to side with the opposition. When Zelaya ordered the top commanders and thirty-three high-level military officers to step down, the Supreme Court ordered their reinstate-ment, which the president refused to comply with. Acting on a secret warrant from the Supreme Court, the military entered the presidential palace, removed Zelaya, put him on an air force airplane, and flew him into exile in Costa Rica. The national Congress then met, and read a resignation they attributed to Zelaya; voted to remove him on grounds of treason, abuse of authority, and usurpation of functions; and replaced him with Roberto Micheletti, the speaker of the House, who constitutionally was next in line. Following these actions, surveys revealed that public opinion remained divided, with a majority undecided about the le-gality of the removal. The new government, after restricting civil liberties and repeatedly declaring states of emergency, especially during clashes when Zelaya returned in September and it took refuge in the Brazilian embassy, announced that presidential elections would take place in November 2009.

The Honduran delegation to OAS had requested a meeting of the Permanent Council two days before the coup d'état, as the situation had turned ominous. This meeting concluded with an agreement on establishing a special commission to "to gather additional information regarding the situation, to encourage a dialogue between the parties, and to report back to the Permanent Council." The OAS's decision was unsuccessful in preventing the president's loss of power. When Zelaya was removed from office, other regional IGOs, including MERCOSUR, UNASUR, and ALBA, issued statements demanding Zelaya's reinstatement. The OAS acted in solidarity with the other organizations, condemning the actions taken and passing Resolution 953, which demanded the reinstatement of the deposed head of state. After granting the Honduran government seventy-two hours to yield to the demand, when the government failed to do so, the OAS unanimously voted to suspend Honduras's membership. This instance of attempted intervention produced ambiguous results. On a positive note, it illustrated that OAS was capable of acting in a timely manner, trying to affect an unfolding situation. However, it also revealed that without more than a diplomatic strategy of intervention, the OAS was ineffective in preventing the coup or reversing the situation, even though it put momentary pressure on the new power holders by suspending their country from its membership in the OAS. The OAS also designated Costa Rica's president Oscar Arias—a veteran mediator in Central America—to mediate in the crisis. After months of diplomatic missions and negotiations, the parties signed an accord in October 2009, aimed at "achieving reconciliation and strengthening democracy":

> These expectations included the creation of a government of national unity composed of representatives of different political parties and social organizations, the authorization of international electoral observers at the general election, and the expectation that there would be a renunciation of the calls for a National Constituent Assembly and for the amendment of the "unamenable" articles of the Honduran Constitution.[24]

> She also notes that a Verification Commission intended to measure compliance, but the international community failed to enforce it. In November 2009, elections took place and Porfirio Lobo, the candidate of the conservative party, won the presidency. While the country remained divided, a new round of mediation brought the Lobo government and Zelaya to reach an agreement, The Cartagena Accord of May 2011, which enabled Zelaya to live freely in Honduras and allowed to his allies participate in politics. Only then did the OAS lifted the suspension of Honduras from its membership in the organization.

In Dilma Rousseff's congressional impeachment in 2016, it was UNASUR that expressed vocal condemnation, yet without apparent impact on the resolution of the crisis. Nonetheless, UNASUR's Secretary General used strong language, describing the presidential removal as posing "a danger to the democratic stability of Brazil and a risk for the entire region."[25]

The case of Bolivia's president Morales is an example of the most assertive intervention by the OAS. Elected three times since 2006, Morales had decided to run for a fourth term in 2019. In order to win the election in a first round, Morales needed to have a ten-point lead over his opponent. As results were pouring in, he was short of that lead, but after Bolivia's Electoral Board suspended the count, a new result was announced granting Morales a clear-cut victory. The apparent lack of electoral integrity generated massive protest, resulting in many casualties and wounded. The military then stepped in and demanded Morales's resignation to prevent further violence. Playing perhaps its most significant role ever while events unfolded, the OAS was called upon to audit the election, suggesting a way out of a polarizing situation. After publishing its report just ten days after the election, OAS concluded, based on the use of technology, the chain of custody, the tally sheets, and some statistical projections, that major irregularities had occurred. In its conclusion, the OAS also suggested conducting a new election to ensure fair electoral results. This statement resulted in Morales leaving Bolivia for asylum in Mexico, to return only in November 2020, following an election that returned his movement to power a year after he had fled the nation.

The Drive for State Accountability

I have discussed here the role of the IACHR and the Court of Human Rights in providing avenues of support for citizens willing to protest abusive or arbitrary state decisions and hold administrations accountable. In addition to this recourse for demanding state accountability on grounds of abuse of human rights, Latin American citizens have been increasingly concerned with the question of how to tackle state corruption. Surveys and polls have consistently registered low citizen confidence in elected politicians and government officials, who are perceived as betraying the public interest, thus spreading distrust and cynicism about the workings of institutions and the rule of law. In 2019, Transparency International published a report on citizens' views and experiences of corruption based on national representative samples from eighteen countries, covering more than seventeen thousand interviewees. The findings indicated that a majority of people in the region lacked confidence in institutions, with only 21 percent expressing trust in government, 27 percent in the courts, and 33 percent in the police. Eighty-five percent thought government corruption was a big problem, and over

50 percent were of the opinion that corruption was on the rise and the government was doing poorly in combating it. On average, one in five respondents who had used a public service in the previous twelve months reported having paid a bribe. Moreover, sexual extortion was also widely reported.[26]

Usually the combination of horizontal and vertical forms of accountability is key to a successful reinvigoration of citizen trust in state and public institutions. In recent years, the region has witnessed the creation of innovative transnational mechanisms to address this issue and push for state accountability. Transparency International suggested a series of recommendations to tackle public corruption, including advocating for stronger political integrity, improving transparency of political finance, reducing the need for enablers as citizens interact with agencies providing public services, strengthening judicial institutions, empowering and protecting those who report corruption, and recognizing and addressing specific gendered forms of corruption and sexual extortion. Transparency International also mentioned that it was equally important to hold governments accountable and report on their actions to meet regional goals agreed upon by the countries attending the VIII Summit of the Americas, which identified fifty-seven actions needed to achieve public administrations clean of corruption.[27] These are targeted goals, yet often undermining their achievement is the lack of will or capacity of state officials, agencies, and executives to implement them, and even actions by them to curtail transnational attempts at state reform. Such signs became visible in recent years, affecting the lives of journalists and prosecutors who were challenging those in power or constraining the mode of operation of innovative bodies and agencies targeting corruption.

The bright and grim aspects of the transnational efforts to support the countries' efforts against corruption have been evident in the case of the International Commission against Impunity in Guatemala (Comisión Internacional contra la Impunidad en Guatemala; CICIG). The CICIG was created in December 2006 as an independent body, charged with supporting the Guatemalan criminal justice system in overcoming judicial incompetence, fighting corruption, and moving forward in major investigations and prosecutions. Established by an agreement between the United Nations and the Guatemalan government and approved by the Guatemalan congress in August 2007, the initiative could not have been achieved without the massive transnational and national work of a coalition of Guatemalan NGOs and external NGOs such as the Washington Office for Latin America (WOLA). The coalition that started the initiative in 2001 included various networks, among them the Center for Legal Action on Human Rights (Centro para la Acción Legal en Derechos Humanos), the International Human Rights Research Center (Centro Internacional para Investigaciones en Derechos Humanos), the Myrna Mack Foundation (Fundación Myrna Mack), the Mutual Support Group (Grupo de Apoyo Mutuo), the Rigoberta Menchú Tum

Foundation (Fundación Rigoberta Menchú Tum), the Institute of Comparative Studies in Criminal Sciences of Guatemala (Instituto de Estudios Comparados en Ciencias Penales de Guatemala), the Human Rights Office of the Archdiocese of Guatemala (Oficina de Derechos Humanos del Arzobispado de Guatemala), and Security in Democracy (Seguridad en Democracia).[28]

Several transnational factors led to the adoption of this mechanism for tackling state-related corruption and violence in Guatemala. The first was the paradigmatic example of the Salvadoran experience in launching an investigative commission connected to the United Nations, the Joint Group for the Investigation of Illegal Armed Groups with Political Motivation in El Salvador, or Grupo Conjunto, which was created in late 1993. Even though the work of the Joint Group for El Salvador did not lead to a single prosecution, it showed that sectors of civil society could project their activism in new directions in a postwar environment. The Salvadoran example inspired Guatemalan activists to join forces and generate transnational support through dense advocacy networks, thus reaching momentum in pushing their own government to act. Key actors and social forces within the country were also led to understand that only by seeking the help of the international community in confronting internal security and state-related violence could they circumvent the compromised work of some national institutions in that transitional period.

The ratification of the mandate proved difficult, due to the many hurdles it encountered in Congress. In the final stages of putting pressure on congressional representatives to approve the CICIG, another transnational event would ultimately lead to its approval. The embarrassing involvement of Guatemalan police in the assassination of three Salvadoran politicians and their driver on the outskirts of the Guatemalan capital in February 2007, followed by the murder of the suspects in a Guatemalan prison, generated momentum for the movement. This turned out to be the final push, as it signaled the inability to reach accountability by addressing the problem of state-related violence within national boundaries and under the often-professed allegations of defending national sovereignty.

The CICIG was an international commission embedded in the Guatemalan judicial system and funded by the UN, whose mandate was to improve the capacity of the Guatemalan administration to eradicate impunity. Starting operations in September 2007 with a two-year provision, its mandate was extended several times until 2019. From its inception, the International Commission against Impunity in Guatemala took center stage, criticizing state agencies and government procedures openly in an attempt to put pressure on existing institutions, with the professed aim of strengthening them. The CICIG's mandate allowed it to file criminal charges and act as a private prosecutor during court proceedings, although the domestic judicial system was in charge of conducting them. That is, even if the CICIG could launch its own investigations, it worked through the Public Prosecutor's Office as it probed leads or prosecuted suspects. The three commissioners of the CICIG have been Carlos Castresana from Spain (2007–10), Francisco Dall'Anese from Costa Rica (2010–13), and Iván Velásquez from Colombia (2013–19). All three had investigative and prosecutorial experience in high-profile corruption cases in their home countries. The UN's choice of foreign citizens to head the CICIG was intended to preclude any involvement in local crime networks that would compromise its operation.[29]

Another important part of the mandate was proposing reforms for the judicial system and the security forces. The CICIG could recommend those reforms to the government, so that its agencies might endorse transparency and fight abuse of power and impunity, although the government was under no obligation to follow the recommendations. The effectiveness of these reforms was reflected in the substantial public trust that the CICIG enjoyed (70 percent), which was even greater than the trust placed in the attorney general's office and the judicial system. With the CICIG's support, the Guatemalan judicial system successfully convicted four hundred individuals implicated in corruption. In conjunction with the Public Prosecutor's Office, the CICIG conducted several investigations into corrupt practices within the state administration and the security apparatus. Furthermore, the government approved several reforms recommended by the CICIG, including investigative procedures and techniques such as wiretapping, surveillance, confidential informants, undercover agents, and plea bargaining. The CICIG also oversaw the implementation of the Witness Protection Program and Courts for High-Risk Crimes, designed to protect eyewitnesses and judicial officials involved in serious, potentially life-threatening cases.[30]

Among the high-profile cases the CICIG handled were investigations involving former president Alfonso Portillo (2000–2004) on charges of money laundering and corruption. Another example is a 2010 case against five high-ranking officials in security institutions and various state agencies, as well as police officers and military personnel involved in extrajudicial killings of prison inmates during Oscar Berger's presidential term (2004–2008). The judicial system thus set a precedent with respect to the type of people that the commission was willing to confront. Many high-level officials were arrested, signaling that nobody was above the law. Likewise, in 2015 the CICIG uncovered one of Guatemala's largest scandals, involving President Otto Pérez Molina, Vice President Roxana Baldetti, and the latter's private secretary, who had engaged with impunity in murky transactions, including money laundering and drug trafficking, as well as corrupt interventions in the judiciary. Although those implicated denied these allegations, the release of wiretapped evidence confirmed their involvement.[31]

The CICIG derived much of its support from civil society and the media rather than the government. From the beginning of the CICIG mandate, the

Guatemalan Congress erected obstacles to the efforts to end corruption and strengthen institutional procedures. In 2018 the CICIG launched an investigation into the 2015 presidential campaign, based on information on illegal financing sources. Also in mid-2018, former foreign affairs minister and political analyst Edgar Gutiérrez accused President Jimmy Morales (2016–20) of sexually abusing at least ten women working in the public administration. In that tainted environment, President Morales barred CICIG commissioner Iván Velásquez's entrance into Guatemala and announced that he would not renew the CICIG mandate, a decision that the Constitutional Court considered unconstitutional. Although Morales cited the CICIG's ineffectiveness, biases, and failures and criticized the constitutionality of the CICIG's reform proposals as bases for his decision, many saw this as part of a smear campaign spreading rumors, motivated by retaliation. The sworn in president, Alejandro Giammattei, mentioned the creation of "a national anti-corruption commission," yet his own alleged involvement in the 2010 extrajudicial killings case and his strong stance against the CICIG did not augur a strong state commitment to the anticorruption cause.[32]

Another facet of the mandate relates to designing mechanisms of regional cooperation to control the impact of illicit and criminal rings that ravaged countries to varying degrees, by entering into agreements to implement transnational practices of prevention and regulation. The extent of the problem prompted this cooperation. Although violence has many origins and conditioning factors, it has been increasingly connected to the struggle over controlling access to the illegal transnational trafficking of persons, drugs, and arms, as well as the control of illegal markets. In Central America, citizens have linked the increase in criminality to the presence of *maras*. The Salvadoran National Police reported that there were almost 70,000 gang members in Central America, with a distribution of approximately 36,000 in Honduras, 14,000 in Guatemala, 11,000 in El Salvador, 4,500 in Nicaragua, 2,700 in Costa Rica, 1,400 in Panama, and 100 in Belize. Although the Salvadoran *maras* MS-18 and MS-13 are the largest, many more operate in the region. These gangs expanded by the end of the twentieth century, some through their links to illegal transnational trafficking networks. Packs of minors on corners and neighborhood gangs have been around for a long time, robbing or assaulting people who cross their territory, stealing from small businesses, and painting graffiti on the walls.[33] The massive transnational displacement and migration prompted by the civil wars from the 1970s through the 1990s transformed that dynamic by creating an interface between gang behavior and organized crime.

Uprooted from Central America, many migrants ended up in Los Angeles, California, a city known to be the home of numerous gangs, most of them divided along racial and ethnic lines. The immigrants arrived mainly from war zones and had been fighting in the army or with guerrillas; some had knowledge of arms, and they or their children soon joined the urban gangs. Changes in US federal immigration policies adopted after the violent disturbances of 1992 in Los Angeles determined that jailed gang members were to be deported to their countries of origin after serving jail time. Violence related to these markets and the circuits of drug and human trafficking was then spread by deported individuals, who transferred their knowledge and criminal networks back to the countries of origin, mainly, but not exclusively, Honduras and El Salvador. Their repatriation consolidated such networks in Central America, and some became integrated into transnational transport circuits of drugs, people, and arms, in addition to forms of local criminality.

With the increased importance of Central America as a corridor for drug and humantrafficking to the United States, the arms trade, coercion, extortion, and murders were also augmented. These activities thrived in the framework of state weakness and conflicts surrounding the control of access to routes and markets for illegal trade, often reinforcing public corruption and spreading fear throughout the population. A decisive factor in the entrenchment and radicalization of gang violence has been the substratum of the routinization of violence from previous decades. After the civil wars, societies in El Salvador, Guatemala, and Honduras were left traumatized by generalized violence. The prolonged civil struggle produced cultures of violence of variable historical depth across the isthmus. Another conditioning factor was that the states, along with enacting repressive policies, also weakened their regulating presence in society, thus creating vacuums that were filled by illegal networks in their interface with local gangs and *maras*. When the *maras* connected with organized crime and illegal circuits and markets, they were able to consolidate economic power, exercise violence, and control territories, which recreated the atmosphere of gang rule that many had known in the United States. Gangs could easily recruit new members in the context of poverty, unemployment, and distrust of police agencies and administrative organs, a situation that prevailed then in the region, with the partial exception of Costa Rica and, until recently, Nicaragua.

The interface between local criminality and the illegal transnational markets generated much violence and public insecurity, which has been ongoing for decades. The movement of drugs, people, and arms across borders using maritime and air transport has converted the *maras* into operational networks. One of the most serious problems in trying to lower the level of illicit activities and violence is the lack of alternative opportunities for people to sustain themselves; therefore extortion, human trafficking, and prostitution have continued to be extensive problems in Latin America. Alongside tourism, and occasionally in combination with it, there has been a noted increase in human trafficking for sexual exploitation. The interest of employers in the North in securing cheap labor for their businesses drove the development of illicit networks of Mexican coyotes, who were ready to facilitate the irregular transit and crossing of undocumented transmigrants from Mexico and Central America toward the United States.

On those transit routes, numerous transmigrants were deceived by the coyotes, kidnapped by organized crime networks, forced to pay a ransom, compelled to commit crimes, tortured, abused, sexually assaulted, and even detained by the police and turned over to networks of criminals. The broad scope of this type of exploitation included female stripteases and pornography with women and children. The relaxing of border controls in the 1990s facilitated the activity of human trafficking networks, especially those that moved along northern Nicaragua, passing through Honduras and possibly through El Salvador, and ending in Guatemala and Belize, and in the other direction, moving southward, trying to enter places of greater affluence in Costa Rica and Panama.

All across Central America, as well as in cities like Cartagena on Colombia's Caribbean coast, these phenomena emerged in the "tolerance zones" of tourist circuits, ports, casinos, and transnational transportation routes. Prostitution was also amply apparent in border zones and public markets, as well as in agricultural areas with temporary male crop workers. Attracted by the lure of tourists' dollars, the owners of bars, taxi drivers, hotel personnel, market sellers, and independent procurers all provided "intermediation services" to clients. Among such services are access to sex and drugs. While in the poorest regions prostitution is often carried out in family settings (Honduras) or related to gangs (El Salvador and Honduras), in the richest areas of Costa Rica, Panama, and Mexico there were reports of marriage fraud and deceptive entrapment. On the other hand, kidnappings and unfortunate accidents have been the result of human trafficking in all countries in the region. What has changed occasionally, under different contextual circumstances, has been the location of such networks.

According to the Center for Research on Organized Crime, gangs in El Salvador have been behind most cases of prostitution and extortion, or, as they call it, the "rent": a fee for "protection" of homes, businesses, and bus drivers. In an effort at rehabilitation, some *maras* have attempted to create "sanctuaries" and create sources of work and sustenance, such as bakeries or other stores. In conjunction with the government and institutions like the Catholic Church, attempts have been made to create "liberated" districts and "peace zones," free from crimes such as extortion, robbery, and kidnapping, where police presence can be minimal. The success rate has been uneven, as evidenced by the ups and downs in the truces and the occurrence of new outbursts of violence. Panama has also developed a program called Friendly Hand to facilitate access to theater works and sports for some ten thousand young people as an alternative to gang activities. Guatemala also established several programs for the prevention of delinquency, such as working with former gang members and with young people likely to join gangs. It also has added several thousand reserve troops to the streets to assist the police.

In Central America, states have begun such assessments in recent decades, amid a growing recognition of the need to implement transnational mechanisms to curtail the reach of criminal networks and illicit markets through the cooperation of nations on the isthmus. In January 2004, officials from Nicaragua, Honduras, Guatemala, El Salvador, and the Dominican Republic launched a database of information on criminals in order to follow the movements of clandestine organizations within the region. Over the last decade, security plans have been elaborated as part of the Central American Integration System, which was devised to combat the dangers of terrorism, drug trafficking, and related crimes, frequently combining efforts with those of the United States and Mexico. The police forces of El Salvador and Guatemala have cooperated on the border, coordinating actions for the detention of gang members, independently of where the crimes were committed. The countries have agreed to conduct joint actions within their borders and to common provision of resources to surmount limitations imposed by each country's internal laws and resources. Facing the illicit transnational networks and a deficit in public security, countries have moved to cooperate transnationally. It has also been suggested that NGOs and religious groups should create rehabilitation programs to help former gang members reintegrate into normal life, in addition to programs of obligatory rehabilitation designed for future recruitment of gang (*mara*) members into the armed forces.

Likewise, in South America there has been a belated effort of intelligence cooperation across borders, probably due to the memory of regional repressive cooperation during the Cold War and the ideological divide between countries. All South American countries have military and police intelligence agencies, and several also have other intelligence units: Brazil, Colombia, Ecuador, Paraguay, and Uruguay have financial intelligence agencies; Brazil, Peru, and Uruguay have such units at their ministries of foreign affairs; and Ecuador has customs and tax intelligence units. Most UNASUR countries participate in regional intelligence forums, in addition to INTERPOL, including the Foro Iberoamericano de Directores de Servicios de Inteligencia, the Comunidad Latinoamericana y del Caribe de Inteligencia Policial (CLASIP), the Red Sudamericana de Comunicaciones Protegidas (SURNET), the Grupo de Acción Financiera Latinoamericana (GAFILAT), and the Oficina Regional de Enlace de Inteligencia de Aduana (RILO). Nonetheless, researchers in this domain, such as Carolina Sancho Hirane and Fredy Rivera Vélez, have indicated that in spite of UNASUR's declaration of principles about the need to target transnational threats on a regional level, a region-wide strategic intelligence effort remains a pending item on the agenda of the organization.[34]

Transnational Movements Breaking New Ground

Perhaps more than the top-down mechanisms, bottom-up efforts by transnational movements have worked innovatively in Latin America. Due to the work of the social movements, the thematic agenda of human rights has broadened substantially in recent decades to include rights that were previously ignored, among them gender and diversity rights, the rights of original peoples, and the effective defense of economic and cultural rights. Transnational feminist movements in particular have targeted a persistent problem in the region, namely, gender inequality, discrimination, and violence against women and LGBTTQ individuals, including domestic violence.

To this day, women and gender-diverse individuals are more likely to become victims of violent crime in Latin America, including rape, a trend also reflected in differential rates based on race. Femicide and feminicide, gender-based hate crimes rooted in dominant male structures and misogyny, male control, and sexism, are still widespread phenomena, present in the entire region. In the decade and a half after 1993, most Latin American countries adopted laws prohibiting domestic violence and violence against women, prompted particularly by the work of OAS's Inter-American Commission of Women and the Inter-American Commission on Human Rights' Rapporteurship on the Rights of Women. Still, ECLAC Gender Equality Observatory for Latin American and the Caribbean compiled official data that at least 1,678 women were victims of femicide or feminicide in 2014; the numbers for 2016 were 1,831 women murdered for reasons of gender in thirteen countries in Latin America and three in the Caribbean; for 2019, ECLAC reported the figure of 4,555 to 4,640 victims of feminicide or femicide in fifteen Latin American states and four Caribbean countries.[35] In 2014, Brazil and Mexico showed high levels of feminicide in terms of both absolute numbers and the number of feminicides per 100,000 inhabitants.[36] In September 2018, the UN reported that Latin America was home to fourteen of the twenty-five countries with the highest rates of femicide in the world, with 98 percent of gender-related killings going unprosecuted. For 2019, the ECLAC Gender Equality Observatory reported that "the highest rates of feminicide per 100,000 women are observed in the case of Honduras (6.2), El Salvador (3.3), the Dominican Republic (2.7) and the Plurinational State of Bolivia (2.1)."[37] Thus, the problem is rather severe in Central America and has been aggravated by factors such as poverty, migration, and networks of drug trafficking and criminality.[38] In 2017, Gallup reported that only 35 percent of the poll's respondents in the region thought society respected women, far behind the average global assessment of 65 percent of respondents.[39] Likewise, lesbians of all social classes have faced hidden discrimination, resulting in being fired and a lack of job opportunities. Transvestites and transsexuals are the group most discriminated against, marginalized, and stereotyped as a pathology on the entire continent. Violent crimes against individuals of different sexual orientations continue to occur, with several hundred homicides each year in Brazil, for example. It is important to point out that it is difficult to judge if sexual orientation and gender identity are the main cause for those crimes or, depending on each case, there were other motives, such as the collection of debts or conflicts over disputed resources. Accordingly, transnational feminist movements have increasingly combined gender issues and systemic structural constraints imposing discriminatory policies with an intersectional impact on marginal populations.

Starting in one country, these movements have reached out to groups of feminist organizers in other settings, which in turn have used their transnational influence to advance issues of fundamental global and local relevance. The UN conferences on women that started in the mid-1970s and the global conferences of the 1990s allowed feminists from the Global South to meet one another along with activists from the Global North, to debate and articulate an expanding global vision of not only female rights but gender equality. Feminist activists worked their way into coalitions of organizations and networks, organized campaigns with other advocacy groups, and politicized women's rights and gender equality issues across nation-state boundaries. Later on, the new communications technologies allowed connections and cyber activism to develop between groups from multiple nations, inspiring each other as they advanced shared goals, from women's human rights to health issues and social justice. Indeed, as Rachel O'Donnell has indicated, Latin American feminists have consistently politicized the private sphere, campaigning against domestic violence, sexual harassment, gender violence, and the feminization of poverty. She described a massive protest against gendered violence in Santiago in November 2019 that shifted the blame away from the victim and onto the state. Going viral, it inspired similar protests elsewhere in the Americas:

> The women danced while declaring [that] "it was not my fault, or where I was, or how I was dressed!" . . . The protest went viral, and activists in Puerto Rico and Mexico have since used the same phrasing to bring attention to the ongoing local struggles against femicides and continued colonial exploitation, and even to advocate for education that prioritizes a gendered perspective.[40]

Likewise, the movement NiUnaMenos in Mexico, embodying the call for "*ni una mujer menos, ni una muerte más*" ("not even one woman less, not even one more death"), has gathered momentum and has resonated not just in Mexico. According to the Mexican Commission of Defense and Promotion of Human Rights (CMDPDH), violence against women has been normalized and perpetuated in family roles, schools, the labor market, politics, and religion. Although

Mexico took part in international conferences focused on the eradication of gendered violence, forced disappearances, abuse, and killing of women were on the rise in the decades following the 1990s. Violence against women pervaded Mexican socioeconomic and political structures, without much accountability. One of the events that sparked national and international interest in the feminicides in Mexico was the case of the Campo Algodonero in the city of Juárez, Chihuahua. In November 2001, eight bodies of women aged between fifteen and nineteen were found in an open field. The mothers of the victims presented a petition against Mexico before the Inter-American Commission on Human Rights, which found Mexico guilty of investigative negligence and ordered the government to compensate the families and build a memorial for the victims. The rise in feminicides can be attributed to organized crime and drug wars, the introduction of women in the labor market, and structural deficiencies in the judicial system. In 2007, the state promulgated a law on women's access to a life free of violence, and in 2009, the government created the National Commission for the Prevention and Eradication of Violence against Women (CONAVIM). Yet feminicide continues, and Ni Una Menos has gained momentum. Started by Mexican poet and activist Susana Chávez Castillo in response to the unsolved murders in Ciudad Juárez, Chihuahua, the movement gained media attention due to the passionate nature of protestors. In response to the news of a seventeen-year-old who was raped by four policemen in August 2019, more than three hundred women in Mexico City marched to the attorney general's office to ask the government to reshape and strengthen the legislation on violence against women. Using both peaceful and violent tactics, protesters were able to gain the attention of the media at least for a few days before their demonstrations were overshadowed by alarms about the pandemic. In terms of the most recent measures taken to diminish the rate of feminicides, Mexico still faces various internal obstacles to ensuring full accountability.[41]

Similarly, organizers of the International Women's Strike (IWS) in major Latin American capitals have tried to call attention to the many forms of unacknowledged and undercompensated labor mostly performed by women, such as child care, elder care, and intimate labor. On the day of the strike in March 2020, thousands of women in Argentina, Colombia, and Chile, and elsewhere in the world, withheld their labor at work, at school, and in the home. Marches and rallies planned in Buenos Aires coincided with the fight for reproductive rights and legalization of abortion in Argentina. A strong movement aligned in favor of reforming the 1921 criminal code that allowed legal abortion only under very narrow circumstances. With their green bandanas, the movement organized massive demonstrations outside Congress, where senators finally passed the law, thus overcoming the staunch resistance of the Catholic Church and evangelical denominations against it. Having managed to push through the hoped-for reform of abortion, the "green wave" movement was hopeful it would have some domino effect in other countries. The Argentine Senate also passed a law intended to provide better healthcare for pregnant women and mothers of young children.[42]

In recent years, advances have also taken place in the recognition of equal rights for the LGBTTQ community, which is composed of a variety of groups and sectors of sexual orientations: lesbians, gays, bisexuals, transsexuals, transvestites, and queers. Argentina was a pioneer in this area, recognizing same-sex marriage in 2010, following a 1996 statute adopted by the autonomous city of Buenos Aires that condemned all forms of discrimination, including discrimination based on sexual orientation. Outside the metropolitan area, homophobia continued to prevail, and lesbian activists argued that even homosexual men are *machistas* and hold prejudices against other manifestations of sexual diversity, including lesbianism. Finally, there have been criticisms of the concentrated attention on work benefits and marriage rights, topics of concern primarily for middle-class feminists, while issues such as discrimination against popular class individuals with reduced work opportunities have been ignored, for instance the hardship of those forced to work in prostitution. In Brazil, the Supreme Court voted in June 2019 to make discrimination based on sexual orientation and gender identity a criminal offense.[43]

The Covid-19 Pandemic, Politics, and Populist Leaderships

The coronavirus outbreak has added to human suffering in Latin America as much as anywhere else worldwide. The outbreak has produced loss of human life, reduced market activity, and increased rates of unemployment. Popular sectors have been especially vulnerable due to their dwelling and working conditions, and their lack of savings forces them to continue interacting in formal and informal markets, making it difficult for them to keep appropriate distance and observe hygiene precautions. In Peru, for example, more than two-thirds of the population works in the informal sector; more than 40 percent of households do not have a refrigerator, and people must go out repeatedly to stock up; people must go in person to the bank to cash a check, because they lack a bank account; and about 12 percent of poor households live in overcrowded homes.[44] Throughout Latin America, less than two-thirds of the workforce have some form of social protection benefit in case of unemployment, and only 23 percent of jobs can be conducted via "telework," mostly at large companies. In 2019, unemployment insurance was only available in Argentina, Brazil, Chile, Colombia, Ecuador, and Uruguay. Moreover, in some of these countries, like Chile, unemployment insurance becomes effective only under extreme circumstances, such as when the authorities order work to be suspended.[45] Moreover, in a region where only limited segments of the population have internet access, the transition to telework at government offices, schools, and other public institutions can be particularly difficult for popular sectors. Add to that the need to ask for and process a special transit permit to go out of home lockdown, as enforced in Argentina in 2020, and the situation can become extremely stressful.[46]

For Latin American countries, the pandemic also led to major reductions in remittances, an important transnational source of income for those inhabitants whose relatives worked in developed economies and used to send them money regularly from abroad. For decades individuals pooled earnings from their work in the United States and other locations to support their families and build public projects back in their home countries. The loss of economic activity in the United States and Europe led to the loss of this cash flow, which for years had improved life back home and provided a safety net during economic downturns.[47]

Another major impact has been a lack of adequate attention to other illnesses and diseases. For instance, in the state of Paraná, Brazil, the first five months of 2020 witnessed an explosion of cases of dengue, while federal financial support and hospital beds had been earmarked for expected Covid-19 cases.[48] The same applied to many other illnesses, which due to lack of proper attention remained largely untreated for the length of the global pandemic outbreak.

Less obvious yet equally significant are the political impacts. The pandemic put to the test Latin American multilateralism, since the width and severity of the crisis could have been, as Arie Kacowicz, Exequiel Lacovksy, and Daniel F. Wajner have indicated, "an excellent occasion to strengthen the mechanisms of dialogue, coordination, and cooperation in the region." Instead, the crisis showed up the deficiencies of Latin American regionalism, trapped in a huge gap between professions of faith and rhetorics of multilateralism and integration and the policies of national closure and regional lack of cooperation:

> There has not been much progress in this respect, beyond the obvious rhetorical level. For instance, despite the existence of the Pan-American Health Organization (since 1902, well before the WHO!), the OAS has not been very effective beyond some token initiatives. Similarly, Mercosur has been dysfunctional because of the rising tensions and animadversion between the Argentine and Brazilian Presidents. Furthermore, SEGIB might issue positive and well-taken declarations, but it cannot replace an alternative CELAC as the all-encompassing Latin American organization in identity terms, whereas CELAC is currently malfunctioning, if not non-existent.[49]

At the national level, some parliaments and judicial systems have closed their doors. In others, heads of state have threatened to constrain the leeway of the other branches of government, under the guise of ruling effectively. The pandemic may likely also affect the support of Latin American citizens for their leadership, particularly populist leaders. While leaders projected claims of being the true representatives of the common good, some—like Jair Bolsonaro and Daniel Ortega—downplayed the severity of the Covid-19 epidemic and disregarded the adoption of prompt and strict measures to cut down the contagion curve, unlike more effective leaderships.[50] Instead, they accused political oppositions and the media of oversensationalizing the threat, which proved to be detrimental to public trust when the number of severe cases and deaths spiraled. Bolsonaro's whimsical attitude to the health crisis, often at odds with scientists, academics, and even his own ministers, has made Brazil one of the most heavily affected countries worldwide. In 2020, two health ministers resigned from their posts in disagreement with the Brazilian president's dismissive attitude and lack of adoption of bold measures to prevent the spread of the virus, and the president's image has deteriorated. Polls have tracked a growing disenchantment with the president's performance. Just as the virus spread, so has discontent with the government's response, although short-term financial relief has mitigated such negative assessments recently. Notably, state governors have received higher approval ratings than the president and the federal administration, reflecting the fact that the latter was bearing most of the disapproval for the policy of disregarding the threat, which became evident when Bolsonaro himself contracted the virus.[51]

Populist responses to the pandemic met with less success than these leaders had anticipated. Since democratization, populist leaders had portrayed themselves as the embodiment of popular wisdom and defenders of the common good, of the "people" and their pressing needs. Relying symbolically on anti-establishment messages, populist leaders achieved power by making promises of immediate and simple solutions to old and new unsolved problems. The appropriation of voice by leaders preaching a "politics of anti-politics" weakened other branches of government and institutions of representative democracy. The current health and economic crisis has found some of these leaders, both on the Right and on the Left, at the head of their countries' governments, in a period that requires effective and timely responses and prompt calibration of health measures. The strategy of populist leaders to put the blame of this crisis on conspiracies while preaching disinformation and misinformation has only deepened the inner division between their staunch supporters and major sectors disenchanted with the tragic consequences of leaders' dismissive strategy during the pandemic.

Uruguay, Paraguay, and Costa Rica have stood out for their relatively successful measures taken to cope with the pandemic, in contrast to Brazil, Mexico, and Ecuador. Leaders and administrations that acted swiftly in these strenuous times have received far higher rates of approval, irrespective of their ideological-political leanings, stretching from populist leftist to conservative leaderships. In Peru, the popularity of President Martín Alberto Vizcarra (2018–20) during the crisis reached an approval rate of 82 percent, due to his efforts to contain the spread of the virus. However, even Vizcarra's prompt response at the beginning of the pandemic could not halt the rise in mortality, due to structural constraints such as poverty, overcrowding, and the need of many Peruvians to participate daily in the informal sector for their economic survival. In Argentina, President Alberto Fernández (2019–) also saw his popularity rise, even if theoretically the policies of economic closure damaged his political base. His approval rate reached almost 80 percent, with 94.7 percent of respondents indicating they approved of the "shelter-at-home" policies.[52] Likewise, comparing Brazil with Mexico is instructive of the difference between two populist leaderships, correlated with the perception of efficacy or lack of efficacy of the policies implemented. Both countries have responded with negligence and slow and inconsistent measures, resulting in very high mortality rates. Nonetheless, whereas in Brazil polls registered the growing disapproval of the president's performance, in Mexico President Andrés Manuel López Obrador's approval rates were still high in 2020, even though there was a drop compared to 2019. While multiple factors may account for this, one may assume that his sincere commitment to securing a basic livelihood and security for all Mexicans, even in times of crisis, carried weight with the popular classes and earned their support.[53]

The current crisis has challenged Latin American leaders, most of whom have learned to acknowledge the limits of their power in one way or another. While attempting to bypass or bend the rules of the game, for example by closing parliament or attacking the courts, they faced an increased opposition, as in El Salvador or most recently in Brazil. Accordingly, in their discourse, politicians in power claimed to be working to restore order and "democratize democracy," which made sense in terms of the huge socioeconomic gaps persisting under democracy. The logic of neopopulism has thus become entrenched in the perception of direct participatory democracy as "true" democracy. Still, the crisis has revealed the limits of the populist rhetoric as balanced by aggregate citizen power. In these societies, widespread unfulfilled expectations for responsible policymaking can easily erupt into mass demonstrations and occupation of public spaces. The mounting of such popular mobilizations has been rather effective in forcing national leaders to abdicate power in the past. While muted under Covid-19 conditions, popular social protest and mobilization can easily rekindle and become a boomerang against those in power.

Epilogue

As I write these last pages, Latin America has become an epicenter of contagious diseases and is increasingly living through an economic impasse. The rate of contagion has spiraled in many countries, and not only those that delayed or avoided imposing restrictive contact measures. "Peru's government responded quickly with a strict lockdown [and adopted a comprehensive aid package of cash transfers and loans to help citizens stay at home], but deaths have spiked there, much as they have in Brazil and Mexico, where leaders underplayed the virus's threat."[1] In Peru as much as in Brazil, Mexico, Ecuador, and Nicaragua, the number of sick and dead has risen exponentially, even if statistics have tended to register only part of the casualties. The economic toll is equally considerable. Some 72 million Latin Americans had escaped poverty between 2003 and 2013, yet currently between 35 and 52 million people are at risk of falling into poverty again, especially in Colombia, Guatemala, Mexico, and Peru. In March 2020, ECLAC forecasted that out of the 620 million inhabitants of the region, the pandemic could increase the number of poor from 185 to 220 million people, and those in extreme poverty from 67.4 to 90 million people.[2]

All the economies of the region have been affected by the economic deceleration, even those like Nicaragua where no lockdown or distancing measures have been adopted.[3] Some economies, such as those of Guatemala, Honduras, Nicaragua, and Venezuela, have continued to contract. The collapse in the global demand for oil has hit Venezuela, Ecuador, and Colombia, with the Venezuelan economy almost completely disarticulated, and Ecuador is facing a major challenge with no access to credit markets, no reserves, and a dollarized economy. With reserves, Colombia has been better equipped to face its crisis. Argentina, on the other hand, has failed to timely develop its major reservoirs of gas and oil in Vaca Muerta, Patagonia, while its economy has entered free fall and it is on the verge of defaulting on its huge external debt. Mexico's national oil company, PEMEX, is similarly facing deep financial troubles.[4] Millions of people throughout the region are out of work or subsisting precariously in the informal markets. Hundreds of thousands are destitute, suffering hunger and looking frantically for any livelihood survival net, irrespective of whether state or non-state actors provide it, including opportunities provided by illicit networks.

The health and economic conundrum also has added political repercussions that have further weakened the vitality of these democracies. In a note in the

Transnational Perspectives on Latin America. Luis Roniger, Oxford University Press. © Oxford University Press 2022.
DOI: 10.1093/oso/9780197605318.003.0012

Folha de São Paulo, political scientist Manuel Alcántara characterized this as a transition "from tired to quarantined democracies," in which the pandemic added even more pressures to the persistent structure of socioeconomic inequalities and weakness of representative democracies. In this stage, he indicates, the pandemic situation has generated opportunities for personalist executives to concentrate even more decision-making powers in the center, postponing elections or putting on hold other popular consultations, while once again imposing exceptional measures to control the population.[5]

From a long-term perspective, the tensions inherent in performing politics within such a logic are increasingly visible in Latin America. First, there is a weakening of representative democracy, as political parties and parliaments have been ineffective in balancing authoritarian decision-making, with the executive concentrating powers and overriding checks and balances. Second, the persisting appeal of organicist narratives from populist figures claiming to represent the common good of the sovereign "people" is combining with renewed citizen expectations of social justice, which is very appealing during political campaigns. Nonetheless, once these leaders are in power, these expectations are often abandoned for the logic of free markets, and their governments have become more open to private initiatives, which remain burdened by inefficacy and political corruption. Countries such as Ecuador and Brazil had slashed their healthcare budgets and accordingly, their hospitals are underfunded and their medical supplies unfit to meet the challenge of such a health crisis. In addition, governments failed to manage the Covid-19 crisis, partly because they could not outbid more affluent countries when they sought to purchase such supplies, but also because of corruption. The acute crisis allegedly enabled overpricing of testing kits by Ecuadorian officials and the inflated purchase of ventilators by Bolivian officials with Inter-American Development Bank funds.[6] The deficiencies of these countries' medical systems in dealing with the current pandemic have been made evident, for example, in Brazil, Mexico, and Ecuador, where patients have died from lack of timely intervention and care, scarce medical equipment, and mistakes.[7]

Yet as discussed earlier, the region has a strong tradition of highly participatory societies pressing demands and making their voices heard in the public arena. One should expect outbursts of popular mobilization and unrest to develop that will challenge the style of personalist rule and decision-making, most likely supported by countervailing visions of democracy that reverberate cyclically in the public sphere. These popular mobilizations are likely to continue as affected social sectors may raise again the banners of social justice and egalitarian development. The visions of communitarian and participatory democracy, which have been reinforced and betrayed cyclically by various leaders, can be expected to persist, buttressed by outbursts of popular mobilization, a trend that the combination of populist rhetoric and ineffective policies recreates at the center of Latin American politics and public spheres.

As for transnational spillovers, we have witnessed border closings due to the fear of spreading the coronavirus, and the situation of those who move and settle across borders has been dire. Countries fearing contagion moved to close their borders, as Brazil did with eight South American countries, among them Argentina and Paraguay, in March 2020, in addition to the already closed border with Venezuela. Furthermore, the divide between center-Left and center-Right governments and social forces has added problems, as it has affected the ability of sister nations to cooperate in the framework of multiple and often competing regional intergovernmental organizations. This situation became critical for thousands of Venezuelans in the area of Cúcuta, Colombia and Central Americans stuck south of the Mexican-US border. Even when remaining in a sister nation, as aliens, these migrants have become vulnerable to exploitation, sex trafficking and prostitution, domestic servitude, and portering of heavy loads across borders for minimal wages. Often a contradiction has deepened between the professed recognition of universal human rights and the actual bounded life conditions of these alien residents, who find themselves without a political voice, likely to be banished at the will of the authorities. Thus, at the onset of the coronavirus pandemic, in addition to pressure due to unemployment, Colombia decided to bus hundreds of incoming Venezuelans beyond its borders into Ecuador. More recently, however, the new Colombian administration has reversed direction and indicated a willingness to grant permanent resident status for a ten-year period to a million Venezuelans living in the country undocumented.

Balancing these trends, however, are several trends analyzed in this book. Among them, persisting diasporas have connected migrants to both networks in their home countries and the countries of residence, as in the case of Bolivians and Paraguayans in Argentina, Peruvians in Chile, and Nicaraguans in Costa Rica and other nations. The current crisis has already triggered several massive waves of return migration, including unemployed Venezuelans in Colombia returning to their home country. In addition, Venezuela and Cuba have sent physicians abroad to help deal with the humanitarian crises in sister nations. Thus, in return for national revenues, these transnational bonds remained in place. Also, transnational alliances of Afro-Americans, indigenous peoples, and gender-diverse groups have continued to make their mark, contesting existing policies and attempting to effect policy changes across the region, in cooperation with regional IGOs and issue networks.

In Latin America, regionalism retains its high rhetorical pitch in declarations by IGOs and state governments alike, which call for the support of multilateral cooperation and respect for international norms, concern for social justice and equity, inclusion of subaltern groups, and recognition of intersectionality and multiple collective identities. Practically, multilateral governance has been found wanting. Nonetheless, citizens across the region are likely to continue living in a matrix of entangled histories due to geopolitics, territorial closeness, and their shared cultural and linguistic affinity. As the world becomes multipolar, regional reconfiguration of alliances and blocks will likely continue to play an important role in the future. Challenges such as drug trafficking or the curtailment of corruption and feminicide will likely prompt new transnational mobilizations and international solutions. Culturally, Latin American nations also continue to reflect on the effectiveness or failings of each other's policies in facing geopolitical challenges and developmental priorities. The media have long reported on events, trends, and cultural creation in the sister nations, and the new forms of digital and social media have merely increased the virtual connections and increased the likelihood of imagined communities of citizens projecting ideas and interacting with each other across borders in this multistate region.

Notes

Introduction

1. Shmuel N. Eisenstadt and Luis Roniger, *Patrons, Clients, and Friends: Interpersonal Relations and the Structure of Trust in Society* (Cambridge: Cambridge University Press, 1984); Luis Roniger, "Modern Patron-Client Relations and Historical Clientelism: Some Clues from Ancient Republican Rome," *Archives Européennes de Sociologie* 24, no. 1 (1983): 63–95; Luis Roniger, *The Study of Caciquismo: Patterns of Patron-Brokerage in Oaxaca*, Occasional Papers in Latin American Studies No. 13 (Berkeley: University of California and Stanford University Joint Center for Latin American Studies, 1986); Luis Roniger, "Coronelismo, Caciquismo, and Oyabun-Kobun: Divergent Implications of Hierarchical Trust in Brazil, Mexico, and Japan," *British Journal of Sociology* 38, no. 2 (1987): 310–330; Luis Roniger and Ayşe Güneş-Ayata, eds., *Democracy, Clientelism and Civil Society* (Boulder, CO: Lynne Rienner, 1994); and Luis Roniger, "Patron-Client Relations: Anthropological Study of," in *The International Encyclopedia of the Social and Behavioral Sciences*, ed. Neil Smelser and Paul Baltes (Amsterdam: Elsevier, 2001), 16:11118–11120.
2. Luis Roniger and Mario Sznajder, eds., *Latin American Paths: Constructing Collective Identities and Shaping Public Spheres* (Brighton, UK: Sussex Academic Press, 1998); Luis Roniger and Tamar Herzog, eds., *The Collective and the Public in Latin America: Cultural Identities and Political Order* (2000; Brighton, UK: Sussex Academic Press, 2014); and Luis Roniger and Carlos H. Waisman, eds., *Globality and Multiple Modernities: Comparative North American and Latin American Perspectives* (Brighton, UK: Sussex Academic Press, 2002).
3. Luis Roniger, "Democracy in Latin America: The 'Only Game in Town'?," in *Comparing Modernities: Pluralism Versus Homogeneity*, ed. Eliezer Ben-Rafael and Yitzhak Sternberg (Leiden: Brill, 2005), 553–580; Mario Sznajder, Luis Roniger, and Carlos Forment, eds., *Shifting Frontiers of Citizenship: The Latin American Experience* (Leiden: Brill, 2013); and Luis Roniger, *Historia mínima de los derechos humanos en América Latina* (Mexico City: : Colegio de México, 2018).
4. Luis Roniger and Mario Sznajder, *The Legacy of Human-Rights Violations in the Southern Cone: Argentina, Chile and Uruguay* (New York: Oxford University Press, 1999); Mario Sznajder and Luis Roniger, "The Crises beyond Past Crisis: The Unsolved Legacy of Human-Rights Violations in the Southern Cone," *Human Rights Review* 1, no. 1 (1999): 48–68; L. Roniger, "U.S. Hemispheric Hegemony and the Descent into Genocidal Practices in Latin America," in *State Violence and Genocide in Latin America: The Cold War Years*, ed. Marcia Esparza, Daniel Feierstein, and Henry Huttenbach (New York: Routledge, 2010), 23–43.

5. Mario Sznajder and Luis Roniger, *The Politics of Exile in Latin America* (New York: Cambridge University Press, 2009); and Mario Sznajder and Luis Roniger, *La política del destierro y el exilio en América Latina* (Mexico City: Fondo de Cultura Económica, 2013).

6. Luis Roniger, James N. Green, and Pablo Yankelevich, eds., *Exile and the Politics of Exclusion in the Americas* (Brighton, UK: Sussex Academic Press, 2012); Luis Roniger, *Destierro y exilio en América Latina: Nuevos estudios y avances teóricos* (Buenos Aires: Editorial Universitaria de la Universidad de Buenos Aires, 2014); and Arturo Aguirre, Antolín Sánchez Cuervo, and Luis Roniger, *Tres estudios sobre el exilio: Condición humana, experiencia histórica y significación política* (Puebla and Madrid: Universidad Autónoma de Puebla [Mexico] and EDAF [Spain], 2014).

7. Luis Roniger, Leonardo Senkman, Saúl Sosnowski, and Mario Sznajder, *Exile, Diaspora and Return: Changing Cultural Landscapes in Argentina, Chile, Paraguay and Uruguay* (New York: Oxford University Press, 2018).

8. Luis Roniger, *Transnational Politics in Central America* (Gainesville: University Press of Florida, 2011).

Chapter 1

1. José Mauricio Domingues, "Modernity and Modernizing Moves: Latin America in Comparative Perspective," *Theory, Culture and Society* 26 (2009): 208–227; and Mario Sznajder, Luis Roniger, and Carlos Forment, eds., *Shifting Frontiers of Citizenship* (Leiden: Brill, 2013).

2. Peter A. Hall and Sidney Tarrow, "Globalization and Area Studies: When Is Too Broad Too Narrow?," *Chronicle*, January 23, 1998.

3. Michel Gobat, "The Invention of Latin America: A Transnational History of Anti-Imperialism, Democracy, and Race," *American Historical Review* 118, no. 5 (2013): 1345–1375. See also his *Empire by Invitation* (Cambridge, MA: Harvard University Press, 2018).

4. For a fascinating example of such cultural presence, see Coco Fusco, *English Is Broken Here: Notes on Cultural Fusion in the Americas* (New York: New Press, 1995).

5. Peter Winn, "A View from the South," in *Americas: The Changing Face of Latin America and the Caribbean* (Berkeley: University of California Press, 1992), 1–32.

6. José Luis de Imaz, *Sobre la identidad iberoamericana* (Buenos Aires: Sudamericana, 1979), 233–236.

7. Akira Iriye, *Global and Transnational History: The Past, Present and Future* (London: Palgrave Macmillan, 2012); and Diego Olstein, *Thinking History Globally* (London: Palgrave Macmillan, 2014).

8. Sanjay Subrahmanyam, "Connected Histories: Notes towards a Reconfiguration of Early Modern Eurasia," *Modern Asian Studies* 31, no. 3 (1997): 735–762; Steven Vertovec, "Conceiving and Researching Transnationalism," *Ethnic and Racial Studies* 22, no. 2 (1999): 447–462; and Sanjay Subrahmanyam, *Explorations in Connected History: From the Tagus to the Ganges* (Oxford: Oxford University Press, 2005).

NOTES TO PAGES 11–14   263

9. Michael Werner and Bénédicte Zimmermann, "Beyond Comparison: *Histoire croisée* and the Challenge of Reflexivity," *History and Theory* 45 (2006): 30–50.

10. Iriye, *Global and Transnational History*; Pierre Yves Saunier, *Transnational History* (London: Palgrave Macmillan, 2013); and "Borders and Frontiers in Global and Transnational History," ed. Erik Van der Vleuten and Torsten Feys, special issue, *Journal of Modern European History* 14, no. 1 (2016).

11. Michelle Pace, *Politics of Regional Identity* (London: Routledge, 2006); Donatella Della Porta and Sidney Tarrow, eds., *Transnational Protest and Global Activism* (Lanham, MD: Rowman and Littlefield, 2005); and Galia Press-Barnathan, Ruth Fine, and Arie M. Kacowicz, eds., *The Relevance of Regions in a Globalized World* (Abingdon, UK: Routledge; Notre Dame: University of Notre Dame Press, 2019).

12. Thomas Risse-Kappen, ed., *Bringing Transnational Relations Back In* (Cambridge: Cambridge University Press, 1995), 3.

13. Arie M. Kacowicz and Daniel F. Wajner, "Alternative World Orders in an Age of Globalization: Latin American Scenarios and Responses" (unpublished manuscript, December 2019). See also Arie M. Kacowicz, *The Impact of Norms in International Society: The Latin American Experience, 1881–2001* (Notre Dame: University of Notre Dame Press, 2005); and Carlos Escudé, "Who Commands, Who Obeys, and Who Rebels: Latin American a Security in a Peripheral-Realist Perspective," in *Routledge Handbook of Latin American Security*, ed. David R. Mares and Arie M. Kacowicz (London: Routledge, 2016), 56–66.

14. Micol Seigel, "Beyond Compare: Comparative Method and the Transnational Turn," *Radical History Review* 91 (2005): 62–92. See also "The Nation and Beyond: Transnational Perspectives on United States History," special issue, *Journal of American History* 86 (1999): esp. 965–975.

15. Craig Calhoun, "Social Theory and the Politics of Identity," in *Social Theory and the Politics of Identity*, ed. Craig Calhoun (Oxford: Blackwell, 1994), 9–36; and Adrienne Rich, "Notes towards a Politics of Location," in *Blood, Bread and Poetry* (New York: Norton, 1986), 210–231. See also, for example, *Signs* 26, no. 3 (2001); and Sylvanna M. Falcón, "Transnational Feminism as a Paradigm for Decolonizing the Practice of Research," *Frontiers: A Journal of Women Studies* 37, no. 1 (2016): 174–194.

16. Werner and Zimmermann, "Beyond Comparison," 43. These scholars develop their approach more fully in "Vergleich, Transfer, Verflechtung: Der Ansatz der *Histoire croisée* und die Herausforderung des Transnationalen," *Geschichte und Gesellschaft* 28 (2002): 607–636.

17. Barbara Weinstein, "Erecting and Erasing Boundaries: Can We Combine the 'Indo' and the 'Afro' in Latin American Studies?," *Estudios interdisciplinarios de América Latina y el Caribe* 19, no. 1 (2008): 129–144.

18. Ana María Alonso, "The Politics of Space, Time and Substance: State Formation, Nationalism, and Ethnicity," *Annual Review of Anthropology* 23 (1994): 379–405; and Ralph Lee Woodward Jr., *Central America: A Nation Divided* (New York: Oxford University Press, 1999).

19. Anupama Mande, "Subaltern Studies and the Historiography of the Sandinista-Miskitu Conflict in Nicaragua, 1979–1990" (paper presented at LASA 2000 Congress), lasa.international.pitt.edu/Lasa2000/Mande.PDF.

20. Luis Roniger, *Transnational Politics in Central America* (Gainesville: University of Florida Press, 2011); and Ori Preuss, *Transnational South America: Experiences, Ideas, and Identities, 1860s–1910s* (New York: Routledge, 2015).

21. Claus Leggewie, "Transnational Citizenship: Cultural Concerns," in *International Encyclopedia of the Behavioral and Social Sciences* (Saint Louis, UK: Elsevier, 2001), 15857–15862; Adrian Bailey, Richard A. Wright, Alison Mountz, and Ines M. Miyares, "(Re)producing Salvadoran Transnational Geographies," *Annals of the Association of American Geographers* 92, no. 1 (2002): 125–144; and Eliezer Ben-Rafael and Yitzhak Sternberg, eds., *Transnationalism: Diasporas and the Advent of a New (Dis)order* (Leiden: Brill, 2009).

22. Gabriel Sheffer, ed., *Modern Diasporas in International Politics* (London: Croom Helm, 1986); Gabriel Sheffer, *Diaspora Politics: At Home and Abroad* (Cambridge: Cambridge University Press, 2003); Judit Bokser Liwerant et al., eds., *Identities in an Era of Globalization and Multiculturalism* (Leiden: Brill, 2008); and William Safran, "The Diaspora and the Homeland: Reciprocities, Transformations, and Role Reversals," in Ben-Rafael and Sternberg, *Transnationalism*, 75–100.

23. Kacowicz and Wajner, "Alternative World Orders," 6. See also Gary Goertz, Paul F. Dihel, and Alexandru Balas, *The Puzzle of Peace: The Evolution of Peace in the International System* (Oxford: Oxford University Press, 2016).

24. Kathryn Sikkink, "Latin American Countries as Norm Protagonists of the Idea of International Human Rights," *Global Governance* 20, no. 3 (2014): 389–404; Pilar González Bernaldo de Quirós, "Primeras iniciativas de regulación global de las migraciones: Estanislao Zeballos y la doctrina argentina del 'derecho privado humano' (1873–1923)," *História Unisinos* 22, no. 2 (2018): 170–184; Luis Roniger, *Historia mínima de los derechos humanos en América Latina* (Mexico City: COLMEX, 2018).

25. Richard Snyder and Angelica Duran-Martinez, "Does Illegality Breed Violence? Drug Trafficking and State-Sponsored Protection Rackets," *Crime, Law and Social Change* 52, no. 3 (2009): 253–273.

26. Max Paul Friedman, *Rethinking Anti-Americanism: The History of an Exceptional Concept in American Foreign Relations* (New York: Cambridge University Press, 2012), 66–67.

27. Luis Roniger and Mario Sznajder, *The Legacy of Human Rights Violations in the Southern Cone: Argentina, Chile and Uruguay* (Oxford: Oxford University Press, 1999); and Cecilia Menjivar and Nestor Rodriguez, eds., *When States Kill: Latin America, the U.S., and Technologies of Terror* (Austin: University of Texas Press, 2005).

28. Edward Blumenthal, *Exile and Nation-State Formation in Argentina and Chile, 1810–1862*, Palgrave Macmillan Transnational History Series (London: Palgrave Macmillan, 2019), chs. 6–7; 219–316.

29. Mario Sznajder and Luis Roniger, *The Politics of Exile in Latin America* (New York: Cambridge University Press, 2009), 33–34, 81–82, and 105–117.

30. Ori Preuss, *Bridging the Island: Brazilians' Views of Spanish America and Themselves, 1865–1912* (Madrid: Iberoamericana Vervuert, 2011); Ori Preuss, "Brazil into Latin America: The Demise of Slavery and Monarchy as Transnational Events," *Luso-Brazilian Review* 49, no. 1 (2012): 96–126; and Ori Preuss, *Transnational South America: Experiences, Ideas, and Identities, 1860s–1910s* (London: Routledge, 2015).

31. Jaime Moreno Tejada and Bradley Tatar, eds., *Transnational Frontiers of Asia and Latin America since 1800* (London: Routledge, 2017).

32. On the 1937 massacre in the Dominican Republic, see Richard Lee Turits, "A World Destroyed, a Nation Imposed: The 1937 Haitian Massacre in the Dominican Republic," *Hispanic American Historical Review* 82, no. 3 (2002): 589–635; and Lauren Derby, *The Dictator's Seduction* (Durham, NC: Duke University Press, 2009). For an analysis of the conspiracy theories constructed to justify the massacre, see Luis Roniger and Leonardo Senkman, *Conspiracy Theories and Latin American History* (London: Routledge, 2021).

33. Mónica Gatica, *¿Exilio, migración, destierro? Trabajadores chilenos en el noreste de Chubut (1973–2010)* (Buenos Aires: Prometeo, 2013).

34. See, among others, Claudia García, "The Past in the Present: The Social Construction of Miskitu Identity in Sandinista Nicaragua," in *The Collective and the Public in Latin America: Cultural Identities and Political Order*, ed. Luis Roniger and Tamar Herzog (Brighton, UK: Sussex Academic Press, 2000), 95–114; Sandra Brunnegger, "From Conflict to Autonomy in Nicaragua: Lessons Learnt," Minority Rights Group International, 2007, www2.ohchr.org/english/bodies/cescr/docs/infongos/mrginicaragua39wg.pdf; and Roniger, *Transnational Politics in Central America*, 75–81.

35. Judit Liwerant, "Being National, Being Transnational: Snapshots of Belonging and Citizenship," in Sznajder, Roniger, and Forment, *Shifting Frontiers of Citizenship*, 343–365; Leonardo Senkman, "The Latin American Diasporas: New Collective Identities and Citizenship Practices," in Sznajder, Roniger, and Forment, *Shifting Frontiers of Citizenship*, 385–407; and Luis Roniger, Leonardo Senkman, Saúl Sosnowski, and Mario Sznajder, *Exile, Diaspora and Return: Changing Cultural Landscapes in Argentina, Chile, Paraguay and Uruguay* (New York: Oxford University Press, 2018).

36. Blanca G. Silvestrini, "New National Spaces in the Spanish Caribbean: A Methodological Inquiry," in *Beyond Fragmentation: Perspectives on Caribbean History*, ed. Juanita de Barros, Audra Diptee, and David Vincent Trotman (Princeton, NJ: M. Wiener, 2006), 235.

Chapter 2

1. The concept is Martin Wright's in *System of States* (Norwich, UK: Leicester University Press, 1977), 126, cited in Carsten-Andreas Schulz, "Civilisation, Barbarism and the Making of Latin America's Place in 19th-Century International Society," *Millenium* 42, no. 2 (2014): 837–859, 844.

2. Aníbal Quijano, "Coloniality of Power and Eurocentrism in Latin America," *International Sociology* 15, no. 2 (2000): 215–232.

3. Enrique Dussel, "Europe, Modernity, and Eurocentrism," *Nepantla: Views from South* 1, no. 3 (2000): 465–478.

4. See José Mauricio Domingues, *Latin America and Contemporary Modernity* (New York: Routledge, 2008).

5. Jeremy Smith, *Europe and the Americas: State Formation, Capitalism and Civilizations in Atlantic Modernity* (Leiden: Brill, 2006).

6. Thomas E. Skidmore and Peter H. Smith, *Modern Latin America* (New York: Oxford University Press, 2004); Lawrence A. Clayton and Michael Conniff, *A History of Modern Latin America* (Belmont, CA: Thomson-Wadsworth, 2005); S. N. Eisenstadt, "The First Multiple Modernities: Collective Identity, Public Spheres and Political Order in the Americas," in *Globality and Multiple Modernities. Comparative North American and Latin American Perspectives*, ed. Luis Roniger and Carlos Waisman (Brighton, UK: Sussex Academic Press, 2002), 7–28; and Mabel Moraña, Enrique Dussel, and Carlos A Jáuregui, eds. *Coloniality at Large: Latin America and the Postcolonial Debate* (Durham, NC: Duke University Press, 2008).

7. Nicola Miller and Stephen Hart, eds., *When Was Latin America Modern?* (London: Palgrave Macmillan, 2007).

8. Among other things, Knight bemoans the danger of conflating the subjective perceptions of actors with the analytical concepts used by social scientists and historians, indicating that only rarely and recently has the term become "emicized" and used as a popular notion or in political discourse, whereas progress or civilization figured prominently in the vernacular. Alan Knight, "When Was Latin America Modern? A Historian's Response," in Miller and Hart, *When Was Latin America Modern?*, 91–117.

9. Laurence Whitehead, "Conclusion: When Was Latin America Modern?," in Miller and Hart, *When Was Latin America Modern?*, 191–209.

10. Recognition is due to one of the anonymous readers of the book manuscript for this wording.

11. James Dunkerley, *Americana* (London: Verso, 2000).

12. Esteban Krotz, "'The Alienating Utopia': European Modernity and Latin American Identity," *Folk* 34 (1992): 84.

13. Ernest Gellner, *Plough, Sword and Book* (Chicago: University of Chicago Press, 1990).

14. See, for example, S. N. Eisenstadt, "Multiple Modernities—A Paradigma of Cultural and Social Evolution," *Protosociology* 24 (2007): 154–159; Gerhard Preyer, "Introduction: The Paradigm of Multiple Modernities," *Protosociology* 24 (2007): 5–18; and Jóhann Páll Árnason and Björn Wittrock, eds., *Nordic Paths to Modernity* (Oxford: Berghahn Books, 2012). Amy Kaminsky has suggested that even postmodernism—with all its irony and deconstruction—cannot but presuppose what it intends to supersede. Kaminsky, *After Exile: Writing the Latin American Diaspora* (Minneapolis: University of Minnesota Press, 1999), 2.

15. It is not superfluous to recall in this connection that the series of waves of Western-led globalization—and the ambivalent attitude that the centers of such developments

generate—are only a specific case of a wide range of historical globalizations that have included, among others, earlier Persian, Hellenistic, Roman, Chinese, classical Islamic, and Hinduist waves of globalization.

16. Laurence Whitehead, "Latin America as a Mausoleum of Modernities," in Roniger and Waisman, *Globality and Multiple Modernities*, 29–65. See also Laurence Whitehead, *Latin America: A New Interpretation* (London: Macmillan, 2006).

17. John H. Elliott, "A Europe of Composite Monarchies," *Past and Present* 137 (1992): 48–71.

18. Formally, Spanish-American territories were not colonies but parts of the Crown of Castilla and, since the 1560s, quasi-autonomous kingdoms in the framework of Greater Spain, along with Aragon, Naples, and the Netherlands. Brazil followed a similar pattern within the Portuguese realms. See Nicholas Canny and Anthony Pagden, *Colonial Identity in the Atlantic World, 1500–1800* (Princeton, NJ: Princeton University Press, 1987), 15–93.

19. Margalit Bejarano, "The Sephardic Communities of Latin America: A Puzzle of Sub-Ethnic Fragments," in *Contemporary Sephardic Identity*, ed. Margalit Bejarano and Edna Aizenberg (Syracuse, NY: Syracuse University Press, 2012), 3–30; Matthew D. Warshawsky, *The Perils of Living the Good and True Law: Iberian Crypto-Jews in the Shadow of the Inquisition in Colonial Hispanic America* (Newark, DE: Juan de la Cuesta, 2016); Ronnie Perelis, *Narratives from the Sephardic Atlantic: Blood and Faith* (Bloomington: Indiana University Press, 2016); and Luis Roniger, "The Western Sephardic Diaspora: Ancestral Birthplaces and Displacement, Diaspora Formation and Multiple Homelands," *Latin American Research Review* 54, no. 4 (2019): 1031–1038.

20. Tamar Herzog, "A Stranger in a Strange Land: The Conversion of Foreigners in Colonial Latin America," in *Constructing Collective Identities and Shaping Public Spheres*, ed. Luis Roniger and Mario Sznajder (Brighton, UK: Sussex Academic Press, 1998), 57. See also her *Defining Nations: Immigrants and Citizens in Early Modern Spain and Spanish America* (New Haven, CT: Yale University Press, 2003).

21. Alberto Flores Galindo, *Buscando un Inca: Identidad y utopía en los Andes* (Lima: Instituto de Apoyo Agrario, 1987); and David Cahill, "After the Fall: Constructing Incan Identity in Late Colonial Cuzco," in Roniger and Sznajder, *Constructing Collective Identities and Shaping Public Spheres*, 65–99.

22. Enrique Giménez López, *Expulsión y exilio de los Jesuitas españoles* (Alicante: Universidad de Alicante, 1997).

23. Antonello Gerbi, *La disputa del Nuevo Mundo* (Mexico City: Fondo de Cultura Económica, 1960); and Leopoldo Zea, *America en la historia* (Madrid: Ediciones de la Revista de Occidente, 1957). Others, primarily exiled Peruvian Jesuit Juan Pablo Viscardo y Guzmán, called for independence, exhorting his compatriots to rebel against the Spanish Crown, rejecting its arbitrary and despotic rule that "ignored the unalienable rights of man and the indisputable duties of all governments." He tried unsuccessfully to attract British support for expeditions to liberate South America. See David Brading, *The First America* Cambridge: Cambridge University Press, 1991), 535–540.

24. Claudio Lomnitz, *Modernidad indiana: Nueve ensayos sobre nación y mediación en México* (Mexico City: Planeta, 1998).

25. S. N. Eisenstadt and Bernhard Giesen, "The Construction of Collective Identity," *Archives Europeennes de Sociologie* 36 (1995): 72-102.

26. "Europeans have said, let's form a happy society and we will all be happy, I speak of the most well organized. The Incas on the other hand have said: Let us make each individual happy to see you that no one can without injustice wish for a better state. By this means, the society will be powerful and happy." *El dilatado cautiverio bajo el gobierno español de Juan Bautista Tupamaru, 5° nieto del último emperador del Perú* (Buenos Aires, [1826]), in Marie-Danielle Demélas, *La invención política* (Lima: Instituto de Estudios Peruanos, 2003), 377.

27. This assertion may sound strange regarding Paraguay, often parochialized in analyses, but even there universal and of course Iberoamerican horizons existed since colonization and the Jesuit missions. Even José Gaspar de Francia's and López's policies were more dialectically connected to globalism than is usually claimed. See Julio César Chávez, *El supremo dictador* (Madrid: Ediciones A, 1964); and Helio Vera, *En busca del hueso perdido* (Asunción Paraguay: Expolibro and RP Ediciones, 1999).

28. Rodrigo Uprimny, "The Recent Transformation of Constitutional Law in Latin America: Trends and Challenges," *Texas Law Review* 89 (2011): 1587-1609; and Mauricio García Villegas, "Constitucionalismo aspiracional," *Araucaria: Revista Iberoamericana de Filosofía, Política y Humanidades* 15, no. 29 (2013): 77-97.

29. Eduardo Posada-Carbó and Iván Jaksić, "Shipwrecks and Survivals: Liberalism in Nineteenth-Century Latin America," *Intellectual History Review* 23, no. 4 (2013): 479-498, 482.

30. Posada-Carbó and Jaksić, "Shipwrecks and Survivals," 492.

31. Anthony Pagden, *Spanish Imperialism and the European Imagination* (New Haven, CT: Yale University Press, 1990), 133-153.

32. *Registro Yucateco* (1846), in James Dunkerley, *Americana* (London: Verso, 2000), 32, from Marie Lapointe, *Los mayas rebeldes de Yucatán* (Zamora, Michoacán, Mexico: El Colegio de Michoacán, 1983), 32. This quotation is fully in line with Carlos A. Forment, *Democracy in Latin America, 1760-1900*, vol. 1, *Civic Selfhood and Public Life in Mexico and Peru* (Chicago: University of Chicago Press, 2003).

33. James E. Sanders, *The Vanguard of the Atlantic World* (Durham, NC: Duke University Press, 2014), 6-7. See also Demélas, *La invención política*.

34. Referring to a later period, Laurence Whitehead makes a distinction that applies to liberalism in general as well as to other ideas and institutional trends incorporated from the core societies of the West. "Even during the [post-1930] Depression there was an important difference (understood by those who experienced it at first hand) between the *achieved* liberalism of developed capitalist/market economies, and the *rhetorical* and *aspirational* liberalism of Latin American societies." Laurence Whitehead, "State Organization in Latin America since 1930," in *The Cambridge History of Latin America*, ed. Leslie Bethell (Cambridge: Cambridge University Press, 1993), 5. See also his *Latin America: A New Interpretation* (London: Palgrave-Macmillan, 2006).

In the same line and from a culturalist perspective, see Octavio Paz, "A Literature without Criticism," *Times Literary Supplement*, August 6, 1976, 979–980.

35. Whereas Sarmiento relied on the style of Spanish *costumbristas* to unravel the character of the Argentinean people, his framework of comparison was the world as a whole, freely comparing the gauchos in the pampas to the Bedouins in the Middle East and the Tartars in central Asia.

36. Brading, *The First America*, 620–647.

37. Hilda Sabato, *Republics of the New World* (Cambridge, MA: Harvard University Press, 2018).

38. Leopoldo Zea, *Pensamiento positivista latinoamericano* (Caracas: Biblioteca Ayacucho, 1980).

39. Tulio Halperin Donghi, "En busca de la especificidad del pensamiento político hispanoamericano," *Cuadernos americanos* 6, no. 66 (1992): 31–46.

40. Roberto Schwarz, *Misplaced Ideas: Essays on Brazilian Culture* (London: Verso, 1992).

41. Nicola Miller, *Reinventing Modernity in Latin America. Intellectuals Imagine the Future, 1900–1930* (London: Palgrave-Macmillan, 2008), 20.

42. Demélas, *La invención política*, 355.

43. Leoncio López Ocón, *Biografía de 'La América* (Madrid: Consejo Superior de Investigaciones Científicas, 1987).

44. Luis Roniger and Mario Sznajder, *The Legacy of Human Rights Violations in the Southern Cone* (Oxford: Oxford University Press, 1999); and Roniger, "Transitional Justice and Protracted Accountability in Re-Democratized Uruguay (1985–2011)," *Journal of Latin American Studies* 43, no. 4 (November 2011): 693–724.

45. Antonio Luis Hidalgo-Capitán and Ana Patricia Cubillo-Guevara, "Deconstruction and Genealogy of Latin American Good Living (*Buen Vivir*)," *International Development Policy* 9 (2017): 23–50. ; David Lehmann, "Intercultural Universities in Mexico: Identity and Inclusion," *Journal of Latin American Studies* 45, no. 4 (2013): 779–811; Deby Babis, "The Role of Civil Society Organizations in the Institutionalization of Indigenous Medicine in Bolivia," *Social Science and Medicine* 123 (2014): 287–294; and John Stolle-McAllister, *Intercultural Interventions: Politics, Community, and Environment in the Otavalo Valley* (Amherst, NY: Cambria Press, 2019).

46. See Serge Gruzinski, *The Conquest of Mexico* (Cambridge, UK: Polity Press, 1992) and Pierre Duviols, *Cultura andina y represión* (Cusco: Centro de estudios rurales y andinos Bartolomé de las Casas, 1986).

47. Gerardo Leibner, "Pensamiento radical peruano: González Prada, Zulen, Mariátegui," *Cuadernos americanos* 66 (1992): 47–66 (Zulen followed moral idealism, and Mariátegui elaborated a blend of Sorel and Marxism, which he adopted while in Europe). On other countries see Nancy Grey Postero and Leon Zamosc, eds., *The Struggle for Indian Rights in Latin America* (Brighton, UK: Sussex Academic Press, 2004); Deborah Yashar, *Contesting Liberal Citizenship in Latin America* (New York: Cambridge University Press, 2005). On the Shining Path, its ideology and practice see Carlos Iván Degregori, *How Difficult Is to Be God: Shining Path's Politics of War in Peru, 1980–1999* (Madison: University of Wisconsin Press, 2012).

48. Margarita López Maya, "The Venezuelan Caracazo of 1989: Popular Protest and Institutional Weakness," *Journal of Latin American Studies* 35, no. 1 (2003): 117–137.
49. Leon Zamosc, "The Indian Movement and Political Democracy in Ecuador," *Latin American Politics and Society* 49, no. 3 (2007): 1–34; Carlos de la Torre, "The Resurgence of Radical Populism in Latin America," *Constellations* 14, no. 3 (2007): 384–397; Steve Ellner, *Rethinking Venezuelan Politics: Class, Conflict, and the Chavez Phenomenon* (Boulder, CO: Lynne Rienner, 2008); and Raanan Rein, "From Juan Perón to Hugo Chávez and Back: Populism Reconsidered," in *Shifting Frontiers of Citizenship*, ed. Mario Sznajder, Luis Roniger, and Carlos A. Forment (Leiden: Brill, 2013), 289–309.
50. Peter Winn, *Americas: The Changing Face of Latin America and the Caribbean* (Berkeley: University of California Press, 2006), 24.
51. Miller, *Reinventing Modernity in Latin America*, 24.
52. On Rodó and the modernists see Jean Franco, *The Modern Culture of Latin America* (Harmondsworth, UK: Penguin, 1970). On Quebec see Gerard Bouchard, *Genèse des nations et cultures du Nouveau Monde* (Montréal: Editions du Boréal, 2001); and Karen Dubinsky, Adele Perry, and Henry Yu, *Within and without the Nation: Canadian History as Transnational History* (Toronto: University of Toronto Press, 2015).
53. See David Lehmann, *Democracy and Development in Latin America* (Philadelphia: Temple University, 1990); and David Lehmann, *Struggle for the Spirit: Religious Transformation and Populist Culture in Brazil and Latin America* (Cambridge, UK: Polity, 1996).
54. Batia Siebzhener and Leonardo Senkman, "Drawing the Boundaries of Non-Catholic Religions in Argentina and Brazil: Conversion to Islam and the Return to Orthodox Judaism (*Teshuva*)," *International Journal of Latin American Religions* 3 (2019): 40–67.
55. Luis Roniger and Daniel F. Wajner, "El auge del ciclo 'nuestramericano': Analizando el rol discursivo del proyecto chavista en la integración transnacional," *Pacarina del Sur* 10, no. 40 (2019): 1–43.
56. Eduardo Mendieta, "Remapping Latin American Studies: Postcolonialism, Subaltern Studies, Post-Occidentalism and Globalization Theory," in *Coloniality at Large. Latin America and the Postcolonial Debate*, ed. Mabel Moraña, Enrique Dussel, and Carlos A. Jáuregui (Durham, NC: Duke University Press, 2008), 287–306.
57. Leon Zamosc, "Popular Impeachments: Ecuador in Comparative Perspective," in Sznajder, Roniger, and Forment, *Shifting Frontiers of Citizenship*, 237–265.
58. Luis Roniger, "U.S. Hemispheric Hegemony and the Descent into Genocidal Practices," in *State Violence and Genocide in Latin America: The Cold War Years*, ed. Marcia Esparza, Daniel Feierstein, and Henry Huttenbach (New York: Routledge, 2010), 23–43.
59. Luis Roniger, "Global Times Once Again: Representative Democracy and Countervailing Trends in Iberoamerica," *Iberoamericana* (Berlin), 17 (2005): 66–85.
60. Jorge Castañeda, "Any Number of Tempests Could End Latin America's Calm," *Daily Star* June 22, 2010, accessed June 24, 2010, http://www.dailystar.com.lb/ArticlePrint.aspx?id=121519&mode=print .

61. Mario Sznajder and Luis Roniger, *The Politics of Exile in Latin America* (New York: Cambridge University Press, 2009).

Chapter 3

1. Marie-Danielle Demélas, *La invención política* (Lima: Instituto de Estudios Peruanos, 2003).

2. In Latin America, it meant that the independent states would inherit the territories that were within the realm of administrative units at the end of colonial times. Following independence, Bolivarianism, predicated on the idea of refraining from territorial gain as the result of war, aimed to create a region of peaceful coexistence among republican states emerging from Spanish American imperial rule.

3. Roberto Querejazu Calvo, *Guano, Salitre y Sangre* (La Paz-Cochabamba: Los Amigos del Libro, 1979); Ronald D. Crozier, "El salitre hasta la Guerra del Pacífico: Una revisión," *Historia* (Santiago) 30 (1997): 53–126; and Carlos Contreras Carranza, *La economía pública en el Perú después del guano y del salitre* (Lima: Instituto de Estudios Peruanos, 2012), ch. 1.

4. "Día del Mar (23 de marzo de 1879)," 2017, http://bit.ly/2YZBzoP.

5. Luis Roniger and Leonardo Senkman, *Conspiracy Theories and Latin American History. Lurking in the Shadows* (New York: Routledge, 2021), ch. 5.

6. Tulio Halperin Donghi, "Party and Nation-State in the Construction of Collective Identities: Uruguay in the Nineteenth Century," in *The Collective and the Public in Latin America*, ed. Luis Roniger and Tamar Herzog (Brighton, UK: Sussex Academic Press, 2000), 158–173.

7. As late as 1851, Uruguay renounced its claims over the Eastern Missions, an area equaling nearly 100,000 square kilometers, or 37 percent of its territory, in favor of imperial Brazil.

8. David McLean, *War, Diplomacy and Informal Empire. Britain and the Republics of La Plata 1836–1853* (London: British Academic Press, 1995); and John Street, *Artigas and the Emancipation of Uruguay* (Cambridge: Cambridge University Press, 1959).

9. The black legend of Artigas was invigorated in the 1880s, especially with the publication of a work by Francisco Berra. Some official and academic circles defended and nearly beatified him. In September 1884, the Congress declared the day of his death a day of national mourning. By the early 1950s, a national cult of Artigas had crystallized. In the aftermath of the civilian-military dictatorship, historical revisionism critically assessed that veneration. See Arturo Ardao, *¿Desde cuándo el culto artiguista?* (Montevideo: Biblioteca de Marcha, 2001); and Guillermo Vázquez Franco, *La historia y sus mitos* (Montevideo: Cal y canto, 1994).

10. Hugo Achúgar, ed., *La fundación por la palabra: Letra y nación en América Latina en el siglo XIX* (Montevideo: Universidad de la República, FHCE, 1998).

11. Doris Sommer, "Irresistible Romance: The Foundational Fictions of Latin America," in *Nation and Narration*, ed. Homi K. Bhabha (London: Routledge, 1990), 71–98.

12. Juan E. Pivel Devoto, *Historia de los partidos políticos en el Uruguay*, 2 vols. (Montevideo: Ediciones de la Cámara de Representantes, 1994).

13. Cited in Carlos Demasi, "La dictadura military: Un tema pendiente," in *Uruguay: Cuentas pendientes*, ed. Alvaro Rico (Montevideo: Trilce, 1995), 29 and 47–48.

14. Gustavo Verdesio. *Forgotten Conquests: Rereading New World History from the Margins* (Philadelphia: Temple University Press, 2001).

15. José Pedro Barrán, Gerardo Caetano, and Teresa Porzecanski, eds., *Historias de la vida privada*, vols. 1–2 (Montevideo: Santillana, 1996).

16. Jens R. Hentschke, *Philosophical Polemics, School Reform, and Nation-Building in Uruguay: Reforma Vareliana and Batllismo from a Transnational Perspective, 1868–1915* (Baden-Baden, Germany: Nomos, 2016).

17. Miguel Angel Centeno, "Blood and Debt: War and Taxation in Nineteenth-Century Latin America," *American Journal of Sociology* 102, no. 6 (1997): 1565–1605; and see the discussion on the conservative leanings of postindependent elites in Howard Wiarda, *The Soul of Latin America* (New Haven, CT: Yale University Press, 2001), 112–145.

18. Ana María Alonso, "The Politics of Space, Time and Substance: State Formation, Nationalism, and Ethnicity," *Annual Review of Anthropology* 23 (1994): 379–405.

19. See Anupama Mande, "Subaltern Studies and the Historiography of the Sandinista-Miskitu Conflict in Nicaragua, 1979–1990" (paper presented at LASA 2000 Congress, accessed July 11, 2008, lasa.international.pitt.edu/Lasa2000/Mande.PDF.

20. Luis Roniger, *Transnational Politics in Central America* (Gainesville: University of Florida Press, 2011).

21. Luis Roniger, "Identidades colectivas: Avances teóricos y desafíos políticos," in *Identidad, sociedad y olítica*, ed. Judit Bokser Liwerant and Saúl Velasco Cruz (Mexico City:UNAM, 2008), 45–68; Sherry B. Ortner, "On Key Symbols." *American Anthropologist* 75 (1973): 1338–1346; Anthony Smith, *The Symbolic Construction of National Identities* (Paris: Euroconference on Collective Identity and Symbolic Representation, 1996); and Michael E. Geisler, ed., *National Symbols, Fractured Identities: Contesting the National Narrative* (Hanover, NH: University Press of New England, 2005).

22. S. N. Eisenstadt and Bernhard Giesen, "The Construction of Collective Identity," *Archives Europeennes de Sociologie* 36 (1995): 72– 102, esp. 85–93.

23. Eisenstadt and Giesen, "The Construction of Collective Identity," 93–102.

24. See Guntram H. Herb and David H. Kaplan, eds., *Nations and Nationalisms in Global Perspective*, 4 vols. (Santa Barbara, Ca: ABC-CLIO, 2008).

25. Benedict Anderson, *Imagined Communities* (London: Verso, 1991).

26. Robert H. Holden, *Armies without Nations. Public Violence and State Formation in Central America, 1821–1960* (New York: Oxford University Press, 2004).

27. Among important contributions are Steven Palmer, "Hacia la 'auto-inmigración': El nacionalismo oficial en Costa Rica, 1870–1930," in *Identidades nacionales y Estado moderno en Centroamérica*, ed. Arturo Taracena and Jean Piel (San José: Editorial de la Universidad de Costa Rica, 1995), 75–86 and other contributions to that volume;

Frances Kinloch Tijerino, ed., *Nicaragua en busca de su identidad* (Managua: Instituto de Historia de Nicaragua, Universidad Centroamericana, 1995); Marta Casaús Arzú and Oscar Guillermo Peláez Almengor, eds., *Historia intelectual de Guatemala* (Guatemala City: CEUR/UAM/AECI, 2001); Arturo Taracena Arriola, *Etnicidad, estado y nación en Guatemala, 1808–1944*, vol. I (Guatemala City: CIRMA, 2002; and Darío A Euraque et al., *Memorias del mestizaje: Cultura política en Centroamérica de 1920 al presente* (Guatemala City: CIRMA, 2005).

28. See Consuelo Cruz, "Identity and Persuasion: How Nations Remember Their Pasts and Make Their Futures," *World Politics* 52 (2000): 275–312; and Consuelo Cruz, *Political Culture and Institutional Development in Costa Rica and Nicaragua: World Making in the Tropics* (New York: Cambridge University Press, 2005).

29. Clifford Geertz, *The Interpretation of Cultures* (New York: Basic Books, 1973).

30. Cruz, "Identity and Persuasion," 278–279.

31. Pablo Antonio Cuadra, *El nicaragüense* (Managua: Hispamer, 2004), esp. 203–205.

32. Thomas M. Leonard, "Central America and the United States: Overlooked Foreign Policy Objectives," *The Americas* 50, no. 1 (1993): 6; and Michel Gobat, "The Invention of Latin America: A Transnational History of Anti-Imperialism, Democracy, and Race," *American Historical Review* 118, no. 5 (2013): 1345–1375, esp. 1346–1347.

33. Charles W. Domville-Fife, *Guatemala and the Status of Central America* (London: Francis Griffiths, 1913).

34. *Gaceta de Nicaragua* no. 38 (September 20, 1873), 140, cited in Patricia Fumero Vargas, "De la iniciativa individual a la cultura oficial: El caso del General José Dolores Estrada, Nicaragua, década de 1870," in *Nicaragua en busca de su identidad*, ed. Frances Kinloch Tijerino (Managua: Instituto de Historia de Nicaragua, Universidad Centroamericana, 1995), 324–325.

35. Víctor Hugo Acuña Ortega, "Autoritarismo y democracia en Centroamérica: La larga duración," in Kinloch Tijerino, *Nicaragua en busca de su identidad*, 535–571.

36. Another trend was the split between public popular ceremonies and the ceremonies conducted in the secluded environment of recently established "clubs" reserved for the elite. See Patricia Fumero Vargas, "De la iniciativa individual a la cultura oficial: El caso del General José Dolores Estrada, Nicaragua, década de 1870," in Kinloch Tijerino, *Nicaragua en busca de su identidad*, 307–325.

37. Eisenstadt and Giesen, "The Construction of Collective Identity"; Eric Hobsbawn and Terence Ranger, eds., *The Invention of Tradition* (New York: Cambridge University Press, 1983); and Anthony Smith, *The Nation in History: Historiographical Debates about Ethnicity and Nationalism* (Lebanon, NH: University Press of New England, 2000).

38. See Roniger, *Transnational Politics in Central America*, ch. 8.

39. *Centro-América* 12 no. 2 (1920): 1.

40. I am following here the studies by Marta Elena Casaús Arzú and Teresa García Giráldez, *Las redes intelectuales centroamericanas: Un siglo de imaginarios nacionales (1820<n>1920)* (Guatemala: F&G Editores, 2005), as integrated in Roniger, *Transnational Politics in Central America*, ch. 8.

41. A. Luna, "San Salvador," *La Quincena*, June 1, 1906, 129–131; Alejandro Bermúdez, *Lucha de razas* (Mexico City: Tipografía Económica, 1912), 34; and Carlos Serpas, *Diario de Hoy*, San Salvador, May 8, 1954, in Mario Monteforte Toledo, "Los intelectuales y la integración centroamericana," *Revista Mexicana de Sociología* 29, no. 4 (1967): 844–845.

42. See, for example, Salvador Mendieta, *La enfermedad de Centro América*, 3 vols., *Descripción del sujeto y síntomas de la enfermedad, Diagnóstico y orígenes de la dolencia, Terapéutica* (Barcelona: Tipografía Maucci, 1934).

43. Margarita Silva H., "Salvador Mendieta y la unión centroamericana (1879–1958)," Colegio de México, https://shial.colmex.mx/assets/salvador_mendieta_1.pdf.

44. Marta Casaús Arzú, "Las redes intelectuales centroamericanas y sus imaginarios de nación (1890–1945)," *Circunstancia. Revista de Ciencias Sociales del Instituto Universitario de Investigación Ortega y Gasset* no. 9 (2006), https://ortegaygasset.edu/wp-content/uploads/2019/05/Circunstancia_Numero_9_Enero_2006.pdf.

45. Teresa García Giráldez, "La Patria Grande Centroamericana: La elaboración del proyecto nacional por las redes unionistas," in Casaús Arzú and García Giráldez, *Las redes intelectuales centroamericanas*, 123–205.

46. Donald Clark Hodges, *Sandino's Communism: Spiritual Politics for the Twenty-First Century* (Austin: University of Texas Press, 1992). Hodges's interpretation is not endorsed by other analyses of Sandino's worldview. On Sandino's complex positions in the late 1920s and early 1930s, see also Cruz, *Political Culture*, 201–206.

47. Among them are *La tribuna, El unionista, Tiempos nuevos, Electra, Studium, Claridad, Vida, La campaña, La hora*, and many more. See García Giráldez, "La Patria Grande Centroamericana," esp. 148.

48. Federación Universitaria de Córdoba, "Manifiesto liminar," June 21, 1918.

49. See among others Ingrid E. Fay and Karen Racine, eds., *Strange Pilgrimages: Exile, Travel and National Identity in Latin America, 1800–1990s* (Wilmington, DE: Scholarly Resources, 2000).

50. Alexandra Pita González, *La Unión Latino Americana y el Boletín Renovación: Redes intelectuales y revistas culturales en la década de 1920* (Mexico City: Colegio de México, 2009).

51. Martín Bergel, coord., *Los viajes latinoamericanos de la reforma universitaria* (Rosario, Argentina: Humanidades y Artes Ediciones, 2018).

52. Roniger, *Transnational Politics in Central America*, 67–86.

53. Ori Preuss, "Discovering 'os ianques do sul': Towards an Entangled Luso-Hispanic History of Latin America," *Revista brasilera de política internacional* 56, no. 2 (2013): 157–176, 170.

54. Ori Preuss, *Transnational South America: Experiences, Ideas, and Identities, 1860s–1910s* (New York: Routledge, 2015).

55. José Luis de Imaz, "De la deficiente solidaridad internacional," in *Sobre la identidad iberoamericana* (Buenos Aires: Sudamericana, 1979).

Chapter 4

1. See, for instance, Mario Sznajder and Luis Roniger, *The Politics of Exile in Latin America* (New York: Cambridge University Press, 2009); and Edward Blumenthal, *Exile and Nation-State Formation in Argentina and Chile* (New York:Palgrave-Macmillan, 2019).

2. For work on different diasporas of exiles and émigrés, see Denise Rollemberg, *Entre raízes e radares* (Rio de Janeiro: Record, 1999); "Exilios: Historia reciente de Argentina y Uruguay," *América Latina Hoy: Revista de Ciencias Sociales* (Universidad de Salamanca) vol. 34 (August 2003): 15-143; Pablo Yankelevich, coord., *Represión y destierro: Itinerarios del exilio argentino* (La Plata, Argentina: Ed. al Margen, 2004); José del Pozo Artigas, coord., *Exiliados, emigrados y retornados chilenos en América y Europa, 1973-2004* (Santiago: RIL, 2006); Silvia Dutrénit-Bielous, coord., *El Uruguay del exilio: Gente, circunstancias, escenarios* (Montevideo: Trilce, 2006); Pablo Yankelevich and Silvina Jensen, coords., *Exilios: Destinos y experiencias bajo la dictadura militar* (Buenos Aires: Libros del Zorzal, 2007); Luis Roniger and James N. Green, coords., "Exile and the Politics of Exclusion in Latin America" (dossier), *Latin American Perspectives* 34, no. 4 (July 2007): 3-108; Pilar González Bernaldo de Quirós, coord., "Emigrar en tiempo de crisis al país de los derechos humanos. Exilios latinoamericanos en Francia en el siglo XX" (dossier), *Anuario de Estudios Americanos* (Sevilla) 64, no. 1 (2007): 15-172; and Silvia Dutrénit Bielous, Eugenia Allier Montaño, and Enrique Coraza de los Santos, *Tiempos de exilios: Memoria e historia de españoles y uruguayos* (Colonia Suiza, Uruguay: CeAlCI—Fundación Carolina e Instituto Mora, 2008). See also Silvina Jensen and Soledad Lastra, eds., *Exilios: Militancia y represión: Nuevas fuentes y nuevos abordajes de los destierros de la Argentina de los años setenta* (La Plata, Argentina: Editorial de la Universidad Nacional de La Plata, 2014); Enrique Coraza de los Santos and Soledad Lastra, eds., *Miradas a las migraciones, las fronteras y los exilios* (Buenos Aires: CLACSO, 2020).

3. Among them, see Paul Estrade, *La colonia cubana de París, 1895-1898* (La Habana: Editorial de Ciencias Sociales, 1984); Erasmo Saenz Carrete, *El exilio latinoamericano en Francia 1964-1979* (Mexico City: Potrerillos Editores, 1995); François-Xavier Guerra, "La lumière et ses reflets: Paris et la politique Latino-Americain," in *Le Paris des Etrangers* (Paris: Edition de l'Imprimerie Nationale, 1989), 171-182; Hebe Pelossi, *Argentinos en Francia: Franceses en Argentina* (Buenos Aires: Ciudad Argentina, 1999); Ingrid E. Fay and Karen Racine, eds., *Strange Pilgrimages: Exile, Travel and National Identity in Latin America, 1800-1990s* (Wilmington, DE: Scholarly Resources, 2000); Pablo Yankelevich, *México, país refugio: La experiencia de los exilios en el siglo XX* (Mexico City: INAH-Plaza y Valdés, 2002); Anne Marie Gaillard, *Exils et retours: Itineraires chiliens* (Paris: CIEMI y L'Harmattan, 1997); Marina Franco, *Exilio: Argentinos en Francia durante la dictadura* (Buenos Aires: Siglo XXI, 2007); and Silvina Jensen, *La provincia flotante: El exilio argentino en Cataluña (1976-2006)* (Barcelona: Casa de América Cataluña, 2007).

4. Félix Luna, *Historia general de la Argentina* (Buenos Aires: Planeta, 1995), 5:202.

5. Emma Bomilla, *Continuismo y dictadura* (Tegucigalpa, Honduras: Litográfica Comyagüela, 1989), 1–2, cited in Marvin Barahona, *Honduras en el siglo XX: Una síntesis histórica* (Tegucigalpa, Honduras: Guaymuras, 2005), 101.

6. Luis Roniger and Mario Sznajder, "Los antecedentes coloniales del exilio político y su proyección en el siglo XIX," *Estudios Interdisciplinarios de América Latina y el Caribe* 18, no. 2 (2008): 31–51.

7. On Brazil see, for instance, Geraldo Pieroni, *Vadios e ciganos, hereges e bruxos—os degradados no Brasil colonia* (Rio: Bertrand, 2000). On Spanish America see José María Mariluz Urquijo, *Ensayo sobre los juicios de residencia indianos* (Sevilla: Escuela de Estudios Hispanoamericanos, 1952), 208–209; Héctor José Tanzi, "El derecho penal indiano y el delito de lesa majestad," *Revista de Historia de América* 84 (1977): 54–55; Tamar Herzog, *La administración como un fenómeno social: La justicia penal de la ciudad de Quito (1650–1750)* (Madrid: Centro de Estudios Constitucionales, 1995); Gabriel Haslip, "Crime and the Administration of Justice in Colonial Mexico City 1696–1810" (PhD diss., University Microfilm International, 1982), 203–227.

8. In other publications, as sole author and as coauthor with political scientist Mario Sznajder and historians James N. Green and Pablo Yankelevich, I have discussed major perspectives, including semantic, semiotic, and cultural analyses as well as historical, sociological, and political approaches. See, for example, Luis Roniger, "Destierro y exilio político en América Latina: Un campo de estudio transnacional e histórico en expansión," *Pacarina del Sur*, no. 9 (October–December 2011): 1–18, http://www.pacarinadelsur.com/home/abordajes-y-contiendas/318-destierro-y-exilio-en-america-latina-un-campo-de-estudio-transnacional-e-historico-en-expansion; Mario Sznajder and Luis Roniger, *The Politics of Exile in Latin America* (New York: Cambridge University Press, 2009), 11–39; and Roniger, *Destierro y exilio en América Latina: Nuevos estudios y avances teóricos* (Buenos Aires: Editorial Universitaria de Buenos Aires, 2014).

9. José Murilo de Carvalho, *La formación de las almas: El imaginario de la República en el Brasil* (Buenos Aires: Universidad Nacional de Quilmes, 1997).

10. The urban elites of Spanish America soon embarked on a move toward independence, albeit in ways that retained an in-built tension between political fragmentation and a hoped-for reconstituted regional unity. See Roniger, *Transnational Politics in Central America*, 24–37.

11. Tamar Herzog, *La administración como un fenómeno social*, 252.

12. Still, such denial was far from universal, and territorial displacement of lower class individuals continued to be used in the Andean area in late colonial and early independent times. Ricardo Melgar Bao, "Exile in the Andean Countries: A Historical Perspective", in *Exile and the Politics of Exclusion in the Americas*, ed. Luis Roniger, James N Green, and Pablo Yankelevich (Brighton, UK: Sussex Academic Press, 2012), 100–118.

13. Mario Sznajder and Luis Roniger, "Political Exile in Latin America," *Latin American Perspectives* 34, no. 4 (2007): 7–30.

14. William H. Katrak, *The Argentine Generation of 1837* (London: Associated University Presses, 1996). Whereas Brazil was somehow exceptional in reaching early stability

under the aegis of Emperor Pedro II and thus became a center of attraction for exiles escaping from persecution in the Spanish American republics, with the founding of the republic the emperor and his family were banished and forbidden to own property in Brazil, and they were forced into exile with a small entourage. See Roderick J. Barman, *Citizen Emperor: Pedro II and the Making of Brazil, 1825–1891* (Stanford, CA: Stanford University Press, 1999), 364–397.

15. Roberto J. Lovera De-Sola, *Curazao, escala en el primer destierro del Libertador* (Caracas: Monte Avila Editores, 1992), esp. 23–36 and 67–68.

16. See Aline Helg, "Simón Bolívar and the Spectre of *Pardocracia*: José Padilla in Post-Independence Cartagena," *Journal of Latin American Studies* 35 (2003): 447–471.

17. Mario Sznajder and Luis Roniger, *The Politics of Exile in Latin America* (New York: Cambridge University Press, 2009), 27–28.

18. Francisco de Paula Santander to the President of the Republic, Ocaña, March 17, 1828, in Roberto Cortázar, *Cartas y Mensajes de Santander* (Bogotá: Talleres Editoriales de la Librería Voluntad, 1953/1956), 7:403.

19. Archivo Santander Bogotá: Academia de Historia y Aguila Negra, n.d., vol. XVIII, p. 96.

20. Horacio Rodríguez Plata, *Santander en el exilio* (Bogotá: Editorial Kelly, 1976), 76–79, cited in Pilar Moreno de Angel, *Santander* (Bogotá: Planeta, 1989), 467; and see Francisco de Paula Santander, *Diario del General Francisco de Paula Santander en Europa y los Estados Unidos 1829–1832* (Bogotá: Banco de la República, 1963).

21. Timothy E. Anna, *The Fall of the Royal Government in Mexico City* (Lincoln: University of Nebraska Press, 1978), 189–215.

22. Brian Loveman and Elizabeth Lira, *Las suaves cenizas del olvido: Vía chilena de reconciliación política (1814–1932)* (Santiago: LOM, 1999), 85–95.

23. Rebecca Earl, ed., *Rumours of Wars: Civil Conflict in Nineteenth Century Latin America* (London: Institute of Latin American Studies, 2000).

24. Another prominent example is Francisco de Morazán, president of the Central American Federation in the 1830s, who was executed in San José de Costa Rica in 1842 after returning from Panamá. His execution signaled the final death of the Federation. See Angel Zúñiga Huete, *Morazán* (Tecigualpa [AQ: Please provide the country]: Editorial Universitaria, 1982); and Leslie Bethell, *Central America since Independence* (Cambridge: Cambridge University Press, 1991), 13–22.

25. David Brading, "Nationalism and State-Building in Latin American History," *Ibero-Amerikanisches Archiv* 20 (1994): 83–108; and David Brading, "Patriotism and the Nation in Colonial Spanish America," in *Constructing Collective Identities and Shaping Public Spheres*, ed. Luis Roniger and Mario Sznajder (Brighton, UK: Sussex Academic Press, 1998), 14–45.

26. For a broader analysis of these circuits, see Sznajder and Roniger, *The Politics of Exile*, 91–192.

27. Herbert Klein, *Bolivia* (New York: Oxford University Press, 1982).

28. Rossana Barragán, Dora Cajías, and Seemin Qayum, eds., *El Siglo XIX: Bolivia y América Latina* (La Paz: Coordinadora de Historia e I.F.E.A., 1997).

29. Luis Mariano Guzmán, *Historia de Bolivia* (Cochabamba, Bolivia: Imprenta del Siglo, 1983), 78.

30. Modesto Basadre y Chocano, *Diez Años de Historia Política del Perú* (Lima: Editorial Huascarán, 1953), 7-20 and 272-275; Evaristo San Cristóval, *El Gran Mariscal Luis José de Orbegoso* (Lima: Gil S.A. Editores, 1941), 54; Ronald B. St. John, *The Foreign Policy of Peru* (Boulder, CO: Lynne Rienner, 1992), 23-43; and Charles F. Walker, *Smoldering Ashes: Cuzco and the Creation of Republican Peru, 1780-1840* (Durham, NC: Duke University Press, 1999), 124-128.

31. François-Xavier Guerra, "The Implosion of the Spanish Empire: Emerging Statehood and Collective Identities," *The Collective and the Public in Latin America*, ed. Luis Roniger and Tamar Herzog (Brighton, UK: Sussex Academic Press, 2000), 71-94; and Federica Morelli, "Territorial Hierarchies and Collective Identities in Late Colonial and Early Independent Quito," in Roniger and Herzog, *Collective and the Public in Latin America*, 37-56.

32. Katrak, *The Argentine Generation of 1837*; and Blumenthal, *Exile and Nation-State Formation in Argentina and Chile*.

33. The United States and Europe also became poles of attraction and asylum for the Latin American exiles. European sites such as Paris attracted other migrants, businesspeople, students, and expatriates, in addition to exiles as part of the diaspora community.

34. Tulio Halperin Donghi, *Proyecto y construcción de una nación* (Caracas: Biblioteca Ayacucho, 1980), 500.

35. Jorge Basadre, *Historia de la República del Perú* (Lima: Editorial Universitaria, 1968), vol. 2.

36. Albert O. Hirschman, *Exit, Voice and Loyalty: Responses to Decline in Firms, Organizations, and States* (Cambridge, MA: Harvard University Press, 1970).

37. Luis Miguel Díaz and Guadalupe Rodríguez de Ita, "Bases histórico-jurídicas de la política mexicana de asilo político," in Silvia Dutrénit Bielous and Guadalupe Rodríguez de Ita, *Asilo diplomático mexicano en el Cono Sur* (Mexico City: Instituto Mora e Instituto Matías Romero, 1999), 68; Pilar González Bernaldo de Quirós, "La Independencia desde una perspectiva global: Soberanía y derecho internacional," *Prismas. Revista de historia intelectual* 13 (2016): 245-253.

38. Linda S. Frey and Marsha L. Frey, "Diplomatic Immunity," in *Sage Handbook of Diplomacy*, ed. Costas M. Constantinou et al. (Newbury Park, CA: Sage, 2016), 197; and see, Linda S. Frey and Marsha L. Frey, *The History of Diplomatic Immunity* (Colombus: Ohio University Press, 1999).

39. Pilar González Bernaldo de Quirós, "Primeras iniciativas de regulación global de las migraciones: Estanislao Zeballos y la doctrina argentina del 'derecho privado humano' 1873-1923," *Historia Unísonos* (Brazil) 22, no. 2 (2018): 170-184.

40. David Alejandro Luna, *El asilo político* (San Salvador: Ed. Universitaria, 1962), 39-40.

41. Unión Panamericana, *Convención sobre asilo diplomático suscrita en la X Conferencia Interamericana: Caracas, 1-28 marzo 1954* (Washington, DC: OEA, 1961); Díaz and Rodríguez de Ita, "Bases histórico-jurídicas," 63-82; Keith W. Yundt, *Latin American States and Political Refugees* (New York: Praeger, 1988); Leonardo Franco et al.,

"Investigación: El asilo y la protección de los refugiados en América Latina; Acerca de la confusión terminológica 'asilo-refugio'; Informe de progreso," in *Derechos humanos y refugiados en las Américas: Lecturas seleccionadas* (San José de Costa Rica: ACNUR-IIDH, 2001).

42. "Declaration on Territorial Asylum," http://www.unchr.ch/html/menu3/b/ o_asylum.htm.

43. In the late twentieth century the major events were the meeting of Tlatelolco in 1981, the declaration of Cartagena in 1984, the conference of Guatemala in 1989, the meeting of San José de Costa Rica in 1994, and the meeting of Tlatelolco in 1999. Franco et al., "Investigación," 176–177.

44. Barry Carr, "Across Seas and Borders: Charting the Webs of Radical Internationalism in the Circum-Caribbean, 1910–1940," in Roniger, Green, and Yankelevich, *Exile and the Politics of Exclusion in the Americas*, 217–240.

45. Julio C. Lamónaca and Marcelo N. Viñar, "Asilo político: Perspectivas desde la subjetividad," in *Asilo diplomático mexicano en el Cono Sur*, ed. Silvia Dútrenit Bielas and Guadalupe Rodríguez de Ita (Mexico City: Instituto Mora and SRE, 1999), 84. The decision about exile affects family members unrelated to the political circumstances that produced the exile, including life partners, parents, children, brothers, and sisters. Children are particularly vulnerable, as they generally are not part of the decision to leave the home environment yet suffer its consequences.

46. Ariel Dorfman, *Heading South, Looking North: A Bilingual Journey* (New York: Farrar, Straus and Giroux, 1998), 236–239.

47. In this period, when exile becomes a massive phenomenon, it is often difficult to trace a clear-cut line between political exile and economic migration. Thomas Faist, *The Volume and Dynamics of International Migration and Transnational Social Spaces* (Oxford: Clarendon Press, 2000)). In earlier periods, such a distinction was rather sharp, with political exile distinguished from the wide movements of migrant workers settling in neighboring regions in search of a livelihood. See, for example, Julio Pinto Vallejos and Verónica Valdivia Ortiz de Zárate, "Peones chilenos en tierras bolivianas: la presencia laboral chilena en Antofagasta (1840–1879)," in Barragán, Cajías, and Qayum, *El Siglo XIX*, 179–201.

48. For a full treatment see Luis Roniger, "Exilio massivo, inclusão e exclusão política no século XX," *DADOS—Revista de Ciências Sociais* (Brazil) 53, no. 1 (2010): 35–65.

49. David Sheinin, "How the Argentine Military Invented Human Rights in Argentina," in *Spanish and Latin American Transitions to Democracy*, ed. Carlos H Waisman and Raanan Rein (Brighton, UK: Sussex Academic Press, 2005), 190–214; and Luis Roniger and Mario Sznajder, *The Legacy of Human-Rights Violations in the Southern Cone* (Oxford: Oxford University Press, 1999), 38–49.

50. Thomas Risse and Kathryn Sikking, "The Socialization of International Human Rights Norms into Domestic Practices: Introduction," in *The Power of Human Rights*, comp. Thomas Risse, S. Ropp, and K. Sikking (New York: Cambridge University Press, 1999), 1–38; Alison Brysk, comp., *Globalization and Human Rights* (Berkeley: University of California Press, 2002); and Saskia Sassen, *Territory, Authority, Rights* (Princeton, NJ: Princeton University Press, 2006).

51. On the transformation of such discourses and the role of intellectuals in the Southern Cone, see Luis Roniger and Leandro Kierszenbaum, "Los intelectuales y los discursos de derechos humanos: La experiencia del Cono Sur," *Estudios Interdisciplinarios de América Latina y el Caribe* 16, no. 2 (2005): 5–36.

52. See the work by Vania Markarian, *Left in Transformation: Uruguayan Exiles and the Latin American Human Rights Networks, 1967–1984* (New York: Routledge, 2005); Roniger and Sznajder, *The Legacy of Human Rights Violations*; and Thomas Wright, *State Terrorism in Latin America: Chile, Argentina, and International Human Rights* (Lanham, MD: Rowman & Littlefield, 2007).

53. Judith N. Shklar, "The Bonds of Exile," in *Political Thought and Political Thinkers*, comp. Stanley Hoffman (Chicago: University of Chicago Press, 1998), 56–72. See also her piece "Obligation, Loyalty, Exile," in Hoffman, *Political Thought and Political Thinkers*, 38–55.

54. José María Torres Caicedo, *Ensayos biográficos y de crítica literaria* (Paris, Segunda serie, 1868), 274.

55. Arturo Ardao, *Génesis de la idea y el nombre de América Latina* (Caracas: Centro de Estudios Latinoamericanos Rómulo Gallegos, Consejo Nacional de la Cultura, 1980).

56. Jorge Arias Gómez, *Farabundo Martí* (San Salvador: Editorial Abril Uno, 2005), 35–42, 129–180, 231–288; Carr, "Across Seas and Borders"; Jeffrey L. Gould and Aldo A. Lauria-Santiago, *To Rise in Darkness. Revolution, Repression, and Memory in El Salvador, 1920–1932* (Durham, NC: Duke University Press, 2008); and Héctor Lindo-Fuentes, Erik Ching, and Rafael A. Lara-Martínez, *Remembering a Massacre in El Salvador* (Albuquerque: University of New Mexico Press, 2007).

57. Teresa García Giráldez, "La patria grande centroamericana: La elaboración del proyecto nacional por las redes unionistas," in Marta Elena Casaús Arzú and Teresa García Giráldez, *Las redes intelectuales centroamericanas: Un siglo de imaginarios nacionales (1820<n>1920)* (Guatemala: F&G Editores, 2005), esp. 148.

58. Thomas M. Leonard, *Central America and the United States* (Athens: University of Georgia Press, 1991), 13; see also Arturo Taracena Arriola, "Liberalismo y poder político en Centroamérica (1870–1929)," in *Historia General de Centroamérica*, coord. Víctor Hugo Acuña Ortega (Madrid: Sociedad Estatal Quinto Centenario and FLACSO, 1993), 4:223–225.

59. Volker Wünderich, *Sandino en la costa: De las Segovias al litoral Atlántico* (Managua: Editorial Nueva Nicaragua, 1989). As another illustration, when Sandino traveled in 1929 from Nicaragua to Mexico to try to secure military support, he used a Honduran passport and crossed the Salvadoran and Guatemalan territories under the understanding of the respective governments.

60. Jan Knippers Black, *Sentinels of Empire: The United States and Latin American Militarism* (New York: Praeger, 1986), 4.

61. Benedict Anderson, *Long-Distance Nationalism: World Capitalism and the Rise of Identity Politics* (Amsterdam: Centre for Asian Studies, 1992). See also Nina Glick Schiller, "Long Distance Nationalism," in *Encyclopedia of Diasporas* (New York: Springer, 2005), 570–580; and Daniele Conversi, "Irresponsible

Radicalisation: Diasporas, Globalisation and Long-Distance Nationalism in the Digital Age," *Journal of Ethnic and Migration Studies* 38, no. 9 (2012): 1357–1379.

Chapter 5

1. See, for example, Mark Fenster, *Conspiracy Theories: Secrecy and Power in American Culture* (Minneapolis: University of Minnesota Press, 1999); and Paul McCaffrey, *Conspiracy Theories* (Ipswich, UK: EBSCO Publishing, 2012). For a comprehensive discussion, see Leonardo Senkman and Luis Roniger, *América Latina tras bambalinas: Teorías conspirativas, usos y abusos* (Pittsburgh: Latin Ametrican Research Commons, 2019), https://doi.org/10.25154/book2.
2. Ricardo Piglia, "Teoría del complot" (2007), in http://bit.ly/2T82LR8 and http:/bit.ly/2YpaOyK (accesed July 6, 2018); and Arndt Graf, Schirin Fathi, and Ludwig Paul, *Orientalism and Conspiracy* (London: Taurus, 2011).
3. See Michael Barkun, *A Culture of Conspiracy* (Berkeley: University of California Press, 2003); Hugo Antonio Pérez Hernaiz, "The Uses of Conspiracy Theories for the Construction of a Political Religion in Venezuela," *International Scholarly and Scientific Research and Innovation* 2, no. 8 (2008): 970–981; Jane Parish, "The Age of Anxiety," in *The Age of Anxiety: Conspiracy Theory and the Human Sciences*, ed. Jane Parish and Martin Parker (London: Blackwell and Sociological Review, 2001), 1–16; and Rob Brotherton, *Suspicious Minds: Why We Believe Conspiracy Theories* (New York: Bloomsbury, 2015).
4. Vitor Izecksohn, "State Formation and Identity: Historiographical Trends Concerning South America's War of the Triple Alliance," *Historical Compass* 17, no. 9 (2019), in https://onlinelibrary.wiley.com/doi/10.1111/hic3.12589. Works mentioned are Carlos Guido y Spano, *El Gobierno y la Alianza* (Buenos Aires: Editorial la América de Vedia, 1866); and Juan Bautista Alberdi, *La Guerra del Paraguay* (1869; Buenos Aires: Editorial Sudamericana, 1988).
5. Juan E. O'Leary, *Nuestra Epopeya* (Asunción: Biblioteca Paraguaya del Centro de Estudiantes de Derecho, 1919).
6. Alfredo da Mota Menezes, *Guerra do Paraguai: Como construímos o conflito* (Cuiabá, Brazil: Editora da Universidade Federal de Mato Grosso, 1998).
7. For bibliographical details on these works see Esteban Chiaradía, "El debate historiográfico sobre la Guerra de la Triple Alianza (1864–1870)," *Entornos* 31, no. 1 (2018): 69–80.
8. León Pomer, *La Guerra del Paraguay: Estado, política y negocios* (Buenos Aires: CEAL, 1968); and Julio José Chiavenato, *Genocidio americano: La guerra del Paraguay* (Asunción, Paraguay: Carlos Schauman Editor, 1979). See also Rodolfo Ortega Peña and Luis Eduardo Duhalde, *Felipe Varela contra el Imperio Británico* (Buenos Aires: Shapire, 1975).
9. Laura Scoppetta and Pablo Torres, "La guerra del Paraguay en la retina de la izquierda argentina," *Revista Paraguay desde las ciencias sociales* 3 (2013): 1–18.

10. Eduardo Galeano, *Las Venas Abiertas de América Latina* (Buenos Aires: Siglo XXI, 1971).

11. Izecksohn, "State Formation and Identity." References are to Milcíades Peña, *La Era de Mitre: De Caseros a La Guerra de La Triple Infamia* (Buenos Aires: Ediciones Fichas, 1968); and José Fornos Peñalba, *The Fourth Ally: Great Britain and the War of the Triple Alliance* (PhD diss., University of California Los Angeles, 1979).

12. Jorge Abelardo Ramos, *Historia política del Ejército argentino* (Buenos Aires: Peña Lillo, 1959); and Jorge Abelardo Ramos, *Del patriciado a la oligarquía* (Buenos Aires: Ed. del Mar Dulce. Buenos Aires, 1982).

13. Milcíades Peña, *Historia del pueblo argentino* (Buenos Aires: Ed. Emecé, 2012).

14. Scoppetta and Torres, "La guerra del Paraguay," 16.

15. Moniz Bandeira, *O Expansionismo Brasileiro e a Formação dos Estados na Bacia do Prata: Argentina, Uruguai e Paraguai; Da colonização à Guerra da Tríplice Aliança* (1985; Brasília: Revan/UNB, 1998), 181–212.

16. Ricardo Caballero Aquino, *Las causas de la guerra* (Asunción, Paraguay: El Lector, 2013), ch. 9, http://bit.ly/2MXiwco.

17. Alfredo da Mota Menezes, *Guerra é nossa: A Inglaterra não provocou a Guerra do Paraguai* (São Paulo: Contexto, 2012), 164. Also important is Francisco Doratioto, *Maldita guerra: Nueva historia de la Guerra del Paraguay* (Buenos Aires: Emecé, 2008).

18. This section mostly reproduces materials from "Fuel for Oil: Conspirationism and the War of Chaco in the Americas," *Journal of Politics in Latin America* 11, no. 1 (June 2019): 1–20, doi/10.1177/1866802X19843008, published under CC-by-NC license and used here by permission of Sage.

19. Herbert Klein, *Orígenes de la revolución nacional boliviana* (Mexico City: Grijalbo, 1993), 223; Robert Alexander, *Prophets of the Revolution* (New York: Macmillan, 1962), 199.

20. Tristán Marof, *La tragedia del altiplano* (Buenos Aires: Claridad, 1934), 206.

21. Carlos R. Santos, *Conflicto paraguayo-boliviano* (Asunción, Paraguay: Segunda edición a beneficio de la Cruz Roja Paraguaya, 1932), 17 and 29.

22. Marof, *La tragedia del altiplano*, 2–3.

23. Marof, *La tragedia del altiplano*, 3.

24. Unidad Internacional de los Trabajadores—Cuarta Internacional, "Las petroleras provocaron un enfrentamiento fraticida," accessed November 20, 2017, http://uit-ci.org/index.php/donde-encontrarnos/bolivia/186-a-80-anos-de-la-guerra-del-chaco.

25. Raúl Scalabrini Ortiz, *Política británica en el Río de la Plata* (1940; Barcelona: Plus Ultra, 2001), 138.

26. Gregorio Selser, *Cronología de las intervenciones extranjeras en América Latina 1899–1945* (1994; Mexico City: UNAM, Centro de investigaciones interdisciplinarias, 2001), 539.

27. Eduardo Galeano, *Memoria del fuego 3* (Mexico City: Siglo XXI, 1986), 94.

28. Manuel Frontaura Argandoña, *La Revolución Boliviana* (1974; La Paz: Rolando Diez de Medina, 2012), 18.

29. Frontaura Argandoña, *La Revolución Boliviana*, 18 and 38.

30. Porfirio Díaz Machicao, *Historia de Bolivia: Salamanca, La Guerra del Chaco, Tejada Sorzano, 1931–1936* (La Paz: Gisbert y Cía, 1955), esp. 38–39, 57–58, and 83–85.

31. Soon-to-be Argentine president Arturo Frondizi's assessment that oil interests were behind the belligerent countries is still used today in Bolivian educational texts as proof of veracity (http://www.educabolivia.bo/files/textos/TX_Guerra_del_Chaco. pdf). See also Arturo Frondizi, *Petróleo y política* (Buenos Aires: Raigal, 1954).

32. Maximiliano Zuccarino, "Los intereses argentinos en Paraguay durante la Guerra del Chaco (1932–1935): Razones de un apoyo incondicional," *Estudios interdisciplinarios de América Latina y el Caribe* 28, no. 1 (2017): 82–101, relying on the following works: Sergio Almaraz, *Petróleo en Bolivia* (La Paz: Juventud, 1958); Julio José Chiavenato, *A Guerra do Chaco (Leia-se petróleo)* (São Paulo: Brasiliense, 1979); Alfredo Seiferheld, *Economía y petróleo durante la Guerra del Chaco* (Asunción, Paraguay: El Lector, 1983); and Stephen Cote, *Oil and Nation: A History of Bolivia's Petroleum Sector* (Morgantown: West Virginia University Press, 2016).

33. Enrique Mariaca Bilbao, *Mito y realidad del petróleo boliviano* (La Paz: Editorial Los amigos del pueblo, 1966), 43–65.

34. Herbert Klein, *Parties and Political Change in Bolivia, 1880–1952* (New York: Cambridge University Press, 1969), esp. 194–197 and 217–218.

35. Leslie B. Rout Jr., *Politics of the Chaco Peace Conference 1935–1939* (Austin: University of Texas Press, 1970).

36. Augusto Bunge, *La guerra del petróleo en la Argentina* (Buenos Aires: La Gráfica, 1933), 72–93.

37. Rout, *Politics of the Chaco Peace Conference*, 45–48.

38. Jorge Muñoz Reyes, *La caducidad de las concesiones otorgadas a the Standard Oil Company of Bolivia*, Cuartillas informativas no. 5 (La Paz: Departamento Nacional de Propaganda Socialista, March 23, 1937), in Klein, *Parties and Political Change*, 260–264.

39. Frank O. Mora and Jerry Cooney, *Paraguay and the United States: Distant Allies* (Athens: University of Georgia Press, 2007), 78; and Bridget María Chesterton, *The Grandchildren of Solano López: Frontier and Nation in Paraguay, 1904–1936* (Albuquerque: University of New Mexico Press, 2013).

40. Mora and Cooney, *Paraguay and the United States*, 64; and Stephen Cote, "A War for Oil in the Chaco, 1932–1935," *Environmental History* 18, no. 4 (2013): 748.

41. Mora and Cooney, *Paraguay and the United States*, 79–81; and Efraím Cardozo, *Breve historia del Paraguay* (Buenos Aires: EUDEBA, 1965), 136.

42. Juan Stefanich, *La guerra del Chaco y la misión de la Sociedad de las Naciones* (Asunción Paraguay: Self-published, 1934), 21–22, 28–29, 100, and 113.

43. Klein, *Parties and Political Change*, p. 187.

44. This official claim was disputed by those suggesting that Dr. Weiss had also been a victim in a wider conspiracy plot by the "powers that be," whose identity remains a controversial issue to this day. See http://www.nola.com/politics/index.ssf/2010/09/controversy_mystery_still_surr.html.

45. Raúl Scalabrini Ortiz, "El petróleo argentino," *Cuadernos de FORJA* II, no. 4 (1938): 8, and Raúl Scalabrini Ortiz, *Política británica*, 155–56.

46. Cote, "A War for Oil in the Chaco."
47. Spruille Braden, *Diplomats and Demagogues: The Memoirs of Spruille Braden* (New Rochelle, NY: Arlington House, 1971), 25–27.
48. Sergio Almaraz, *Petróleo en Bolivia* (La Paz: Juventud, 1958), 97–98.
49. Cardozo, *Breve historia del Paraguay*, p. 134.
50. Mora and Cooney, *Paraguay and the United States*, 66–77.
51. Francisco Barrero, *Conducción político-diplomática de la guerra con Paraguay* (La Paz: self published, 1979), 285; and L. A. Moniz Bandeira, "A Guerra do Chaco," *Revista Brasilera de Política Internacional* (Brasilia) 41, no. 1 (1988), n160, accessed November 18, 2017, http://www.scielo.br/scielo.php?script=sci_arttext&pid=S0034-73291998000100008.
52. Juan Luis Hernández, "Una guerra fratricida: El conflicto por el Chaco Boreal (1932–1935)," *Pacarina del Sur*, accessed November 22, 2017, http://www.pacarinadelsur.com/home/abordajes-y-contiendas/370-una-guerra-fratricida-el-conflicto-por-el-chaco-boreal-1932-1935.
53. This section is based on Senkman and Roniger, *América Latina tras bambalinas: Teorías conspirativas, usos y abusos*, 121–145, https://doi.org/10.25154/book2.
54. Alberto Ostria Gutiérrez, *The Tragedy of Bolivia: A People Crucified* (New York: Devin-Adair, 1958), 10 (translation of *Un pueblo en la cruz: El drama de Bolivia*).
55. Enrique Amayo, *La política británica en la Guerra del Pacífico* (Lima: Editorial Horizonte, 1988).
56. Genaro Figueroa Fajardo, Comentario a la nota de Estefanía Araya, "El dossier boliviano a La Haya y el futuro de la agenda," *La Segunda*, April 5, 2014, http://bit.ly/2Tng9Rk.
57. Luis E. Vásquez Medina, *La verdad detrás de la Guerra del Pacífico: El Imperio británico contra el Sistema americano de economía en Sudamérica* (Lima: Arquitas, 2012), back cover. Vásquez Medina defined himself as a "historian and politician, founder of the philosophical and political current of Lyndon LaRouche Jr. in Peru," the latter being a vocal supporter of conspiracy theories, even the most implausible and fanciful ones. See Mark Fenster, *Conspiracy Theories* (Minneapolis: University of Minnesota Press, 1999), 59–60, 183–188, and 191.
58. Vásquez Medina, *La verdad detrás de la Guerra del Pacífico*, 176 and 176–191.
59. Vásquez Medina, *La verdad detrás de la Guerra del Pacífico*, 11–12.
60. Heraclio Bonilla, "La dimensión internacional de la Guerra del Pacífico," in *Un siglo a la deriva. Ensayos sobre el Perú, Bolivia y la guerra* (Lima: Instituto de Estudios Peruanos, 1980), 171. See also V. G. Kiernan, "Foreign Interest in the War of the Pacific," *Hispanic American Historical Review* 35 (1955): 14–36.
61. Roberto Querejazu Calvo, *Guano, Salitre y Sangre* (La Paz-Cochabamba: Amigos del Libro, 1979); Ronald D. Crozier, "El salitre hasta la Guerra del Pacífico: Una revisión," *Historia* (Santiago), 30 (1997): 53–126; and Carlos Contreras Carranza, *La economía pública en el Perú después del guano y del salitre* (Lima: Instituto de Estudios Peruanos, 2012), ch. 1.

62. Alonso Barros, "Revolución chilena, Litoral boliviano: La Patria, La Compañía de Salitres y los prolegómenos de la Guerra del Pacífico en el Desierto de Atacama," *Revista de Antropología Experimental* 15 (2015): 483–520, 510.

63. Barros, "Revolución chilena," p. 490.

64. Benjamín Vicuña Mackenna, *Historia de la campaña de Tarapacá: desde la ocupación de Antofagasta hasta la proclamación de la dictadura en el Perú* (Santiago: Rafael Jover, 1880), 248–249.

65. Because of space limitations, I do not examine other threads of the conspiracy plot as suggested by Vásquez Medina, such as what he defines as the "suspicious murder of Manuel Pardo, on November 16, 1878, five months after the Anglo-Chilean invasion of Peru [where] the murderer, a obscure sergeant, conspired with his uncle, a tailor who sewed for the English military delegation in Callao" Vásquez Medina, *La verdad detrás de la Guerra del Pacífico*, 153.

66. Vásquez Medina, *La verdad detrás de la Guerra del Pacífico*, 133 and 20, respectively.

67. Lawrence A. Clayton, *Peru and the United States: The Condor and the Eagle* (Athens: University of Georgia Press, 1999).

68. Jorge Basadre, *Historia de la República del Perú, 1822–1933, 1983*, 11 vol. (Lima: Editorial Universitaria, 1983, 7th edition); reference is to vol. 5, 122–136.

69. Clayton, *Peru and the United States*, 53–60.

70. Kiernan, "Foreign Interest in the War."

71. Clayton, *Peru and the United States*, 66–67.

72. Clayton, *Peru and the United States*, 67.

73. Clayton, *Peru and the United States*, 68–71.

74. Hernán Dinamarca,"Bolivia, Chile y Perú: Conflicto de emociones," *El Mostrador*, October 31, 2010, http://bit.ly/2YZVg46; and "La Guerra del Pacifico, 1879–1883," *Perú Cultural*, May 16, 2013, http://bit.ly/2ZWwBL0.

75. Patricio Rivera Olguín, *La enseñanza de la guerra de 1879 en la región de Tarapacá* (PhD thesis, Universitat Autònoma de Barcelona, 2016), 132.

76. See E. Jorge Abastoflor Frey, "Mitos de la guerra del Pacifico," 2013, http://bit.ly/33pg3gK.

77. Jaime Bayly, "Peruano Jaime Bayly se ríe de Evo Morales y le recuerda que fue Bolivia la que declaró la Guerra a Chile en 1879," 2015, http://bit.ly/2TnNfR8.

78. Martin Brienen, "Interminable Revolution: Populism and Frustration in 20th Century Bolivia," *SAIS Review of International Affairs* 27, no. 1 (2007): 21–33.

79. "Decapitan bustos de héroes chilenos en la Guerra del Pacífico," July 12, 2017, http://bit.ly/2GZ8Avq; and "Chile advierte a Bolivia que no lo involucre en su campaña por la demanda marítima," March 17, 2017, http://bit.ly/2MYfpB4.

80. "Chile advierte a Bolivia."

81. "Argentinos mataré, bolivianos fusilaré, peruanos degollaré," February 6, 2013, https://youtu.be/NsVVXJwDxWk; and BBCMundo, February 7, 2013, https://youtu.be/IgT8_k3YHd8.

82. "Argentinos mataré."

83. Eduardo Cavieres y Cristóbal Aljovín de Losada, *Chile-Perú Perú-Chile, 1820–1920: Reflexiones para un análisis histórico de Chile-Perú en el siglo xix y la Guerra*

del Pacífico (Valparaíso: Pontificia Universidad Católica de Valparaíso, 2015), www.educarchile.cl.

84. "Miles de bolivianos forman una 'Marea azul' por demanda marítima a Chile," March 21, 2017, http://bit.ly/2ZWwKhw.

85. "Armada Boliviana celebra 191 años con una demostración militar en el Titicaca," 2017, http://bit.ly/2TnpVD7.

86. F. Artaza y E. Montesinos, "Perú recuerda la Guerra del Pacífico como antecedente en su demanda," December 3, 2012, in http://bit.ly/2YZmUKc.

87. John Ranson García, "El fallo de la corte internacional de justicia sobre el límite marítimo entre Chile y Perú: Sus efectos," *Revista Enfoques: Ciencia Política y Administración Pública* (Universidad Central de Chile) 12, no. 21 (2014): 45–68, ICJ Ruling 2017.

88. As when Bolivian, Peruvian, and Chilean individuals cooperated in the production of the documentary *Epitafio a una guerra* (2010), as discussed earlier.

89. Luis Roniger and Carlos H. Waisman, eds., *Globality and Multiple Modernities. Comparative North American and Latin American Perspectives* (Brighton: Sussex Academic Press, 2002); and Laurence Whitehead, *Latin America as a Mausoleum of Modernities* (London: Macmillan, 2006).

90. See, for instance, Enrique Santos Molano, *Grandes conspiraciones de la historia de Colombia* (Bogotá: Debate, 2011); and Jaime Guerrero and Tere Vale, *De conspiraciones, ambiciones y elecciones: Los grandes mitos de la política mexicana* (Mexico City: Planeta, 2012).

91. Mario Sznajder and Luis Roniger, *The Politics of Exile in Latin America* (New York: Cambridge University Press, 2009).

92. Pérez Hernaiz, "The Uses of Conspiracy Theories"; and David Kelman, *Countefeit Politics: Secret Plots and Conspiracy Narratives in the Americas* (Lewisburg, Pennsylvania: Bucknell University Press, 2012).

93. Ernesto Bohoslavsky, *El complot patagónico: Nación, conspiracionismo y violencia en el sur de Argentina y Chile (siglos XIX y XX)* (Buenos Aires: Prometeo, 2009), 17; and Geoffrey Cubitt, *The Jesuit Myth. Conspiracy Theory and Politics in Nineteenth Century France* (Oxford: Clarendon Press and Oxford University Press, 1993).

94. Peter Smith, *Talons of the Eagle. Dynamics of US-American Relations* (New York: Oxford University Press, 2000); and Luis Roniger, "U.S. Hemispheric Hegemony and the Descent into Genocidal Practices in Latin America," in *State Violence and Genocide in Latin America: The Cold War Years*, ed. Marcia Esparza, Daniel Feierstein and Henry Huttenbach (New York: Routledge, 2010), 23–43.

95. Felipe Fernández-Armesto, *The Americas: A Hemispheric History* (New York: Modern Library, 2003), p. 165.

96. Eldon Kenworthy, *America/Americas: Myth in the Making of U.S. Policy toward Latin America* (Philadelphia: Pennsylvania State University, 1995), 163.

97. Agustín Cueva, "A Summary of 'Problems and Perspectives of Dependency Theory,'" *Latin American Perspectives* 3, no. 4 (1976): 12–16; and Erasmo Sáenz Carrete, "El exilio brasileño en Chile, Francia y México: La teoría de la dependencia," II Jornadas

de trabajo sobre Exilios políticos en el Cono Sur en el siglo XX, SEDICI, Repositorio documental de la Universidad de La Plata, 2014.

98. André Gunder Frank, *Capitalismo y subdesarrollo en América Latina* (Buenos Aires: Siglo XXI, 1970); Eduardo Galeano, *Las venas abiertas de América Latina* (Buenos Aires: Siglo XXI, 1971); Theotonio Dos Santos, *Socialismo o Fascismo: El nuevo carácter de la dependencia y el dilema latinoamericano* (Santiago: Pla, 1972); and Vania Bambirra, *El capitalismo dependiente latinoamericano* (Mexico City: Siglo XXI, 1974).

99. Benedetta Calandra and Marina Franco, eds., *La guerra fría cultural en América Latina: Desafíos y límites para una nueva mirada de las relaciones interamericanas* (Buenos Aires: Editorial Biblos, 2012); Max Paul Friedman, *Rethinking Anti-Americanism* (New York: Cambridge University Press, 2012); Avital Bloch and Rosario Rodríguez, eds., *La Guerra Fría y las Américas* (Mexico City: Universidad de Colima and Universidad Michoacana de San Nicolás de Hidalgo, 2014).

100. Carlos Escudé, *El realismo de los estados débiles* (Buenos Aires: GEL, 1995).

Chapter 6

1. Robert H. Holden and Eric Zolov, *Latin America and the United States: A Documentary History* (New York: Oxford University Press, 2000).

2. Jan Knippers Black, *Sentinels of Empire: The United States and Latin American Militarism* (New York: Greenwood Press, 1986), 27–28.

3. Robert H. Holden, *Armies without Nations: Public Violence and State Formation in Central America, 1821–1960* (New York: Oxford University Press, 2004), esp. 27.

4. Juan Pablo Scarfi, *The Hidden History of International Law in the Americas: Empire and Legal Networks* (New York: Oxford University Press, 2017).

5. Black, *Sentinels of Empire*, 4.

6. Arie M. Kacowicz, "Latin America as an International Society," *International Politics* 37 (2000): 143–162.

7. The belated exception is Argentina, which did not break off diplomatic relations with the Axis until 1944 and only declared war in 1945 as an implicit condition for joining the United Nations. Similarly, Argentina remained economically attached to the United Kingdom longer than other sister nations, as exemplified in a 1933 preferential commercial agreement known as the Roca-Runciman Agreement.

8. James Lockhart, *Chile, the CIA and the Cold War* (Edinburgh: Edinburgh University Press, 2019), esp. chs. 3–4.

9. Lockhart, *Chile*, 114, relying on Carlos Humeeus, *La guerra fría chilena: Gabriel González Videla y la ley maldita* (Santiago, Chile: Random House Mandadori, 2008), 15–16, 355–371.

10. Benedetta Calandra, *La guerra fredda culturale* (Verona: Ombre corte, 2011).

11. Alberto Martín Álvarez and Eduardo Rey Tristán, "La dimensión transnacional de la izquierda armada," *América Latina Hoy* 80 (2018): 9–28, 18; and Thomas C

Field, Stella Krepp, and Vanni Pettinà, eds., *Latin America and the Global Cold War* (Chapel Hill: University of North Carolina Press, 2020).

12. Prudencio García, *El Drama de la Autonomía Militar* (Madrid: Alianza Editorial, 1995).

13. Frederick Nunn, "The South American Military and (Re)democratization: Professional Thought and Self-Perception," *Journal of Interamerican Studies and World Affairs* 37, no. 2 (1995): 7–9.

14. Christopher Darnton, "Asymmetry and Agenda-Setting in U.S.–Latin American Relations: Rethinking the Origins of the Alliance for Progress," *Journal of Cold War Studies* 14, no. 4 (2012): 55–92, 62.

15. Darnton, "Asymmetry and Agenda-Setting," 64.

16. Kenneth D. Lehman, *Bolivia and the United States: A Limited Partnership* (Athens: University of Georgia Press, 1999).

17. The United States did so especially since the discourse that attributed corruption to the civilian administrations in Latin America struck a chord in the minds of decision makers in Washington, DC. John Johnson, *Latin America in Caricature*. (Austin: University of Texas Press, 1980).

18. Lehman, *Bolivia and the United States*, 141. Juan Lechín (1914–2001), a leftist political figure of Trotskyist leanings, was head of the Federation of Bolivian Mine Workers from 1944 to 1987 and served as vice president of Bolivia in 1960–64.

19. Eduardo Galeano, *Las Venas Abiertas de América Latina* (Montevideo: Ediciones del Chanchito, 1987), 435–436.

20. Ana Pizarro, *De Ostras y Caníbales. Ensayos sobre la Cultura Latinoamericana* (Santiago, Chile: Editorial Universidad de Santiago, 1994), 173.

21. G. V. Correa, "Otros rasgos históricos de la derecha," *La Segunda* (Santiago), February 27, 1966.

22. José Murilo de Carvalho, *Cidadania no Brasil: O Longo Caminho* (São Paulo: Civilização Brasileira, 2001).

23. Enrique Padrós, "Como el Uruguay no hay . . . Terror de Estado e Segurança Nacional Uruguai (1968–1985)" (PhD thesis, Federal University of Rio Grande do Sul—UFRGS, 2005), 702.

24. Manoel Pio Corrêa, *O mundo em que vivi* (Rio de Janeiro: Expressão e Cultura, 1996), 1:848 and 2:869–870. The same dynamics operated with Argentina, where the armed forces took power in 1966–73.

25. Ananda Fernandes, "Quando o inimigo ultrapassa a fronteira: As conexões repressivas entre a ditadura civil-militar brasileira e o Uruguai (1964–1973)" (MA thesis, Federal University of Rio Grande do Sul—UFRGS, 2009); and Marla Barbosa Assumpção, "Fronteiras territoriais versus fronteiras ideológicas: A geopolítica do anticomunismo no marco das discussões sobre terrorismo de estado no Cone Sul," *Espaço Plural* 13, no. 27 (2012): 178–194.

26. Tim Weiner, *Legacy of Ashes: The History of the CIA* (New York: Doubleday, 2007), 357–58.

27. *Church Report* (Washington, DC: US Senate, 1975), section I.A. See also "Covert Action in Chile 1963–1973" Senate Select Committee on Intelligence Activities.

Declassified secret staff report. Washington, DC: US Government Printing Office, 1975, in https://www.archives.gov/files/declassification/iscap/pdf/2010-009-doc17.pdf; *Foreign Relations of the United States, 1969–1976*, vol. XXI, Chile, 1969–73, ed. James McElveen and James Siekmeier, in https://history.state.gov/historicaldocuments/frus1969-76v21Paul E. Sigmund, "The 'Invisible Blockade' and the Overthrow of Allende," *Foreign Affairs* 52, no. 2 (1974): 322–340; and Paul E. Sigmund, *The United States and Democracy in Chile* (Baltimore. MD: Johns Hopkins University Press, 1993).

28. *Informe de la Comisión Nacional de Verdad y Reconciliación* (Santiago: Corporación Nacional de Reparación y Reconciliación), vol. 1, 36–37, in http://bit.ly/33rj402.

29. Peter Kornbluh, *The Pinochet File: A Declassified Dossier on Atrocity and Accountability* (Washington, DC: National Security Archive and New Press, 2003), xiii.

30. Peter Kornbluh, "The Chile Coup—the U.S. Hand," *If Magazine*, October 25, 1998.

31. *Church Report*, section III.E.1.

32. Luis Corvalán Márquez, *La secreta obscenidad de la historia de Chile contemporáneo: Lo que dicen los documentos norteamericanos y otras fuentes documentales, 1962–1976* (Santiago: Ceibo, 2012); Kristian Gustafson, *Hostile Intent: U.S. Covert Operations in Chile, 1964–1974* (Washington, DC: Potomac Books, 2007); see also Carlos Basso, *La CIA en Chile, 1970–1973* (Santiago: Aguilar, 2013).

33. Seymour Hersh, *The Price of Power: Kissinger in the Nixon White House* (New York: Summit Books, 1983); Chistopher Hitchens, *The Trial of Henry Kissinger* (London: Verso, 2001); and Patricia Verdugo, *Allende: Cómo la Casa Blanca provocó su muerte* (Santiago: Catalonia, 2003), 59.

34. *Hinchey Report, CIA Activities in Chile* (Washington, DC: US State Department, 2000); Pablo Leighton, "Archives and Narratives for the Recent Coup-History of Chile," *Neo Journal* (Macquarie University) 2008, 20 pp. pdf in https://researchdirect.westernsydney.edu.au/islandora/object/uws.

35. Joaquín Fermandois, "Pawn or Player? Chile in the Cold War (1962–1973)," *Estudios Públicos* 72 (1998): 1–23.

36. Tanya Harmer, *El gobierno de Allende y la Guerra Fría Interamericana* (Santiago: Universidad Diego Portales, 2013), 22.

37. Harmer, *El gobierno de Allende y la Guerra Fría Interamericana*, 288.

38. Emilio Crenzel, "Tanya Harmer. El gobierno de Allende y la guerra fría interamericana," *Contemporánea (Montevideo)*, 5 (2014): 192–193.

39. Tanya Harmer, *El gobierno de Allende y la Guerra Fría Interamericana* (Santiago, Chile: Universidad Diego Portales, 2013), 176.

40. Harmer, *El gobierno de Allende*, 184, 303.

41. John Dinges, *The Condor Years* (New York: The New Press, 2005), esp. 41–81.

42. The initiative was Chilean. See letter from Manuel Contreras, head of National Intelligence in Chile, inviting South American police and intelligence delegations to a secret meeting aimed at coordinating cross-national intelligence, to be held in Santiago on November 25–December 1, 1975. M. Contreras, Document 00143F0011–0022, 1975, accessed September 26, 2008, http://http://www.pj.gov.py/cdya (currently unavailable).

43. These factors have been thoroughly studied by political scientists and Latin Americanists such as Giovanni Sartori, Laurence Whitehead, Guillermo O'Donnell, Philippe Schmitter, Juan Linz, and Alfred Stepan.

44. According to J. Patrice McSherry, "[T]op U.S. officials and agencies, including the State Department, the Central Intelligence Agency, and the Defense Department, were fully aware of Condor's formation and its operations from the time it was organized in 1975 (if not earlier). The U.S. government considered the Latin American militaries to be allies in the Cold War and worked closely with their intelligence organizations. U.S. executive agencies at least condoned, and sometimes actively assisted, Condor 'counter-subversive' operations." J. Patrice McSherry, "Operation Condor: Clandestine Inter-American System," *Social Justice* 26, no. 4 (1999): 144–145; and J. Patrice McSherry, *Predatory States: Operation Condor and Covert War in Latin America* (Lanham, MD: Rowman and Littlefield, 2005).

45. There were differences in the way de facto rulers carried out policies in tandem with a lack of political freedoms and civil rights. In Brazil, authoritarian rulers did not obliterate all the formalities of democracy, such as the Congress and political parties, in order to retain legitimacy. Instead, they carried out intermittent repression along with attempts to enlarge social rights, while restricting the hold of political rights (the suspension of habeas corpus, violation of privacy, censure of media, etc.). In addition, there were exceptions to such visions, as in the case of the Peruvian developmental military rule by General Juan Velasco Alvarado, especially in the first years following the 1968 coup.

46. Jorge Tapia Valdés, *El Terrorismo de Estado* (Mexico City: Editorial Nueva Imagen, 1980); and David Pion-Berlin, *The Ideology of State Power* (Boulder, CO: Lynne Rienner, 1989).

47. Manuel A. Garretón, *The Chilean Political Process* (Boston: Unwin Hyman, 1989), 70.

48. See the declarations of Colonel Juan Deichler Guzmán in Pablo Politzer, ed., *Fear in Chile: Lives under Pinochet* (New York: Pantheon Books, 1989), 20–39; and A. J. Letelier, "Los Intelectuales-políticos Chilenos," in *Intelectuales y Política en América Latina*, ed. W. Hofmeister and H. C. F. Mansilla (Rosario, Argentina: Homo Sapiens Ediciones, 2003), 171–198, esp. 171–179.

49. Mario Sznajder, "Entre autoritarismo y democracia: El legado de violaciones de derechos humanos," in *El Legado del Autoritarismo*, ed. Leonardo Senkman and Mario Sznajder, with the cooperation of E. Kaufman (Buenos Aires: Grupo Editor Latinoamericano, 1995), 16–17; and Luis Roniger, "Sociedad civil y derechos humanos: Una aproximación teórica en base a la experiencia argentina," in Senkman and Sznajder, *El Legado del Autoritarismo*, 37–54.

50. Ricardo Piglia, "Los pensadores ventrílocuos," in *Rebeldes y Domesticados*, ed. Raquel Angel (Buenos Aires: Ediciones el Cielo por el Asalto, 1992), 32.

51. John Simpson and Jana Bennett, *The Disappeared: Voices from a Secret War* (London: Robson Books, 1985), 66.

52. Daniel Feierstein, "Political Violence in Argentina and Its Genocidal Characteristics," *Journal of Genocide Research* 8, no. 2 (2006): 149–168. On the ambiguity of defining the enemy and its genocidal consequences in Argentina, see G. Levy, "Considerations

on the Connections between Race, Politics, Economics and Genocide," *Journal of Genocide Research* 8, no. 2 (2006): 137–148.

53. Frederick M. Nunn, *Time of the Generals. Latin American Professional Militarism in World Perspective* (Lincoln: University of Nebraska Press, 1992); Simpson and Bennett, *The Disappeared*, 66. In recent years, the armed forces have left behind this narrative of saving the nation and their views of society's collective blame. Their sustained effort to project blame onto others was reflected in their attempt to assume a new narrative according to which they too had been victims of terrorism. See Valentina Salvi, "Memoria y justificación: Consecuencias de la auto-victimización del ejército argentino" (paper presented at the Second International Congress on Genocidal Practices, Universidad Tres de Febrero, November 2007).

54. For a detailed analysis, see Luis Roniger, *Historia mínima de los derechos humanos en América Latina* (Mexico City: Colegio de México, 2018).

55. Accordingly, "Henry Kissinger declared that Santiago's human rights abuses strained Chile's diplomatic relations with the United States. If the Moneda's policy failed to change, Kissinger warned, the damage would be considerable. By then, however, Washington had lost much of its leverage on Chile. So much foreign private capital— nearly three billion dollars from 1974 to 1978 [*sic*]—had flowed into Santiago that Pinochet not only did not require American economic assistance, but he even publicly belittled the American offer of twenty-five million dollars in aid. Nor did the U.S. arms embargo discommode Santiago. . . . Santiago encountered little difficulty in replacing American weapons [with German, British, French, Spanish and Brazilian acquisitions]. . . . Increasingly Santiago manufactured its own weapons as well as assault and armored vehicles." William F. Sater, *Chile and the United States: Empires in Conflict* (Athens: University of Georgia Press, 1990), 191–192.

56. Peter Kornbluh, "Finding the Pinochet File: Pursuing Truth, Justice, and Historical Memory through Declassified US Documents," in *Democracy in Chile: The Legacy of September 11, 1973*, ed. Silvia Nagy-Zekmi and Fernando Leiva (Brighton, UK: Sussex Academic Press, 2005), 16 . See also Peter Kornbluh, *The Pinochet File* (New York: The New Press, 2003).

57. Sater, *Chile and the United States*, 194–95.

58. David Sheinin, *Argentina and the United States: An Alliance Contained* (Athens: University of Georgia Press, 2006), 150–180.

59. Cecilia Menjivar and Néstor Rodríguez, *When States Kill* (Austin: University of Texas Press, 2005), esp. Aldo Lauria-Santiago, "The Culture and Politics of State Terror and Repression in El Salvador," 85–114; and Rachel Sieder, "War, Peace and Memory Politics in Central America," in *The Politics of Memory: Transitional Justice in Democratizing Societies*, ed. Alexandra Barahona de Brito, Carmen González-Enríquez, and Paloma Aguilar (Oxford: Oxford University Press, 2001), 161–189.

60. S. S. Volk, "Chile and the United States Thirty Years Later: Return of the Repressed?," in Nagy-Zekmi and Leiva, *Democracy in Chile*, 24–40.

61. Donald E. Schulz, "Ten Theories in Search of Central American Reality," in *Revolution and Counterrevolution in Central America and the Caribbean*, ed. Donald E. Schulz

and Douglas H. Graham (Boulder, CO: Westview, 1984), 55. See also Kathryn Sikkink, *Mixed Signals* (Ithaca, NY: Cornell University Press, 2004), 79–105.

62. National Security and International Affairs Division (N. Toolan, M. Forster, K. Handley, F. J. Shafer, and N. Ragsdale), *School of the Americas US Military Training for Latin American Countries* (Washington, DC: US General Accounting Office, 1996), www.fas.org/asmp/resources/govern/gao96178.pdf; and Leslie Gill, *The School of the Americas* (Durham, NC: Duke University Press, 2004), esp. 71–73.

63. Dana Priest, "U.S. Instructed Latins on Executions, Torture," *Washington Post*, September 21, 1996.

64. Lisa Haugaard, "Declassified Army and CIA Manuals Used in Latin America: An Analysis of Their Content," Latin American Working Group, February 18, 1997, https://newtotse.com/oldtotse/en/politics/central_intelligence_agency/162408.html.

65. Gill, *School of the Americas*, 212; and Haugaard, "Declassified Army and CIA Manuals."

66. Baldwin Brown, "School for Scandal," *Commonwealth* 22, no. 125 (1998): 10–11; and Kathrine E. McCoy, "Trained to Torture? The Human Rights Effects of Military Training at the School of the Americas," *Latin American Perspectives* 32, no. 6 (2005): 47–64.

67. Gill, *School of Americas*, p. 152.

68. In 1984, the SOA moved to Fort Benning, Georgia, where it operated until its replacement by the Western Hemisphere Institute for Security Cooperation in 2001.

Chapter 7

1. For a systematic review of the literature of comparative democratization, see Luis Roniger, "Democratization," in *Concise Encyclopedia of Comparative Sociology*, ed. Masamichi Sasaki, Ekkart Zimmermann, Jack Goldstone, and Stephen Sanderson (Leiden: Brill, 2014), 342–351.

2. Manuel Alcántara Sáenz, "Tras un cuarto de siglo de democracia en América Latina," in *Alternativas para el siglo XXI*, ed. Alfonso Guerra and José Félix Tezanos (Madrid: Sistema, 2003), 519–550. The same applied to Southern Europe, East Asia, and Africa; South Korea, Singapore, and South Africa were democratizing, while other societies in the same region were entering periods of tightened control and repression. Moreover, progress was often reversed. Democratization soon led to renewed authoritarianism in Zimbabwe, Armenia, and Russia, and to various political crises and massive violence, such as in the Philippines, Ukraine, Kenya, Ethiopia, Thailand, Syria, and even some states in India, the most populated democracy in the world.

3. See also Luis Roniger and Carlos H. Waisman, eds., *Globality and Multiple Modernities. Comparative North American and Latin American Perspectives* (Brighton, UK: Sussex Academic Press, 2002); and Laurence Whitehead, *Latin America: A New Interpretation*. (London: Macmillan, 2006).

4. Carlos H. Waisman and Raanan Rein, eds., *Spanish and Latin American Transitions to Democracy* (Brighton, UK: Sussex Academic Press, 2005); and Mario Sznajder and Luis Roniger, *The Politics of Exile in Latin America* (New York: Cambridge University Press, 2009).

5. Laurence Whitehead, *The International Dimensions of Democratization* (Oxford: Oxford University Press, 2001), 3–25.

6. Dietrich Rueschemeyer, Evelyne Huber Stephens, and John D. Stephens, *Capitalist Development and Democracy* (Chicago: University of Chicago Press, 1992); Juan J. Linz and Alfred Stepan, *Problems of Democratic Transition and Consolidation: Southern Europe, South America and Post-Communist Europe* (Baltimore, MD: Johns Hopkins University Press, 1996); and Whitehead, *The International Dimensions of Democratization*.

7. See D. A. Crocker, "Reckoning with Past Wrongs: A Normative Framework," *Ethics and International Affairs* 13 (1999): 43–64; Luis Roniger and Mario Sznajder, *The Legacy of Human Rights Violations in the Southern Cone* (Oxford: Oxford University Press, 1999); Alexandra Barahona de Brito et al., eds., *The Politics of Memory: Transitional Justice in Democratizing Societies* (Oxford: Oxford University Press, 2001), especially Rachel Sieder, "War, Peace and Memory Politics in Central America," 161–189; Richard Wilson, "Justice and Legitimacy in the South African Transition," 190–217; and Nanci Adler, "In Search of Identity: The Collapse of the Soviet Union and the Recreation of Russia," 248–264; and Kathryn Sikkink, *The Justice Cascade* (New York: WW Norton, 2011).

8. International Center for Transitional Justice, "What Is Transitional Justice," in http://ictj.org/en/tj/; and Alexandra Barahona de Brito, "Transitional Justice and Memory: Exploring Different Perspectives" (paper presented at the IPSA Congress in Santiago de Chile, July 2009).

9. See, for example, Elin Skaar, "Truth Commissions, Trials: Or Nothing? Policy Options in Democratic Transitions," *Third World Quarterly* 20, no. 6 (1999): 1109–1128; Richard Falk, *Human Rights Horizons* (New York: Routledge, 2000), 199–216; and Priscilla B. Hayner, *Unspeakable Truths: Confronting State Terror and Atrocity* (New York: Routledge, 2001).

10. Only Bolivia started the process earlier, albeit almost on the verge of civil war and with continuing social tensions and economic crisis, which reduced its regional appeal as a model to replicate elsewhere.

11. Resembling the Uruguayan case, about which the SERPAJ published a partial and unofficial report in 1989 (*Uruguay Nunca Más: Human Rights Violations, 1972–1985*), Brazil had only an unofficial report prepared by the Archdiocese of Sao Paulo, covering abuses from 1964 to 1979, made public in 1998 in book-length form (*Nunca mais*; Torture in Brazil). In 2000 Uruguay launched a peace commission of inquiry (*Informe final de la Comisión para la Paz* was published on April 2003, archivo. presidencia.gub.uy), and Brazil created an official commission of truth covering the 1964–85 dictatorship, whose report was released on December 2014.

12. See, for example, "Transitional Justice and Protracted Accountability in Re-Democratized Uruguay (1985–2011)," *Journal of Latin American Studies* 43,

no. 4 (2011): 693–724; and "How a Shattered Civil Religion Is Rebuilt through Contestation: Uruguay in Comparative Perspective," *Revista de Ciencia Política* (Santiago) 36, no. 2 (2016): 411–432.

13. For a comprehensive analysis, see Roniger and Sznajder, *The Legacy of Human Rights Violations in the Southern Cone*7

14. Agenda setting is defined as "the politics of selecting issues for active consideration." See R. W. Cobb and M. H. Ross, *Cultural Strategies of Agenda Denial* (Lawrence: University Press of Kansas, 1997), 3–6; and David Dery, "Agenda Setting and Problem Definition," *Policy Studies* 21, no. 1 (2000): 37–48.

15. Ernesto González Bermejo, "Las singulares opiniones del ciudadano Medina," *Brecha* (Montevideo), March 27, 1987, 3.

16. Interview with Sanguinetti, *El país* (Madrid), April 19, 1989, 6.

17. Guillermo Chifflet, "Poder military o poder popular," *Brecha*, April 24, 1987, 32.

18. Horacio Verbitsky, *El vuelo* (Buenos Aires: Planeta, 1995); and Samuel Blixen, "Por supuesto que no me voy a callar," *Brecha* (Montevídco), May 7, 1996.

19. "Tedeum Evangélico: Gobierno debe hacer prioritaria la reconciliación," *El Mercurio* (Santiago), September 18, 1995, 1.

20. *Página/12* (Buenos Aires), July 12, 1995, 10–11.

21. *El Soldado* (Montevideo), May–June 1989, 35.

22. Interview with Emiliano Cotclo, *Radio El Espectador*, May 24, 1996, 09:10 a.m.

23. Horacio Verbitsky, "Fuerzas armadas y sociedad civil," *Página/12*, July 16, 1995, 10–11 (from an interview for *Time* magazine).

24. This section follows closely the analysis in Mario Sznajder and Luis Roniger, "The Crises beyond Past Crisis: The Unsolved Legacy of Human-Rights Violations in the Southern Cone," *Human Rights Review* 1, no. 1 (1999): 48–68.

25. Museo de la Justicia, Centro de Documentación y Archivo para la Defensa de los Derechos Humanos de la Corte Suprema de Justicia del Paraguay, http://www.pj.gov.py/contenido/132-museo-de-la-justicia/132; and Alfredo Boccia Paz, Rosa Palau Aguilar, and Osvaldo Salerno, *Paraguay: Los archivos del terror; Papeles que resignificaron la memoria del stronismo*, 2nd ed. (Asunción, Paraguay: Editorial Servilibro, 2008).

26. See Centro de Documentación y Archivo para la Defensa de los Derechos Humanos de la Corte Suprema de Justicia del Paraguay, http://www.pj.gov.py/contenido/132-museo-de-la-justicia/132; and Myriam González Vera, "Los archivos del Terror del Paraguay: La historia oculta de la represión," in *Los archivos de la represión: Documentos, memoria y verdad*, ed. Ludmila da Silva Catela and Elizabeth Jelin (Buenos Aires: Siglo XXI, 2002), 85–115.

27. Interview with Alfredo Boccia Paz, Asunción, April 12, 2010; Alfredo Boccia Paz, Carlos Portillo, and Carlos Arestivo, *Médicos, ética y tortura en el Paraguay* (Asunción, Paraguay: Editorial RP, 1992); Alfredo Boccia Paz, Myriam Angélica González, and Rosa Palau Aguilar, *Es mi informe: Los archivos secretos de la policía de Stroessner* (Asunción, Paraguay: CDE, 1994); Alfredo Boccia Paz, Rosa Palau Aguilar, and Osvaldo Salerno, *Paraguay: Los archivos del terror* (Asunción, Paraguay: Servilibro, 2008).

28. That progress was also channeled through a reform of the judicial system, accelerated in 1994 through a governability pact between the presidential office and the opposition. The discovery of the archives of repression also generated broad support for the enactment of the Law on Compensation for Victims of Dictatorship, which would be implemented years later. By August 2011, the state had paid—through the Ministry of Finance and the Office of the Ombudsman—almost $10 million in compensation to victims of repression, those persecuted, and the families of the disappeared.

29. Balza made that statement on live television on April 25, 1995, in the program *Tiempo Nuevo*, hosted by Bernardo Neustadt.

30. Olga Wornat, "Increible, pero cierto: Las confesiones de Massera," *Gente* (Buenos Aires), July 27, 1995, 48–56. For Díaz's declarations see *Página/12*, August 13, 1995.

31. Among them are Nobel Prize winner Adolfo Pérez Esquivel and Hebe de Bonafini, president of the Mothers of Plaza de Mayo. See *Madres de Plaza de Mayo* 118 (April 1995). The statements of Emilo Mignone, Adolfo Pérez Esquivel, Nora Cortinas, and Domingo Quarracino can be seen in "Culpas que debe asumir la Iglesia," *Página/12*, April 25, 1995.

32. "Malestar en el gobierno por el discurso de un jefe militar," *Clarín*, April 3, 1996, 6.

33. *Posdata* (Montevideo), April 26, 1996; Jorge Tróccoli, "Yo asumo . . . yo acurso," *Brecha* (Montevideo), May 10, 1996; see also Jorge Néstor Tróccoli, *La ira de Leviatán* (Montevideo: Caelum, 1996).

34. Maria Rosaria Stabili, "*Oparei*: La justicia de transición en Paraguay," *América Latina Hoy* 61 (2012): 148–149.

35. Centro de Documentación y Archivo para la Defensa de los Derechos Humanos (CDyA) de la Corte Suprema de Justicia del Paraguay, http://www.pj.gov.py/cdya.

36. *Comisión Verdad y Justicia, Informe final: Anive hagua Orko* (Asunción, Paraguay: CVJ, 2008), 1:24–25.

37. *Comisión Verdad y Justicia, Informe final*, 1:45–57.

38. *Comisión Verdad y Justicia, Informe final*, 1:61–62.

39. "Histórica sesión por la memoria" (2009), http://www.radionacional.com.ar/audios/uruguay-histrica-sesin-por-la-memoria.html.

40. Due to the civil law character of the legal system of Uruguay, this decision has no binding effect on future adjudication and did not nullify the patterned hold of the Law of Expiry.

41. See the testimony of Juan Gelman on his years-long struggle and the attitudes of the various Uruguayan administrations, in an interview with Victoria Ginzberg in *Página/12* (Buenos Aires), November 25, 2010, http://notas.desaparecidos.org/2010/11/el_poeta_juan_gelman _habla_de.html.

42. Raúl Olivera Alfaro, "Sobre el futuro de la impunidad en Uruguay, también miremos hacia Brasil," http://www.pvp.org.uy/?p=1749 (originally from http://raulolivera.blogspot.com/2011/01/sobre-el-futuro-de-la-impunidad-en.html).

43. See, among others, "Impunidades y cuestiones legales," *Página/*, March 6, 2011, http://www.pagina12.com.ar/diario/elmundo/4-163557-2011-03-06.html.

44. Interview with political scientist Oscar Bottineli, Montevideo, April 26, 2011.

Chapter 8

1. "Habla Maduro en Argentina," *Quebracho*, May 10, 2013; and "Rodilla en tierra! No nos arrebatarán la revolución bolivariana," *Quebracho*, April 15, 2013 (both found at http://www.quebracho.org).
2. Alfredo Oliva, "Comandante Inmortal," *Aporrea*, March 6, 2013, www.aporrea.org/ideologia/a160587.html; Kenneth Chávez and Yader Prado Reyes, "OCLAE destaca al Presidente Daniel como 'soldado histórico de las causas del movimiento estudiantil,'" *El 19 Digital*, August 21, 2014; and MPPRE, "Mercosur y la integración nuestramericana," *PortalAlba*, July 30, 2014.
3. Milos Alcalay, "Nuestramérica: El Neo-Lenguaje Bolivariano," June 19, 2012, https://runrun.es/ internacional/diploos/46928/nuestramerica-el-neo-lenguaje-bolivariano-por-milos-alcalay/.
4. "VI Cumbre Extraordinaria Declaración Conjunta," *PortalAlba*, June 24, 2009, www.portalalba.org.
5. Luis Roniger, "Estructurando bienes y servicios públicos en Argentina, Chile y Brasil: Prácticas e imágenes contemporáneas," *Estudios Interdisciplinarios de América Latina* 13, no. 1 (2002): 89–116.
6. Luis Roniger and Leonardo Senkman, *Conspiracy Theories and Latin American History* (New York: Routledge, 2021), ch. 6.
7. The election of Andrés Manuel Ló, pez Obrador (AMLO) as Mexican president in 2018 is a later development, occurring when other countries had already turned to the center Right.
8. Juan Agulló, "La forja del chavismo," *Estudios Latinoamericanos* 32, no. 24 (2009): 89–113.
9. Max Azicri, "The Castro-Chávez Alliance," *Latin American Perspectives* 36, no. 1 (2009): 99–110; and Michael Shifter, "In Search of Hugo Chávez," *Foreign Affairs*, May–June 2006, 99.
10. Andrés Malamud, "A Leader without Followers? The Growing Divergence between the Regional and Global Performance of Brazilian Foreign Policy," *Latin American Politics and Society* 53 (2011): 1–24; Sean W. Burges, "Building a Global Southern Coalition: The Competing Approaches of Brazil's Lula and Venezuela's Chávez," *Third World Quarterly* 28 (2007): 1343–1358; and Mario E. Carranza, "Can Mercosur Survive? Domestic and International Constraints on Mercosur," *Latin American Politics and Society* 45, no. 2 (2003): 67–103.
11. See Joseph S. Nye and Robert O. Keohane, "Transnational Relations and World Politics: An Introduction," *International Organization* 25, no. 3 (1971): 329–349; Kathryn Sikkink, "Transnational Politics, International Relations Theory and Human Rights," *PS: Political Science and Politics* 31, no. 3 (1998): 516–523; Thomas Risse, *Bringing Transnational Relations Back* (New York: Cambridge University Press, 1995); Sydney Tarrow, "Transnational Politics: Contention and Institutions in International Politics," *Annual Review of Political Science* 4, no. 1 (2001): 1–20; D. Fitzgerald, *Negotiating Extra-territorial Citizenship: Mexican Migration and the Transnational Politics of Community* (Boulder, CO: Lynne Rienner, 2000); and Shari

M. Huhndorf, *Mapping the Americas: The Transnational Politics of Contemporary Native Culture* (Ithaca, NY: Cornell University Press, 2009).

12. Luciana Gil and Damián Paikin, "Mapa de la Integración Regional en América Latina: Procesos e instituciones," *Nueva Sociedad*, September 2013, 1–34; and Thomas Muhr, "The Politics of Space in the Bolivarian Alliance for the Peoples of Our America–Peoples' Trade Agreement (ALBA–TCP): Transnationalism, the Organized Society, and Counter-Hegemonic Governance," *Globalizations* 9, no. 6 (2012): 767–782.

13. Jorge G. Castañeda, "Latin America's Left Turn," *Foreign Affairs* 85, no. 3 (2006): 28–43. For an analysis of moderates and more radical sectors in this period, see also Kurt Weyland and Wendy Hunter, *Leftist Governments in Latin America: Successes and Shortcomings* (New York: Cambridge University Press, 2010); Martha Harnecker, "Latin America and Twenty-First Century Socialism: Inventing to Avoid Mistakes," *Monthly Review* 62, no. 2 (2010): 1–83; Kurt Weyland, "The Rise of Latin America's Two Lefts: Insights from Rentier State Theory," *Comparative Politics* 41, no. 2 (2009): 145–164; and Maxwell A. Cameron and Eric Hershberg, *Latin America's Left Turns: Politics, Policies, and Trajectories of Change* (Boulder, CO: Lynne Rienner, 2010).

14. See Jean Grugel, "Regionalist Governance and Transnational Collective Action in Latin America," *Economy and Society* 35, no. 2 (2006): 209–231; Peter Hakim, "Is Washington Losing Latin America?," *Foreign Affairs* 85, no. 1 (2006): 39–53; Diana Tussie, "Latin America: Contrasting Motivations for Regional Projects," *Review of International Studies*, no. 35 (2009): 169–188; J. M. Gomez, *América Latina y el (des)orden global neoliberal: Hegemonía, contra hegemonía, perspectivas* (Buenos Aires: CLACSO, 2004); S. Gratius and H. Fürtig, *Iran and Venezuela: Bilateral Alliance and Global Power Projections, 2009*, www.maximsnews.com/news2009050 3frideiranvenezuela10905030102.html; José Briceño Ruiz and Rosalba Linares, "Más allá del chavismo y la oposición: Venezuela en el proceso del ALCA y la propuesta ALBA," *Geoenseñanza* 9, no. 1 (2004): 19–45; and Gerardo Caetano, Introducción to *MERCOSUR: 20 años* (Montevideo: CEFIR, 2011), 21–71, http://library.fes.de/pdf-files/bueros/uruguay/07904.pdf.

15. See respectively Pía Riggirozzi and Diana Tussie, *The Rise of Post-Hegemonic Regionalism: The Case of Latin America* (New York: Springer, 2012); and José Antonio Sanahuja, "Del 'regionalismo abierto' al 'regionalismo post-liberal': Crisis y cambio en la integración regional en América Latin," *Anuario de Integración Regional de América Latina y el Gran Caribe* 7 (2008–2009): 11–54.

16. José Briceño Ruiz, "Strategic Regionalism and Regional Social Policy in the FTAA Process," *Global Social Policy* 7, no. 3 (2007): 294–315.

17. Reports on Summits of America, http://www.summit-americas.org/iv_summit_sp.html; Héctor de la Cueva, "Mar del Plata: El ALCA no pasó; Una victoria de la Cumbre de los Pueblos," *Observatorio Social de América Latina* 6, no. 18 (2005): 81–91, http://biblioteca.clacso.edu.ar/clacso/osal/20110318071958/7delaCueva.pdf; Marcelo Saguier, "The Hemispheric Social Alliance and the Free Trade Area of the Americas Process: The Challenges and Opportunities of Transnational Coalitions

against Neo-liberalism," *Globalizations* 4, no. 2 (2007): 251–265; and Masiel Fernández-Bolaños, "Sepelio del ALCA en Mar del Plata," *Bolpress*, November 4, 2011, www.bolpress.com/art.php?Cod=2011110406.

18. Secretaría de Formación Político Sindical, "Clase trabajadora, nuestra lucha," *Suteba*, November 9, 2013, www.suteba.org.ar/4-y-5-de-noviembre-no-al-alca-11473.html.

19. De la Cueva, "Mar del Plata"; Gonzalo Patrone, "El Alca ... ¡al carajo!," *Puntonoticias*, March 5, 2013, www.puntonoticias.com/el-alca-al-carajo-hugo-chavez-dejo-su-huella-en-mar-del-plata/#ixzz37Xs2XHKk.

20. Sanahuja, "Del 'regionalismo abierto' al 'regionalismo post-liberal': Mario Vargas Llosa, 'La careta del gigante,'" *El País*, July 13, 2014.

21. Jorge I. Domínguez, "International Cooperation in Latin America: The Design of Regional Institutions by Slow Accretion," in *Crafting Cooperation: Regional Institutions in Comparative Perspective*, ed. Amitav Achayra and Alistair Iain Johnston (New York: Cambridge University Press, 2007), 83–128; Muhr, "The Politics of Space in the Bolivarian Alliance"; and Riggirozzi and Tussie, *The Rise of Post-Hegemonic Regionalism*.

22. Carlos Malamud, "La salida venezolana de la Comunidad Andina de Naciones y sus repercusiones sobre la integración regional" (1ª parte), *Análisis del Real Instituto Elcano* 54 (2006), http://www.realinstitutoelcano.org.

23. Richard Feinberg, "Recent Tendencies in Latin American Multilateralism: Implications for the Inter-American System and the OAS," in *Latin American Multilateralism: New Directions*, ed. Thomas Legler and Lesley Burns Ottawa: Canadian Foundation for the Americas—FOCAL, 2010), 23–26.

24. Caetano, Introducción to *MERCOSUR: 20 años*, 21–71.

25. On UNASUR, see Thomas Legler, "Multilateralism and Regional Governance in the Americas," in Legler and Burns, *Latin American Multilateralism*, 12–17; Brigitte Weiffen, Leslie Wehner, and Detlef Nolte, "Overlapping Regional Security Institutions in South America: The Case of OAS and UNASUR," *International Area Studies Review* 16, no. 4 (2013): 370–389; Tussie, "Latin America: Contrasting Motivations for Regional Projects"; Gian Luca Gardini, "Proyectos de Integración Regional Sudamericana: Hacia una Teoría de Convergencia Regional," *Relaciones Internacionales*, no. 15 (2010): 11–31; Feinberg, "Recent Tendencies in Latin American Multilateralism"; Arie Kacowicz, "The Rio Group and the South American Union as Tools of Regional Security," in *The New Security Equation in the Americas*, ed. Gordon Mace and Catherine Durepos (Montreal: Université Laval, Center of Interamerican Studies, 2007); 96–111; and Ricardo Lagos, *América Latina: ¿integración o fragmentación?* (Buenos Aires: Edhasa, 2008).

26. See Dexter Boniface, "Latin American Multilateralism: The U.S. Perspective," in Legler and Burns, *Latin American Multilateralism*, 44–47; and Roberto Russell and Juan Gabriel Tokatlian, "Modelos de política exterior y opciones estratégicas: El caso de América Latina frente a Estados Unidos," *Revista CIDOB d'afers internacionals*, nos. 85–86 (2009): 211–249.

27. Roberto Porzecanski, *No voy en tren: Uruguay y las perspectivas de un TLC con Estados Unidos (2000–2010)* (Montevideo: Random House Mondadori, 2010).

28. Javier Corrales, "Using Social Power to Balance Soft Power: Venezuela's Foreign Policy," *Washington Quarterly* 32, no. 4 (2009): 97–114, https://doi.org/10.1080/01636600903232285; and Steve Ellner, "The Distinguishing Features of Latin America's New Left in Power: The Chávez, Morales, and Correa Governments," *Latin American Perspectives* 39, no. 1 (2012): 96–114.

29. Raúl Andrés Sanhueza Carvajal, *Las cumbres iberoamericanas: Comunidad de naciones o diplomacia clientelar* (Santiago de Chile: Editorial Universitaria, 2003).

30. On CELAC and its creation, see Francisco Rojas Aravena, *América Latina y el Caribe: Multilateralismo vs. Soberanía: La Construcción de la Comunidad de Estados Latinoamericanos* (Buenos Aires: Teseo, 2012); Raúl Bernal-Meza, *Modelos o esquemas de integración y cooperación en curso en América Latina* (Berlin: Ibero-Americhaniskes Institut, 2013); Andrés Malamud and Gian Luca Gardini, "Has Regionalism Peaked? The Latin American Quagmire and Its Lessons," *International Spectator: Italian Journal of International Affairs* 47, no. 1 (2012): 116–133; Andrés Serbín, "Old Facts and New Challenges in Regional Multilateralism: A Latin American Idiosyncrasy?," in Legler and Burns, *Latin American Multilateralism*, 8–11; and Thomas Legler, "Post-hegemonic Regionalism and Sovereignty in Latin America: Optimists, Skeptics, and an Emerging Research Agenda," *Contexto Internacional* 35, no. 2 (2013): 325–352.

31. R. Sanders, "Venezuela in the Caribbean: Expanding Its Sphere of Influence," *Round Table* 96 (2007): 465–476.

32. Félix Peña, "La integración regional en América Latina: Hacia una estrategia nacional acorde con nuevas realidades regionales y globales," *Archivos del Presente* 17, no. 61 (2014), in http://www.felixpena.com.ar (accessed July 27, 2021).

33. Moisés Naím, "Experimento en Latinoamérica," *El País*, February 15, 2014; and Beatriz Ramacciotti, "Alianza del Pacífico ¿un intento más para la integración regional?," *América Economía*, July 17, 2013.

34. Félix Peña, "La diplomacia económica multi-espacial e interregional: el caso de las relaciones entre América Latina y la Unión Europea," in *Después de Santiago: Integración Regional y Relaciones Unión Europea-América Latina*, ed. J. Roy (Miami, FL: Thomson Publishing, 2013), 181–192; and J. Monnet Chair, "Cancilleres del MERCOSUR avanzan en presentación de la oferta del bloque regional para acuerdo con Unión Europea," *La Red* 21 (December 20, 2015), www.lr21.com.uy/politica/1269077-canciller-mercosur-avanzan-presentacion-oferta-bloque-union-europea.

35. Salvador Martí i Puig, "The Adaptation of the FSLN: Daniel Ortega's Leadership and Democracy in Nicaragua," *Latin American Politics and Society* 52, no. 4 (2010): 79–106; Juan Montes and José de Córdoba, "Nicaragua's Leftist Ortega Embraces Business and Authoritarianism," *Wall Street Journal*, November 4, 2016; and Héctor Cruz Feliciano, "The Perils of Reconciliation: Achievements and Challenges of Daniel Ortega and the Modern FSLN," *Latin American Perspectives* 46 (2019): 247–262.

36. Thomas Muhr, "(Re)constructing Popular Power in Our America: Venezuela and the Regionalisation of 'Revolutionary Democracy' in the ALBA–TCP Space," *Third World Quarterly* 33, no. 2 (2012): 225–241; Ernesto Laclau, "La deriva populista y

la centroizquierda latinoamericana," *Nueva Sociedad* 205 (2006): 56–61; and Agulló, "La forja del chavismo," 108–109.

37. See Kirk A. Hawkins and David R. Hansen, "Dependent Civil Society: The Círculos Bolivarianos in Venezuela," *Latin American Research Review* 41, no. 1 (2006): 102–132; Steven Ellner, "Revolutionary and Non-Revolutionary Paths of Radical Populism: Directions of the 'Chavista' Movement in Venezuela," *Science & Society* 69, no. 2 (2005): 160–190; Daniel Hellinger, "When 'No' Means 'Yes to Revolution': Electoral Politics in Bolivarian Venezuela," *Latin American Perspectives* 32, no. 2 (2005): 8–32; Agulló, "La forja del chavismo," 104; Noam Lupu, "Who Votes for Chavismo? Class Voting in Hugo Chávez's Venezuela," *Latin American Research Review* 45, no. 1 (2010): 7–32; and Damarys Canache, "From Bullets to Ballots: The Emergence of Popular Support for Hugo Chávez," *Latin American Politics and Society* 44, no. 1 (2002): 69–90.

38. Silvio Waisbord, "Between Support and Confrontation: Civic Society, Media Reform, and Populism in Latin America," *Communication, Culture & Critique* 4, no. 1 (2011): 97–117, esp. 100; José Pedro Zúquete, "The Missionary Politics of Hugo Chávez," *Latin American Politics and Society* 50, no. 1 (2008): 91–121, esp. 91–93; and Ernesto Laclau, "La deriva populista y la centroizquierda latinoamericana," *Nueva Sociedad* 205 (2006): 56–61.

39. "Declaración Final del VI Encuentro Hemisférico de Lucha contra los TLCs y por la Integración de los Pueblos," *La Habana*, May 5, 2007, www.alainet.org/es/active/ 17361; "Conclusiones de la Cumbre Antiimperialista," Cochabamba, July 2013, http://eju.tv/2013/08/conclusiones-de-cumbre-antiimperialista-evo-morales-lder-mundial-de-movimientos-sociales/; and "Daniel clausura el XVII Congreso de la OCLAE," *Radio La Primerísima*, August 22, 2014, https://www.alainet.org/es/active/ 76431https://www.alainet.org/es/active/76431

40. Ellner, "The Distinguishing Features of Latin America's New Left," 107.

41. Because of space limitations, the analysis here is only synoptic and cannot fully reflect the nuanced treatment of a burgeoning research domain. Among important contributions see Andrés Serbín, "Etnicidad y política: Los movimientos indígenas en América Latina," *Nueva Sociedad* 49 (1980): 57–71; John Antón, Álvaro Bello, and Marta Rangel, "La equidad y la exclusión de los pueblos indígenas y afrodescendientes en América Latina y el Caribe," *Revista de la CEPAL* 76 (2002): 39–54; Robert Andolina, Nina Laurie, and Sarah Radcliffe, *Indigenous Development in the Andes: Culture, Power, and Transnationalism* (Durham, NC: Duke University Press, 2009); Yashar, *Contesting Citizenship in Latin America* (New York: Cambridge University Press, 2005); and David Lehmann, *The Crisis of Multiculturalism in Latin America* (London: Palgrave-Macmillan, 2016).

42. Emillienne Ireland, "Neither Warriors nor Victims: The Wauja Peacefully Organize to Defend Their Land," *Latin American Anthropological Review* 2, no. 1 (1990): 3–12.

43. Leon Zamosc, "Agrarian Protest and the Indian Movement in the Ecuadorian Highlands," *Latin American Research Review* 29, no. 3 (1994): 37–68; and Heidi Brandenburg and Mathew Orzel, dirs., *When Two Worlds Collide*(2016; documentary film).

44. There was also a parallel commodification of identities, as studied by anthropologists and sociologists since the late 1980s. See Stanley Brandes, *Power and Persuasion: Ritual and Social Control in Rural Mexico* (Philadelphia: University of Pennsylvania Press, 1988); and Néstor García Canclini, *Transforming Modernity: Popular Culture in Mexico* (Austin: University of Texas Press, 1993).

45. Andrea Muehlebach, "'Making Place' at the United Nations: Indigenous Cultural Politics at the U.N. Working Group on Indigenous Populations," *Cultural Anthropology* 16, no. 3 (2001): 415–448; and Salvador Martí Puig, "The Emergence of Indigenous Movements in Latin America and Their Impact on the Latin American Political Scene: Interpretive Tools at the Local and Global Levels," *Latin American Perspectives* 37, no. 6 (2010): 74–92.

46. Erick D. Langer, Introduction to *Contemporary Indigenous Movements in Latin America*, ed. Erick D. Langer with Elena Muñoz (Wilmington, DE: Scholarly Resources, 2003), xxv.

47. Daniel Mato, "Transnational Networking and the Social Production of Representations of Identities by Indigenous Peoples' Organizations of America," *International Sociology* 15, no. 2 (2000): 343–360; and Donna Lee Van Cott, "Broadening Democracy: Latin America's Indigenous Peoples," *Current History* 103 (2004): 80–85.

48. For illustrations, see Daniel F. Wajner and Luis Roniger, "Transnational Identity Politics in the Americas: Reshaping "Nuestramérica" as Chavismo's Regional Legitimation Strategy," *Latin American Research Review* 54, no. 2 (2019): 458–475, in https://doi.org/10.25222/larr.43.

49. Iván Novotny, "Venezolanos en Argentina realizarán campaña por Nicolás Maduro," *Pressenza*, March 29, 2013, www.pressenza.com/es/2013/03/venezolanos-en-argentina-realizaran-campana-por-nicolas-maduro.

50. "Los movimientos indígenas latinoamericanos estamos avanzando no sólo para liberarnos sino para caminar junto a los otros pueblos y liberarlos. No somos excluyentes ni vengativos, por eso hemos llegado a la presidencia de Bolivia, para re-solver los problemas de todos [. . .]. La solidaridad entre nuestros pueblos está por encima de todo, y en América Latina los pueblos indígenas y los pueblos en general somos una gran familia." Kintto Lucas, "Evo Morales propone refundar América Latina," *Rebelión*, June 17, 2006, www.rebelion.org/noticia.php?id =33236.

51. "Por estos senderos de la patria grande está caminado nuestro Simón Bolívar, con todas las canciones y los cambios profundos, camina por las calles Manuelita Sáenz, con los trabajadores, con los obreros y las plazas se visten de colores [. . .] por América Latina está flameando el grito de Túpac Catari, acertando que después de la muerte vuelve en millones; de Túpac Amaru, que se levanta y convoca para que los pueblos ancestrales rompan el silencio de siglos y sean parte sustancial de estos procesos libertarios." "Correa rinde homenaje a Chávez en inauguración de XII Cumbre Presidencial del Alba," *AVN*, July 30, 2013, http://m.avn.info.ve/contenido/correa-rinde-homenaje-ch%C3%A1vez-inauguraci%C3%B3n-xii-cumbre-presidencial-del-alba.

52. Constitución Política de Nicaragua y sus reformas (August 2003), www.ilo.org/dyn/travail/docs/2134/Constitucion.pdf.

53. Constitución de Ecuador (2008), www.asambleanacional.gov.ec/documentos/constitucion_de_bolsillo.pdf.

54. Constitución de Ecuador (2008), 15: "Celebrando a la naturaleza, la Pacha Mama, de la que somos parte y que es vital para nuestra existencia [...] decidimos construir una nueva forma de convivencia ciudadana, en diversidad y armonía con la naturaleza, para alcanzar el buen vivir, el sumak kawsay."

55. On the lesser advances of Afro-American movements compared to the indigenous movements, see Andrés Serbín, "¿Por qué no existe el poder negro de América Latina?," *Nueva Sociedad* 111 (1991): 148–157; and Álvaro Antón, J. Bello, Fabiana Del Popolo, Marcelo Paixão, and Marta Rangel, *Afrodescendientes en América Latina y el Caribe: Del reconocimiento estadístico a la realización de derechos* (Santiago de Chile: CEPAL, 2009).

56. John Antón and Fabiana Del Popolo, "Visibilidad estadística de la población afrodescendiente de América Latina: Aspectos conceptuales y metodológicos," in *Afrodescendientes en América Latina y el Caribe: Del reconocimiento estadístico a la realización de derechos*, ed. J. Antón et al. (Santiago de Chile: CEPAL, 2009), 13–38.

57. M. Becerra and D. Buffa, "Nuevos espacios de participación de los afrodescendientes en América Latina y el Caribe," *Astrolabio* 3 (2003), www.iidh.ed.cr/BibliotecaWeb/Varios/Documentos.

58. Marta Rangel, "Una panorámica de las articulaciones y organizaciones de los afrodescendientes en América Latina y el Caribe," in Antón et al., *Afrodescendientes*, 87–97.

59. Andrés Serbín, *De la ONU al ALBA: Prevención de conflictos y espacios de participación ciudadana* (Barcelona: Icaria, 2011).

60. Rodrigo Valenzuela Fernández, "Pueblos Indígenas y MERCOSUR," ponencia presentada en las Primeras Jornadas de Políticas Sociales del MERCOSUR (2000), www.mapuche.info/mapuint/Indigenas_Mercosur.html.

61. Gil and Paikin, "Mapa de la Integración Regional," 18–23; and "Mercosur Cultural reconoció lucha integracionista del Comandante Hugo Chávez," *AVN*, June 6, 2013, www.avn.info.ve/contenido/mercosur-cultural-reconoci%C3%B3-lucha-integracionista-del-comandante-hugo-ch%C3%A1vez.

62. "MERCOSUR Indígena: Declaración de Ciudad Bolívar," *Notiindigena*, October 15, 2010; "El estado Bolívar será sede del Mercosur indígena," *Noticias* 24, October 9, 2013; Felipe Silva, "El carácter indígena en el Mercosur es importante para la integración de los pueblos de América," *MINPPC*, October 13, 2013; and K. Beberache, "Encuentro MERCOSUR Indígena, 'Vamos a la victoria y reivindicación de nuestros pueblos,'" *FCCR Mercosur*, October 12, 2013.

63. Mercosur-CMC 14/14, "Plan de Trabajo del Mercosur Indígena 2015–2016," December 2014; and "Declaración Conjunta de los Estados Miembros del MERCOSUR," *Cámara de Comercio e Industria Venezuela-Brasil*, August 8, 2014. See also K. Beberache, "Representantes de pueblos indígenas del Mercosur se reunirán en Bolívar," *FCCR Mercosur*, October 8, 2013; K. Cordova, "Comisión presidencial

se reúne para establecer introducción del tema indígena en el Mercosur," *FCCR Mercosur*, September 2, 2013; and "Pueblos indígenas del Mercosur realizarán encuentro en el estado Bolívar," *Aporrea*, August 10, 2013.

64. Ministerio del Poder Popular para la Energía y el Petróleo de Venezuela, "Antecedentes: Comunidad Sudamericana de Naciones"; Correo Sindical Latinoamericano, "Unión Sudamericana de Naciones"; "Legado del Libertador Simón Bolívar," *TeleSur*, July 24, 2015; and "Unión de Naciones Suramericanas (UNASUR)," *Agencia Boliviana de Información*, May 24, 2008.

65. "Declaración del Cusco sobre la Comunidad Sudamericana de Naciones," *III Cumbre Presidencial Sudamericana* (Cusco), December 8, 2004.

66. "Programa de Acción" de la Primera Reunión de Jefes de Estado de la Comunidad Sudamericana de Naciones, Brasilia, September 30, 2005.

67. UNASUR, *Declaración de Cochabamba*, 2006, available at: www.latinreporters. com/amlatpol10122006DeclaracionCochabamba.html; and "Un Nuevo Modelo de Integración de América del Sur Hacia la Unión Sudamericana de Naciones," *Documento final de la Comisión Estratégica de Reflexión* (2006), www.camiri.net/ ?p=19189.

68. "Declaración de los derechos de los Pueblos Indígenas de la Organización de Naciones Unidas," Cochabamba, Bolivia, December 9, 2006, www.comunidadandina.org/ documentos/ dec_int/dec_cochabamba_indigenas.htm.

69. Correo Sindical Latinoamericano, "Unión Sudamericana de Naciones."

70. "Nosotros, desde las raíces profundas de la hoy llamada 'Sudamérica', nos dirigimos a los Presidentes de los Estados Nación, que son posteriores a nuestras orgullosas civilizaciones, eficaces y autónomas, que dieron y siguen dando forma a estas tierras desde el inicio de los tiempos, para reiterarles nuestras propuestas concretas para que sea posible otra forma de integración sudamericana distinta a la del neoliberalismo en todas sus variantes." "Llamamiento y propuestas desde la visión de los pueblos indígenas y naciones originarias: Comunidad Sudamericana de Naciones: Para 'Vivir Bien' Sin Neoliberalismo," *Cumbre de Cochabamba* (Bolivia), December 7, 2006, http://www.comunidadandina.org/unasur/ llamamiento_cochabamba.htm.

71. UNASUR, *Tratado Constitutivo de la Unión de Naciones Suramericanas*, Quito, March 11, 2011.

72. CEPAL, *Integración regional: Hacia una estrategia de cadenas de valor inclusivas* (Santiago de Chile: CEPAL, 2014), in https://repositorio.cepal.org/bitstream/handle/ 11362/36733/1/S2014216_es.pdf, 88–89; H. Moldiz Mercado, "La CELAC, por el camino de las rebeliones indígenas y las luchas independentistas," *Rebelión*, December 5, 2011, www.rebelion.org/noticia.php?id=140716; and M. Verón, Politicaspublicas. net, February 10, 2012.

73. CELAC, "Special Declaration on the World Conference on Indigenous Peoples," II Cumbre CELAC, January 29, 2014; and CELAC, "Declaración," II Cumbre CELAC, January 29, 2014.

74. CELAC, "CELAC Cultural Action Plan 2015–2020," UNESCO Workshop on the Adoption of a Culture Work-Plan, September 18–19, 2015; Prensa Latina, "CELAC defiende en Cuba diversidad cultural, integración y patrimonio," *SELA*, September

21, 2015, www.sela.org/es/prensa/servicio-informativo/ 2015/09/20150921/celac-defiende-en-cuba-diversidad-cultural; and A. Duarte de la Rosa, "Aprueban por primera vez un plan de acción de la Celac," *Granma*, September 19, 2015, http://www.granma.cu/cuba/2015-09-19/iii-reunion-de-ministros-de-cultura-de-la-celac.

75. CELAC, "Declaración política de Belén," III Cumbre CELAC, January 29, 2015; Jesús García, "CELAC reconoce decenio afrodescendiente," *Aporrea*, February 2, 2014; and Diógenes Díaz, "CELAC fue la primera en reconocer pueblos indígenas," *Alainet*, October 1, 2014, www.radiolaprimerisima.com/ noticias/70910/celac-fue-la-primera-en-reconocer-pueblos-indigenas.

76. Muhr, "The Politics of Space," 776–77; and Gil and Paikin, "Mapa de la Integración Regional," 6–8.

77. Grupo Parlamentario Venezolano, "Logros de Gestión" (2012), http://www.parlatino.org.ve/wp-content/uploads/2018/10/Encarte-de-Logros-2012-1.pdf.

78. AP, "Instauran primer Parlamento Negro de América," *Emol*, August 31, 2015, www.emol.com/noticias/internacional/2005/08/31/193987/instauran-primer-parlamento-negro-de-america.html; Parlamento Negro de las Américas, "Resultados de la reunión de trabajo," April 28, 2006, www.alainet.org/es/active/11423; and Parlamento Negro de las Américas, "Carta de Santiago de Cali," March 16, 2008.

79. Quebracho, "Participamos del tercer encuentro internacional por la integración de los pueblos," April 7, 2013.

80. José Pedro Zúquete, "The Missionary Politics of Hugo Chávez," *Latin American Politics and Society* 50, no. 1 (2008): 91–121, 103.

81. Mark Dinneen, "The Chávez Government and the Battle over the Media in Venezuela," *Asian Journal of Latin American Studies* 25, no. 2 (2012): 27–53; Max Azicri, "The Castro-Chávez Alliance," *Latin American Perspectives* 36, no. 1 (2009): 99–110, 100; Michael Shifter, "In Search of Hugo Chávez," *Foreign Affairs*, May–June 2006; and Silvio Waisbord, "Between Support and Confrontation: Civic Society, Media Reform, and Populism in Latin America," *Communication, Culture & Critique* 4, no. 1 (2011): 97–117, esp. 101–102.

82. MINCI, "Cofundador de Telesur propone creación de plataforma comunicacional latinoamericana," June 6, 2014, www.minci.gob.ve/cofundador-de-telesur-propone-creacion-de-plataforma-comunicacional-latinoamericana/.

83. Alison Brysk, "Turning Weakness into Strength: The Internationalization of Indian Rights," *Latin American Perspectives* 23, no. 2 (1996): 38–57.

84. Eric D. Weitz, "Self-Determination: How a German Enlightenment Idea Became the Slogan of National Liberation and a Human Right," *American Historical Review* 120, no. 2 (2015): 462–496; and Lehmann, *The Crisis of Multiculturalism*.

85. Marta Rangel, *Organizaciones y articulaciones de los afrodescendientes de América Latina y el Caribe* (Santiago de Chile: CEPAL, 2008), 19.

86. D. Andreucci, "'Asfaltar Bolivia': El conflicto que cambió Bolivia," *Rebelión*, March 11, 2015, www.rebelion.org/noticia.php?id=196319; A. Canessa, "Conflict, Claim and Contradiction in the New 'Indigenous' State of Bolivia," *Critique of Anthropology* 34, no. 2 (2014): 153–173; G. Ángel . Lorenzo, "Marcha indígena por el TIPNIS en Bolivia: ¿más que un simple problema?," *Revista Andina de Estudios Políticos* 1, no.

9 (2011): 3–17; and AFP, "Violenta represión de gobierno boliviano contra marcha indígena," *El Universo*, September 25, 2011.

87. "Bolivia: Unasur, OEA y ONU investigarán la salvaje represión a indígenas," *Infobae*, October 7, 2011; and "Conflicto por el TIPNIS: Se rompe el diálogo y el MAS da paso a consulta previa," *La Razón*, October 11, 2011.

88. TeleSur, "Unasur y OEA califican de histórica consulta boliviana en el Tipnis," *Aporrea*, July 30, 2012; "Tribunal Electoral ratifica que la ONU no tiene veedores en TIPNIS," *Página Siete*, October 11, 2011; P. Pedraza, "Observadores de Unasur, Uniore y la OEA ya están en Santa Cruz," *El Deber*, August 11, 2015; and CLACPI, "Bolivia: Relator de ONU llega por indígenas y otros grupos vulnerables" (2015).

89. "Brutal represión y cacería de indígenas guaraníes en Bolivia," *Monitor VB*, August 21, 2015, https://agenciadenoticiaspueblosoriginarios.wordpress.com/ 2015/08/21/brutal-represion-y-caceria-de-indigenas-guaranies-en-bolivia; and "Bolivia: Represión en el Territorio Indígena de Takovo Mora," *IWGIA*, August 20, 2015, www.iwgia.org/noticias/buscar-noticias?news_id=1242. See also Andolina, Laurie, and Radcliffe, *Indigenous Development in the Andes*, which registered in the 2000s the limits to indigenous empowerment in Bolivia and Ecuador.

90. Natalia Fátima Ríos, "La irrupción india en la movilización social jujeña: el caso de la Organización Barrial Tupac Amaru," *VII Jornadas de Jóvenes Investigadores* (Buenos Aires: UBA-Instituto de Investigaciones Gino Germani, 2013), www.aacademica. org/000-076/61.pdf; "Llega la Marcha de los Pueblos Originarios," *Página/12*, May 20, 2010, www.constituyentesocial.org.ar/article697.html?lang=es; and Raúl Noro, "Marcha de los Pueblos Originarios," *Redacción Popular*, May 12, 2010, www. redaccionpopular.com/content/marcha-de-los-pueblos-originarios.

91. "Mauricio Macri: 'Vamos a trabajar juntos para atender las necesidades de los pueblos originarios,'" *La Nación*, December 17, 2015.

92. S. Constante, "La protesta indígena llega a Quito tras 11 días de marcha," *El País*, August 13, 2015; G. Esquivada, "Las protestas indígenas en Ecuador y el silencio de Evo Morales," *Infobae*, August 30, 2015; and "Indígenas y trabajadores de Ecuador anuncian protestas desde el 11 de noviembre,'" *El Universo*, October 5, 2015.

93. V. Davies, "El reto de la Celac: Que sean respetados los derechos indígenas," *Correo del Orinoco*, June 18, 2011, www.correodelorinoco.gob.ve/nacionales/ reto-celac-que-sean-respetados-derechos-indigenas.

94. R. Rojas, "Control indígena, exigen pueblos originarios para organismos de desarrollo en Sudamérica," *La Jornada*, November 1, 2009.

95. "Organizaciones políticas de 39 países expresan respaldo al presidente Maduro," *r-evolucion.es*, April 2, 2014, http://r-evolucion.es/2014/04/02/ organizaciones-politicas-de-39-paises-expresan-respaldo-al-presidente-maduro.

96. "Sindicatos y organizaciones sociales marchan en Montevideo en apoyo a Gobierno de Venezuela," *r-evolucion.es*, April 8, 2014.

97. "Organizaciones sociales viajarán a Venezuela para respaldar democracia," *TeleSur*, March 13, 2014.

98. "Rodilla en tierra! No nos arrebatarán la revolución bolivariana," *Quebracho*, April 15, 2013; and "Habla Maduro en Argentina," *Quebracho*, May 10, 2013.

99. Daniel F. Wajner, "Primavera en América Latina," *Real Instituto Elcano-Blog*, February 25, 2014, www.blog.rielcano.org/primavera-en-america-latina; Carlos Montaner, "La CELAC contra la Carta Democrática Interamericana," *Infobae*, January 25, 2014; UNASUR, "Comunicado de la I Reunión de la Comisión de Cancilleres de UNASUR," *Prensa Unasur*, March 26, 2014; K. Beberache, "Ministras y Ministros de RREE de Unasur emiten resolución sobre la violencia presentada en Venezuela," *FCCR Mercosur*, March 12, 2014; O. Calderón, "CELAC aboga por diálogo en Venezuela y rechaza la violencia," *CB24*, February 18, 2014, http://cb24.tv/celac-aboga-por-dialogo-en-venezuela-y-rechaza-la-violencia/; and K. Beberache, "Declaración de la OEA sobre Venezuela," *FCCR Mercosur*, March 8, 2014, www.fccrmercosur.org/web/declaracion-de-la-oea-sobre-venezuela.

100. "ALBA denuncia campaña contra Venezuela para detener integración regional," *TeleSur*, February 25, 2014; and "Asociación de Estados del Caribe condena violencia fascista en Venezuela," *TeleSur*, February 14, 2014.

101. "Países latinoamericanos rechazan violencia y se solidarizan con Gobierno de Venezuela," *Noticiero Venevisión*, February 13, 2014; and "Embajador de Venezuela agradece solidaridad y llama a la unidad de los pueblos," *Prensa Bolivariana*, February 21, 2014, http://prensabolivariana.com/2014/02/21/embajador-de-venezuela-agradece-solidaridad-y-llama-a-la-unidad-de-los-pueblos.

102. "Venezuela le respondió a Macri: Somos un país modelo en derechos humanos," *La Nación*, December 21, 2015; and A. Oppenheimer, ¡Se despertó la OEA!, *Nuevo Herald*, November 11, 2015.

103. For some of those interpretations, see Daniel F. Wajner, "La inminente era del neo-progresismo en Latinoamérica," *Foreign Affairs Latinoamerica*, January 28, 2016; Mario Vargas Llosa, "La muerte lenta del chavismo," *El País*, May 5, 2013; and Agustina Larrea, "Entrevista a Ignacio Ramonet: En Europa no entienden a América Latina," *Ámbito Financiero*, November 8, 2013.

104. Latinobarómetro, *Oportunidades de Cooperación Regional: Integración y Energía*, 2007.

105. Guadalupe González González, Jorge A. Schiavon, David Crow, and Gerardo Maldonado, *Las Américas y el Mundo 2010–2011* (Mexico City: CIDE, 2011).

106. PNUD, *1ª Encuesta Iberoamericana de Juventudes: Informe Ejecutivo* (Mexico City: OIJ, PNUD, CEPAL, and UNAM, 2013), in https://www.undp.org/content/dam/undp/library/Democratic%20Governance/Spanish/PNUD_Encuesta%20Iberoamericana%20de%20Juventudes_%20El%20Futuro%20Ya%20Llego_Julio2013.pdf ; for earlier public opinion surveys, see Carmen Estrades, "Opinión Pública y Mercosur: Conocimiento y apoyo de los uruguayos al proceso de integración regional," *Revista Uruguaya de Ciencia Política* 15, no. 1 (2006): 107–127; CARI, *La Opinión Pública Argentina sobre Política Exterior y Defensa 2010* (Buenos Aires: Gráfica Andrea, 2010); Martín Puchet Anyul, Juan Carlos Moreno-Brid, and Pablo Ruiz Nápoles, "La integración regional de México: condicionantes y oportunidades por su doble pertenencia a América del Norte y a Latinoamérica," *Economíaunam* 8, no. 23 (2011): 3–36.

107. Not by chance, Mauricio Macri promoted in December 2015 a meeting with Félix Díaz, the chief of the Qom community, and members of thirty other indigenous peoples, with whom C. F. Kirchner herself had refused to meet. Perhaps even more significant was his decision to spread this information on his Twitter account, in which he declared, "We are going to work together to meet the needs of indigenous peoples and achieve the goal of zero poverty," and "For this government, recognition of indigenous communities and policies towards indigenous peoples are State policies." DON'T HAVE IT! Sorry!*La Nación*, December 17, 2015.

Chapter 9

1. Shmuel Noah Eisenstadt, *Jewish Civilization: The Jewish Historical Experience in Comparative Perspective* (Albany: State University of New York Press, 1992).
2. Based on religious practice rather than on ethnic, linguistic, or geographic characterizations, most non-Ashkenazi communities consider Joseph Karo's *Shulhan Aruch* the core guidebook for religious practice, setting them apart from the Ashkenazi Jews, who have followed the doctrinal exegesis of rabbi Moshe Iserlisch. Margalit Bejarano, "Comunidad y religiosidad: Cambios en la identidad colectiva de los sefardíes en América Latina," in *Pertenencia y alteridad: Judíos en/ de América Latina*, coord. Haim Avni, Judit Bokser Liwerant et al. (Frankfurt and Madrid: Iberoamericana/Vervuert/Bonilla Artigas, 2011), 603–620.
3. The most synthetic systematic analysis of Sephardic Jews remains Margalit Bejarano, "'The Sephardic Communities of Latin America. A Puzzle of Sub-Ethnic Fragments," in *Contemporary Sephardic Identity in the Americas*, by Margalit Bejarano and Edna Aizenberg (Syracuse, NY: Syracuse University Press, 2012), 3–30.
4. Bejarano and Aizenberg, *Contemporary Sephardic Identity in the Americas*, xiii.
5. David Scott FitzGerald and Dabid Cook-Martin, *Culling the Masses: Immigration Policy in the Americas* (Cambrdige, MA: Harvard University Press, 2014).
6. Magnus Mörner, *Adventurers and Proletarians* (Philadelphia: UNESCO/University of Pittsburgh Press, 1985), 50.
7. Judith Laikin Elkin, *The Jews of Latin America* (Boulder, CO: Lynne Rienner, 2014); and Haim Avni, *Argentina and the Jews: A History of Jewish Immigration* (Tuscaloosa: University of Alabama Press, 1991).
8. In Argentina and Brazil, by the 1970s Yiddish had disappeared from primary and secondary Jewish education, replaced by Hebrew, which subsequently underwent a similar fate, even though it is still taught in primary schools and some high schools. Yossi Goldstein reported that in many high schools the study of Hebrew has been reduced to a few weekly hours—as in the ORT network in Argentina or the Renascence School in Sao Paulo—or has been replaced altogether by the study of Judaism in English—as in some Jewish private schools such as Brazil's Arlene Fern School. See Yossi Goldstein, "Jewish Communal Life in Argentina and Brazil at the End of the 20th Century and the Beginning of the 21st: A Sociological

Perspective," in *Identities in an Era of Globalization and Multiculturalism*, ed. Judit Bokser-Liwerant, Eliezer Ben-Rafael, Yossi Gorny, and Raanan Rein (Leiden and Boston: Brill, 2008), 185–202, 192.

9. Judit Bokser Liwerant, "Fuentes de legitimación de la presencia judía en México: El voto positivo de México a la ecuación sionismo=racismo y su impacto sobre la comunidad judía," *Judaica Latinoamericana*, no. 3 (Jerusalem: AMILAT and Magnes Press, 1997), 319–349; and DellaPergola, Sergio, Uzi Rebhun, and Mark Tolts, "Contemporary Jewish Diaspora in Global Context: Human Development Correlates of Population Trends," *Israel Studies* 10, no. 1 (2006): 61–95, esp.: 63–64 and 93; see also Sergio Della Pergola, "Changing Cores and Peripheries: Fifty Years in Socio-Demographic Perspective," in *Terms of Survival: The Jewish World Since 1945*, ed. Robert S. Wistrich (London: Routledge, 1995), 13–43.

10. Bokser Liwerant, "Fuentes de legitimación."

11. Luis Roniger and Mario Sznajder, *The Legacy of Human Rights Violations in the Southern Cone* (Oxford: Oxford University Press, 1999), 7–38.

12. Luis Roniger and Mario Sznajder, "Israel and the Escape of the Victims of Military Repression in Argentina (1976–1983)," *Soziologia Israelit* 6, no. 2 (2005): 233–263; and Mario Sznajder and Luis Roniger, "From Argentina to Israel: Escape, Evacuation and Exile," *Journal of Latin American Studies* 37, no. 2 (2006): 351–377.

13. Illustrative are Brazilian jurist and twice minister of foreign affairs Celso Lafer; former president of Panama Eric Arturo Delvalle Cohen-Enríquez, who served in that capacity in the late 1980s; Benjamín Teplitzky, a prominent supporter of Salvador Allende in Chile; Brigadier General José Berdichevsky, who was actively involved in the Pinochet regime of 1973–1990; Eliane Karp de Toledo, first lady of Peru in 2001–2006; Eduardo Stein Barillas, who served as foreign minister and vice president of Guatemala in 1996–2000 and 2004–2008, respectively; his co-national Gert Rosenthal, who fulfilled many diplomatic roles in CEPAL, as ambassador to the UN and as foreign minister of Guatemala; Brazilian film director, screenwriter, and producer Héctor Babenco; leading Mexican TV anchorman Jacobo Zabludovsky; writer Marcos Aguinis; economist Mario Blejer, who became chair of the Central Bank of Argentina; and politician José Alperovich, elected governor of the Argentine province of Tucumán in 2003 and reelected in 2007. Alperovich has been married to Beatriz Rojkés, who holds the position of deputy president of the Partido Justicialista of their province in Argentina.

14. Deborah Yashar, *Contesting Liberal Citizenship in Latin America* (New York: Cambridge University Press, 2005).

15. Carlos Forment, "Working for Citizenship in Argentina: Recuperated Factories and Democratic Rights in the Wake of Globalization" (paper presented at the International Workshop on Contesting Liberal Citizenship in Latin America, Institute of Advanced Studies, Jerusalem, July 6–9, 2009).

16. Leon Zamosc, "Popular Impeachments: Ecuador in Comparative Perspective," in *Shifting Frontiers of Citizenship: The Latin American Experience*, ed. Mario Sznajder, Luis Roniger, and Carlos A. Forment (Leiden and Boston: Brill, 2013), 237–265.

17. Robert Albro, "The Culture of Democracy and Bolivia's Indigenous Movements," *Critique of Anthropology* 26, no. 4 (2006): 387–410; and Steve Ellner, *Rethinking Venezuelan Politics: Class, Conflict, and the Chávez Phenomenon* (Boulder, CO: Lynne Rienner, 2008).
18. Bokser Liwerant, "Fuentes de legitimación," esp. 340–344.
19. The following analysis is based on research first published in Luis Roniger, *Antisemitism: Real or Imagined? Chavez, Iran, Israel and the Jews*, ACTA Paper no. 33 (Jerusalem: Vidal Sassoon International Centre for the Study of Antisemitism, 2009).
20. Javier Monagas Maita, "The Palestinean Holocaust Will Bury You: You, Zionists, Jews, Fascists, Murderers, Failed," January 15, 2009, accessed March 5, 2009, www.aporrea.org/tiburon/a70440.html(the URL is no longer available).
21. Pedro Méndez, "Jews, Plotting and Murderers," January 7, 2009, accessed March 5, 2009, www.aporrea.org/tiburon/a69910.html.
22. Evaristo Marcano Marín, "To Hunt Jews," January 9, 2009, accessed March 5, 2009, www.aporrea.org/tiburon/a70050.html.
23. Roniger, *Antisemitism: Real or Imagined?*; and Claudio Lomnitz and Rafael Sánchez, "United by Hate: The Uses of Anti-Semitism in Chavez's Venezuela," *Boston Review*, July–August 2009 .
24. Leonardo Senkman, "Klal Ysrael at the Frontiers: The Transnational Jewish Experience in Argentina," in *Jewish Identities in an Era of Multiculturalism*, in Bokser-Liwerant, Ben-Rafael, Gorny, and Rein, 125–152.
25. Maritza Corrales Capestany, "Revolution, Ethnicity and Religions in Cuba: Similarities, Differences and Dichotomies in the Case of the Jews," in Bokser-Liwerant, Ben-Rafael, Gorny, and Rein, *Jewish Identities in an Era of Multiculturalism*, 203–219.
26. Corrales Capestany, "Revolution, Ethnicity and Religions," 218.
27. Christine Folch, "Trouble in the Triple Frontier: The Lawless Border Where Argentina, Brazil and Paraguay Meet," *Foreign Affairs*, September 6, 2012, accessed April 10, 2020, https://www.foreignaffairs.com/articles/argentina/2012-09-06/trouble-triple-frontier.
28. Ignacio Klich, comp., *Árabes y judíos en América Latina: Historia, representaciones y desafíos* (Buenos Aires: Siglo XXI and Asociación por los Derechos Civiles, 2006); and Lorenzo Agar et al., *Contribuciones árabes a las identidades iberoamericanas* (Madrid: Casa Árabe-IEAM, 2009).
29. They added that small but growing Muslim populations also existed in twelve other Latin American countries. Ella Shohat and Evelyn Alsultany, "The Cultural Politics of 'the Middle East' in the Americas: An Introduction," in *Between the Middle East and the Americas: The Cultural Politics of Diaspora*, ed. Evelyn Alsultany and Ella Shohat (Ann Arbor: University of Michigan Press, 2013), 18–19.
30. John Tofik Karam, "Crossing the Americas: The U.S. War on Terror and Arab Cross-Border Mobilizations in a South American Frontier Region," *Comparative Studies of South Asia, Africa and the Middle East* 31, no. 2 (2011): 251–266, 256. On the internal rifts, see also Omri Elmaleh, "¡Bienvenidos a la Triple Frontera! La generación fundacional de la colectividad libanesa-musulmana entre Argentina, Brasil y

Paraguay, 1950–1975," *Contra Relatos desde el Sur* 13, no. 15 (2017): 5–16; and Omri Elmaleh, "Together Yet Apart: The Institutional Rift among Lebanese-Muslims in a South American Triple Frontier and Its Origins," *Anuario de Historia de América Latina* 56 (2019): 97–121.

31. Omri Elmaleh, personal communication with the author, July 6, 2020.

32. John Tofik Karam, "Anti-Semitism from the Standpoint of Its Arab Victims in a South American Border Zone," *Latin American and Caribbean Ethnic Studies* 6, no. 2 (2011): 141–167.

33. Alejandro Simonoff, "Analizando a Cristina Fernández: Interpretaciones sobre la política exterior desde el segundo gobierno kirchnerista (2007–2013)," in *La política exterior de Cristina Fernández al finalizar su mandato*, ed. Alfredo Bruno Bologna (Argentina: Editorial de la Universidad Nacional de Rosario, 2014), 431–452; and Anabella Bussom, "Los ejes de la acción externa de Cristina Fernández: ¿cambios hacia un nuevo horizonte o cambios para consolidar el rumbo?," *Relaciones Internacionales* 50 (2016): 143–170.

34. L. Senkman and L. Roniger, *América Latina tras bambalinas: Teorías conspirativas, usos y abusos* (Pittsburgh: Latin America Research Commons, 2019), 225–248, https://doi.org/10.25154/book2.

35. Omri Elmaleh, "Together Un-United: Muslims in the Triple Frontier on the Defensive against Accudations of Terrorism," in *Migrants, Refugees and Asylum Seekers in Latin America*, ed. Raanan Rein, Stefan Rinke, and David Sheinin (Leiden and Boston: Brill, 2020), 242–263, 242.

36. A. F. Trevisi, "Assessing the Terrorist Threat in the Triborder area of Brazil, Paraguay and Argentina," IDC Herzlia and International Institute for Counter-Terrorism, October 2013, https://www.ict.org.il/UserFiles/Trevisi-2014.pdf; and Alma Keshavarz, "Iran and Hezbollah in the Triborder areas of Latin America: A Look at the 'Old TBA' and the 'New TBA,'" *Small Wars Journal*, November 12, 2015, accessed April 10, 2020, https://smallwarsjournal.com/jrnl/art/iran-and-hezbollah-in-the-triborder-areas-of-latin-america-a-look-at-the-%E2%80%9Cold-tba%E2%80%9D-and-the.

37. Karam, "Crossing the Americas," 255 and 263. Among the sources mentioned by the author are Jeffrey Goldberg, "In the Party of God," *New Yorker*, October 28, 2002, 75–80; "Bin Laden Reportedly Spent Time in Brazil in '95," *Washington Post*, March 18, 2003; "Bin Laden esteve em Foz do Iguaçu e até deu palestra em mesquita" [Bin Laden was in Foz do Iguaçu and even gave a speech at a mosque], *O Estado de São Paulo*, March 16, 2003; and Júnior Policarpo, "Ele esteve no Brasil" [He was in Brazil], *Veja*, March 19, 2003.

38. Sarah Nielsen, "Fighting Terror in the Triborder Area," Wilson Center Latin American Program, December 9, 2019, accessed April 27, 2020, https://www.wilsoncenter.org/article/fighting-terror-the-tri-border-area.

39. Charles Taylor, *Philosophical Arguments* (Cambridge, MA: Harvard University Press, 1995), 257–287; Will Kymlicka, *Multicultural Citizenship* (New York: Oxford University Press, 1995); Will Kymlicka, *Politics in the Vernacular: Nationalism, Multiculturalism, Citizenship* (New York: Oxford University Press, 2001); and

Bikkhu Parekh, *Rethinking Multiculturalism: Cultural Diversity and Political Theory* (Cambridge, MA: Harvard University Press, 2000).

40. Shmuel Noah Eisenstadt, "The First Multiple Modernities: Collective Identity, Public Spheres and Political Order in the Americas," in *Globality and Multiple Modernities*, ed. Luis Roniger and Carlos H. Waisman (Brighton, UK: Sussex Academic Press, 2002), 7–28; Noah Eisenstadt, "Multiple Modernities—A Paradigm of Cultural and Social Evolution," *Protosociology* (Frankfurt) 24 (2007): 20–370; and Luis Roniger, "Identidades colectivas: avances teóricos y desafíos políticos," in *Identidad, sociedad y política*, ed. Judit Bokser Liwerant and Saúl Velasco Cruz (Mexico City: Universidad Nacional Autónoma de México, 2008), 45–68.

41. See e.g., Nancy Fraser, "From Redistribution to Recognition: Dilemmas of Justice in a Post-Socialist Age," *New Left Review* 212 (1995): 68–93; and Nancy Fraser, "Rethinking the Public Sphere: A Contribution to the Critique of Actually Existing Democracy," in *Habermas and the Public Sphere*, ed. Craig Calhoun (Cambridge, MA: MIT Press, 1999), 109–142.

42. James Tully, *Strange Multiplicity: Constitutionalism in an Age of Diversity* (Cambridge: Cambridge University Press, 1995); James Tully, "Recognition and Dialogue," *Critical Review of International Social and Political Philosophy* 7, no. 3 (2004): 84–106; and Michael Kenny, *The Politics of Identity* (Cambridge, UK: Polity Press, 2004), 149–168.

43. Bénédicte Susan and Jean-Marc Dreyfus, *Muslims and Jews in France: Communal Conflict in a Secular State*, US-France Analysis Series (Washington, DC: The Brookings Institution, 2004); and Roland Goetschel, "Jews and Muslims in Contemporary France," in *Transnationalism: Diasporas and the Advent of a New (Dis) order*, ed. Eliezer Ben-Rafael and Yitzhak Sternberg (Leiden: Brill, 2009), 441–444.

Chapter 10

1. Caio de Souza Gomes, "Cada verso é uma semente no deserto do meu peito: Exílio, resistência e conexões transnacionais na canção engajada latino-americana (anos 1970)" (PhD thesis, University of Sao Paulo, 2018).

2. Alison Brysk, *Speaking Rights to Power* (New York: Oxford University Press, 2013).

3. César Gamboa, "Los derechos colectivos de los pueblos indígenas en la Comunidad Andina (CAN)," in César Gamboa et al., *Aportes andinos sobre derechos humanos* (Universidad Andina Simón Bolívar, Unión Europea, COSUDE, Ediciones Abya-Yala, 2005), 11–52.

4. The concept follows Leon Zamosc, "Popular Impeachments: Ecuador in Comparative Perspective," in *Shifting Frontiers of Citizenship* (Leiden: Brill, 2013), ch. 13.

5. Heidi Brandenburg and Mathew Orzel, dirs., *When Two Worlds Collide* (Rickmandworth, UK: Yachaywasi Films and First Run Features, 2016), documentary.

6. Mario Sznajder, "Dilemmas of Economic and Political Modernisation in Chile: A Jaguar That Wants to Be a Puma," *Third World Quarterly* 17, no. 4 (1996): 725–736; and Mario Sznajder, "¿Adaptando el Estado al Mercado, o el Mercado al Estado?

Reformas constitucionales en Chile, Brasil y Argentina hacia fines del siglo XX," *Estudios interdisciplinarios de America Latina y el Cribe* 13, no. 1 (2002): 61-87.

7. Patricio Navia, "Chile's Riots: Frustration at the Gate of the Promised Land," *Americas Quarterly*, October 21, 2019, accessed May 14, 2020, https://www.americasquarterly.org/article/chiles-riots-frustration-at-the-gate-of-the-promised-land/; and Guillermo Guajardo Soto, "Neoliberalism as a Capitalist Revolution in Chile: Antecedents and Irreversibility," *PSL Quarterly Review* 72, no. 289 (2019): 135-148.

8. Kirsten Sehnbruch and Sofia Donoso, "Social Protests in Chile: Inequalities and Other Inconvenient Truths about Latin America's Poster Child," *Global Labour Journal* 11, no. 1 (2020): 52-58.

9. Pablo Abufom, "It's Not about 30 Pesos, It's about 30 Years," *Jacobin*, October 21, 2019, accessed May 14, 2020, https://www.jacobinmag.com/2019/10/chile-protests-pinera-repression.

10. Sarah Jones, "A Chilean Activist Explains the Protests: 'People in the Streets Are Experiencing an Awakening,'" *New York Magazine*, November 7, 2019.

11. Evelyn Dagnino, "Meaning of Citizenship in Latin America," *Canadian Journal of Latin American and Caribbean Studies* 31 (2006): 15-52; Mario Sznajder, Luis Roniger, and Carlos A. Forment, *Shifting Frontiers of Citizenship* (Leiden: Brill, 2013); and Luis Roniger, *Historia mínima de los derechos humanos en América Latina* (Mexico City: Colegio de México, 2018).

12. CEPAL, *Integración regional: Hacia una estrategia de cadenas de valor inclusivas* (Santiago de Chile: CEPAL, 2014), https://repositorio.cepal.org/bitstream/handle/11362/36733/1/S2014216_es.pdf.

13. Thomas Legler, *Latin American Multilateralism: New Directions* (Ottawa: FOCAL, 2010), esp. 12-17.

14. C. D. Malamud Rikles, "La cumbre de UNASUR, un nuevo intento de relanzar la integración suramericana," *Infolatam*, December 7, 2014; and C. Moreno, "Correa hace un llamado en la Celac a acelerar el proceso de integración y la unidad de los pueblos," *Aucalatinoamericano*, January 30, 2015.

15. MPPRE, "Mercosur y la integración nuestramericana," *PortalAlba*, July 30, 2014, www.portalalba.org/index.php?option=com_content&view=article&id=890:mercosur-y-la-integracion-nuestramericana&catid=23&Itemid=118.

16. Andrés Malamud and Gian Luca Gardini, "Has Regionalism Peaked? The Latin American Quagmire and Its Lessons," in *Regionalism in a Changing World*, ed. Lorenzo Fioramonti (London: Routledge, 2013), 117.

17. See N. Phillips, "Regionalist Governance in the New Political Economy of Development: 'Relaunching' the Mercosur," *Third World Quarterly* 22, no. 4 (2001): 565-583; and Kanishka Jayasuriya, "Regionalising the State: Political Topography of Regulatory Regionalism," *Contemporary Politics* 14, no. 1 (2008): 21-35.

18. OAS AG/Res. 1080 (XXI-0/91), "Representative Democracy," June 5, 1991, https://www.oas.org/sap/peacefund/VirtualLibrary/KeyPeaceInstruments/SantiagoCommitment/SantiagoCommitment.pdf.

19. Betsy Montgomery-Smith, "Democratic Crises in Latin America from 1990–2012: Explaining the Variation in Responses from Regional Intergovernmental Organizations" (PhD diss., Georgia State University, 2015), 19–20, https://scholarworks.gsu.edu/political_science_diss/36.

20. Zamosc, "Popular Impeachments."

21. Jorge Heine and Brigitte Weiffen, *21st Century Democracy Promotion in the Americas: Standing up for the Polity* (New York: Routledge, 2015), pp. 92–93.

22. Craig Arceneaux and David Pion-Berlin, *Transforming Latin America: The International and Domestic Origins of Change* (Philadelphia: University of Pittsburgh Press, 2005); and Craig Arceneaux and David Pion-Berlin, "Issues, Threats, and Institutions: Explaining OAS Responses to Democratic Dilemmas in Latin America," *Latin American Politics and Society* 49, no. 2 (2007): 1–31.

23. Montgomery-Smith, "Democratic Crises," esp. 197–201. See also Barry S. Levitt, "A Desultory Defense of Democracy: OAS Resolution 1080 and the Inter-American Democratic Charter," *Latin American Politics and Society* 48, no. 3 (2006): 93–123, which stresses the uneven record of the OAS and the relevance of domestic factors determining countries' positions as they face democratic crises.

24. Montgomery-Smith, "Democratic Crises," 97–104, 103.

25. Kevin Parthenay, *A Political Sociology of Regionalisms: Perspectives for Comparison* (New York: Springer, 2019), 64.

26. Transparency International, *Global Corruption Barometer, Latin America and the Caribbean 2019: Citizens' Views and Experiences of Corruption*, https://www.transparency.org/en/gcb/latin-america/latin-america-and-the-caribbean-x-edition-2019#.

27. Transparency International, *Global Corruption Barometer*, 6.

28. By reaching out to international human rights organizations, "these eight organizations, often braving death threats and harassment, then sought to garner the support of Guatemalan government officials and representatives of aid-donor governments who were based in Guatemala, often at their respective countries' embassies, for this innovative proposal." Washington Office for Latin America, "Advocates against Impunity: A Case Study in Human Rights Organizing in Guatemala," December 2008, http://www.wola.org/organized_crime /cicig/cicig_advocates_against_impunity.pdf.

29. Yulia Krylova, "Outsourcing the Fight against Corruption: Lessons from the International Commission against Impunity in Guatemala," *Global Policy*, November 29, 2017; and Günther Maihold, "Intervention by Invitation? Shared Sovereignty in the Fight against Impunity in Guatemala," *European Review of Latin American and Caribbean Studies* 101 (2016): 5–31.

30. Andrew Hudson and Alexandra W. Taylor, "The International Commission against Impunity in Guatemala," *Journal of International Criminal Justice* 8, no. 1 (2010): 53–74; Mark L. Schneider, *Democracy in Peril: Facts on CICIG in Guatemala*, in https://www.csis.org/analysis/democracy-peril-facts-cicig-guatemala; and "The International Commission against Impunity in Guatemala: A WOLA Report on the CICIG Experience," https://www.wola.org/analysis/wola-report-on-the-international-commission-against-impunity-in-guatemala-cicig.

31. Arturo Matute, "Ending Corruption in Guatemala," *International Crisis Group*, April 30, 2015, https://www.crisisgroup.org/latin-america-caribbean/central-america/guatemala/ending-corruption-guatemala.

32. Maihold, "Intervention by Invitation?," 15; "Saving Guatemala's Fight against Crime and Impunity," *Crisis Group*, October 24, 2018, https://www.crisisgroup.org/latin-america-caribbean/central-america/guatemala/70-saving-guatemalas-fight-against-crime-and-impunity; and Schneider, *Democracy in Peril*.

33. Thomas C. Bruneau, "The Maras and National Security in Central America: Center for Contemporary Conflicts," *Strategic Insights* 4, no. 5 (2005); and Major Dan Zeytoonian, "Intelligent Design: COIN Operations and Intelligence Collection and Analysis," *Military Review* 86, no. 5 (2006): 30-37.

34. Carolina Sancho Hirane, "Inteligencia y cooperación internacional, desafío para la función estatal de inteligencia en el marco de la coordinación interagencial: Una aproximación desde Suramérica en el siglo XXI," in Mariano Bartolomé, Carolina Sancho Hirane, et al. *Inteligencia estratégica contemporánea: Perspectivas desdhhe la región suramericana*, ed. (Sangolquí, Ecuador: Universidad de las Fuerzas Armadas ESPE, 2016), 24-42, 37-40; and Fredy Rivera Vélez, "Inteligencia estratégica e inteligencia política: Los claro-oscuros del caso ecuatoriano," in Bartolomé, Sancho Hirane, et al., *Inteligencia estratégica contemporánea*, 133-148, 139-140.

35. ECLAC, "Femicide or Feminide," in Gender Equality Observatory for Latin America and the Caribbean, https://oig.cepal.org/en/indicators/femicide-or-feminicide.

36. Alda Facio and Lorena Fries, eds., *Género y derecho* (Santiago, Chile: CIMA y LOM, 1999); Paula Halperin and Omar Acha, comps., *Cuerpos, géneros e identidades* (Buenos Aires: Ediciones del Signo, 2000); Juan Marsiaj, "Social Movements and Political Parties: Gays, Lesbians, and 'Travestis,' and the Struggle for Inclusion in Brazil," *Canadian Journal of Latin American and Caribbean Studies* 31, no. 62 (2006): 167-196; Dossier on "How Pink Is the Pink Tide?," *NACLA Report on the Americas* 40, no. 2 (2007); Elisabeth Jay Friedman, "Re(gion)alizing Women's Human Rights in Latin America," *Politics and Gender* 5, no. 3 (2009): 349-375; and Sharlene Mollett, "Irreconcilable Differences? A Postcolonial Intersectional Reading of Gender, Development and Human Rights in Latin America," *Gender, Place and Culture* 24, no. 1 (2017): 1-17.

37. ECLAC, "Femicide of Feminicide."

38. Latin America Working Group Education Fund, "Left in the Dark: Violence Against Women and LGBTI Persons in Honduras and El Salvador," n.d., https://www.lawg.org/left-in-the-dark-violence-against-women-and-lgbti-persons-in-honduras-and-el-salvador/.

39. Johanna Godoy, "Latin America: Signs of Progress," Gallup.com, April 8, 2020, news.gallup.com/poll/247199/latin-america-signs-progress-change-takes-time.aspx.

40. Rachel O'Donnell, "Transnational Feminist Activism in Latin America and Beyond," Alliance for Sustainable Communities, August 10, 2020, https://www.sustainlv.org/transnational-feminist-activism-in-latin-america-and-beyond/.

41. Tania del Moral, "Feminicides in Mexico" (unpublished manuscript, Wake Forest University, December 2020).

42. "Argentine Abortion: Senate Approves Legalization in Historic Decision," *BBC News*, December 30, 2020, https://www.bbc.co.uk/news/world-latin-america-55475036.

43. This theme will be addressed in greater detail in a book under preparation, *The Politics of Human Rights*, part of *Historia mínima de los derechos humanos en América Latina* (Mexico City: Colegio de México, 2018).

44. Pierina Pighi Bel and Jake Horton, "Coronavirus: What's Happening in Peru?," *BBC News*, July 9, 2020, https://www.bbc.com/news/world-latin-america-53150808. See also the section "COVID-19 Pandemic Strikes across Latin America: Early Assessments," *Middle Atlantic Review of Latin American Studies* 4, no. 1 (2020): 1–44; and Julie Turkievwitz and Sofía Villamil, "In Latin America, the Pandemic Threatens Equality Like Never Before," *New York Times*, July 11, 2020, https://www.nytimes.com/2020/07/11/world/americas/coronavirus-latin-america-inequality.html?referringSource=articleShare.

45. Economic Commission for Latin America and the Caribbean and International Labor Organization, *Work in Times of Pandemic: The Challenges of the Coronavirus Disease (Covid-19)*, Employment Situations in Latin America and the Caribbean no. 22 (UN and CEPAL, May 2020), 24–29, https://repositorio.cepal.org/bitstream/handle/11362/45582/4/S2000306_en.pdf.

46. Personal communication from María Antonia Sánchez, Buenos Aires, June 9, 2020.

47. Megan Janetsky, "How Covi-19 Is Threatening Central America's Economic Lifeline," *BBC News*, May 17, 2020, https://www.bbc.com/news/world-latin-america-52550389.

48. Paolo Marinho de Zanotto and Luciana Cezar de Cerqueira Leite, "The Challenges Imposed by Dengue, Zika, and Chikungunya to Brazil," *Frontiers in Immunology* 9 (2018). There is also a possible successful treatment by biological means carried out, only partially, by Forrest Innovations Company since 2019 (see https://www.forrestinnovations.com/en/news).

49. Arie M. Kacowicz, Exequiel Lacovksy, and Daniel F. Wajner, "The Covid-19 Crisis and Alternative World Orders: The Views from Latin America" (paper presented at the APSA Annual [Virtual] Meeting, September 11, 2020).

50. Frida Ghitis, "The New Divide in a Polarized Latin America: How to Respond to COVID-19," *World Politics Review*, April 2, 2020, www.worldpoliticsreview.com/articles/28650/across-latin-america-coronavirus-responses-are-a-new-dividing-line.

51. Anthony Boadle, "Poll Shows More Brazilians Spurn Bolsonaro's COVID-19 Response," *Reuters*, May 12, 2020, www.reuters.com/article/us-brazil-politics-poll/poll-shows-more-brazilians-spurn-bolsonaros-covid-19-response-idUSKBN22O2DC.

52. Christopher Sabatini, "Latin America's COVID-19 Moment: Differences and Solidarity," *Chatham House*, April 30, 2020, www.chathamhouse.org/expert/comment/latin-america-s-covid-19-moment-differences-and-solidarity.

53. Nacha Cattan, "AMLO's Approval Falls in Two Polls on Mexico's Rampant Violence," *Bloomberg News*, March 2, 2020, https://www.bloomberg.com/news/articles/2020-03-02/amlo-s-approval-falls-in-two-polls-on-mexico-s-rampant-violence.

Epilogue

1. Anatoly Kurmanaev, Manuela Andreoni, Letícia Casado, and Mitra Taj, "Latin America's Outbreaks Now Rival Europe's, But Its Options Are Worse," *New York Times*, May 12, 2020, https://www.nytimes.com/2020/05/12/world/americas/latin-america-virus-death.html.
2. CEPAL, "COVID-19 tendrá graves efectos sobre la economía mundial e impactará a los países de América Latina y el Caribe," March 19, 2020, https://www.cepal.org/es/comunicados/covid-19-tendra-graves-efectos-la-economia-mundial-impactara-paises-america-latina.
3. Isolda Hurtado, "La lección de Nicaragua: Desestimar la gravedad de la pandemia es letal," *Confidencial* (Managua), May 26, 2020, https://confidencial.com.ni/la-leccion-de-nicaragua-desestimar-la-gravedad-de-la-pandemia-es-letal/.
4. Benjamin Gedan, "Q&A with Francisco Monaldi," Wilson Center, June 5, 2020.
5. Manuel Alcántara, "De democracias fatigadas a democracias em quarentena," *Folha de São Paulo*, May 20, 2020, https://www1.folha.uol.com.br/mundo/2020/05/de-democracias-fatigadas-a-democracias-em-quarentena.shtml; and Manuel Alcántara, "América Latina y el Covid-19," *Middle Atlantic Review of Latin American Studies* 4, no. 1: 16–19.
6. "Envían a la cárcel al ex-ministro de Salud de Bolivia por posible compra irregular de respiradores," *El espectador* (Bogotá), May 24, 2020, https://www.elespectador.com/coronavirus/envian-la-carcel-al-exministro-de-salud-de-bolivia-por-posible-compra-irregular-de-respiradores-articulo-921069.
7. "'It's Not the Virus': Mexico's Broken Hospitals Become Killers, Too," *New York Times*, May 28, 2020, https://www.nytimes.com/2020/05/28/world/americas/virus-mexico-doctors.html.

Index